"Read this breakthrough around the results of you

It's not like any other trading book you've ever read before!

In *Mercury, Money and the Markets* you'll discover:

- The money-making truth about Mercury Retrograde periods.
- A detailed analysis of Mercury's impact on the trading patterns of 30 individual blue-chip stocks.
- Three practical ways you can use the wisdom of astrology to help you achieve real market mastery.
- Precision market timing tips based on planetary cycles.
- Back-testing trading results for Mercury cycles in precious metals and international markets.
- A secret trading technique from a mysterious ancient manuscript that's amazingly profitable in the markets today.
- What Mercury in your natal horoscope can tell you about your personal chance of success in the markets.
- Mercury timing techniques from legendary trading masters.
- How to harness the power of Mercury in the First-Trade horoscope.
- Why the Trading Triad is so important-- and exactly what you need to do about it!
- The unique impact of Mercury's relationships with the transneptunian factors-- and how they pinpoint turning points in a major market index!
- A reliable key to deciphering the hidden astro-trading meanings in W. D. Gann's strangest book.
- How to identify the most profitable short-term trading opportunities.
- Dynamic factors in successful astro-traders' natal horoscopes.
- A quick and easy technique for revealing Mercury's real role in activating trading dynamics in any First-Trade chart.

PLUS

A unique cross-indexed 201-year Mercury Station ephemeris you won't find anywhere else - it's a trading tool you'll use for years to come!

And much, much more!

Also by Tim Bost

The Basic Stock Market Astrology Home Study Course

J. P. Morgan's Billion Dollar Secret

How To Find the Money in Your Horoscope

Plan 9 for Inner Space

Creating Personal Wealth with Astrology

Astrology and the Law of Attraction

Finding Riches in Every Zodiac Sign

Gann Secrets Revealed: Beyond Symbolism in Financial Astrology

Profitable Trading with Planetary Timing

Mars Triggers and the Markets at the Cardinal Climax

Beyond the Basics in Stock Market Astrology

8 Billionaire Strategies for Breakthrough Stock Market Success

The Planetary Station Super-Cluster: A Stress Point in the Markets

Mars, Pluto and Big Changes in the Markets

Uranus and Hades: Obscene Corruption and Speculative Surprises

The Uranus/Pluto Waxing Square 2012 - 2015

Mercury, Money and the Markets

*Profitable Planetary Cycles
for
Short-Term Astro-Trading*

Tim Bost

Harmonic Research Associates
Sarasota, Florida, USA
2012

Mercury, Money and the Markets:
Profitable Planetary Cycles for Short-Term Astro-Trading

Copyright © 2012 Timothy L. Bost

All rights reserved under all Copyright Conventions.

No part of this book may be reproduced, stored in a retrieval system, or transmitted by any means, electronic, mechanical, photocopying, recording, or otherwise for public or private use (other than for "fair use" as brief quotations embodied in articles and reviews), without written permission from the author.

While the publisher and author have used their best efforts in preparing this publication, they make no representation or warranties with respect to the accuracy or completeness of its contents, and specifically disclaim any implied warranties or merchantability or fitness for a particular purpose. No warrant may be created or extended by sales representatives or written sales materials. The advice and strategies contained herein may not be suitable for your situation, and you should consult a professional where appropriate. This publication is prepared from astrological information, news and research reports, cycle projections, and market observations which are believed to be accurate and reliable, but which cannot be guaranteed. Even with accurate information, past performance is no guarantee of future results. Speculation in securities and commodities involves considerable financial risk, and readers who plan to invest or speculate in any securities or commodities mentioned in this publication have the complete responsibility for making themselves fully aware of all the risks involved before they invest. The information presented in this publication should in no way be understood or construed as a solicitation or an offer to buy or sell any products or securities, nor should it be considered buy/sell advice. Neither the publisher nor author shall be liable for any loss of profit or other personal or commercial damages, including but not limited to special, incidental, consequential, or other damages.

Submit all requests for reprinting to:
Harmonic Research Associates
Post Office Box 1657
Sarasota, Florida 34230-1657 USA

The astrological and market charts in this publication were prepared with the Fibonacci/Galactic Trader software from PAS Inc. (www.galacticinvestor.com) and the Solar Fire and Nova Chartwheels programs available from Astrolabe (www.alabe.com).

Published in the United States of America by Harmonic Research Associates.

www.HarmonicResearchAssociates.com

First Edition

**ISBN-10: 1-933198-38-9
ISBN-13: 978-1-933198-38-5
EAN: 9781933198385**

Acknowledgements

The process of writing a book is by necessity a solitary affair, but the content itself is inevitably a by-product of encounters with, and help from, many other people.

That has certainly been the case with this book, and I'm very grateful for those encounters, and for the insights, inspiration, and practical assistance many others have given me.

Needless to say, I owe a debt of gratitude to countless traders and astrologers past and present, who have inspired and encouraged me through their writing, their teaching, and their willingness to share their wisdom and experiences. While some of them are mentioned in the pages of this book, there are many, many more who deserve recognition. In some cases I've been especially fortunate in having my mentors and role models become my friends and colleagues as well, and I'm particularly grateful for these rewarding connections.

Software designers and computer programmers are the unsung heros of modern research efforts, and their contributions are especially noteworthy in market astrology. Some of the ones who have helped develop the tools that have made this book possible include Carlos Almeida, Gary Christen, Alphee Lavoie, Bill Meridian, Sergei Tarassov, and Ray White.

I also want to acknowledge the huge contributions of the many hundreds of astrological, coaching, and consulting clients and students who have come to me during the past 40 years or so, mainly because they have so often given me opportunities to say to them the exact things that I most needed to hear myself. Special thanks are due to the ones who have Mercury retrograde in their natal horoscopes, but I'm grateful to all of you for trusting me with your secrets, your problems, and your self-esteem.

The months of preparation for this book included a lot of painstaking research and considerable amounts of number-crunching, and if it had all been left to me to do by myself, this book would never have been completed. My heartfelt thanks go to Doug Capehart for his invaluable assistance in that part of the work.

Above all I want to thank Patty Taylor for her passionate and persistent efforts in helping bring this book to completion. My Dear, your sharp eye in proofreading and your courageously candid comments on the text have done a lot to make this a better book. On top of that, your patient and forgiving willingness to put up with a husband who has all too often been hopelessly AWOL in the uncharted territory of writing a book has truly been amazing. Words can never fully express the depth of my gratitude and devotion to you.

Contents

Introduction: The Astro-Trading Advantage   1

Mercury in Myth and the Esoteric Tradition   7
    The Emerald Tablet   11

The Trading Triad   **15**
    The Market   16
    The Trade   17
    The Trader   18
    The Challenge of Mastery   18

Mercury in the Astro-Trader's Natal Horoscope   **21**
    Two Key Mercury Considerations   22
    Mercury Prometheus and Epimetheus   22
    Natal Mercury in Motion   24
    Mercury and the Money Houses   25
    Mercury Ruling Money Houses   27
    Mercury and the Sun   28
    Mercury and the Moon   29
    Mercury and Venus   29
    Mercury and Mars   29
    Mercury and Jupiter   30
    Mercury and Saturn   30
    Mercury and Uranus   31
    Mercury and Neptune   31
    Mercury and Pluto   32
    Example Horoscopes   32
    A Successful Speculator   32
    A Chronic Loser in the Markets   35
    Horoscope Synthesis and the Astro-Trading Advantage   37

Mercury in Money Horoscopes   **39**
    The Free Coinage Act   43

The U.S. Dollar	44
U.S. Treasury	45
U.S. Paper Currency Act	46
Federal Reserve Bank	47
Federal Reserve Operations	48
Bretton Woods Act	49
Dollar/Gold Convertibility Ends	50
Japanese Yen	51
Euro	52
New York Stock Exchange	53
Securities & Exchange Commission	54
Paris Bourse	55
Bombay Stock Exchange	56
Mercury & First-Trade Charts	57

Mercury Aspects and Angles   59

Mercury and the Moon	61
Mercury and the Sun	62
Mercury and Venus	63
Mercury and Mars	64
Mercury and Jupiter	65
Mercury and Saturn	66
Mercury and Uranus	67
Mercury and Neptune	68
Mercury and Pluto	69
Mercury and Cupido	70
Mercury and Hades	71
Mercury and Zeus	72
Mercury and Kronos	73
Mercury and Apollon	74
Mercury and Admetos	75
Mercury and Vulcanus	76
Mercury and Poseidon	77
A Couple of Practical Astro-Trading Reminders	78

Mercury Retrograde   79

A Sobering Lesson	81
A Business Disaster	84
Flash Crash	88
Retrograde Strategies	91
The Internal Component	91
The External Component	95
A Synthetic Approach	98
An 18% Game Plan	99
Re-Energize	99
Refocus and Regroup	99
Revisit	100
Review	100
Research	101
Revise	101
Repair	101
The Empirical Advantage	102

Mercury Cycles and Market Indices — 105

Mercury Retrograde Periods & the Dow 30 Stocks — 129

Emerald Tablet Trades — 195
September 27 2002	197
July 18 2006	198
November 8 2006	199
May 18 2009	200
January 4 2010	201
December 2, 2011	202
Trading Opportunities	203
Mercury/Sun Conjunctions	203

Other Mercury Trading Strategies — 211
W. D. Gann	213
George Bayer	215
Jeanne Long	216
Dr. Alan Richter	217

Larry Pesavento	218
Earik Beann	218
Raymond Merriman	219
Bill Meridian	220
New Directions	221

Mercury Retrograde Periods 1900 - 2100 — **223**

Zodiac Degree Index: Mercury Stations 1900-2100 — **265**
   Mercury Stations Listed by Zodiac Degree — 266

Online Resources — **277**

Introduction:
The Astro-Trading Advantage

The study of planetary cycles and their correlation with market movements has been around for a long time, but for much of its history it has remained hidden in the shadows of the financial world. Market astrology was rarely talked about, and those who did actually discuss it did so in hushed tones, treating it as a closely-guarded secret that shouldn't be exposed to profane ears.

In many cases, those who talked about astrology in the markets at all did so with contempt and ridicule, making fun of it as preposterous superstition. Some others who were generally more open-minded still hesitated at using the term "astrology" in their discussions, preferring instead to talk about "astronomic phenomena" or "geocosmic influences" in the markets rather than to risk using words that might somehow lead to their being associated with psychics or charlatans.

But in many cases market astrology and astro-trading were deliberately preserved as carefully-protected secrets simply because the traders who benefited from astrology just weren't all that eager to share their methods with other people in the markets. They preferred to keep the hidden knowledge – and their personal trading profits – to themselves.

A century ago there were noteworthy traders whose success in the markets became legendary, but they too were rarely very open in explaining the planetary dynamics that lay behind their proprietary trading methods. There have also been many devoted students of astro-trading who have consciously chosen to be secretive about what they were doing, sometimes because of fearing embarrassment and sometimes because they were unsure about the ultimate value of their experimental methods. There have in fact been many traders who have glimpsed the potential of astrology in the markets and have gotten excited by the profitable possibilities that it offers, but who have never developed their understanding of astrological market methodologies well enough to apply them in their personal trading and then profit from the astro-trading advantage themselves.

But all that has radically changed during the past couple of decades. In many respects, the veil of secrecy has been lifted. Astrological trading methods have become much more widely accepted in the trading community as a whole, and have been featured in trading magazines and in books surveying contemporary approaches to market timing. More and more traders have been discovering the benefits of the astro-trading advantage in their own market experiences, and have successfully connected with still other traders who have shared their passion for planetary market timing, forming alliances and networking to support and encourage each others' investigations and trading insights.

Also during the past 25 years or so, the usefulness of astrology as a tool for market timing and forecasting has been extended enormously from the results of expanded research and from more disciplined back-testing. As improved tools and sharper thinking have enhanced the capabilities of mainstream trading, astro-trading has benefited, too. There have been remarkable advances in computerization, and historical market data has become much more accessible than it was in previous times. As a result it has become possible to test a larger variety of astro-trading hypotheses, and to quantify the results of those tests with increasing precision, contributing substantially to both the credibility and the creativity of market astrology as a maturing discipline.

Most important of all, however, is the fact that individual traders have increasingly understood their need for some kind of an edge that would help them compete effectively in a cutthroat market environment that is increasingly skewed by ever more sophisticated high-speed technologies. It is also an environment that is increasingly manipulated by forces which dwarf the resources of individual traders, and is dominated by the leverage of big market players controlling large blocks of trading capital. The astro-trading advantage offers individual traders a unique opportunity to rely on their personal knowledge and resourcefulness in ways that can help them contend with this complex and often challenging market environment as they strive to control their own financial destinies.

I've been fortunate to have been both a witness to and a participant in this growth of astro-trading into a more mature market discipline. I've been involved in astrological study and practice for more than four decades now, and more than three of those decades have been devoted almost exclusively to applying astrology to the markets. For nearly 25 years

I've been publishing the *Financial Cycles Weekly* newsletter (currently available at www.FinancialCyclesWeekly.com), and much of what I have learned about astro-trading has come through that experience.

About a dozen years ago I used what I had learned so far to create the **Basic Stock Market Astrology Home Study Course**. Although some of the specific references in that course are a bit dated now, is still a viable resource. It is certainly worth investigating if you are a newcomer both to astrology and to active trading; you can find additional information at www.BasicMarketCourse.com.

Unlike the broad survey of information presented in the **Basic Stock Market Astrology Home Study Course**, however, **Mercury, Money and the Markets** has a much narrower focus. Much of the past work in market astrology has focused either on long-term outer planet cycles or on the correlation of lunar dynamics with shorter-term market movements. While both of these approaches have given us extremely valuable information that can enhance our effectiveness in the markets, when we turn our attention to Mercury we are dealing with something remarkably different. Because it moves so rapidly, Mercury doesn't share the same characteristics exhibited by Jupiter, Saturn, and the other outer planets in influencing market mega-trends and long-term economic cycles. But at the other extreme, Mercury isn't exclusively a short-term, rapid-fire trading indicator, either (even though it has considerable strength in that capacity), since the patterns displayed by Mercury unfold more slowly than the cycles and phases of the Moon.

Mercury thus plays a unique role in helping us identify short-term trading opportunities, while at the same time it moves just slowly enough to make those opportunities potentially significant milestones in our trading experience. When we understand Mercury and its influence on market behavior, we can gain knowledge and insights that are particularly well-suited to short-term, hit-and-run trading strategies that can give us both the power and the flexibility we need to be profitable and effective in today's complex trading environment.

While this book explores many practical examples of Mercury's role in market dynamics, **Mercury, Money and the Markets** is not intended to be simply a how-to book. Its purpose is to help you understand some of the complex and intriguing ways that Mercury impacts the markets, to get you excited about including Mercury dynamics in your own personal approach to astro-trading, and to provide you with a useful resource as you move forward with your own astro-trading research and design your own astro-trading systems.

With that in mind, this book makes a few assumptions which we should acknowledge at the outset. First of all, it assumes that there is in fact a correlation between the behavior of prices in the markets and planetary cycles and interactions. Our aim here is not to prove that such a correlation exists, nor to explain how and why that correlation functions. There have been many excellent studies that have more than adequately demonstrated that astrology really works, and that it works especially well when it is skillfully applied in active trading. You may want to turn to those studies if you are not already convinced that such a correlation is at work behind the scenes in day-to-day market activity. Once you have done so, return to these pages when you're ready to explore the astro-trading advantage for yourself.

This book also assumes that you are already aware of the basic rules and procedures for sensible trading in the markets, or that you are at least ready to learn and apply those rules before getting into the market yourself. Astro-trading, like any other kind of trading, involves considerable risk. When you put your money into the markets, you can lose all or part of that money.

While the tools and insights provided by astro-trading can give you a considerable advantage in the markets, it is not a magic bullet that effortlessly hits the bulls-eye in your trading target every time, or a mystical shield that will automatically protect you from market losses. While the information in this book is based on extensive research and rigorous back testing, it does not guarantee that the techniques which have worked well in the past will infallibly do so in the future. In other words, you should under no circumstances trade with money that you cannot afford to lose, and you must be willing to assume personal responsibility for understanding the markets that you are trading and the full extent of the risks involved when you trade.

It's worth noting here as well that astro-trading is more than just simply applying astrological paradigms to the markets. To be truly effective, the astro-trader must also understand the fundamentals that lie beneath the stock or commodity being traded, with an eye to the external market forces, geopolitical and economic influences, and other factors which can influence the outcome of a trade, along with some basic knowledge of earnings, cash flow, supply and demand, and the other factors which go into a well-reasoned assessment of the potential for ongoing corporate profitability.

The competent astro-trader also needs to have a good core understanding of technical analysis – the assorted analytical tools and graphic techniques which can help us look at a chart of the historic price performance of a stock or commodity and draw some conclusions about future price trends and their sustainability. While you don't have to be an expert market technician to use astrology profitably in your trading, it's important that you don't ignore key technical indicators as you reach conclusions about what to trade and when to trade it.

Ideally, astro-trading is a seamless integration of fundamental analysis, technical analysis, and astrological insights. When we find sound fundamentals and a technical chart that indicates a potentially profitable trading opportunity, and then add the confirmation of back-tested astrological indicators to the mix, we can be much more confident in entering the markets and we can increase our likelihood of profiting through the astro-trading advantage.

In this book you will find many correlations between Mercury dynamics and important movements in the markets, which have been uncovered through extensive, systematic research and then back-tested to determine their reliability. While this information can be used to develop market forecasts with surprising accuracy, that is not the ultimate goal of this book. The assumption here is that getting real profits from your trading is more important to you than being right about what the markets are doing. If your personal approach to astro-trading includes disciplined money management of your trading capital and a realistic assessment of the risks that you are willing to accept, you will be far more likely to enjoy profitable results from your experiences in the markets.

Use the astrological insights about Mercury in this book to help you make clearer and more confident decisions about what you are trading and when you are trading it, but once you have entered a trade, I encourage you to be willing to surrender your need to be right about your analysis. Instead, pay close attention to what the movements of the market are actually telling you.

Above all, I hope that you will find **Mercury, Money and the Markets** an enjoyable reading experience. You'll encounter lots of pragmatic information here that you can apply to developing and refining your skills as an astro-trader. Along the way, there will also be some digressions and some tangential information that may at first seem to be irrelevant. But if you stay with the process, and have some fun as you do so, you will discover that you can integrate all of the diverse material in this book into a dynamic comprehension of the unique role that Mercury plays in the markets. You will also be well on your way to enjoying the full benefits of the astro-trading advantage for yourself.

Mercury in Myth and the Esoteric Tradition

As we look at the role of Mercury in the markets, we are of course primarily concerned with the practical results we can get in trading and in investing.

That's one of the great benefits of financial astrology. It gives us endless opportunities to test astrological hypotheses and to see in unequivocal, real-world terms what kinds of correlations actually exist between cosmic structures and ancient symbols and the day-to-day flow of contemporary human activities.

The markets are particularly unforgiving in this regard. When we look each day at price fluctuations, we have an opportunity to determine in no uncertain terms whether we have been successful or unsuccessful, whether our trades have brought us wins or losses, and we can keep score with precise numerical accuracy.

Above all, then, financial astrology and astro-trading demand a level of accountability that we rarely find in any other applications of the astrological craft.

But even though most of our work in astro-trading obliges us to focus on concrete results, we can also gain a great deal from the kind of richness that we find in astrological symbolism, and in the esoteric lore that provides the foundation for the astrological wisdom of the ages. When we get a glimpse of the cosmic dimensions of astrology, and when we begin to comprehend the incredible scope of astrological traditions over the passing centuries, it is a truly humbling experience.

That kind of humility is a prerequisite for real learning, and it is a virtue that is all too absent in market behavior. But when the vastness of our astrological heritage leaves us full of wonder, in that humbled and awe-stricken state we are most likely to be at our best in the trading environment.

It is, after all, when we are willing to admit our ignorance as we impartially observe the fluctuations of market activity that we can the greatest opportunities for trading success, rather than in those all too frequent occasions when we are somehow convinced that we actually know what's going on, and insist on using that blind conviction in our vain attempts to tell the market what to do. Mythology gives us an intuitive, right-brain experience that provides a counterpoint to the left-brain analysis we use so much in the markets. When we integrate the two into whole-brain thinking, we become much more effective as traders.

The markets truly have a mind of their own, and so it is even more appropriate that we examine Mercury and the markets to get a core understanding of the ebb and flow of information that creates the divergences and opportunities of the trading environment. And with Mercury we get an added bonus-- a unique grounding in spiritual tradition and esoteric lore that ultimately serves us well in maintaining emotional balance and appropriate intellectual perspective as we seek to understand the vagaries of the markets, and to identify the most salient opportunities that perpetually await us in the never-ending stream of market data.

Before we examine some of the characteristics of Mercury in an astrological context and begin our exploration of the unusual connections between Mercury and the markets, it's thus worthwhile to recall the mythological connections that so enrich the literature of Mercurial lore. Mercury, of course, was the name that the Romans gave to the Messenger of the Gods, a well-known figure even in modern iconography, with his winged feet helping to speed him on his way as he delivers good news, bad news, and unexpected tidings to places near and far. His image remains a familiar one, at least when we visit a florist shop with the intention of having flowers delivered for some special occasion.

But Mercury in the Roman pantheon was part of a wholesale appropriation of deities from the Greek culture, and it was in that context that Mercury was known as Hermes. This Greek antecedent to Mercury is an intriguing figure in mythology, to say the least.

Hermes was the son of Maia, a nymph who lived in a cave and who had become impregnated during a tryst with Zeus, the king of the gods. Hermes was also the brother of Apollo. The Greek story tells us that on the very first day of his life, the infant Hermes decided to steal Apollo's oxen.

In order to escape detection, Hermes got some giant sandals which he tied to the feet of the oxen, with the toes of the sandals pointing backwards. Then, when Hermes led the oxen away, the footprints showed a trail heading in the opposite direction. After he had completed this stunt, Hermes finished the day back in his crib, smiling innocently at his mother.

Apollo, however, soon figured out what had happened to his cattle, and dragged the infant Hermes with him to appear before their father Zeus. As Hermes eventually confessed to his crime, Zeus replaced his initial anger with bemused curiosity, which gradually turned to outright admiration as he learned about the ingenious way that Hermes had disguised his theft. Zeus then gave Hermes a variety of tasks to perform, designed both as penance and as an indoctrination into some of the rudimentary guidelines of civilized society.

Mercury's role as a trickster is an important one, especially in the realm of astro-trading. In this role he is a god and expresses godlike qualities; yet he is not a god at all, acting in all-too-human ways as he exemplifies the fool who is in reality very wise. Like Mercury, the markets have a mind of their own, and we can be severely decieved if we think we can predict their every movement.

As the trickster, Mercury rebels against authority, poking fun at overly serious people and situations, reminding us to step back and reevaluate our most cherished assumptions. In his ability to invent intricate plans and convoluted schemes (which may or may not actually work), his behavior is a reflection of the penchant many traders have for devising complex methods of market analysis, becoming their own worst enemies in the process. When we remain cognizant of Mercury as the trickster, however, we can raise important questions instead of accepting things blindly as we engage with the markets.

It was Zeus who designated Hermes as the Messenger of the Gods. In that role his responsibilities included insuring the rights and safety of travelers, promoting commerce, and assisting in negotiations and treaties. As a guardian of thresholds, Hermes protected sacred spaces, keeping the unworthy out. It was he who allowed passages between the visible and invisble worlds.

The special staff that Zeus gave Hermes was crowned with snakes, and it had the power to cast spells, induce sleep, and aid Hermes in interpreting dreams. This caduceus could also make Hermes invisible, and it had the power to heal the sick (thus its traditional association with the healing arts and medical professions).

In other parts of the Greek mythology, the role of Hermes is decidedly ambiguous. He is both the archetypal thief himself and the opponent of thievery by stealth (as opposed to open robbery by force, which was more or less a fact of life in the ancient world). In essence, then, he was both outlaw and enforcer of the law; a nemesis of the cunning who calls upon his own extraordinary talents at subterfuge in maintaining the forward progress of social interaction.

But the mythological role of Mercury is not limited to the Roman and Greek contexts. The Greeks had active connections with Egypt, and Hermes became part of the Egyptian pantheon as well. It was as Hermes Trismegistus, "Hermes the Triple-Blessed", that he was embodied by Thoth, an officer of the divinely-privileged Egyptian royal court who appeared in a variety of animal forms. Typically Thoth was depicted as a stork, but sometimes he appeared as a jackal or a baboon.

Regardless of his specific appearance, however, Thoth as the Egyptian version of Hermes is much less a prankster and much more an agent of divine justice, social order, and earthly goodwill. He was, above all, an embodiment of a sacred presence in human activities, and an exponent of the underlying truth which transcends the diversity of material forms.

According to some esoteric traditions, Thoth was the first to cognize and systematize the symbolic system that became the basis for the Major Arcana in tarot cards. These symbols have enormous archetypal power and were, as Ishmael Reed suggests in his 1972 novel **Mumbo Jumbo**, an attempt to codify the sacred fertility dance rites of the cult of Osiris. As Reed depicts it, Thoth told Osiris "that if Osiris would execute these dance steps for Thoth, he would illustrate them and then Osirian priests could determine what god or spirit possessed them as well as learn how to make these gods and spirits depart." And thus "Guides were initiated into the Book of Thoth, the 1st anthology written by the 1st choreographer."

It was also Thoth, in his Alexandrian Greek alter-identity Hermes Trismegistus, who was acknowledged as the author of the mysterious Emerald Tablet, which is doubtless the most pivotal ur-text of the ancient esoteric tradition. The Emerald Tablet was the foundation for centuries of alchemical lore, and it provides the philosophical perspective that underlies astrological work as well. Because it contains the core notion of correspondences between the macrocosm and the microcosm, it's also an important antecedent for us as astro-traders, not only because of our efforts to correlate planetary cycles to market movements, but also because it reminds us to look for the fractal relationships of market activities in different time frames, whether we are examining long-term monthly price charts or are trading one-minute price bars in a rapidly moving contract.

The Emerald Tablet itself is a remarkably brief document, so it's worth reproducing here in its entirety. It's useful as a focal point for meditation and reflection as we contemplate the mysteries of the markets, and it gives us a glimpse of the real scope of the power we are confronting when look at the role of Mercury.

The Emerald Tablet

It is Truth; Truth without lies; certain Truth--
That which is above is like that which is below;
And that which is below is like that which is above
To accomplish the miracles of the One Thing.

As all things came into being by the meditation of one,
So all things arose from this One Thing,
By a single act of creative adaptation.

Its father is the Sun, its mother is the Moon.
It was carried in the womb of the wind, and the earth is its nurse.
It is the father of all wonderful works in the universe.
Its power is perfect.

If it is cast on earth it will divide the element of earth from the element of fire,
Separating the subtle from the gross with gentle heat and one-pointed attention.
In its great wisdom it ascends gently from earth to heaven.
Again it descends to earth, then unites in itself
The force from things above to the force from things below.

Thus you shall call the glorious light of the whole world your own.
All obscurity and darkness will fall away from you.

This is the mightiest of all mighty powers,
For it will overcome every subtle thing
And has the power to penetrate every solid substance.

Thus was the world created.

For this reason I am called Hermes the Thrice-Greatest,
One in essence but Three in aspect,
For I posses three parts of the wisdom of the whole universe.

That which I have to say about the work of the Sun is completed.

This rendition of the Emerald Tablet, which I first published in *The Esoteric Review* newsletter in May,1983, is an attempt to capture much of the essential poetry and mystery of earlier translations while at the same time providing a focus on the text as a guide to the validity of the insights that can only come through the practical alchemy of meditative experience and spiritual discipline. As such, it sometimes sacrifices more precise language in favor of aesthetics-- for example, "that which is above" and "that which is below" would perhaps be more accurately translated as "that which is superior" and "that which is inferior", but in our current politically-correct environment those term have connotations which tend to distract attention away from the true importance of the text.

Even so, the Emerald Tablet is not only a piece of inspired poetry and philosophy, and a means of connecting with the archetypal understandings of the ancient world. If it is also something which can have particular significance for us as astro-traders, especially in our examination of the specific ways that Mercury functions in the markets.

The attribution of the text provides our first clue to its understanding. While it was a common practice in the ancient world to attribute various writings to venerated historical figures and or even to deities, the fact that the Emerald Tablet is attributed to Hermes is especially significant in this case. The Emerald Tablet is not just something that was supposedly written by Hermes, it was also actually about Hermes himself, both as a personage and as a planet. We can thus expect to gain valuable insights into hermetic matters like alchemy and astrology when we ponder this document, but we can also expect it to have some correlation with the observable cycles of the planet Mercury itself.

The portions of the text which refer to "that which is above" and "that which is below" are particularly noteworthy in this regard, since Mercury makes two geocentric conjunctions with the Sun as a part of its regular orbital cycle. These are the superior conjunction, when Mercury is on the far side of the Sun as seen from the Earth's perspective, but is aligned with the Sun in the same degree of the zodiac; and the alignment of the Sun and Mercury when Mercury is between the Earth and the Sun, reaching its closest to Earth as it again ruler lines up with the Sun in the same degree of the zodiac (the inferior conjunction).

The superior conjunction of the Sun with Mercury occurs only when Mercury is in direct motion, and the inferior conjunction always takes place while Mercury is retrograde.

The information in the Emerald Tablet can thus give us more than just philosophical insights to ponder. It is also a commentary on physical planetary cycles and alignments, and as such it provides us with specific guidance in our efforts to understand the dynamic potential hidden in a set of observable and predictable planetary phenomena.

The Emerald Tablet is also important for us as astro-traders because it is about the process of change. The author of the document is not just Hermes, but Hermes Trismegistus, the triple-blessed. While triplicities are significant factors in many of the world's cultural and spiritual traditions, this designation of Hermes is more than just an idle affirmation of a cosmic triune nature. Hermes was unique in the ancient pantheon because he could successfully traverse all three worlds – the abode of the gods on Mount Olympus, the underworld of lost souls and hidden things, and the realm of human beings, that zone which is perpetually caught in the balance between the divine and the daemonic. This extraordinary ability to function comfortably in all three worlds was an essential part of Mercury's role as messenger of the gods. But it also gave him a unique part to play as the gatekeeper, as the Guardian of Thresholds in that nebulous realm between the worlds, where one state of being is transformed into another form of reality.

It was, of course, this capacity for transformation embodied by Mercury that made the Emerald Tablet so appealing to the ancient alchemists. As they labored diligently in their efforts to transmute lead into gold, they also sought to transform their own base and unrefined personal characteristics into more perfect expressions of the divine essence.

In doing so, they embraced one of the core paradoxes of what it means to be human – the perpetual struggle to reconcile lowly instincts and animalistic tendencies with the nagging realization that we are called to higher things, that our destiny is to imbue our earthly existence with lofty ideals and ecstatic inspirations. In fact, this is at the root of the word "human" itself; the etymology of the word combines the root word found in "humus", the fertile soil of the earth, with the notion of "manas", the Indo-European term for mind. With Mercury, then, we have an embodiment of our unique mission as sentient humans-- to use our creative intelligence consciously to transform the earth. When we deal with Mercury we come face-to-face with our own essential role as agents of change and transformation.

That association with the hermetic tradition with transformation is a critical factor in our encounter with the markets as well. As astro-traders we are primarily concerned with changes in trend, those occasions when a shift in market direction offer us specific opportunities to realign our thinking and our capital in more profitable ways. The ability to move freely between the worlds, and to embrace the divergences and transformations in mass behavior, are what astro-trading is all about.

Mercury is also associated with the activity of trading by virtue of his connection with commerce and with the transference of information and value. This is above all an active and dynamic process. Since Mercury is the Messenger of the Gods, when we engage in the markets we can gain the greatest benefit by tuning in to the information at hand, repeatedly asking ourselves "What's the real message here? What is the market telling us now about its own current temperament, about the intentions of other traders, and about the unique opportunities we are being offered for our own trading?"

The Emerald Tablet is often erroneously summarized as a simple statement that "as above, so below" is the governing principle of universal will. In actuality, however, the Emerald Tablet makes it clear that the flow of creative intelligence goes both ways – "that which is above is like that which is below, and that which is below is like that which is above." It does not describe a system in which an omnipotent divine force relentlessly imposes its will upon human affairs. Instead, it emphasizes the fact that creativity, communication, and adaptation emanate as much from Earth and from human affairs as they do from the celestial realms.

As astro-traders, when we align ourselves with these ancient hermetic principles and when we engage with Mercury's influence in the markets, we are participating in a primordial tradition of that gives us a very modern advantage in discovering more profitable trading and more profound rewards from our encounter with the markets. While our main focus is on the planetary correlations with the phenomena we can observe and the data we can back-test, if we add an awareness of the esoteric implications of our actions in the markets to our trading toolbox we can combine an intuitive, right-brain dimension with our left-brain analytical skills, creating an extraordinarily powerful whole-brain approach to our trading activity. When we come to the markets with fully integrated whole-brain awareness, we can't help but spontaneously identify remarkable trading opportunities that we might otherwise have missed. And, as we shall see later in this book, having some familiarity with Mercury myths and traditions can guide us toward specific trading strategies as well.

Trading can be an extremely tricky and even deceptive endeavor, and Mercury in his trickster role won't let us forget that fact. But Mercury also encourages the kind of precise thinking and rigorous record-keeping that can help us manage our trades and trading capital more effectively, and in that capacity Mercury guides and directs us toward more consistent trading performance. But it is through Mercury's role as an agent of change and as a guardian of transformational thresholds that we are given the biggest opportunities for experiences that can alter the course of our lives, taking us closer to a completely empowered expression of who we really are. With that kind of rarefied self-knowledge we can reach greater heights of personal fulfillment, and we can become more effective as astro-traders, too.

The Trading Triad

When we step back from the world of myth and move into the realm of modern astro-trading, we immediately become concerned with pragmatic market matters, with precise measurements, and with practical ways of preserving our capital as we maximize our profits. But if we are wise, we don't completely abandon Mercury myths and esoteric paradigms as we consider the trading opportunities that the markets are offering us now. Instead we integrate our right-brain esoteric awareness with our left-brain analysis to use the full power of whole-brain thinking in our trading.

If we pause to reflect on Mercury archetypes from ancient times, we can often find guidance that is surprisingly relevant to our contemporary circumstances, and discover parallels between the tasks performed by the Messenger of the Gods and our own challenges as we go into action in today's sophisticated market environment.

Like Hermes, for example, our role as astro-traders is to move effortlessly between the worlds, transcending thresholds. Market movements are essentially all about thresholds.

Almost before our eyes, a profitable trading position crosses an invisible threshold and suddenly becomes a loss.

A stock breaks out of a congested trading pattern and then gaps upward into a new trading range, crossing a threshold and creating an important technical signal.

An options play experiences the inexorable effects of time decay and begins to slide rapidly toward worthlessness. At some point a threshold is crossed, and it's time to abandon the trade.

Our task as astro-traders is to become adept at anticipating and negotiating thresholds, so that we can match our actions to the shifting moods of the markets and gain the rewards that come with accurate analysis, reliable intuition, precise communication, and speedy engagement in transactions. Comprehending and utilizing thresholds in the markets and in ourselves is unfortunately a skill which many traders miss completely, whether or not they are cognizant of Mercury myths and whether or not they try to apply astrological principles to their trading.

In many cases, the real problem is one of limited perspective. Effective trading is more than just buying and selling. The markets bring us lots of surprises and complexities, and real mastery of the trading process requires a willingness to broaden our perspectives and to develop our skills in three equally important areas.

We refer to those three areas of mastery as the Trading Triad. Each of them requires knowledge, insight, and disciplined practice, and if any of the three are missing from our engagement with the markets we are much more likely to be disappointed with the results we get from our trading. Whether we imagine the Trading Triad as an equilateral triangle or visualize it as a three-legged stool, we need to give attention to all three components, since all three of them are mutually interdependent. At the most basic level, we can refer to them simply as the Market, the Trade, and the Trader.

The Market

If we are going to trade effectively, we must have some understanding of what the Market as a whole is doing. We try to reach that understanding by observing market data and by asking questions: "What is the current mood and temperament of the market that we are trading? What are its characteristic dynamics, and what external and internal factors are influencing them? Is there a discernible market trend, and if so, how likely is it to change?"

Whether we arrive at our answers through exposure to the daily news, through the maze of recommendations and advice offered by market pundits, or through an awareness of the rhythmic influences of planetary cycles, our goal is to arrive at a reasonable understanding (or at least a well-informed opinion) about the current nature of the market as a whole.

As we prepare to enter a trade, it's important that we come to terms with the Market component of the Trading Triad for one essential reason – the biggest factor in the price movement of any individual stock is the movement and trend of the market on a larger scale. The old trading adage tells us that a rising tide floats all boats, and that notion has been substantiated by research summarized in a 1964 Ph.D. dissertation by Benjamin F. King, Jr. at the University of Chicago, which showed that 70% of the tradable price action in an individual equity can be attributed to the predominant market trend. If we decide to trade against that trend we take on more risk than we need to, and unfortunately that greater risk doesn't always bring us greater rewards. But if we consistently include this critical part of the Trading Triad in our approach to the market opportunities that present themselves, we can be far more confident that we will ultimately experience trading success.

The Trade

Once we are satisfied with our analysis of the market as a whole, we can move to the second component of the Trading Triad, which is an analysis of the specific Trade that we are considering. Whether we are dealing with stocks, with commodities, or with options, the questions that we ask in this part of the Trading Triad are fairly simple ones: "Is this the right trade for me? Does it match the profile of my personal trading capital and my level of risk tolerance? Is this the right time for me to enter a position? If I enter a position, should I be long or short? What are the appropriate stop loss levels and price targets for this trade? Does this trade represent the best use of my trading capital right now, or are there better opportunities that I should explore? How long do I anticipate being in this trade?"

While the pertinent questions are direct enough, arriving at answers to them can potentially be complex and confusing. After all, there are innumerable trading tools, analytical tricks, technical indicators, black box trading systems, and other devices at our disposal, and it's often difficult to decide which tool or technique we should be using. In fact, most of the training programs, literature and folklore associated with trading focus on just this one subject – the Holy Grail search for an infallible trading methodology.

In mastering this second component of the Trading Triad, then, our task is to separate the wheat from the chaff, to find the answers that make enough sense to us to empower decisive action in the markets. Arriving at those answers requires rigorous back-testing, personal knowledge and experience, a healthy dose of skepticism and good judgment, and sometimes a little bit of luck as well. It also requires a willingness to submit ourselves to the kind of discipline which is essential for effective trading – an awareness of probabilities and risk-reward ratios, an adherence to disciplined money management, and the humility to make mistakes and learn from them. Without that kind of discipline and the hard work that it inevitably entails, our chances for success in the markets are greatly diminished. But if we wholeheartedly embrace this second component of the Trading Triad and really engage in active analysis of the Trade, the experience can be enormously energizing and often quite profitable as well.

The Trader

The third component of the Trading Triad is the one that is most often overlooked, and if we ignore it we invite disaster into our engagement with the markets. It is all about the Trader, the actual person who is seeking an understanding of the market trend in the first component of the Trading Triad and who is digging into the intricacies of trading analysis and execution while striving to master the second component. No matter how skilled we are at mastering the first two components of the Trading Triad, if we ignore the importance of refining our personal role as traders we will not get the results we seek. When that happens, we ourselves can become the reason for our failure in the markets– as Walt Kelly's cartoon character Pogo famously quipped, "We have met the enemy, and he is us!"

Any seasoned trader who is willing to speak honestly about his or her experience in the markets can attest to the validity and importance of this component of the Trading Triad. The more thoroughly we understand ourselves, the more effective we can be as traders. But at one level or another, we all have the capacity for shooting ourselves in the foot, for taking all of our market experience and wise trading analysis and then ignoring it completely as we execute our trades on impulse, or in an emotional state overshadowed by fear or greed. Understanding ourselves as traders requires an in-depth look at our own psychology, at our habits and prejudices, and at the mental and emotional blockages which allow us to act against our better judgment. When we make self-mastery a part of our personal trading discipline, mastering the Trading Triad becomes a goal that we can actually achieve.

The Challenge of Mastery

When we have all three components of the Trading Triad in place– the Market, the Trade, and the Trader– we will have laid the foundation for a successful and rewarding career in the markets. Giving less than our best to any of the three Trading Triad components can lead to disappointment and frustration, and the process of mastering the Trading Triad can often seem quite challenging. It demands that we stretch ourselves to acquire new knowledge, to reach higher levels of competence, and to confront our most cherished strategies for self-sabotage. And, as in the world of sports competition or professional musical performance, real mastery only comes as a result of seemingly endless repetition and accumulated experience.

Fortunately, however, we have a unique advantage as astro-traders. Astrology is an extremely powerful tool, and when we make it a part of our quest to master all three Trading Triad components, it can help us speed up the process and increase our confidence as we move toward mastery.

When we apply an astrological understanding of planetary cycles to our analysis of long-term price trends, we gain valuable perspectives that can help us clarify and refine our diagnosis of current market conditions. Astrology can help us anticipate critical thresholds in the markets, so that we can be prepared for the profitable opportunities associated with upcoming inflection points and trend reversals.

When we study the dynamic display of planetary aspects and other interactions on a short-term basis, we have a chance to connect with the market's ebb and flow in ways that can help us take advantage of market momentum in positioning our trades. We can be more confident in knowing when to be aggressive in taking profits or protecting our assets, and when to be more tolerant of trading congestion or price consolidation.

And astrology is more than just a potent tool for improving our market timing. It's also a means of gaining a unique understanding of our own psychological makeup. We can use it to identify the unconscious patterns of behavior that might blind-side us if they go unobserved as we engage with the markets, and we can turn a knowledge of our individual horoscope into practical strategies that amplify our strengths for greater trading effectiveness. By using astrology in the markets we can not only time the markets more accurately; we can also time ourselves, so that we can improve our trading performance by capitalizing on our times of strength and by compensating for our times of weakness.

While this book focuses on the role of Mercury in market astrology and astro-trading, it does so with a recognition of the important contributions that astrology can make to mastering all three components of the Trading Triad. With that in mind, we'll begin with a look at Mercury in the astro-trader's natal horoscope. Then we'll explore a variety of ways that Mercury dynamics can be used to enhance our market analysis, and to add to our confidence as we make decisions and take risks in active trading.

Mercury in the Astro-Trader's Natal Horoscope

If you want to gain the full astro-trading advantage as you engage with the markets, it's vital that you look not only at the role that Mercury plays in the markets you are trading, but also at the way that Mercury functions in your own individual horoscope.

If you're a reasonably accomplished astrologer yourself, you probably have the necessary skills and experience to look at Mercury's role in your natal chart as a source of insight into the financial attitudes and trading strategies are most appropriate for you. If that's the case, you can use the information in this chapter to provide you with some guidelines for a Mercury-based analysis of the trading potentials revealed by your natal horoscope.

If you're not an astrologer, however, or if you simply want to focus on Mercury's role in the external trading environment, you may want to skip reading this chapter altogether. But if you make that choice, please don't ignore the importance of understanding your natal horoscope in refining your personal abilities as a trader. You certainly don't have to become an astrologer yourself to gain the benefits that astrology has to offer, just as you don't have to be an automobile mechanic in order to enjoy the benefits of driving a car.

If you're not already well-versed in horoscope analysis, your best course of action is to schedule a consultation with a competent professional astrologer. When you do so, be sure you're working with someone who not only has proven astrological expertise, but who also has personal experience in the markets as well. Come prepared with specific questions about your trading experience and your failures and successes in the markets. An intelligent interaction with a skilled astrologer will help you get in touch with the role that your natal Mercury can play in helping you identify opportunities and potential pitfalls in your trading.

Two Key Mercury Considerations

Mercury, because it is the planet closest to the Sun in the solar system, is never far away from the Sun in the natal horoscope. It is thus impossible for a geocentric natal horoscope to have a Sun/Mercury opposition. It's far more likely that we will find Mercury in the same zodiac sign that the Sun occupies in the natal chart, although it may be in the sign of the zodiac immediately preceding or following that of the Sun.

In understanding the role of Mercury in the natal horoscope, there are two main considerations that can color our individual approach to the markets, and if we fail to take them into account we risk greater liabilities in our trading, simply because we may be blind-sided by our own inability to identify why we do what we do in the markets. The first is the question of natal Mercury's position relative to that of the Sun, and the second is a consideration of the direction of Mercury's motion at the time of birth.

Mercury Prometheus and Epimetheus

When we find Mercury at an earlier degree of the zodiac than that of the natal Sun, no matter where the two bodies happen to fall in the natal horoscope, we can say that Mercury rises before the Sun, or is Mercury Prometheus. If it follows the Sun in zodiacal sequence, it is Mercury Epimetheus. This terminology comes from the mythological story of two brothers, Prometheus, who always faced forward and looked into the future, and Epimetheus, who always looked backwards, observing and codifying events in the past.

In the natal horoscope Mercury Prometheus, rising before the Sun, is the morning star, visible just before dawn as long as it is not so close to the Sun that its glow is obliterated by the solar light. Mercury Epimetheus is an evening star, appearing in the western sky in the dusky twilight after the setting of the Sun.

Because we associate Mercury with mental traits and capacities, this position of Mercury relative to the Sun can give us some valuable insights into the kind of thinking and decision-making that we are most likely to exhibit in our trading activities.

If we are oblivious to this dynamic through our ignorance of the workings of the natal chart, we can find ourselves repeatedly making mistakes in our market behavior because our unexamined patterns of thought create the kind of booby-traps that can sabotage effective market analysis and accurate execution of our trades. But once we become conscious of these natal Mercury dynamics, we are more likely to be more tuned in to our thought processes as we approach the market environment, and we at least have an opportunity to temper or modify our thinking enough to perform more effectively as astro-traders.

With Mercury Prometheus in the natal chart, an astro-trader is likely to approach the markets from an intuitive, and sometimes impulsive, standpoint. More often than not, there will be a highly refined capacity for pattern recognition, which can be a valuable tool in spotting trading opportunities.

The kind of skill at rapid insight bestowed by Mercury Prometheus offers a distinct advantage to day-traders and to others who rely on quick and accurate assessments of possibilities in the market, allowing for speedy decision-making and the ability to enter trades at just the right time when suitable trading setups and confirming indicators appear. Mercury Prometheus focuses on transforming abstract thought into concrete reality, and this can often be a real benefit to traders who rely on quick and assertive action. But at times it can also be a liability, especially when it leads to precipitous action that ignores hidden risks and inconsistent indicators.

The trader with Mercury Epimetheus in the the natal horoscope, however, is typically much more deliberative in the trading process. This position of Mercury in the natal horoscope promotes the ability to gather and assimilate massive amounts of data, and the Mercury Epimetheus trader thus typically requires some time to digest and absorb the full implications of market complexities before committing to a trading position. Rigorous back-testing can be a salient strong point for any Mercury Epimetheus astro-trader, who in most cases will be highly focused on price history and traditional methods of market analysis.

But having Mercury Epimetheus can also promote "analysis paralysis," with the astro-trader becoming so absorbed in the intricacies of assessing opportunities accurately that the opportunities themselves get passed by without being taken advantage of. Without actually putting money on the line, the Mercury Epimetheus astro-trader isn't really a trader at all, but rather but a passive observer of the markets.

Natal Mercury in Motion

While there are many nuances to these distinctions in the relative positions of Mercury and the Sun in the natal horoscope, simply knowing whether Mercury is Promethean or Epimethean can provide a lot of leverage in modifying our trading behavior in appropriate ways. But those distinctions come into even sharper focus when we add a consideration of the kind of motion Mercury is in at the time of birth.

Most of the time, Mercury is in direct motion, moving rapidly through the degrees of the zodiac in ascending sequence. About three times each year, however, Mercury goes into the retrograde motion, and that retrograde phase will last a little more than three weeks, with a maximum duration of about 25 days. Mercury's progress slows down considerably at the time of the planetary stations, those points in its cycle when it moves from direct into retrograde motion (the retrograde station), and when it ceases its apparent backward motion and begins to move forward again (the direct station).

When we add a consideration of whether Mercury is retrograde or direct to our evaluation of the astro-trader's natal Mercury as Mercury Prometheus or Mercury Epimetheus, we can further refine our understanding of the mental predilections that can empower or inhibit effective performance in the markets.

If Mercury in the natal horoscope is both Prometheus and retrograde, we can expect the intuitive and insightful capabilities to be much more self-referred, creating a mental configuration that will sometimes almost defiantly ignore external signals and potentially pertinent information as the astro-trader makes decisions in the market.

The astro-trader with Mercury Prometheus retrograde will somehow just know in advance what the markets are going to do, and may trade impulsively, plunging into market positions solely on the basis of that highly-internalized insight, whether or not that insight matches the reality of the market at the moment.

While there are times when this tendency can manifest itself as spurts of uncanny brilliance in trading behavior, there are unfortunately also many occasions when it will produce major missteps and errors of judgment.

It is thus especially important for astro-traders with Mercury Prometheus retrograde in their natal horoscopes to exercise high levels of discipline in money management, with specific and inviolable strategies for getting out of losing positions rapidly. Mechanical trading systems that compel unwavering compliance with market signals can be especially useful for astro-traders with Mercury Prometheus retrograde in their natal charts.

If an astro-trader has Mercury Epimetheus in retrograde motion in the natal horoscope, the typical Mercury Epimetheus need for analysis and historical understanding doesn't go away. But unlike an astro-trader with Mercury Epimetheus direct, the Mercury Epimetheus retrograde astro-trader will sometimes look at the results of back-testing and will examine traditional approaches to specific trade setups and market circumstances, and then willfully and rebelliously choose to ignore that potentially valuable information. Whether or not a Mercury Epimetheus retrograde astro-trader actually takes a trade, there will often be a powerful inner conviction that even though the carefully-sifted evidence suggests a particular outcome in the markets, somehow "this time it's different", and irrational or erratic trading behavior can be the result.

Should individuals with Mercury Epimetheus retrograde in their natal horoscopes even think about trading at all? Perhaps not, especially if the would-be trader consistently behaves in the damn-the-torpedoes manner just described. But even so, learning to trade effectively is all about recognizing our natural tendencies and prejudices, and then figuring out how to take action consciously in spite of those tendencies, choosing instead to follow specific rules and strategies to get specific results. That decision to go beyond the limits of our predilections may present some real challenges, but it is nevertheless a matter of individual choice and determination. Making that choice is a highly personal matter, and it's of course possible to certain individuals with natal Mercury Epimetheus and retrograde to come to that decision. If they do choose to trade, however, they need to take extra pains to create rigorous trading rules and to follow them relentlessly.

Mercury and the Money Houses

While a consideration of both Mercury's position relative to the natal Sun and of its motion at the time of birth can give us useful insights into trading potential, these are certainly not the only factors that we can consider in evaluating the role of Mercury in the astro-trader's natal horoscope.

While it is always an inadequate exercise when we try to evaluate a natal chart without doing a comprehensive analysis of the many natal factors that combine within it, it's nevertheless useful to look at Mercury's role as a case in isolation, mainly because Mercury plays such an important part in helping us understand the complex thought processes that go into the process of trading. In fact, trading is almost entirely a mental activity, and the more we know about how we think as astro-traders, the more rapidly and comfortably we can move toward real mastery of the markets.

As a basic approach, it's useful to consider Mercury's relationship to the planetary rulers of the money houses in the natal chart: the second house, which is associated with core values and retained resources; the fifth house, which is the focal point in the horoscope that is related to speculation and investments, along with the ability to take chances and to put money at risk; the eighth house, which is about other people's money, indebtedness, and trading on margin; and the eleventh house, which the ancient astrologers referred to as the House of Acquisition, the portion of the natal horoscope that tells us about our ability to acquire wealth and to gain rewards from the risks that we take.

In each case, we are concerned with the planet which rules the zodiac sign on the cusp of the house in question. My personal preference is to use traditional rulerships in natal horoscope analysis, but it's also acceptable to use modern planetary rulerships or even a combination of modern and traditional techniques.

In the traditional system of astrology, Aries is ruled by Mars, Taurus is ruled by Venus, Gemini is ruled by Mercury, Cancer is ruled by the Moon, Leo is ruled by the Sun, Virgo is ruled by Mercury, Libra is ruled by Venus, Scorpio is ruled by Mars, Sagittarius is ruled by Jupiter, Capricorn is ruled by Saturn, Aquarius is also ruled by Saturn, and Pisces is ruled by Jupiter.

The modern system of zodiacal rulerships assigns the same planetary rulers to Aries through Libra and to Sagittarius and Capricorn, but gives rulership of Scorpio to Pluto, of Aquarius to Uranus, and of Pisces to Neptune.

Note that the planetary ruler of a house does not necessarily need to be located in that house itself to claim its rulership. It may show up at any location in the natal chart, and wherever it turns up, it is that planet that we want to look at with regard to its relationship to natal Mercury. That relationship may be expressed as one of the of the approximate angular relationships known as planetary aspects, or it may involve midpoint structures, planetary pictures, mutual receptions, or parallels and contraparallels in declination.

As we examine the relationships of Mercury with the rulers of the money houses in the horoscope, we should ask ourselves all of the key questions that are a part of competent horoscope analysis: "Are the planetary aspects applying or separating? Are they stressful, or are they harmonious? Do they pull in the influences of additional planets as well? Are they a part of chart patterns like T-squares or Grand Trines, or do they activate symmetrical alignments in the horoscope? Are there planetary relationships expressed through dispositorships that give us additional information about Mercury's role?"

The answers to all these questions depends, of course, on the configurations that are found in the particular horoscope under consideration, but just asking the questions while examining the chart will often inspire useful insights into the role that Mercury plays in describing the thought processes and mental biases that we can expect the astro-trader to exhibit.

Mercury Ruling Money Houses

When Mercury is the ruler of one or more of the money houses in the natal horoscope of an astro-trader, it deserves particular attention. Mercury can function as an amplifying force, pumping up the volume on everything that is associated with the particular house that it rules.

The astro-trader may be preoccupied with thinking about those matters, and that thought process is typically externalized as writing or conversation. There can also be cases in which travel is also included as a means of Mercury expression, for example in the case of a trader with Mercury ruling the natal eighth house who frequently travels to conferences and workshops that are about minimizing trading risk and managing tax situations or margin accounts more effectively.

In other cases we may find that the Mercury amplification of a natal money house remains entirely focused on the implications of that house in the trading process itself, and based on the strength of Mercury in the natal chart we can spot the individual's potential for problems in the trading process, or identify the particular strengths that can make him or her unusually successful in the markets.

In every case, however, with Mercury involved as the ruler of a natal money house we need to pay particular attention to Mercury's relationship to other planets in the horoscope. If there is a Mercury aspect, a relationship of dispositorship, or another type of Mercury connection with a specific planet, the role of Mercury will be colored and modified by the nature of the planet involved. The more deeply we can explore Mercury's connection with that planet, the more insights we are likely to gain into the trader's mental makeup and its potential influence on trading behavior.

The role of Mercury as an influence in an astro-trader's natal horoscope is even stronger if Mercury is a both the ruler of a money house and is also unaspected by other natal planets. This condition, which the astrological tradition calls a peregrine planet, is an indication that Mercury is extraordinarily powerful, and will likely become an overwhelming influence in the astro-trader's thinking and behavior.

While having a peregrine Mercury in the natal chart can lend incredible strength and versatility to the astro-trader's capabilities, it can also bring its share of challenges. Astro-traders with a peregrine Mercury ruling a money house in the natal horoscope need to be especially cautious about over-thinking their trades, or about believing that they can outsmart the market. When traders allow themselves to indulge in such excesses, Mercury is quite likely to put in an appearance in his trickster role, offering the trader unanticipated twists and turns that can prove to be both humbling and expensive.

Even so, with Mercury as the ruler of of one or two money houses the natal horoscope, there will always be other money houses which are ruled by different planets. That's why it's important to determine whether or not Mercury has specific connections with those other planets.

When that's the case, an examination of Mercury's interactions with those other planets will typically give us a much greater understanding of the astro-trader's thought processes and their manifestations in market behavior.

Although the purpose of this book is not to provide a comprehensive guide to natal horoscope analysis, it does have the aim of encouraging a thorough examination of the ways that Mercury can interact with other planets and factors in the birth charts of astro-traders. With that in mind, here are some general guidelines for examining Mercury and its relationships with the planets that rule the money houses of a natal chart:

Mercury and the Sun

Because Mercury is in a geocentric horoscope is never more than 28° away from the position of the Sun, we don't have to consider planetary aspects between these two bodies. We should, however, take a look at the other potential dynamics that we have just described, especially mutual receptions, planetary pictures, and symmetrical alignments. Most of all, though, it's useful to get a core understanding of whether Mercury in the natal chart is Prometheus or Epimetheus, and to the factor in the the corresponding characteristics that we have already described.

In each case, the connections between Mercury and the Sun will tell us something about the degree to which the astro-trader personally identifies with the process of market analysis. A strong sense of individual ownership of the conclusions reached about the possibilities for a successful trade will sometimes create potential problems for the trader, who may become so convinced that the analysis is correct that he or she tries to tell the market what to do, rather than simply observing market actions and adjusting trading strategies and positions accordingly.

Mercury and the Moon

When the Moon is the planetary ruler of one of the money houses in the chart, and when Mercury is involved in some kind of notable relationship with the Moon, it's an especially important interaction for us to take into account. The Moon in the astro-trader's chart will tell us a lot about the nature of the individual's emotions, and a great deal of success in trading is connected with our ability to recognize and manage our emotional fluctuations.

If there is a problematical relationship between Mercury and the Moon in the natal horoscope of an astro-trader, we can gain extremely useful insights into potential obstacles to effective trading. Along with those insights we have an opportunity to come up with creative strategies for managing the emotions in ways that can make a profitable difference in trading effectiveness.

Mercury and Venus

As the lesser benefic of traditional astrology, Venus has a role as one of of the money planets in the astro-trader's horoscope. Its relationship to Mercury can help us understand the trader's core sense of values, the ability of the trader to refine and improve trading plans and strategies, and the trader's tendency to be attracted to certain types of market dynamics or specific trade set-ups.

A positive connection between Venus and Mercury can open up lots of profitable opportunities for an astro-trader. But Venus has a strongly magnetic role in the natal horoscope, and there are even times when we can avoid potential trading mistakes by expanding our knowledge of what we find naturally attractive, especially when that attraction is so compelling that it creates blind spots in our ability to analyze market opportunities correctly.

Mercury and Mars

When Mars is the ruler of one of the money houses in the horoscope, it plays a particularly significant role in describing our ability to take action in the markets. Its connection with natal Mercury will let us know how to evaluate our ability to move from trading theory and market analysis into the role of active risk-taking. It is thus a vital factor in understanding our ability to be effective in the markets, since a strong Mercury/Mars connection will typically empower a trader to follow through in translating trading insights into profitable buying and selling.

It's particularly interesting to examine Mercury/Mars dynamics when the astro-trader's Mercury is both Epimetheus and retrograde. When that happens, Mars can either act in a way that is allows the trader to compensate for Mercury's position and motion, or it can exacerbate the circumstances to such an extreme that it makes it obvious that this is an individual who will be likely to face insurmountable difficulties in the trading environment that make it difficult, if not impossible, to succeed at profitable trading.

Mercury and Jupiter

The conventional understanding of Jupiter in a natal horoscope is that it brings lots of good things into the life of the native, and that can certainly be the case as we examine its role in the natal horoscope of an astro-trader. When it is the ruler of one of the money houses in the horoscope, Jupiter expands the emphasis on that part of the chart enormously.

While that can often provide extraordinary opportunities for an astro-trader, it can also be something to watch out for, since a strong Jupiter influence in active connection with natal Mercury can lead to the kind of expansive thinking that may result in over-trading or in taking market positions that are too large for effective money management.

Good trading always involves a clear sense of dedication to specific trading rules, and an overactive Jupiter can sometimes convince us to throw those rules out the window and take chances that we shouldn't be taking.

Mercury and Saturn

It is when we examine connections between Mercury and Saturn as the ruler of one of the horoscope's money houses that we can best get an understanding of the kinds of rules and structures that are most appropriate in promoting the individual's effectiveness in trading.

Traders with strong and positive Mercury/Saturn dynamics in their natal charts are typically deep thinkers, and they tend to take trading rules and responsibilities very seriously. Although Saturn can occasionally indicate major blockages in the trading experience, including big losses in the markets, it can also give us clues about the kinds of approaches to time and money management that can create the limits that are so essential to profitable market activity.

When we look at Mercury/Saturn relationships we come face-to-face with the paradoxical adage which reminds us that "Losers in the markets think about winning, but winners in the markets think about losing." That may seem counter-intuitive, but it is the kind of understanding that encourages us to enter concrete stop-loss orders with our trades, and to take money off the table when our market positions become profitable.

Mercury and Uranus

We take Uranus into consideration only if we are applying modern rulership associations to our analysis of the money houses in the astro-trader's horoscope. When natal Mercury is in an energetic connection with Uranus, the astro-trader's thought processes are typically extremely quick, sometimes to the point of being precipitous and ill-advised.

A positive Mercury/Uranus combination can enhance the trader's capacity for electrifying connections with fast-paced market dynamics, and there is often an "easy come, easy go" mentality that's not completely inappropriate for effective trading, especially for day-trading or short-term swing trades.

This planetary relationship can especially amplify and accelerate the analytical skills of an astro-trader with Mercury Prometheus in the natal chart, but it underscores the need for the precautions that are required for that kind of quick-draw involvement with trading opportunities. Astro-Traders with a strong or significant natal Mercury/Uranus emphasis need to be particularly cautious about innovation simply for the sake of innovation, especially when trading tools and methods are concerned.

Mercury and Neptune

With Neptune as the modern ruler of a money house in an astro-trader's natal horoscope, there can be a strong emphasis on the power of intuition in the trading process, especially when Mercury is in a favorable relationship with Neptune. Experienced traders who have spent years becoming attuned to the ebb and flow of market rhythms can often rely on intuition as a seemingly infallible guide to taking the right action at the right time in the markets, but it's typically not wise to trust intuitive insights too much as an astro-trader, especially if the trader is relatively new to the ins and outs of trading.

A debilitated Mercury connection with Neptune in the natal horoscope can also indicate a susceptibility to get-rich-quick propositions or Ponzi schemes, or even worse, suggest a great capacity for self-deception, and it goes without saying that these tendencies can be fatal to a successful trading career.

Mercury and Pluto

When we find Pluto serving as the modern ruler of a money house in a natal chart, it can give us a hint about the astro-trader's potential for dealing with big money and large-scale trading positions. This is especially true if Mercury has a favorable relationship with Pluto in the natal chart, but even that kind of big-money connection carries a word of warning: unless the trader has an ample supply of trading capital, and unless there is also an ability to take big trading losses in stride, the astro-trader may unwittingly enter positions that can have a devastating impact on the long-term outcome of trading activities, even to the point of bankrupting the trader and putting an end to market activity once and for all. This potential challenge is especially deserving of close examination when Pluto is the ruler of the eighth house in an astro-trader's natal horoscope, which can indicate the possibility of over-extension of margin indebtedness, or for taking on extensive risks with other people's money.

Example Horoscopes

To get a clearer picture of the ways that Mercury can function in a trader's natal horoscope, let's examine a couple of sample charts and explore the Mercury dynamics in them. As we do so, we can see some of the factors which can lead to either success or to failure in the markets.

A Successful Speculator

Our first horoscope is the chart of an individual who had a long and extremely successful career in business and the markets. He had an excellent knack for identifying profitable opportunities, and was able to leverage those opportunities consistently in acquiring and preserving a large personal fortune. Mercury in his natal chart is both Epimetheus and direct, so we can immediately see that he has a tendency to analyze trading situations carefully. Note as well that Mercury is in its dignity in the sign of Virgo, a factor which adds considerable weight to this trader's ability to apply his analytical skills to the markets and then profit from that analysis.

Successful Speculator
Male Chart

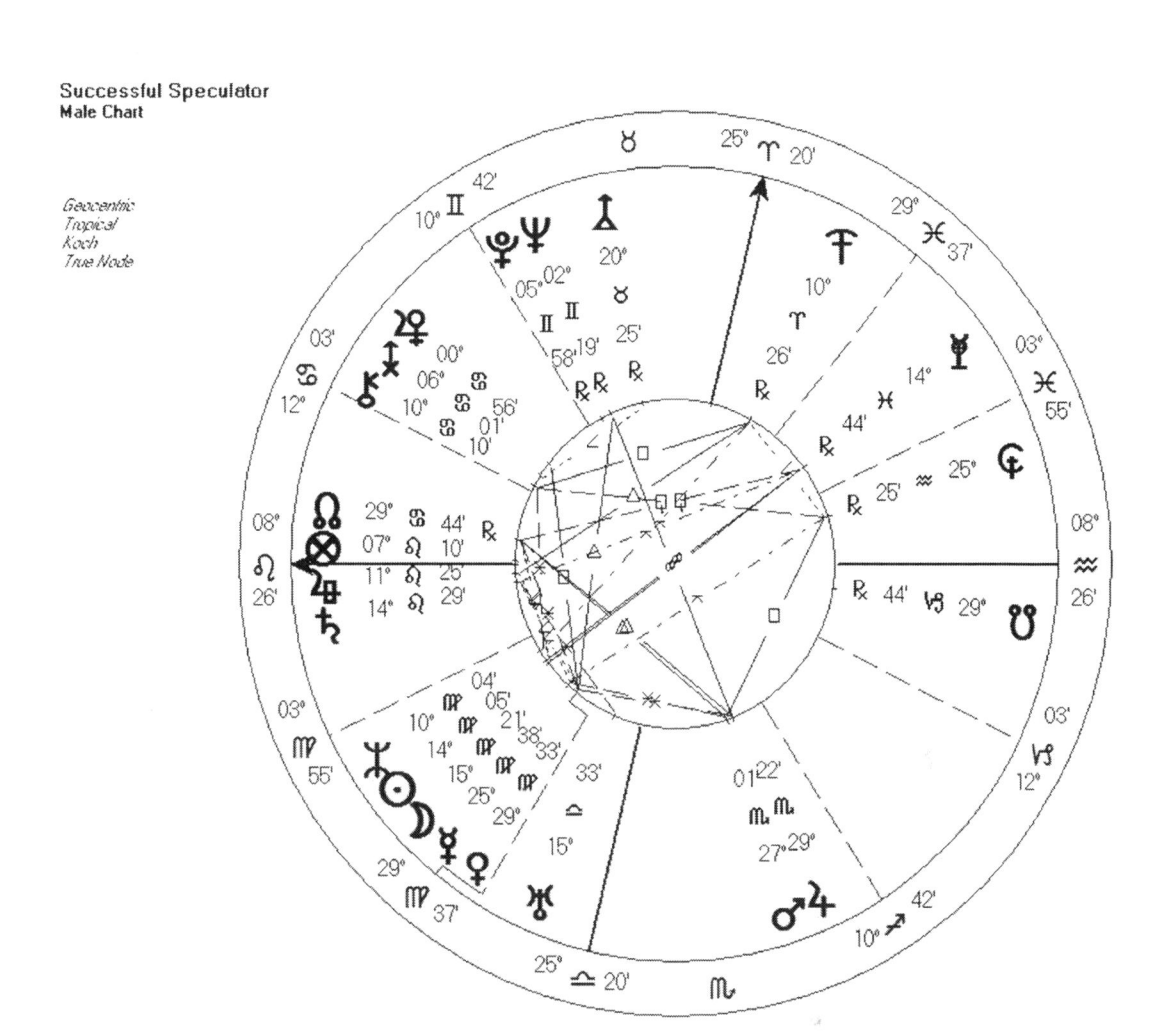

Geocentric
Tropical
Koch
True Node

When we look at the fifth house in this chart, we find Sagittarius on the cusp, ruled by Jupiter, which is conjunct the trader's natal Mars. This combination not only expands the size and scope of the trader's speculative moves, but also contributes to his ability to take successful action in the markets. Although there is no aspect here between Jupiter and Mercury, Mercury in Virgo is in the sign which is the detriment of Jupiter. This factor can keep Jupiter from going completely wild, so even though the trader might take extremely large positions in the markets, he is capable of paying attention to the potential downside in the risks that he takes. This ability to think about the consequences of losing is a vital part of a successful trading career.

With Gemini on the cusp of the eleventh house in the chart, we turn to Mercury as the planetary ruler. Mercury is the strongest planet in this horoscope, so this trader definitely has the ability to take money off the table in order to bring in healthy profits from trading activities. With Mercury conjunct Venus, we can expect those profits to be quite rewarding financially, and their size is enhanced even more by the Mercury/Apollon semi-square. With Mercury trine both Neptune and Vulcanus, this trader is likely to the find imaginative and powerful ways of reaping rewards that might escape others, and with Mercury quincunx Hades he may occasionally have opportunities to cash in on market divergences that have implications which others may find uncomfortable or even repulsive.

The Sun is the ruler of this trader's second house, and the Sun is posited in the second house itself as well. This individual is thus likely to identify quite strongly with the wealth he accumulates, and others are likely to see him first and foremost as someone who is rich without necessarily comprehending the techniques or motivations which lead him to affluence. Mercury doesn't have a strong connection with the Sun in this chart, so it's unlikely that this individual will communicate very much about his real financial status.

Aquarius is on the cusp of the eighth house in this successful speculator's natal horoscope, so we will consider Saturn, the traditional ruler of Aquarius, as well as Uranus, the modern ruler, in understanding this trader's approach to other people's money. Saturn, of course, acts as an inhibiting factor here, so this trader is likely to take financial transactions with others very seriously, especially as a means of defining who he really is. Saturn is extremely weak in this chart, however, so this trader is unlikely to set many limits in using other people's money to his own advantage. With Uranus as the co-ruler of the house, he is capable of making market moves that can take others by surprise. Once again, though, there is not a strong connection between Mercury and Uranus in this chart, so he is unlikely as well to give very much thought to the impact that his actions may have on the counterparties to his trades.

Because Mercury has its strongest association with the eleventh house in this chart, it's clear that this trader's principal preoccupation is with the returns he can get from the risks that he is willing to take. While this horoscope includes many indications of trading ability and financial success, Mercury's key role is in helping this trader use his extraordinary mental abilities to bring in exceptional rewards from his trading activity.

As to the nature of the trader's mental activity itself, we can gain some additional insights by examining Mercury's connection with some key planetary midpoints in the horoscope. Mercury is semi-square the Moon/Zeus midpoint, indicating an extremely lively mind with lots of creative insights and the kind of strong emotional edge of that can sometimes cloud the mental process. This can enhance the awareness of profitable opportunities, but it can also be problematical if too much emotion gets filtered into the trading process. This trader is thus likely to make his share of mistakes in the markets, especially when he becomes too impulsive in following through with some of the profitable opportunities that he discovers. Mercury's activation of the natal Zeus/Admetos midpoint provides a good counterpoint, however, because it strengthens the trader's tendency to think things through carefully, and to prepare thoroughly before committing large amounts of capital.

Even so, with Mercury semi-square the Uranus/Pluto midpoint, this trader is likely to have a strong tendency to change his mind rather quickly. This may be because he spots new and presumably better opportunities which can rapidly lure him away from a planned course of action, but it may also be because he sometimes experiences disappointments with the results he is getting, and then suddenly decides to look for greener pastures. With Mercury in opposition to the midpoint of Hades and the Midheaven in this natal chart, it's clear that this trader is not at all high-minded in his approach to the markets. He is likely to have a very low opinion of the counter-parties in his trades, even though he may keep his negative feelings to himself. Above all, he is clearly capable of the kind of ruthless, cut-throat behavior that will help him make sure that he is getting the big profits that he seeks.

A Chronic Loser in the Markets

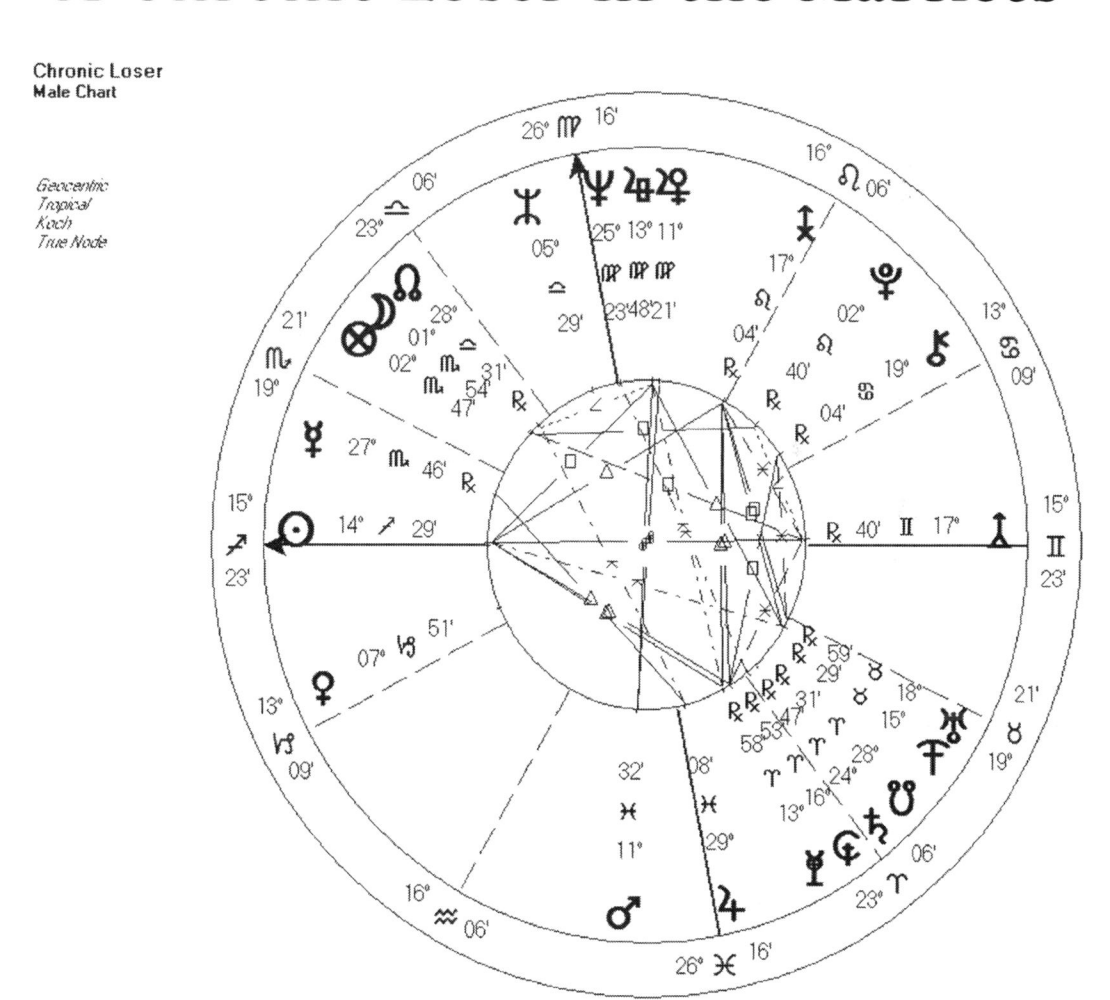

The second natal horoscope that we will examine is the birth chart of an individual whose entire professional life has put him in ongoing contact with the markets and with trading activity, but who has been singularly unsuccessful in his trading efforts. He has

Mercury Prometheus and retrograde, which is the hallmark of the market plunger who impulsively puts money at risk and adamantly refuses to pay attention to the information the market is offering him about potential shifts in trend.

The Mercury Prometheus and retrograde motif in this horoscope is echoed in Mercury's relationships through dispositorship. Neptune has some prominence in this horoscope because of its close conjunction with the Midheaven. This configuration is not unusual in the natal charts of individuals who spend time in the Navy, who have major problems with alcohol or drugs, or who have over-active imaginations. In this case, all three correlations are true for this traders, and much of that planetary energy is transferred to Mercury. Because Neptune in his chart is disposited by Mercury and is in the face of Mercury as well, his thought process is often informed by flights of imaginative fancy or by perceptions muddled by alcohol abuse. But the interplay of planetary influences doesn't stop there. Mercury is in turn disposited by Mars, so this is an individual who spends very little time in thinking things over, but is far more likely to take precipitous action instead. That tendency is reflected in his behavior in the markets.

With Aries on the cusp of the fifth house in this horoscope, it is in fact Mars which drives this individual's push toward risk-taking and speculation. Although the influence of Mercury does little or nothing to slow Mars down in this case, Mars itself is posited in the third house of the horoscope, so the trader is likely to believe that he has given adequate thought to his trading decisions. In fact he may feel that his impulsive traits and the big risks that he takes are actually a means of personal self-expression. That personal identification with his positions in the markets is amplified due to the influence of a separating square of Mars to the Ascendant in the natal chart.

The eleventh house in this trader's horoscope has Venus as its ruler. Mercury is in the triplicity and the face of Venus, and with Venus disposited by Saturn, this individual is likely to feel that the rewards he gets from his trading activity are woefully inadequate. And, with the imbalance between risk and reward that this chart demonstrates, his assessment will be right in many cases.

Saturn is also the ruler of the second house in this trader's natal chart, and Mercury is in the terms of Saturn. This individual is thus likely to experience big shortfalls in personal finances, and it's quite likely that he may find it extremely difficult to get ahead, or even to break even when money matters of any sort are concerned.

While some individuals who have Saturn as a second-house ruler are able to marshal its energies to provide financial structure and security, in this case that seems unlikely, since Saturn is extremely weak and is disposited by Mars. When things get tough financially, the tendency is thus not to institute more checks and balances, but rather to plunge ahead with even bigger risks, in the hopes that a dramatic roll of the dice will magically produce a financial turnaround.

The eighth house also presents its share of challenges. With Cancer on the cusp, this house is ruled by the Moon, so there is considerable emotion involved with this individual's connections to taxes, insurance, indebtedness, trading margin, and other people's money. The Moon is not only disposited by Mars, it is also in the terms and face of Mars, so the emotional expressions can be particularly intense, and are likely to activate bursts of anger or belligerence. Needless to say, such emotional extremes are not congruent with the kind of internal balance required for effective trading.

When we look at Mercury's role as a potential activator of planetary midpoints in this natal horoscope, we find only one significant planetary picture: Mercury is sesquiquadrate to the midpoint of Saturn and the Aries Point in the chart. This planetary picture is the signature of the conclusion of a work project, of the termination of a contract, and of layoffs of a workforce. In the case of this particlar chart, the individual has had repeated experiences with such matters.

But Mercury's activation of the Saturn/Aries midpoint is also important in another context. It is emblematic of the individual's general mindset and attitude, both in approaching the markets and in dealing with life in general-- the belief and core understanding that the world as a whole is a negative place, and that there are severe limits to the benefits that life offers. While other traders may perceive the markets as an endless stream of opportunities, this individual is likely to have extremely low expectations of success, even though his compulsive behavior as a gambler in the markets is driven by the persistent illusion that maybe just this once he'll get lucky and make a big score.

Horoscope Synthesis and the Astro-Trading Advantage

Note that in examining these charts, we aren't looking for particular Mercury signatures that infallibly signal failure or success in the markets. Our goal is instead to come to a comprehensive and dynamic understanding of the way that Mercury functions in the natal chart, particularly with regard to the money houses, and with a special emphasis on the trader's ability to handle risk appropriately. That understanding comes about through a process of synthesis; as we combine observations at different levels, and combine and contrast the indicators we discover in the individual horoscope, we can arrive at a composite picture of the role that Mercury plays. That understanding in turn can become the basis for a more thorough examination of the trader's natal chart, with the aim of developing specific trading disciplines and market strategies that take full advantage of the individual's unique capabilities.

While Mercury clearly plays a different role in each of these natal horoscopes, there is one important point of commonality: an examination of Mercury helps us come to a comprehensive understanding of the mental makeup and characteristic thought processes of the individual trader. That's why connecting with Mercury in the natal chart can offer us such a big advantage in the trading environment. Unless we can understand what we think, how we think, and why we think that way, we have little hope of modifying our thought processes, and instead are likely to become the victims of our habits and prejudices.

Unless we can control the way that we think, we simply can't learn to trade effectively. Someone once commented that "trading is a form of psychological brain surgery," and that observation is even more appropriate in the light of the role that Mercury can play in our behavior as traders. When we understand the unique ways that Mercury functions for us as individual traders, and then observe our trading behaviors from the Mercury perspective, we have an extraordinary opportunity to change our thoughts, to change our actions, and to change the results that we get from our trading.

Mercury in Money Horoscopes

As traders we are concerned with the interaction of price and time in the markets. We use market charts to depict the passage of time on the horizontal axis, and add notations on the vertical axis to record fluctuations in the price of the stock or commodity we are tracking.

In actuality, when we look at a market chart we are not only concerned with the specific price of the stock or commodity we are trading, but also with how that price has changed over time, and what the history of price fluctuations can tell us about the potential for more price fluctuations in the future. Indeed, the current price trend that's reflected in a market chart is not only the result of negotiations between buyers and sellers; it is also a representation of expectations about future value as well.

When we apply astrology to the markets, the most obvious correlations are with the axis of time. After all, planetary alignments take place at specific moments in time, and planetary cycles repeat at regular time intervals. Time itself is something that we measure in clearly-defined increments, and in our work with the markets the relative value of those increments doesn't change.

When it comes to price in the markets, however, things immediately get more complicated. There are of course ways of correlating specific planetary positions in the zodiac with numerical values that can be associated with price values on a market chart, and by tracking a planet's change in position over time we can often gain valuable insights into price trends in a market. But at a fundamental level, there's much more to price than numerical equivalents. Whether the market we are trading is accounted for in dollars, euros, or yen, the current price action is not just about pips or points. Nor is it simply a way of codifying degrees of confidence about the sustainability of prices in the future. It's also intrinsically connected with money, and with our perceptions of monetary value.

The value of money is not static. It fluctuates dramatically over time, and any attempt to assess the value of a currency has to consider that fluctuation if it is to be useful in making decisions in commerce or in the markets. While various economists in the past century have devised formulas for computing the value of money over time, the notion of a time/money connection is in itself not new. In fact, Leonardo of Pisa, popularly known as Fibonacci, specifically included time-value in his monumental work *Liber Abaci*, which was first published in 1202.

While Fibonacci is best remembered as the originator of the Fibonacci series, a numerical sequence that describes geometric patterns of growth in nature (and in the markets as well), *Liber Abaci* is not just a discussion of that concept. It is a comprehensive textbook of basic mathematics, and of the practical applications of mathematical principles in commercial enterprises. The problems and examples in the book display an extremely sophisticated understanding of the fluid complexities of currencies and exchange rates, and of the changing value of money over time.

Shifts in monetary value also influence the action of the markets, and that influence goes beyond the realm of mathematical connections. The impact of the changing value of money on market activity, in particular those shifts in value created by changes in central bank monetary policy, was the subject of a study by Ben S. Bernanke and Kenneth Kuttner in 2003. Bernanke presented their findings in lectures at Widener University in Pennsylvania and at the London School of Economics in October of that year.

"We find that unanticipated changes in monetary policy affect stock prices not so much by influencing expected dividends or the risk-free interest rate," Bernanke said, "but rather by affecting the perceived riskiness of stocks. A tightening of monetary policy, for example, leads investors to view stocks as riskier investments and thus to demand a higher return to hold stocks. For a given path of expected dividends, a higher expected return can be achieved only by a fall in the current stock price."

To get an even richer understanding of the psychological dimensions of value and risk and their connections with money, we can also turn to astrology. Astrology as a symbolic system has a lot to tell us about value, and a study of astrological texts will reveal many planetary associations with money. For example, Venus and Jupiter are sometimes referred to as the money planets in horoscopes, because traditional astrology considered them the lesser and greater benefics, the bringers of good things, including money, in small or large quantities.

In modern astrology Pluto is also associated with money, especially in the context of the kind of transformational power that can be wielded when large amounts of capital come into play. And, as Georgia Stathis has pointed out in her innovative studies of monetary history, long-term Pluto cycles have some significant correspondences with the evolution of currencies and with major shifts in the nature of money itself.

Because monetary value always has some connections with how we feel about certain goods or services, about the wisdom of buying or selling a particular stock, or about other types of monetary transactions between consenting parties, there is also an emotional component to money. While it may be an oversimplification to say that money is nothing more than a crystallization of emotions, when we deal with the role of money in the markets we can't afford to ignore feelings. At least that's a reasonable conclusion when we consider the research done by Bernanke and Kuttner in 2003.

In simpler terms, we can see money's emotional component in everyday commerce as well. A item with a $1,000 price tag may seem exorbitantly over-priced to one individual, while another person may consider it a real bargain-- the dollar amount remains the same, but the two individuals have distinctly different feelings about its worth.

In general, money is a subject that carries a big emotional charge, as is easily demonstrated when we witness a political debate or engage in dinner-table conversation about the family budget. The astrological factor most closely associated with emotional energy is the Moon, and an examination of the role that the Moon plays in a natal horoscope can often provide useful insights into an individual's attitudes about money.

But even though markets are driven by emotional extremes of fear and greed, in this book we are particularly concerned with money's connection to Mercury rather than to any other planets. When we look at Mercury in the horoscope of an individual or a business, we get a glimpse of money as a transactional force in commerce and communication.

Mercury emphasizes one of the key characteristics of money: while it can be accumulated and hoarded, it has its greatest value when it is circulated, fulfilling its function as a medium of exchange.

That characteristic of money is, of course, especially important to us as traders, and it's particularly significant if we intend to bring the astro-trading advantage to our engagement with the markets. Mercury not only connects us to the movement of the markets; it also links us to the money flow that makes up the shifting value which is based in the give-and-take dynamic of the markets themselves, as well as in expectations of price fluctuations and future value.

With that Mercury connection in mind, we can gain valuable information about currencies and financial institutions when we examine their horoscopes with Mercury as a focal point. As we do so, however, we need to remember that Mercury in this context is acting as a messenger, and that the message Mercury is delivering is best understood by examining the other planets that Mercury activates in the horoscope.

The most direct way of examining the horoscope message that Mercury is giving us is by looking at those charts on a 90-degree dial, a horoscopic representation that emphasizes eighth-harmonic planetary relationships. The 90-degree dial has a moveable pointer, and if we align that pointer with the position of Mercury in the chart, we can immediately see the key planets and planetary midpoint structures that Mercury activates in the eighth harmonic, either conjoining the sensitive point or aspecting it in an opposition, a square, a sesquiquadrate, or a semi-square. In each case, those planetary pictures can provide us with useful clues about the true nature of the currency or institution and its potential impact on the trading environment.

Although there are many horoscopes that can provide us with useful information in understanding money and its relationship to the markets, we can get a good sense of the astrological signals we should pay attention to by looking at just a few examples. Two types of charts are presented here: first, some key horoscopes relating to currencies themselves, and secondly, a few representative horoscopes of stock exchanges.

While a quick look at each chart through the Mercury filter will give us some key insights that can give us a starting point for a more thorough investigation, the comments here are not intended as a complete analysis. They are just an illustration of the value we can find when we begin our examination of financial horoscopes by looking at the role that Mercury plays; when we consider current astrological influences on these charts as a tool in forecasting economic or market trends, our task is enormously simplified when we view them through the Mercury lens.

Free Coinage Act
London, England
Dec 30 1666
12:00:00 PM LMT

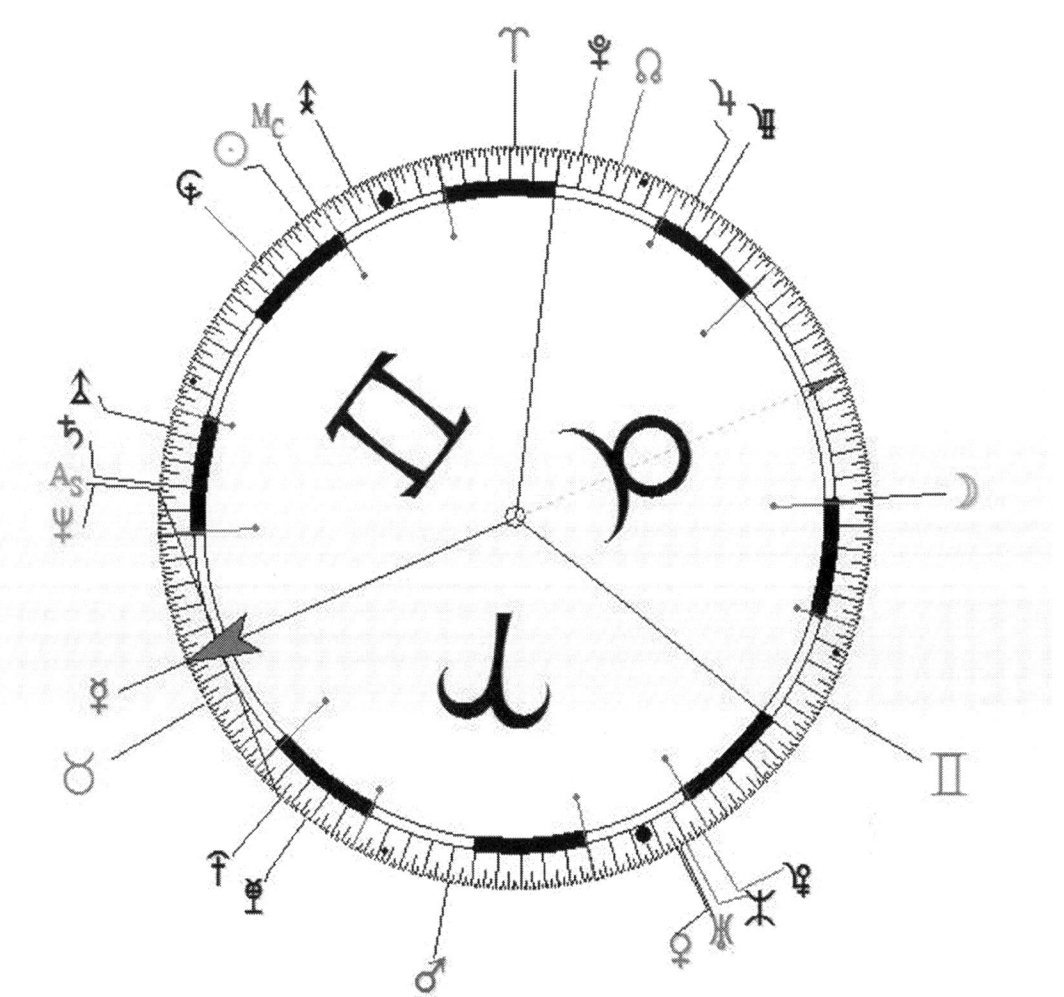

The Free Coinage Act

    This British law effectively transformed global currency structures, for the first time removing coinage as an exclusively royal prerogative and setting the stage for future central banks, currency manipulations, and financial panics. Mercury activates the Neptune/Kronos midpoint in this chart, the astrological signature of large-scale deceptions from the top down. It's also within orb of the Saturn/Admetos midpoint, indicating a total standstill and the creation of long-term structures and relationships.

U.S. Coinage Act
New York, NY
Apr 2 1792
12:00:00 PM LMT

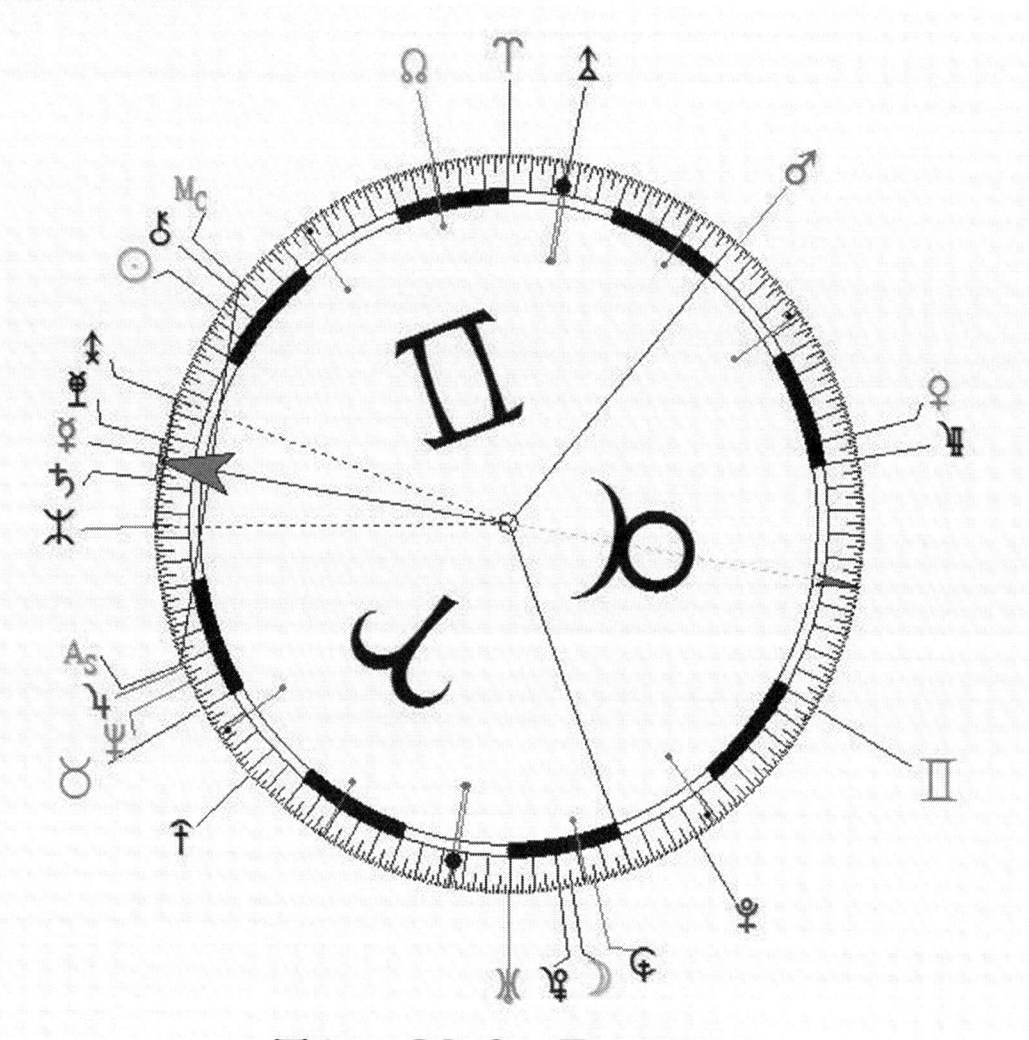

The U.S. Dollar

The birthday of the dollar was the passage of the U.S. Coinage Act in 1792. With a noon chart for the event, Mercury activates the Midheaven/Ascendant midpoint, giving it a solid connection to general commerce and social interactions. The Midheaven/Jupiter connection hints of popularity, wide public acceptance, and positive expectations. But the Saturn/Admetos midpoint that we saw activated in the Free Coinage Act is even more strongly emphasized here, emblematic of scarcity, restriction, and long-lasting structures and institutions.

U.S. Treasury
Washington DC
Sep 2 1789
12:00:00 PM LMT

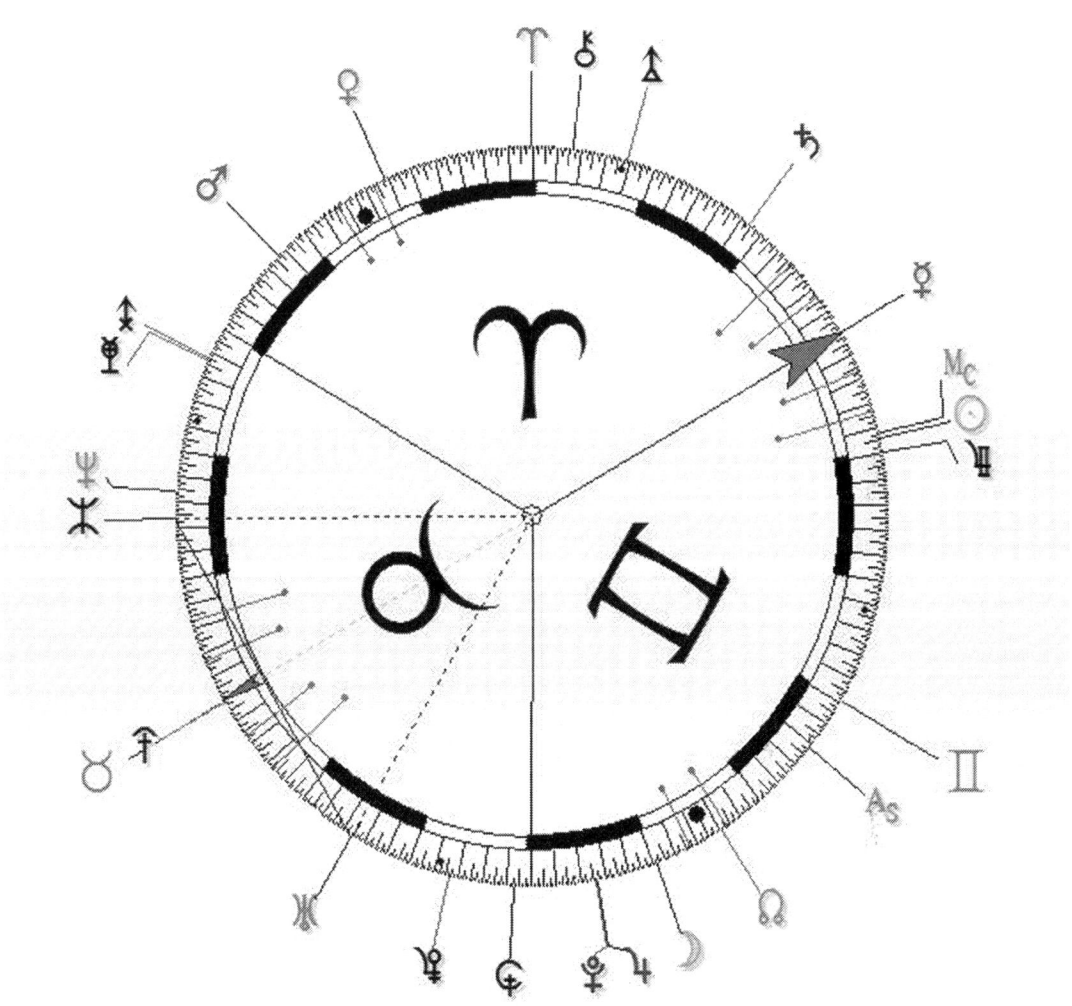

U.S. Treasury

Mercury in this chart precisely aligns with Vulcanus; this is thus first and foremost a picture of the power of the state. With the Venus/True Lunar Node midpoint in play, the public role of the Treasury is generally seen as beneficial, but the activation of the Saturn/Apollon midpoint reveals a role in creating widespread social separations and distinctions. The activation of the Uranus/Poseidon midpoint is also telling-- while the Treasury has a role as a life-sustaining force, it is also an instrument of propaganda.

U.S. Paper Currency Act
Washington DC
Jul 17 1861
12:00:00 PM LMT

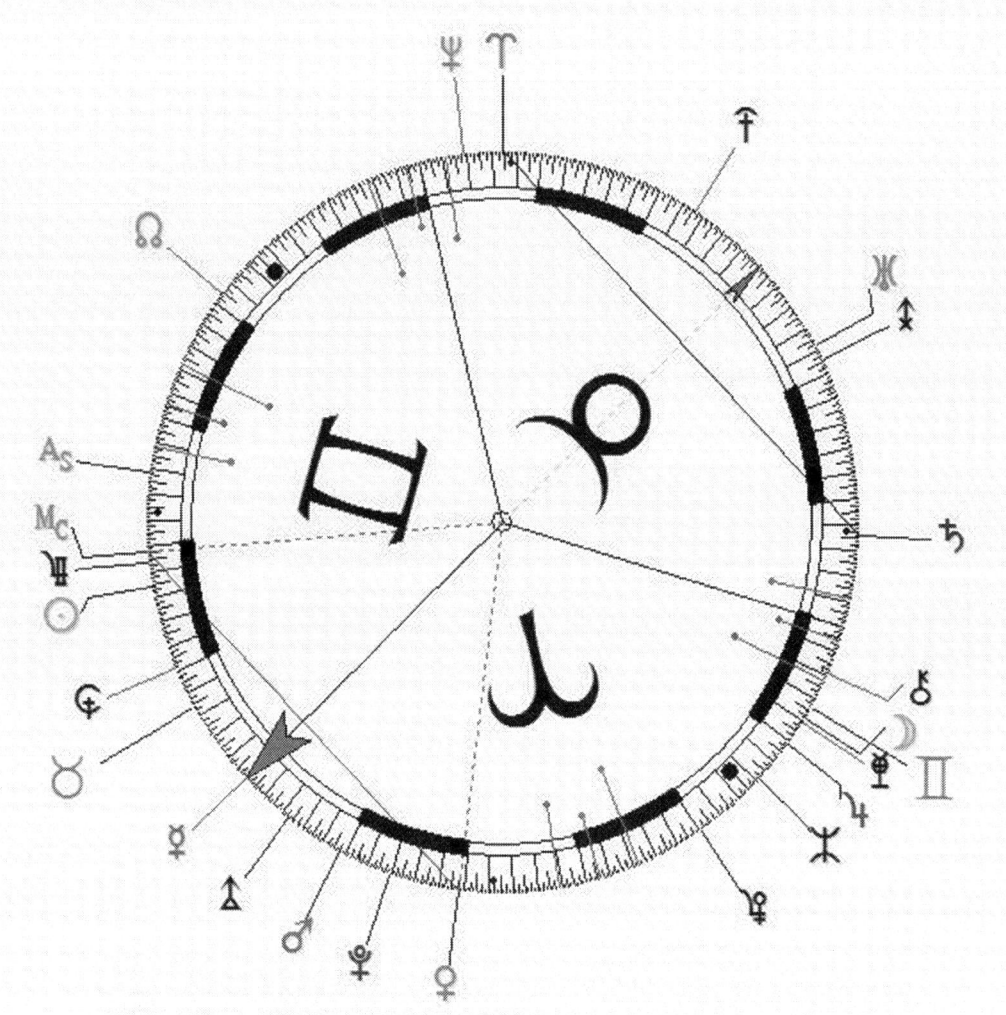

U.S. Paper Currency Act

Congress authorized paper currency in the U.S. to help finance the Civil War; the Mars/Hades midpoint is about slavery, conflict, and atrocities. The sense of separation and desperation is reinforced by the emphasis on the Saturn/Aries Point midpoint. The activation of the Cupido/True Lunar Node midpoint suggests public acceptance of the currency for the common good, while the Venus/Apollon midpoint reveals its inflationary nature. With the Uranus/Kronos midpoint emphasized, the power of the state is suddenly and forcefully imposed.

Federal Reserve Bank
Washington DC
Dec 23 1913
6:02:00 PM EST

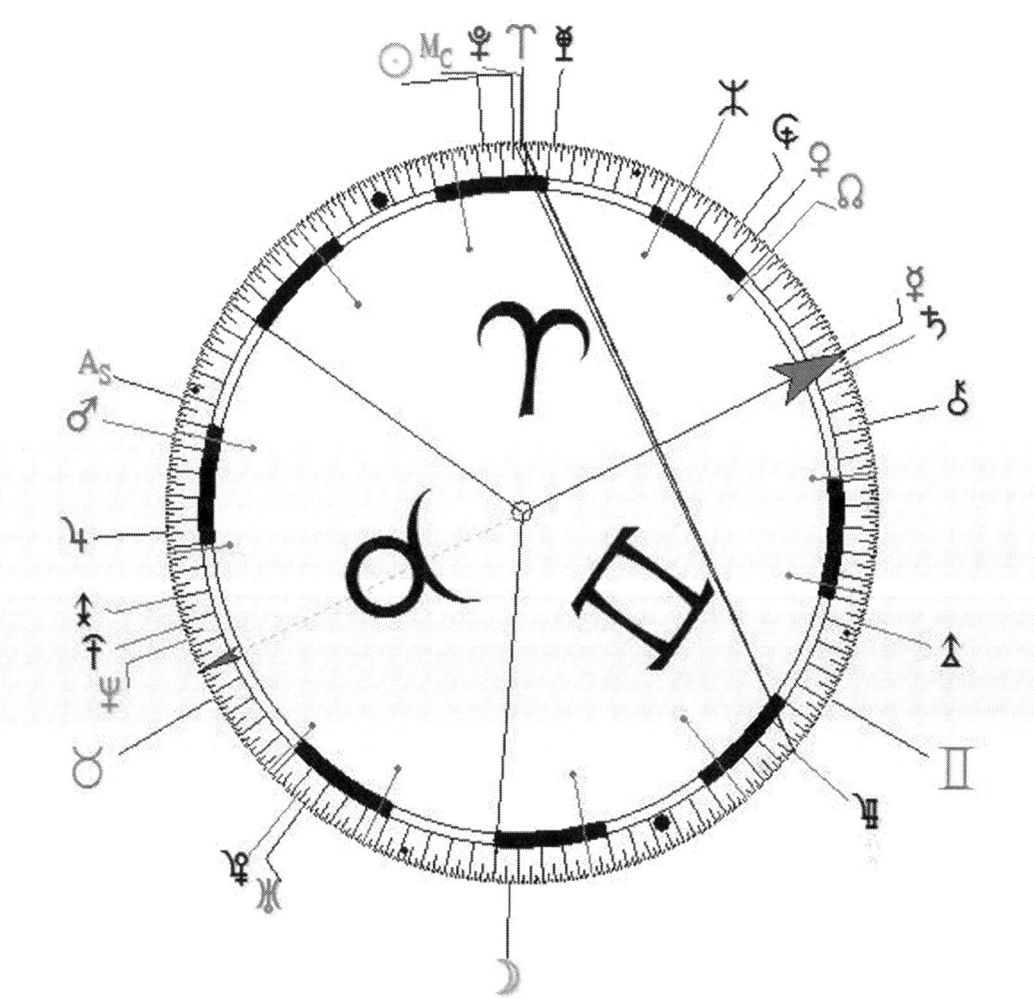

Federal Reserve Bank

    The authorization of the Federal Reserve was a watershed event in financial history, and with Saturn activated in this horoscope a new structure was clearly being created. Looking through the Mercury lens reveals the key role that Apollon plays-- the Pluto/Apollon midpoint indicates a modest beginning that leads to very big consequences; the Sun/Apollon midpoint says that this is an institution that's highly successful in sustaining itself; and the Aries Point/Apollon midpoint reveals its global influence and importance.

Federal Reserve Operatio
Washington DC
Nov 16 1914
12:00:00 PM EST

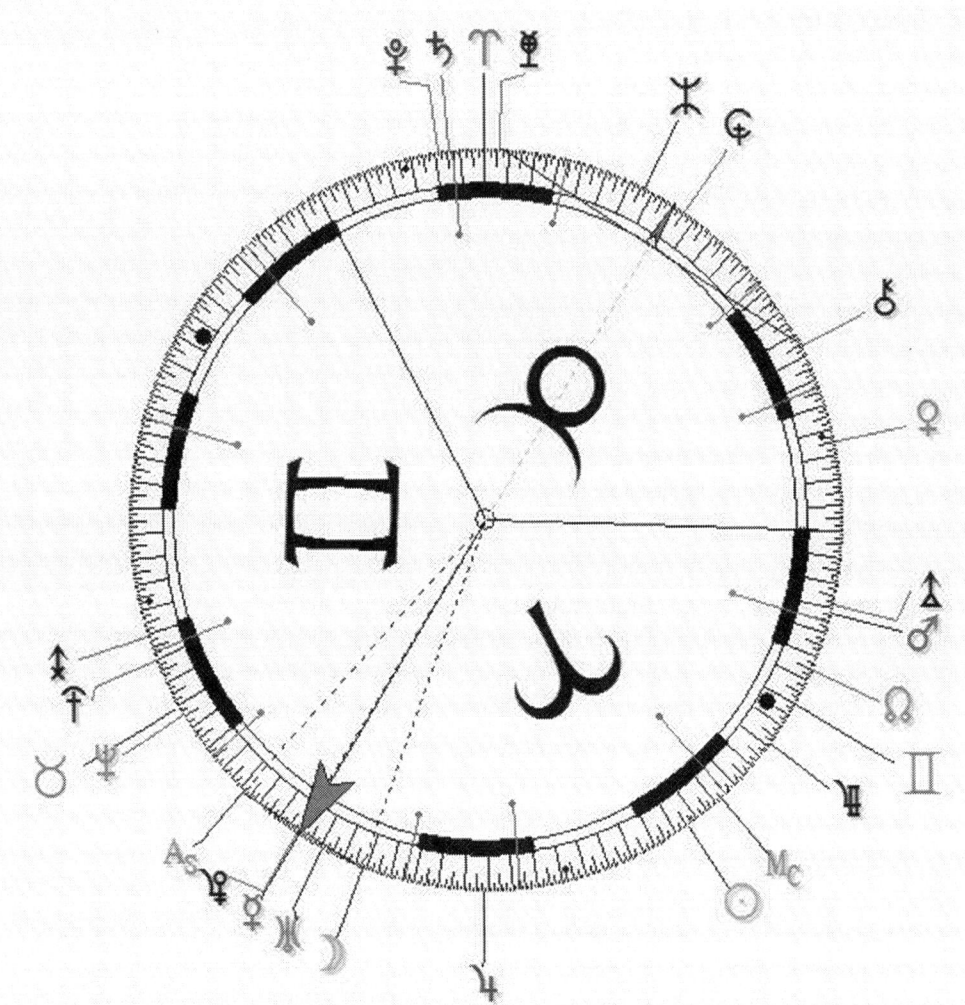

Federal Reserve Operations

    The chart for the start of Fed operations has Mercury aligned with Cupido, which, along with the activation of the Moon/Ascendant midpoint, indicates the central bank's acceptance as a social institution with a lot of public influence. But Mercury also aligns with Hades, so this institution contributes to poverty and corruption, and with the activation of the Chiron/Admetos midpoint it consistently creates problems even as it ostensibly tries to do good.

Bretton Woods Act
Washington, DC
Jul 31 1945
12:00:00 PM

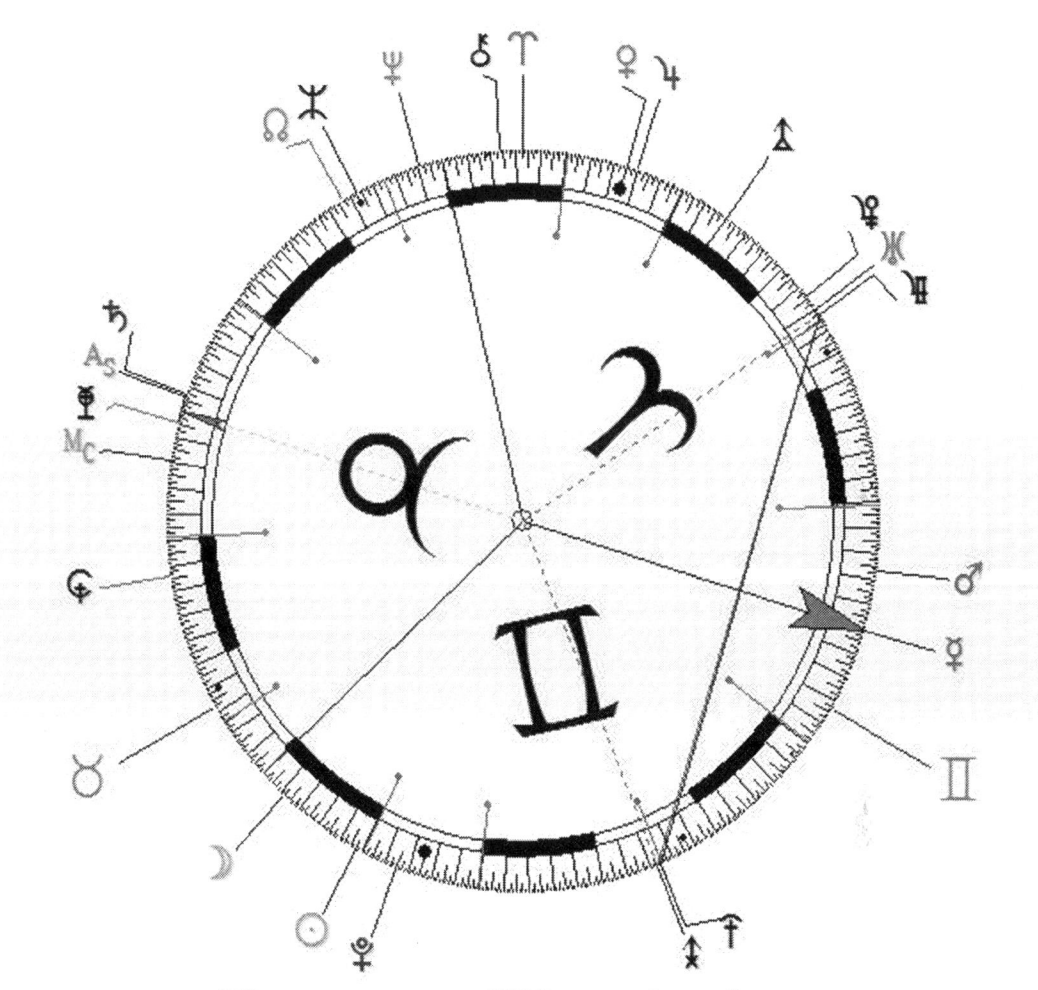

Bretton Woods Act

The Bretton Woods Agreement was reached on July 22, 1944 to fix international currency exchange rates; this chart is for its ratification by the U.S. Congress a year later. It's interesting because Mercury once again activates the Saturn/Admetos midpoint that figured prominently in the Free Coinage Act and U.S. dollar charts. This was an extremely forceful event, as evidenced by the Uranus/Zeus midpoint; with the activation of the Kronos/Apollon midpoint we see the power of the state expanding internationally.

Dollar/Gold Stopped
Washington, DC
Aug 15 1971
12:00:00 PM

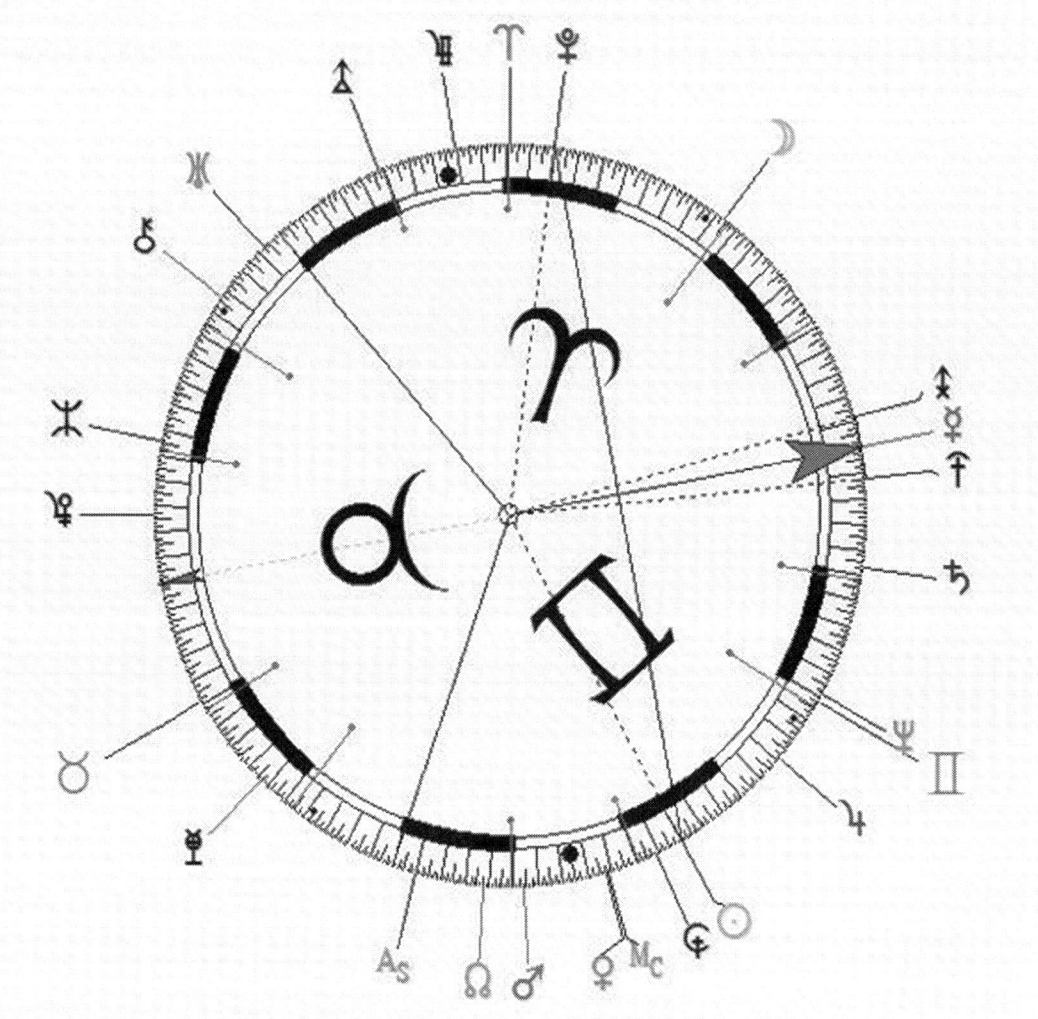

Dollar/Gold Convertibility Ends

U.S. President Richard M. Nixon's surprise announcement that the dollar would no longer be redeemable in gold, and would be allowed to float in value versus other currencies, effectively ended the Bretton Woods Agreement. Mercury at the Zeus/Kronos midpoint is the signature of bold leadership in an act of war (reinforced by the warlike attitude described by Mars/Vulcanus), and the powerful Sun/Pluto midpoint signals an increasing flow of vital substances. The announcement came just three days after a Neptune station; the activation of the Moon/Neptune midpoint indicates deception of the public.

Japanese Yen
Tokyo, Tokyo
May 10 1871
12:00:00 PM LMT

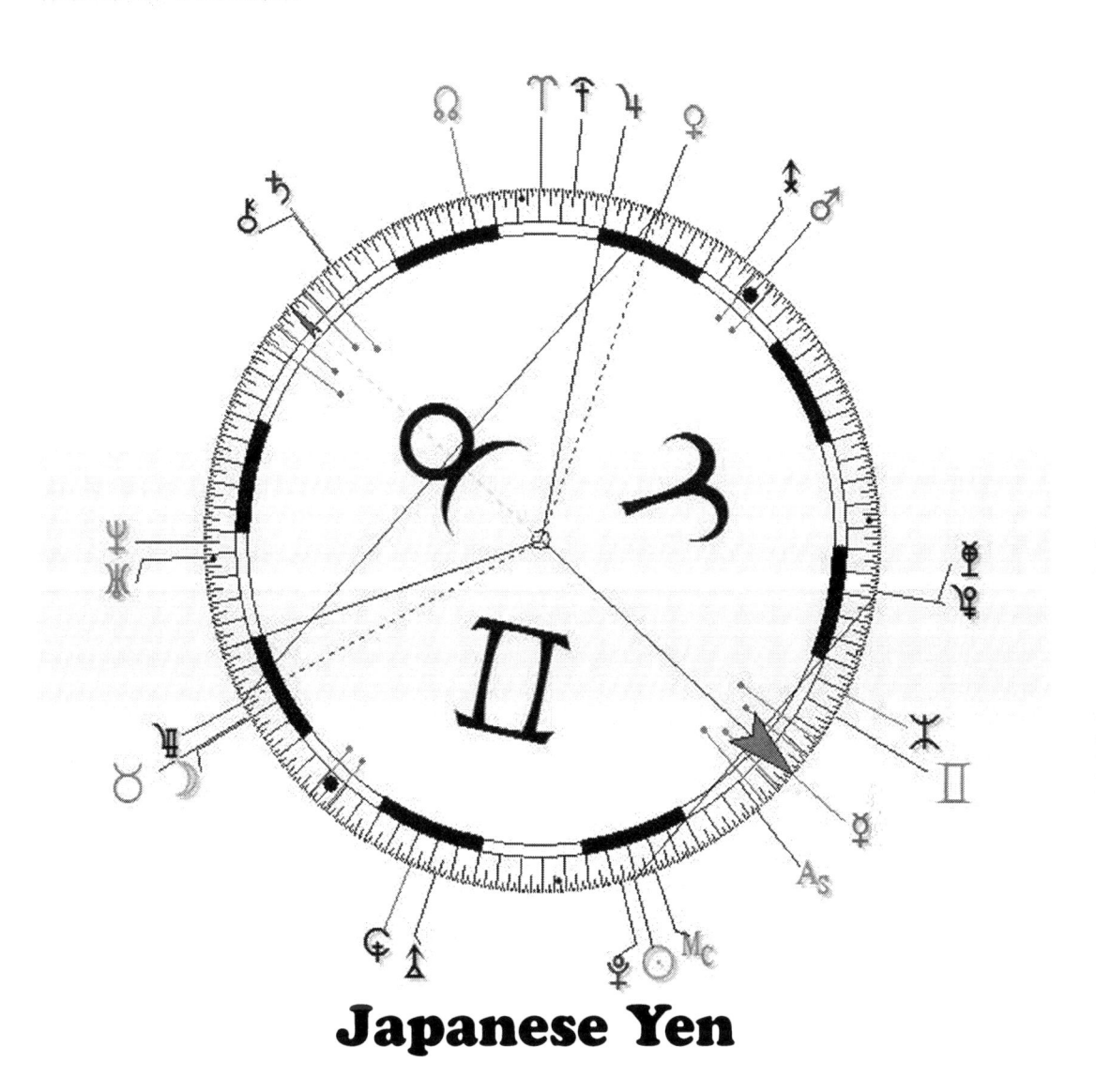

Japanese Yen

The horoscope for the yen reveals that currency's unique relationship to the Japanese social structure. The activation of the Sun/Cupido midpoint shows a strong sense of community, while the Venus/Apollon midpoint emphasizes harmony and equanimity as core values. With Mercury also activating the Sun/Admetos midpoint, there's an indication of perseverance and conservative thinking, with a high value placed on the concept of the homeland in general and on real estate in particular.

Euro First Trade
Frankfurt am Main, Germa
Jan 4 1999
7:00:00 AM CET

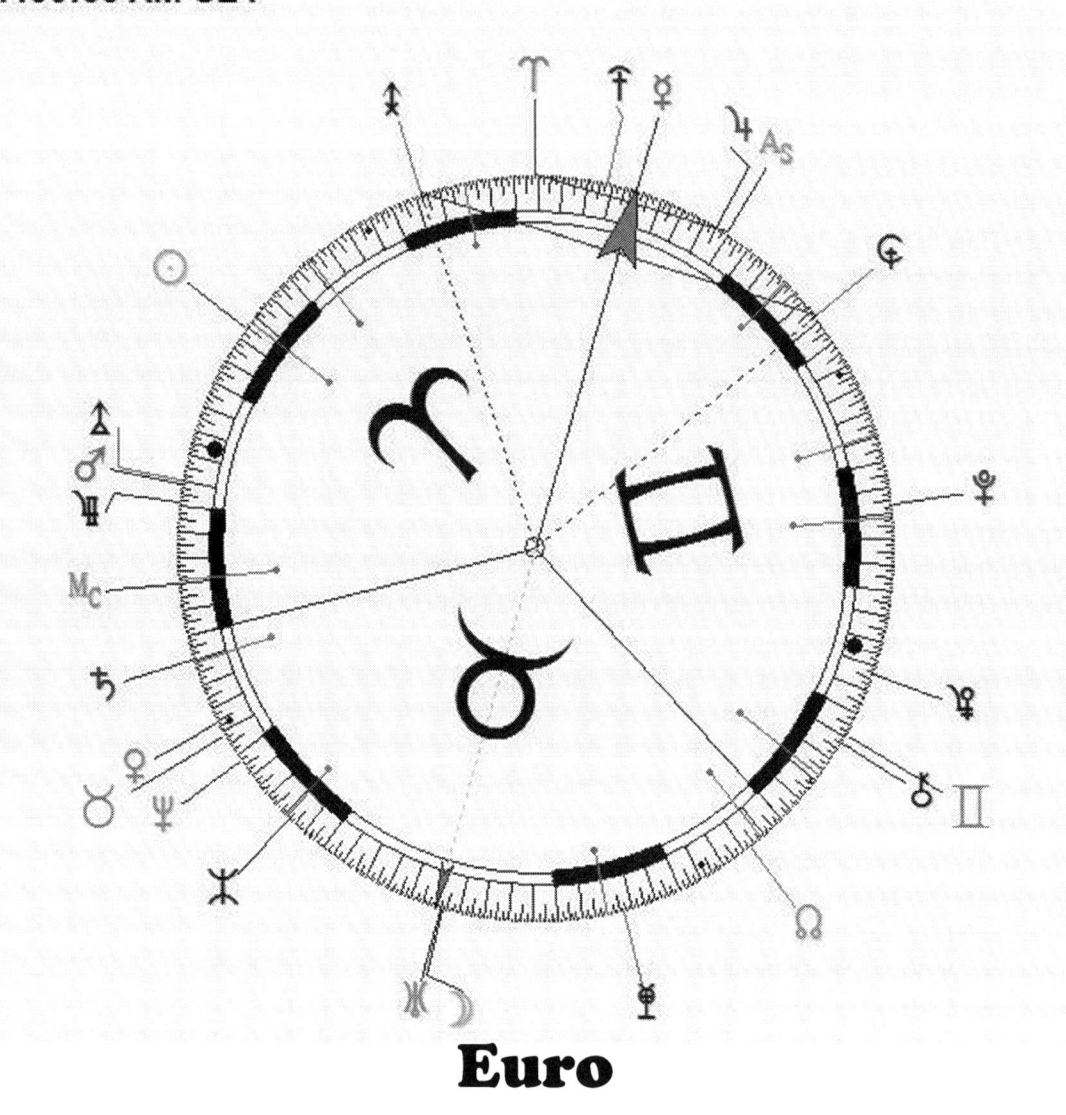

Euro

    There are many precursor charts to the creation of the euro, which went into effect on January 1, 1999; this First-Trade horoscope is especially important, with Mercury triggering the Ascendant/Aries Point, signifying the currency's global role and indicating a constant stream of meetings in a variety of meeting places. The Sun/Pluto midpoint is linked to the distribution of vital resources, but with the activation of the Hades/Zeus midpoint there's a lack of purposeful behavior in favor of compulsory inactivity. The Admetos/Poseidon midpoint suggests that high-minded ideas get rejected, and with the activation of the Moon/Uranus midpoint there's upheaval and unrest among the public, with an ambitious, energetic woman playing a key role.

NYSE_McWhirter
New York, NY
May 17 1792
7:52:00 AM EST

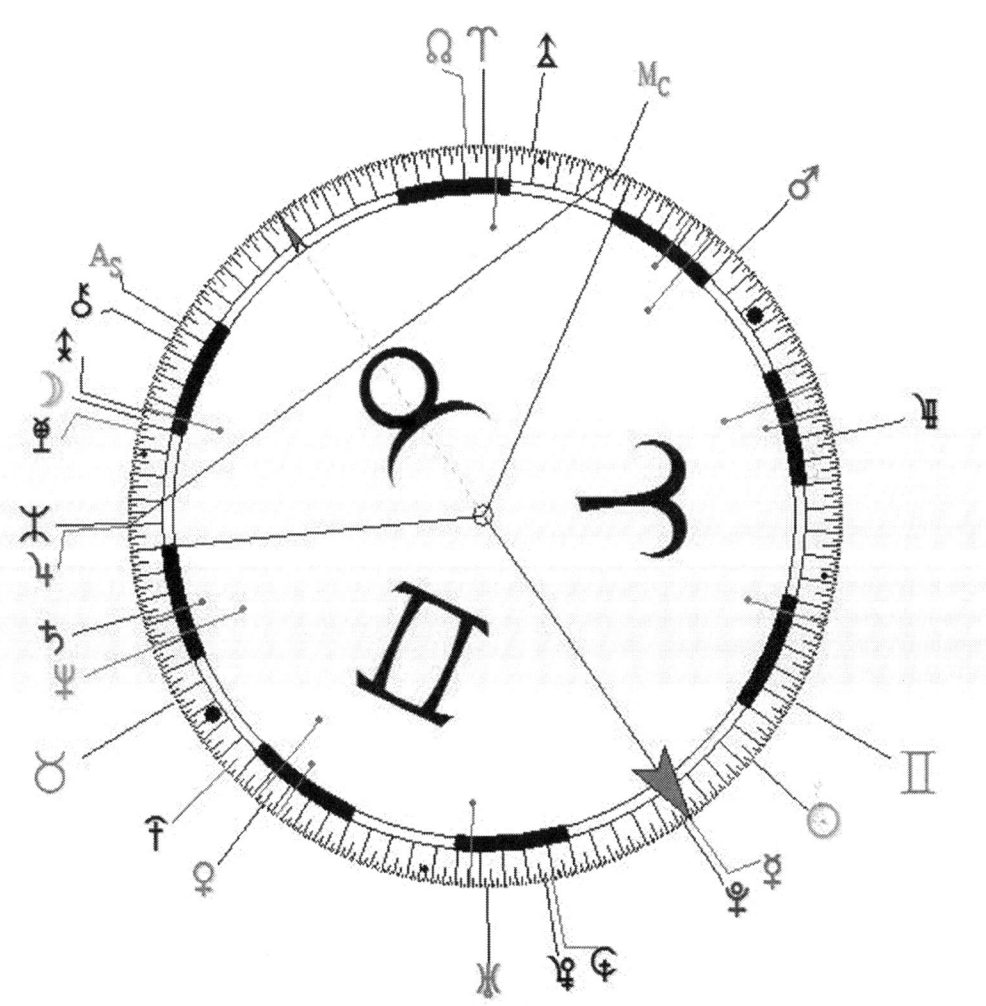

New York Stock Exchange

    The unusual time notation for this chart comes from the work of Louise McWhirter; the chart is remarkably reliable as a forecasting tool. With Mercury's alignment with Pluto, the NYSE is definitely involved with money and power. The activation of the Zeus/Aries Point midpoint indicates an aggressive player on the world stage, strongly linked to the machinery of economics. The Midheaven/Jupiter midpoint signals abiding optimism, while the Midheaven/Poseidon midpoint adds an idealistic dimension. The picture is tempered, however, by the Admetos/Vulcanus midpoint, showing major setbacks and obstacles at the hand of fate.

Securities & Exchange Co
Washington DC
Jun 6 1934
12:00:00 PM EST

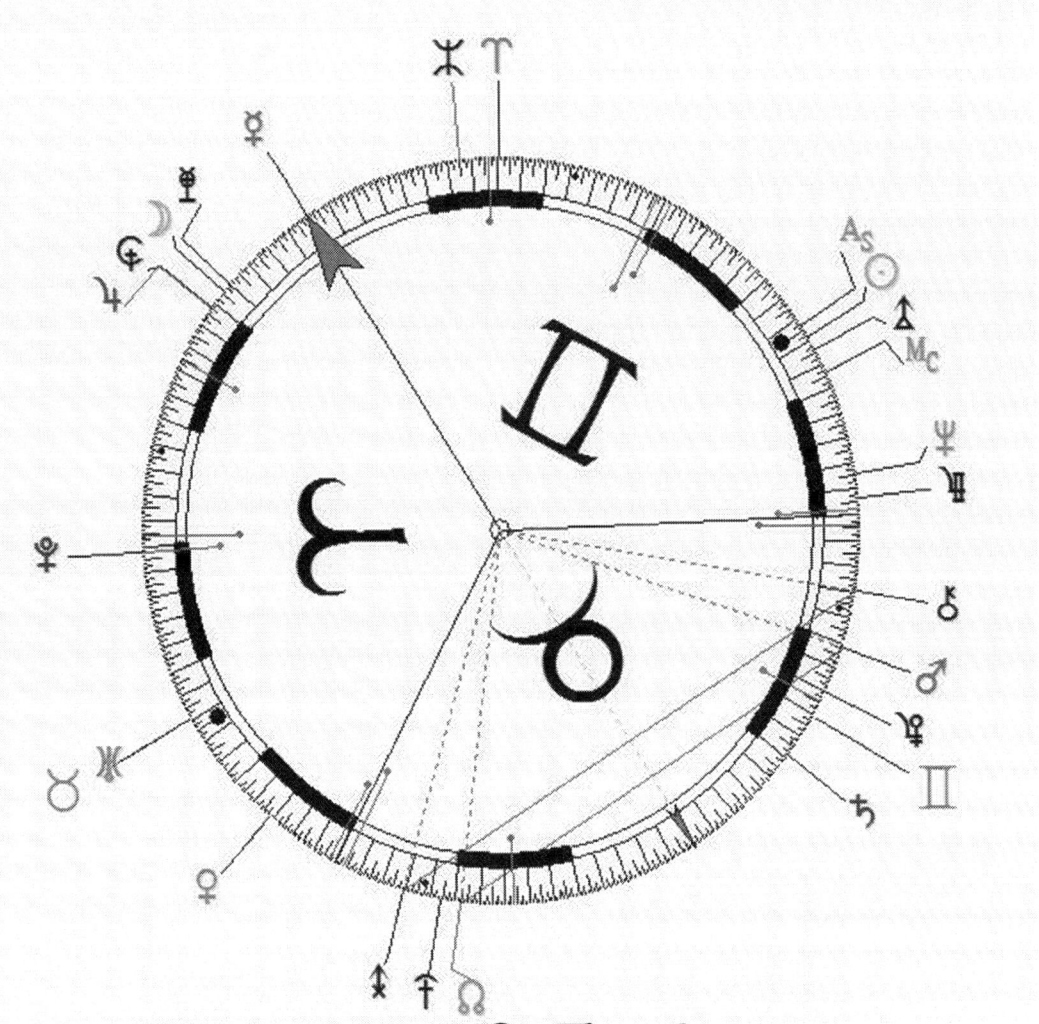

Securities & Exchange Commission

With the Chiron/Zeus midpoint activated, the Securities and Exchange Commission is clearly meant to exhibit forceful regulatory leadership, but often has problems doing so. The Mars/True Lunar Node midpoint provokes a constant pull toward collusion instead of regulation. But the Sun/Uranus midpoint activation indicates that the SEC will sometimes act in surprisingly energetic ways that can impact the direction of the markets.

Paris Bourse
Paris, France
Nov 15 1823
12:00:00 PM LMT

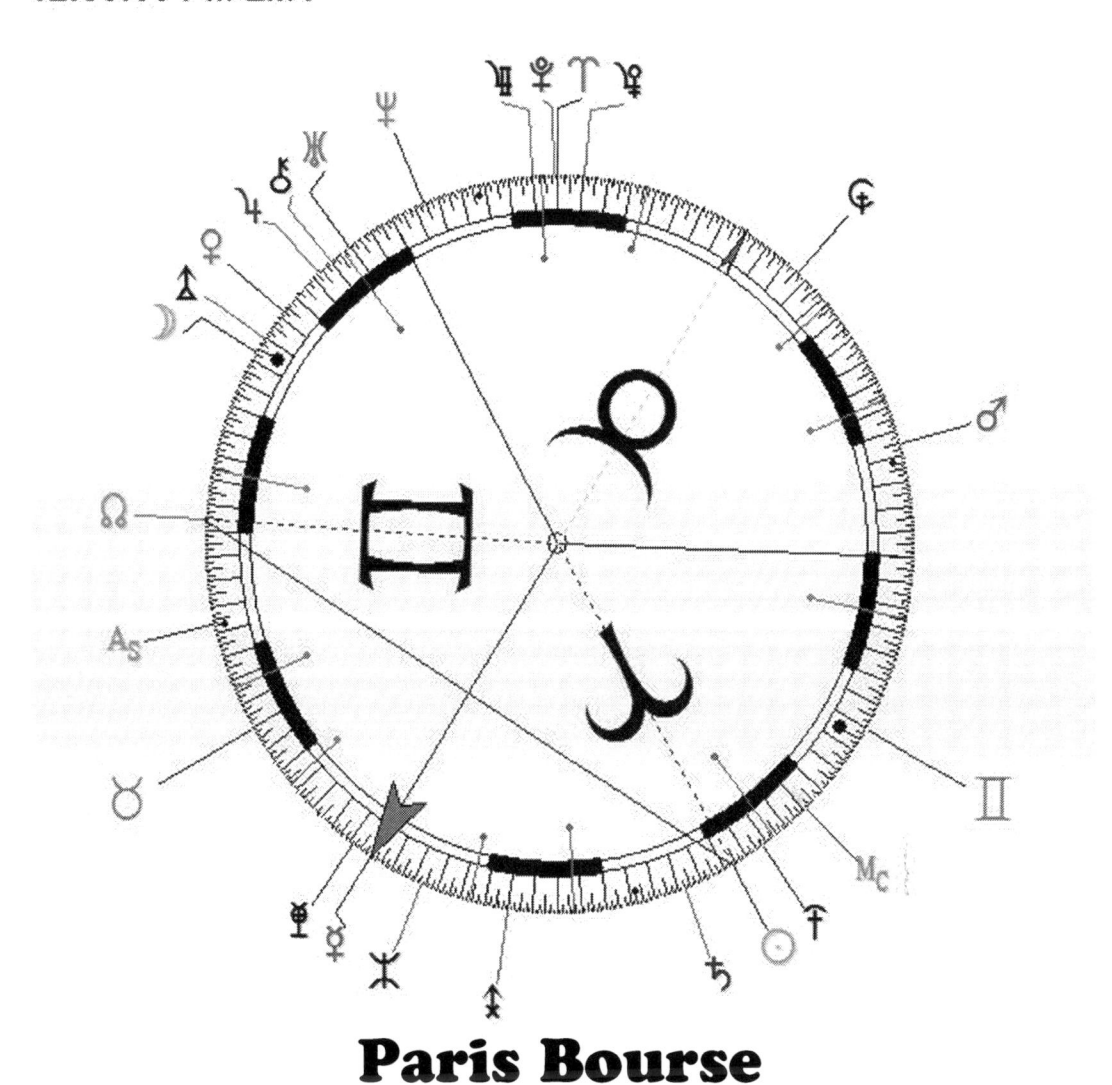

Paris Bourse

The horoscope for the Paris Bourse is included here because it provides an interesting contrast to the NYSE chart. Despite its antiquity, this stock exchange is hardly a major player on the world stage. The activation of the Sun/True Lunar Node midpoint emphasizes its communal connection to the public and its role as a witness to important events rather than as an agent of significant action.

Bombay Stock Exchange
Bombay, India
Jul 9 1875
12:44:00 PM LMT

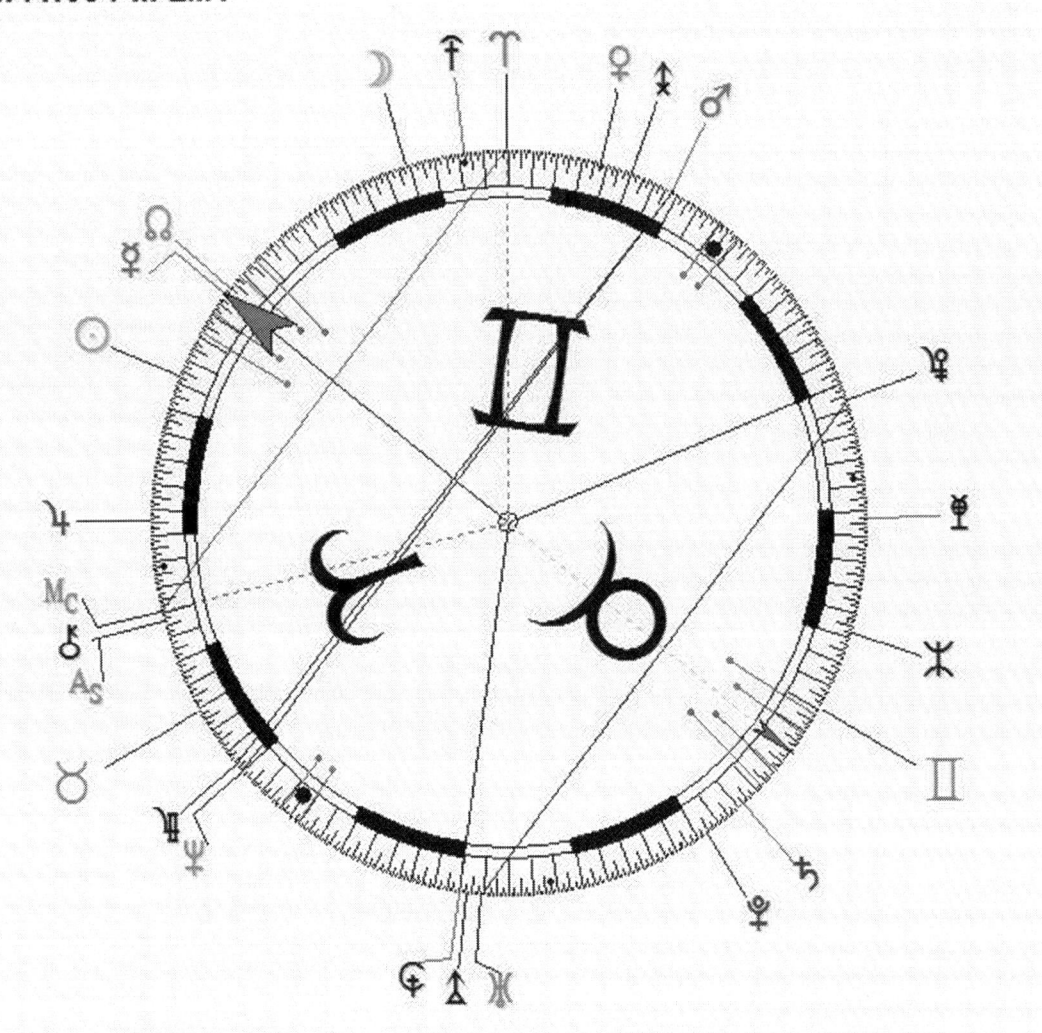

Bombay Stock Exchange

Mercury aligns with the True Lunar Node in this chart, so this stock exchange emphasizes connections and relationships. Mercury triggering the Mars/Apollon midpoint is a sign of accountability, and it also signals a tendency toward rising markets. The activation of the Midheaven/Aries Point midpoint signifies public conversations that can have a global impact, but with Mercury hitting the Uranus/Cupido midpoint, much of that communication is self-congratulatory. With the activation of the Mars/Neptune midpoint, the action on this exchange can at times seem inspired by genius, but it can also appear to be completely insane.

Mercury & First-Trade Charts

One of the key tools that we have for astro-trading analysis is the First-Trade horoscope, which is an astrological chart cast for the time of the opening bell on the day the stock was first publicly traded. The position of Mercury in a First-Trade chart is particularly worth noting, because it is associated with key communications related to the stock.

Mercury in the First-Trade horoscope is especially important when companies make announcements about their quarterly earnings. If Mercury is not strongly aspected at the time of an earnings announcement, the earnings report will not necessarily have a big influence on the price of the stock. But if First-Trade Mercury is strongly aspected when an earnings announcement is made, there can sometimes be significant earnings surprises, either positive or negative ones, depending on the nature of the planetary aspects that occur. The effect can be particularly strong when Jupiter or Saturn are involved, and the most significant earnings surprises can occur when an earnings announcement coincides with either a direct or retrograde station of one of these two planets, with the planet conjoining First-Trade Mercury.

It's worth noting, then, the times and zodiacal positions of Jupiter and Saturn stations, and then scanning your database of First-Trade horoscopes to determine which stocks have Mercury in a position to experience a conjunction with the stationing planet.

This effect on earnings announcements can be especially strong if Mercury is near the ascendant or the midheaven in a First-Trade horoscope, since the chart angles are especially sensitive points. But in every case, paying attention to Jupiter and Saturn stations that align with First-Trade Mercury at the time of an earnings announcement has the potential to open the door to profitable astro-trading opportunities.

Trading with First-Trade Mercury during earnings season can offer some real advantages, but they are limited because of the relative rarity of earnings announcements. But the usefulness of First-Trade horoscopes doesn't stop there. While there are many profitable applications of First-Trade charts in astro-trading, they are most often best used as base charts for evaluating the suitability of specific trades, whether or not earnings announcements are forthcoming.

In making that evaluation, the positions of transiting planets, secondary progressed planets, and converse progressed planets are observed, with special attention to their aspects to key points in the First-Trade horoscope, especially the chart angles as well as the First-Trade Sun and the First-Trade Moon. The primary resource detailing this technique is Bill Meridian's fine book on *Planetary Stock Trading*.

While it is not a substitute for that approach to First-Trade charts, the Mercury method illustrated in this chapter can also be applied to First-Trade horoscopes with good results. By putting a First-Trade chart on a 90-degree dial and moving the pointer to the Mercury position, the astro-trader can get a quick look at significant structures within the chart. If any of the activated midpoints include the key First-Trade planets or points, they will be especially important when they are triggered by transits or progressions.

Mercury Aspects and Angles

Mercury doesn't act in isolation in its connections with market trends and turning points. Some of its most powerful correlations with market behavior coincide with particular interactions between Mercury and other planets.

Traditional astrology puts a great deal of emphasis on specific angular relationships between pairs of planets, known to astrologers as planetary aspects. In the second century A.D. Claudius Ptolemy defined the most important aspects as the conjunction, with the two planets at the same degree of the zodiac; the sextile, with an angle of 60° between the two planets; the square, with a 90° separation between the two planets; the trine, with an angular separation of 120°; and the opposition, with the two planets 180° apart.

Although Ptolemy's work with planetary angles became the basis for a key component of the astrological tradition in mediaeval times and in the modern world as well, astrologers in other eras have added to this set of Ptolemaic aspects some additional specific angular relationships worth noting, including the semisextile, a 30° angle of separation; the semisquare, a 45° angle of separation; the quintile, a 72° angle of separation; the sesquiquadrate, 135° angle of separation; the biquintile, a 144° angle of separation; and the quincunx, a 150° angle of separation.

More recent research in the financial applications of astrology has shown the importance of aspects from the ninth harmonic (multiples of 40°), the twenty-fourth harmonic (multiples of 15°), and the fortieth harmonic (multiples of 9°).

Although the planetary aspects give us convenient signposts in our study of dynamic planetary relationships, coordinating planetary cycles with the movements of the markets requires extensive empirical analysis which is unfettered by a blind adherence to astrological conventions. When we study the angular relationships of Mercury to other planets and look at their correlations to significant market actions, we soon discover that there are far more degrees of arc opening which are active in the markets than those described by the limited set of traditional astrological aspects, and even the more modern additions to the Ptolemaic aspects don't give us the complete picture.

We can thus take two approaches in exploring specific Mercury interactions with other planets as influences in the markets – we can either work with the traditional astrological aspects and back-test the activity of the markets we are studying when those aspects occur, or we can look at the price action of the markets themselves, identifying key turning points, and then observe which specific angular relationships occur at those important times.

When we begin with the traditional planetary aspects, we inevitably find that there are some cases in which clearly delineated shifts in market trend occur. But we also typically find many instances in which there seems to be little or no correlation between a specific Mercury aspect and a key reversal in the markets. When that happens, the best we can do is to determine the statistical probability of rate change in market direction when a particular aspect occurs. This is useful information when there is an extremely high or low correlation between the planets and the markets, but much of the time we wind up with data that has little use to us in pragmatic market forecasting or astro-trading timing.

On the other hand, if we begin with market analysis and then work our way back to a determination of the highest probability angles of separation between Mercury and other planets when noteworthy market activity occurs, we can sidestep many of the inconveniences of dealing with probabilities and focus our attention instead on the specific angular relationships that are most likely to correlate with significant market highs and lows. When we take that approach, the best strategy is is to examine systematically Mercury's relationship with each individual planet in turn, coordinating repeated iterations of each complete synodic cycle with historical price data from the market we are studying.

As an example, here is what we have found in looking at Mercury's relationships with other planets in an analysis of price trends in the S&P 500. Because the cycles of relationship between Mercury and other planets have varying durations, the number of examples that we have been able to examine in each instance also vary. But because Mercury itself moves so rapidly, and because we have an ample amount of data for the S&P 500 to examine, we have been able to reach some potentially useful conclusions about the connections between these Mercury cycles and key turning points in this stock index.

Mercury and the Moon

[Chart: S&P 500 with annotation "Moon/Mercury 150 degrees" — FinancialCyclesWeekly.com]

The Moon moves more rapidly than Mercury, so it is the active factor in determining the length of the cycle of angular relationships, except for some modifications when Mercury is near a station and is thus moving more slowly. Our analysis has shown that the S&P is most likely to reach a trading top when the angle of arc opening between the Moon and Mercury is 54°, with a trading low most likely to occur when that angle is 150°.

Although there is plenty of data on hand to back up this conclusion, it's nevertheless worth noting that since the lunar cycle is only approximately 28 days long we are unlikely to get major tops and bottoms in the S&P with every iteration of the cycle. There are times as well when the Moon/Mercury signals invert, with an expected high becoming a low and vice-versa. Even so, because of the likelihood of short-term trend reversals, it's worth noting these specific Moon/Mercury angles and flagging the dates that they occur when we do our monthly market analysis. If they coincide with other important astro-trading signals, they can be a useful confirming factor in our day-to-day trading decisions.

Mercury and the Sun

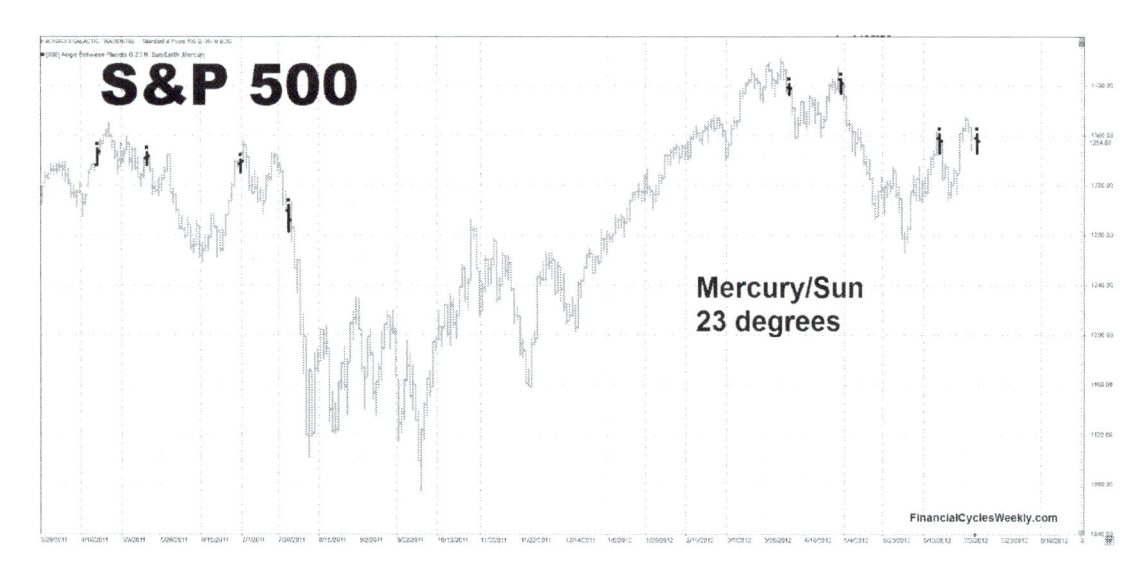

[Chart: S&P 500 with annotation "Mercury/Sun 23 degrees" — FinancialCyclesWeekly.com]

As an inner planet, one which orbits the Sun from within the orbital path of the Earth, Mercury will always appear near the Sun from our geocentric point of view. We thus have a limited range of possible angular relationships to consider in this case.

Our research has shown that highs in the S&P are most likely to occur when Mercury is approaching its conjunction with the Sun and is separated from the Sun by angles of 3°, 14°, or 22°, and also when it is departing from its conjunction with the Sun and is separated by an angle of 23°. On aggregate, then, we can look for the greatest probability of tradable highs in the S&P when Mercury is 22° or 23° away from the Sun, whether the angle is waxing or waning.

Lows in the S&P are most likely to occur when Mercury is moving towards its conjunction and is separated from the Sun by 18° or 25°, and when it is separating from its conjunction and has an angular relationship with the Sun of either 17° for 18°. The Mercury/Sun angle of 18° is thus particularly significant in helping us to identify potential lows in the S&P 500.

[Handwritten note: Merc Sun 23° Spx high / 18° Spx low]

Mercury and Venus

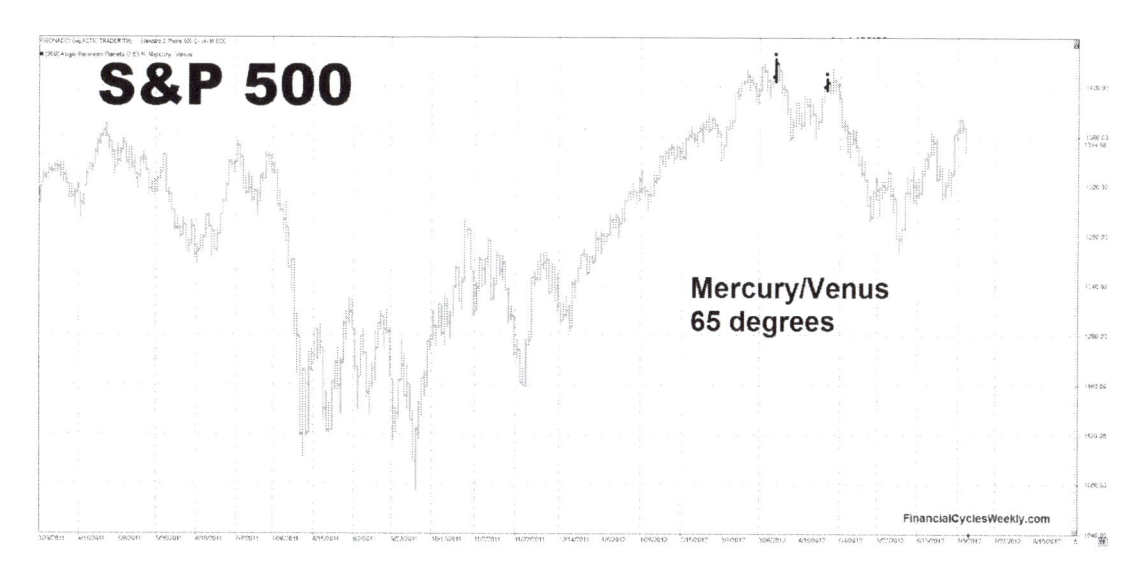

Venus also has its orbit within the orbital path of the Earth, so once again we are limited in the range of potential angular relationships that we can consider.

In all cases, however, the most significant action in the S&P seems to occur when Mercury is moving towards its conjunction with Venus. Potential highs in the S&P are most likely to occur with an angle of separation of 65°, and an angle of 40° between Mercury and Venus is the most likely to bring a trading bottom.

Merc/Venus 65° Spx high
40° Spx low

Mercury and Mars

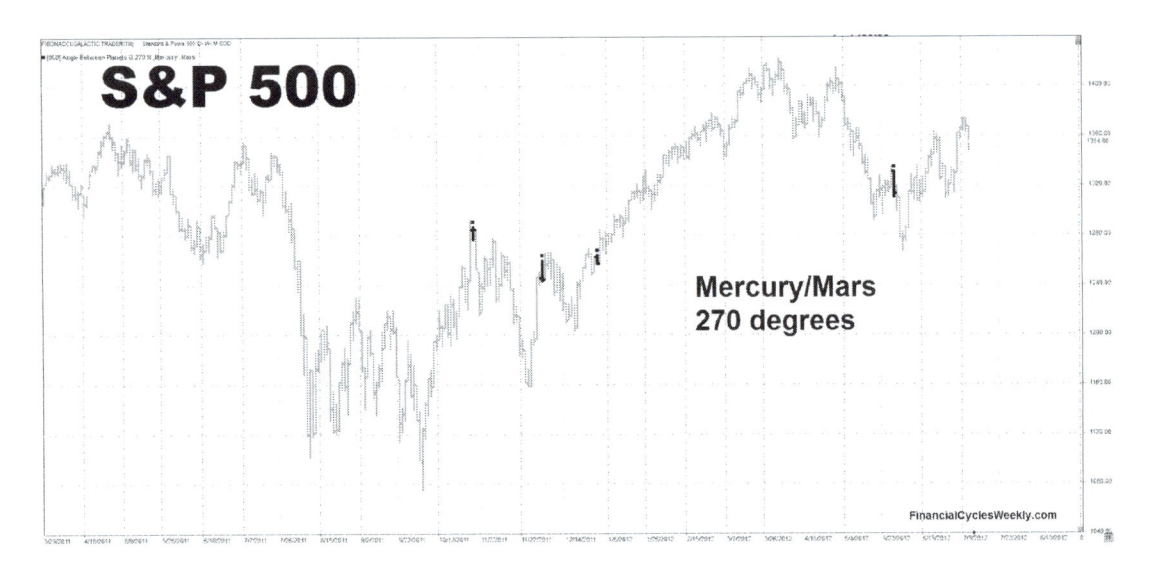

When we get to Mars we begin our considerations of Mercury's relationship with planets outside the orbit of the Earth, so with Mars and with all the planetary bodies that follow we have the full 360° spectrum of potential angular relationships to consider.

Highs in the S&P 500 are most likely to occur with Mercury/Mars angles of 140° and 223°, as well as the degree areas ranging from 268° to 275° and from 290° to 303°. We can look for lows in the S&P 500 when there is a 117° angle of separation between Mercury and Mars, or during the degree ranges of 28° to 35°, 70° to 71°, and 183° to 184°.

Mercury and Jupiter

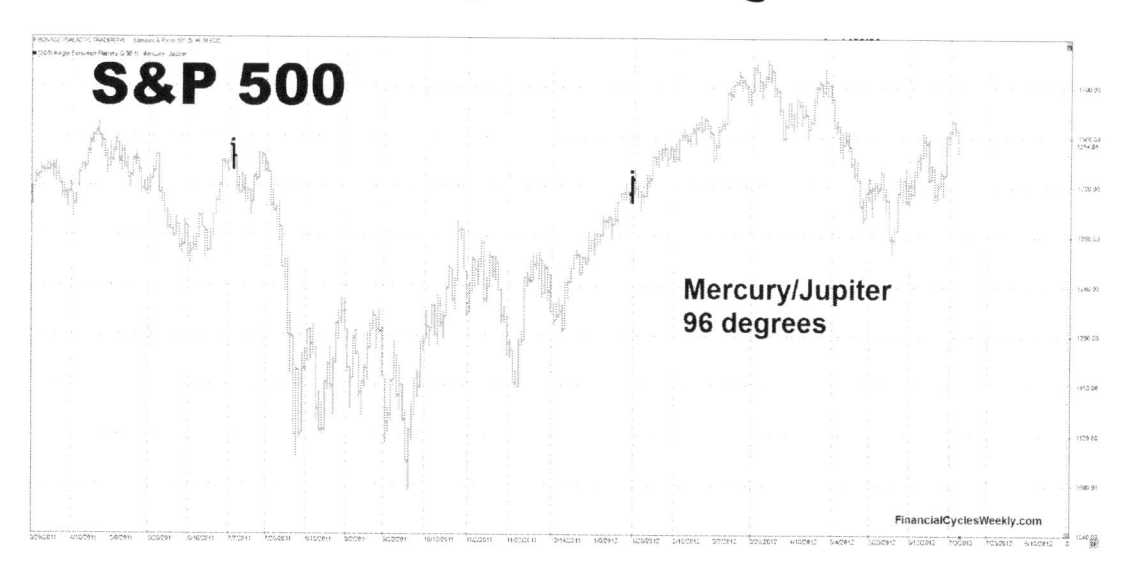

[Chart: S&P 500 with Mercury/Jupiter 96 degrees annotation — FinancialCyclesWeekly.com]

Jupiter is the planet of growth and expansion, so perhaps it's little wonder that we find a lot of correlations between Mercury/Jupiter angles and a high probability of tops and bottoms in the S&P.

The S&P is most likely to hit highs when the angular separation between Mercury and Jupiter is 24°, 96°, 165°, 248°, 300°, or 340°. We are most likely to see lows in the index occur when the Mercury/Jupiter angle is 196°, 218°, or between 44° and 45°.

Mercury and Saturn

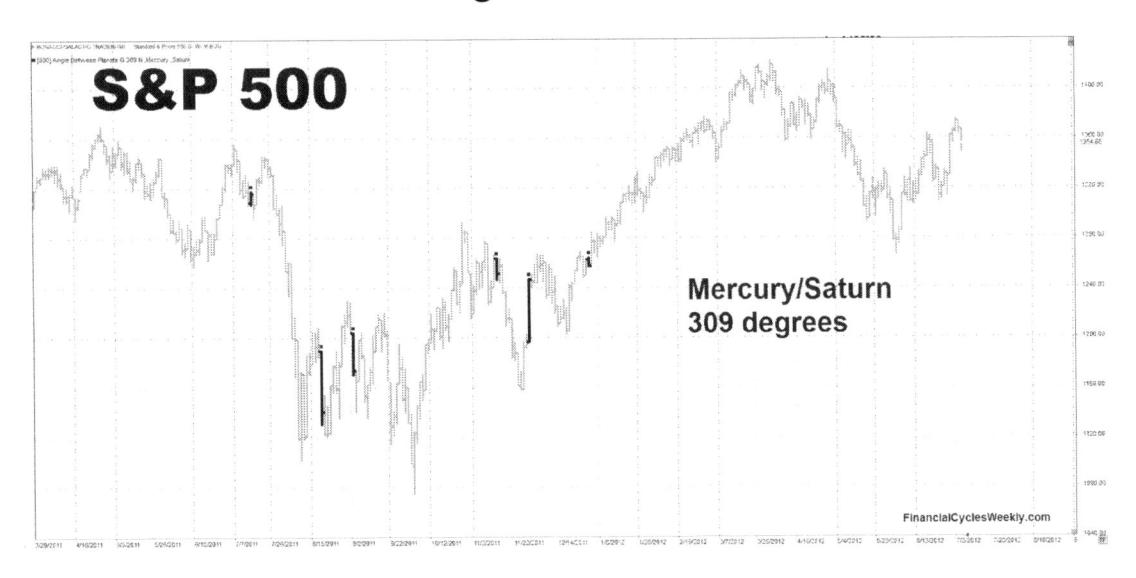

Saturn is all about constriction and limitation, and there are noticeably fewer correlations between market highs and lows in the S&P 500 and the angular relationship between Mercury and Saturn.

When that angle is either 83° or 196°, we are the most likely to see tops in the S&P. We can look for lows in the S&P when the angular relationship between Mercury and Saturn is either 161° or 309°.

Mercury and Uranus

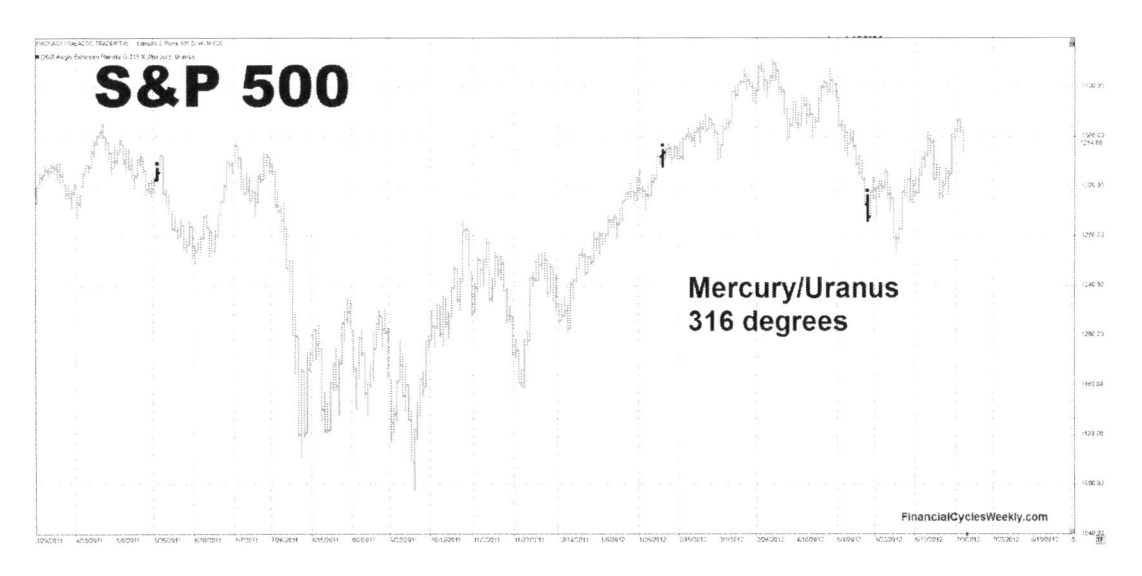

The correlation between Mercury/Uranus angles and the highs and lows in the S&P is even more clear-cut.

When that angle of separation is 67°, the S&P is most likely to hit a high. When it is 316°, we can look for a greater probability of a low in the S&P 500.

Mercury and Neptune

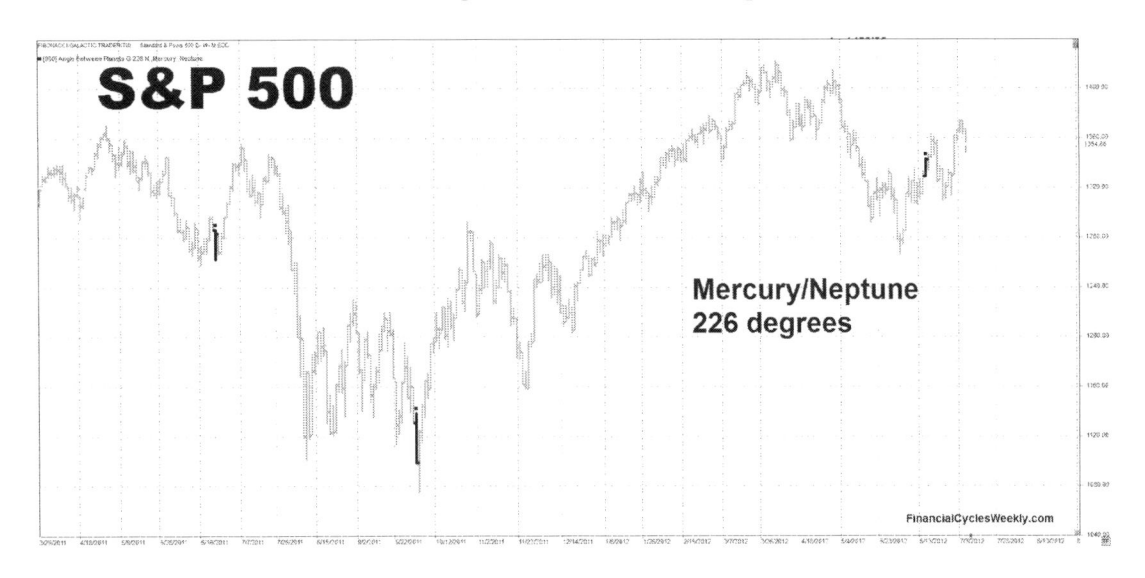

The S&P 500 is most likely to hit a trading top when the angle of separation between Mercury and Neptune is 90°. When that angle is either 226° or 293°, there is the greatest likelihood of seeing the S&P form a significant bottom.

Mercury and Pluto

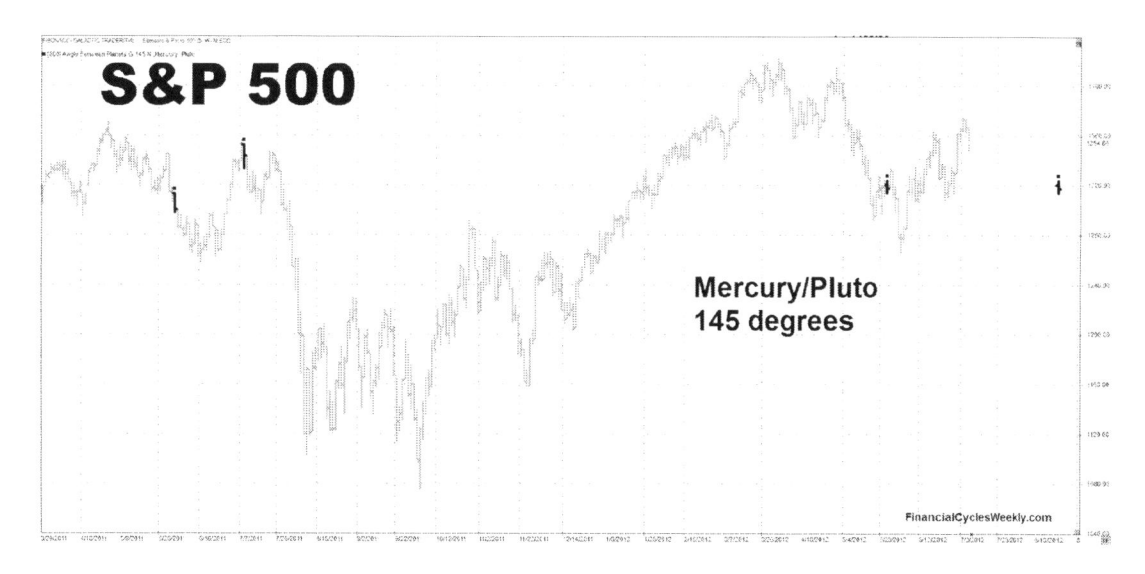

When the angular relationship between Mercury and Pluto is 145°, we are most likely to see a top in the S&P. When the angle is 296°, then we can look for a low in the S&P.

Mercury and Cupido

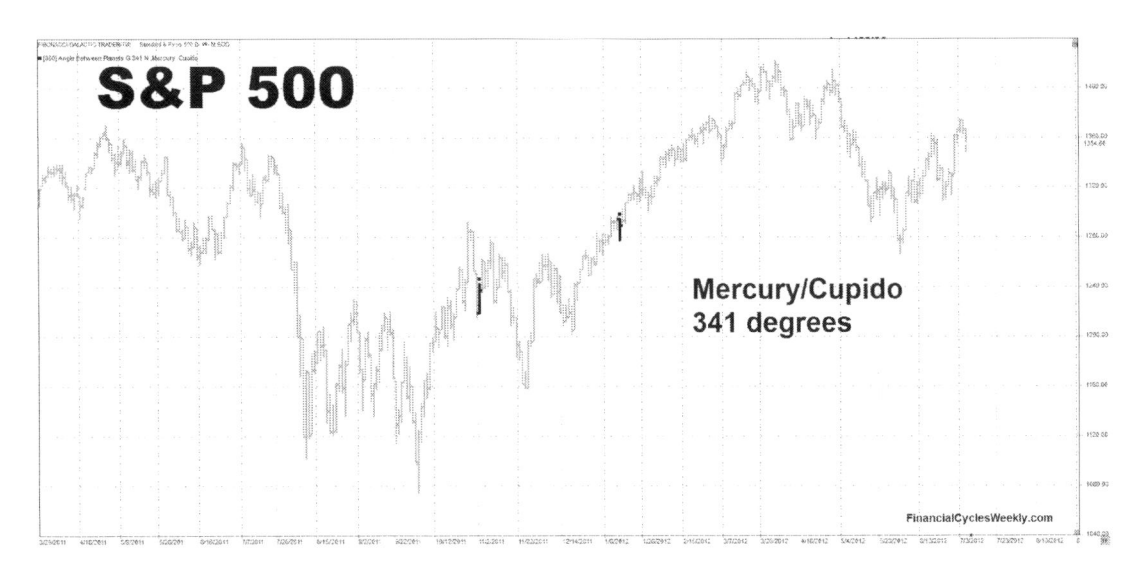

[Chart: S&P 500 with Mercury/Cupido 341 degrees, from FinancialCyclesWeekly.com]

The angular relationships between Mercury and the transneptunian factors are also significant. The transneptunians are the hypothetical planets proposed a century ago by the German astrologer Alfred Witte; ideas about the potential impact of their interactions with other planets can be found in Witte's book ***Rules for Planetary Pictures***.

Cupdio is the innermost transneptunian factor, and when the Mercury/Cupido angle is either 106° or 193°, the S&P 500 has the greatest probability of reaching a high. When the Mercury/Cupido angle is either 305° for 341°, there is a likelihood of a low in the S&P.

Mercury and Hades

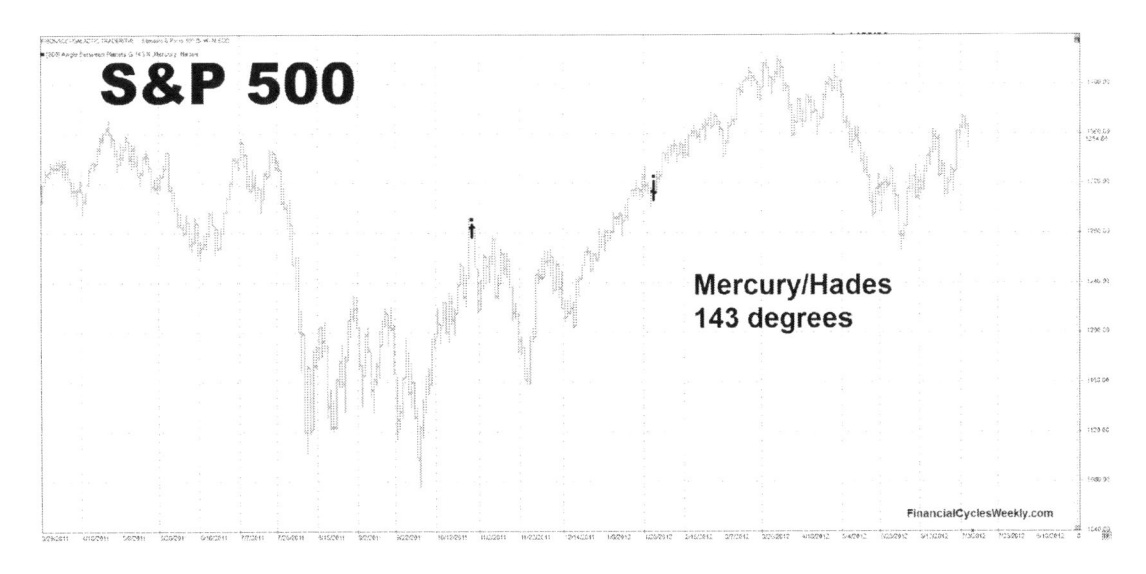

The angular relationship between Mercury and the transneptunian factor Hades is most likely to coincide with a top in the S&P when it is either 178°, 274°, or 354°. There is the highest likelihood of a low in the S&P 500 when the Mercury/Hades angle is 143°.

Mercury and Zeus

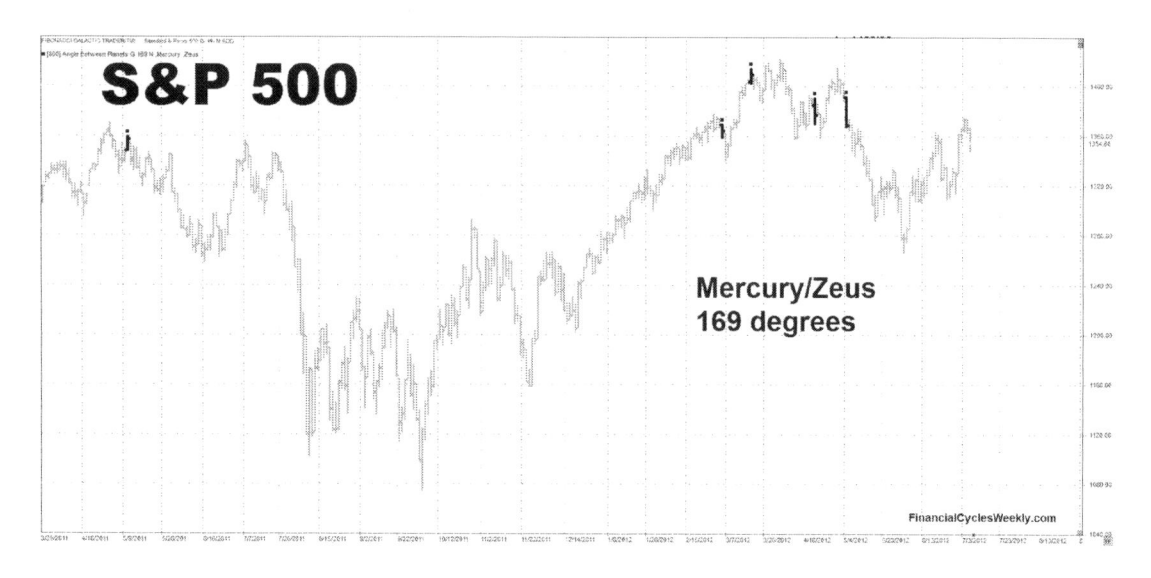

S&P 500 chart labeled "Mercury/Zeus 169 degrees"

Mercury's angular relationship to Zeus seems to be particularly active in coinciding with significant support and resistance in the trading dynamic of the S&P 500.

When the Mercury/Zeus angle of separation is 71°, 169°, or 250°, we are most likely to see the S&P hitting resistance and forming a trading top. When the Mercury/Zeus angle is 356°, or when it falls in the degree range between 34° and 38°, we can look for evidence of support in the S&P and for the formation of trading lows.

Mercury and Kronos

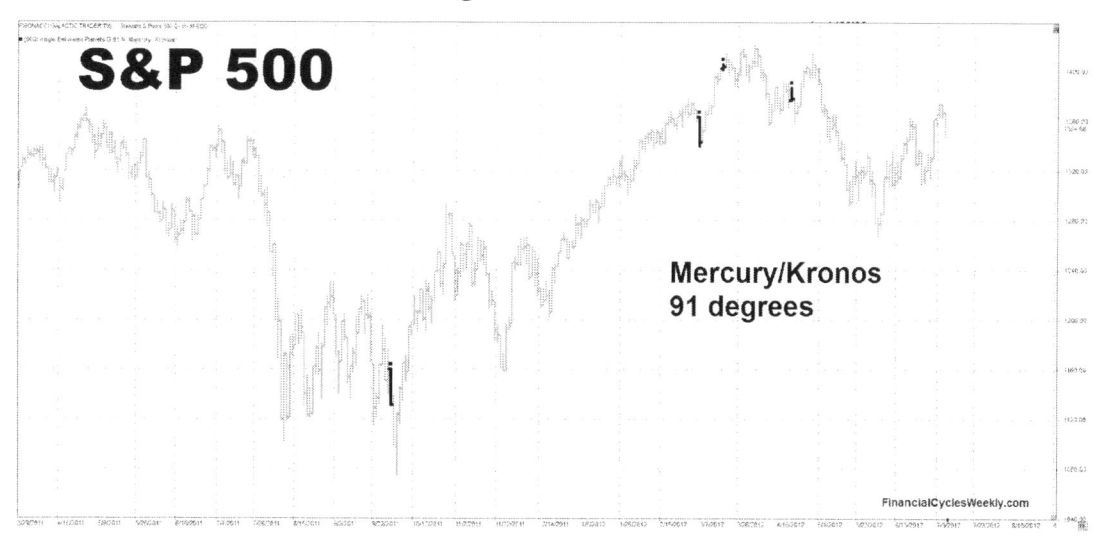

When we find an angular relationship between Mercury and Kronos of 168°, 267°, or 345°, we are likely to see a top in the S&P 500. When the Mercury/Kronos angle of separation is either 91° or 134°, we are the most likely to see a low in the S&P.

Mercury and Apollon

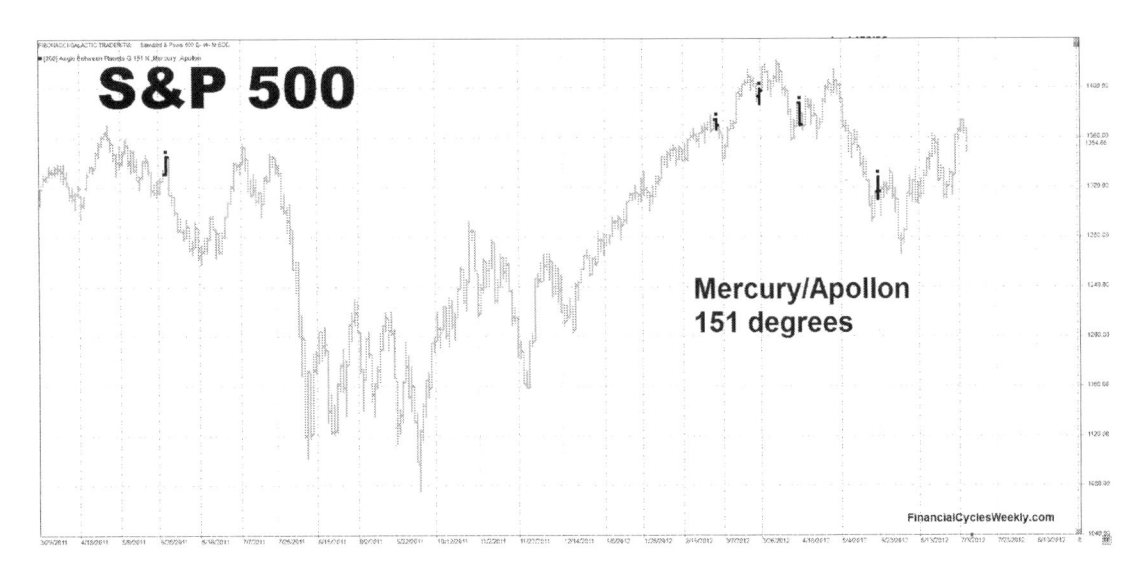

The Mercury/Apollon separation is the most likely to coincide with a high in the S&P 500 when it is 55°, 151°, or 233°. We can look for a greater probability of significant trading lows in the S&P when the Mercury/Apollon angular separation is 338°, or when it falls between 22° and 23°.

Mercury and Admetos

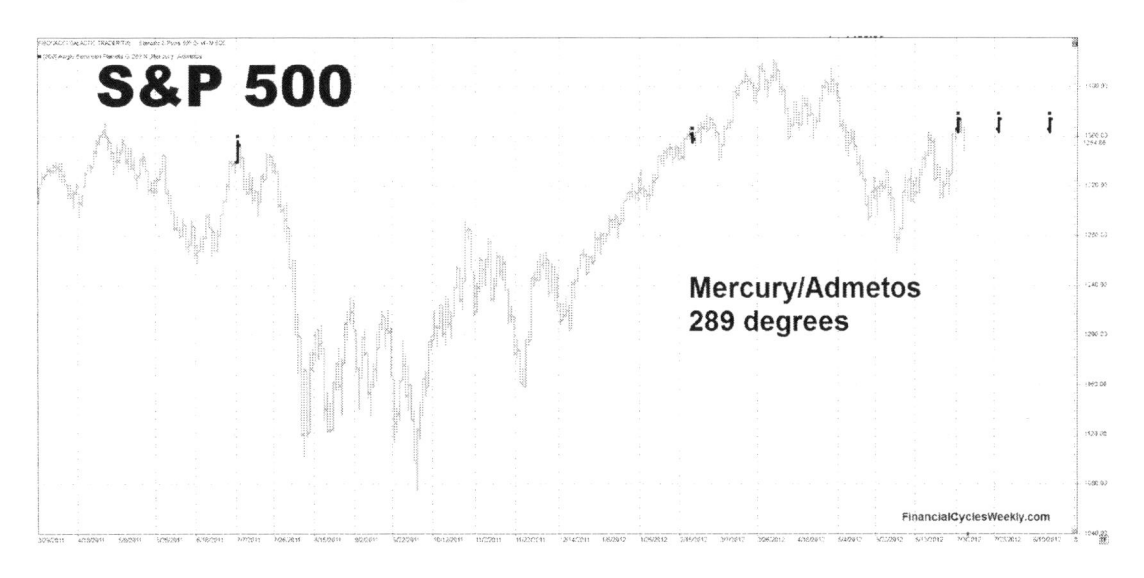

The most significant angular relationships between Mercury and Admetos in terms of their correspondence with highs in the S&P are angles of 23°, 206°, 289°, and 303°. When the Mercury/Admetos angular separation is either 128° or 173°, we have the greatest probability of seeing lows in the S&P 500.

Mercury and Vulcanus

The S&P 500 is most likely to hit a top when there is an angular separation between Mercury and Vulcanus of 145°. However, when that angle is either 67° or 112°, we can typically expect to see a greater likelihood of a low in the S&P.

Mercury and Poseidon

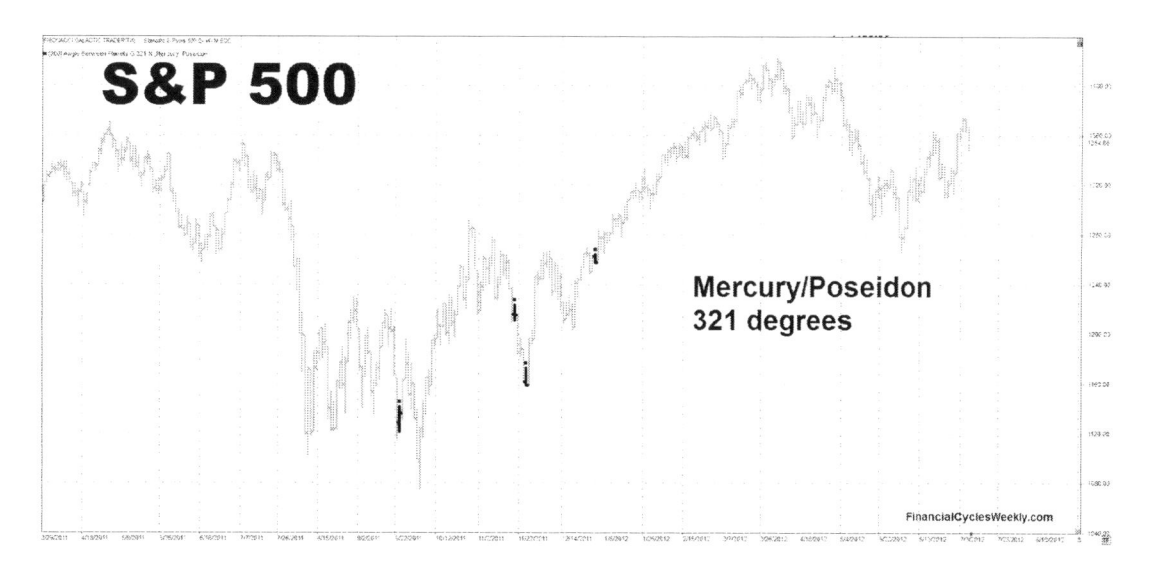

The Mercury/Poseidon angles most likely to coincide with highs in the S&P 500 are 41°, 123°, and 193°. When the Mercury/Poseidon angle is either 9° or 321°, there is the greatest probability of our observing the S&P 500 forming a low.

A Couple of Practical Astro-Trading Reminders

In considering Mercury's angular separations from other planets and their potential relationship with significant turning points in the S&P 500, it's important to keep a couple of facts in mind.

First of all, the angular separations that we have described here are only statements of probability. While they will often coincide with reversal dates in the S&P 500, there are certainly many instances in which no such correspondence is evident or when the signals invert, and we get a high instead of a low, or a low instead of a high. Although these angular relationships can often give us a significant edge in our trading by improving our ability to spot higher-probability opportunities for market tend reversals, they don't coincide with expected shifts in market trend 100% of the time.

Secondly we must remember that even when these Mercury angles prove to be accurate, we shouldn't try to trade solely on the basis of the timing signals they provide. They are best applied as astro-trading tools when we combine them with other astrological and technical indicators. On the occasions when other market timing indicators suggest that a significant turning point is at hand, the consideration of these angular relationships between Mercury and other planets can provide us with additional confirmation for our trading decisions, allowing us to be more confident in entering our trades.

Remember as well that this research on the relationship between Mercury angles and tops and bottoms in the S&P applies only to that specific index. When we are trading individual stocks or commodities, or when we are considering other market indices, then we have to do the back-testing and analysis of those markets as well.

In other words, these examples with the S&P 500 are intended to serve as a model for the kind of analysis that can be applied to any market situation, as long as sufficient historical price data is available. It is only through careful observation and rigorous back-testing that we can reach conclusions about which angular relationships are the most important for any specific market, but once we have done that research, we then have a powerful tool to add to our decision-making process as astro-traders.

Mercury Retrograde

Once you get past the basic introduction to astrology, once you have learned what your Sun sign is and have explored the generic advice delivered by daily Sun sign horoscope columns, one of the first things that you learn about astrology is to beware of Mercury retrograde periods. These are the times when, as seen from the Earth's perspective, Mercury appears to be moving backwards in the sky. It's an optical illusion, of course, created by the varying speeds of planetary orbits around the Sun, but it's nevertheless a significant phenomenon, and one that we need to take into account as we consider Mercury's importance for us as astro-traders.

When Mercury is retrograde, according to the conventional wisdom, everything goes wrong. But even if we don't agree with the conventional wisdom, and choose not to buy into the superstitious notion that a retrograde Mercury inevitably means disastrous doom and gloom, we still have to deal with the phenomenon, and we can do so in creative and productive ways. When Mercury goes into retrograde motion it definitely gives us some challenges. But it also provides some advantages as well, and that's what we need to be aware of as astro-traders.

This phenomenon is not a rare occurrence, since Mercury goes into retrograde motion about three times each year. In fact, Mercury is retrograde roughly 18% of each calendar year, due to the fact that whenever it is retrograde it maintains its apparent backward motion for about three weeks each time. Knowing that Mercury will be retrograde 18% of the time reminds us of the Pareto principle, the famous 80/20 rule which tells us that we can get about 80% of our results from 20% of our effort. Based on this approximation of the

80/20 principle, the times when Mercury is in retrograde motion can actually be opportunities for us to work on the important decisions and preparations that help us be in positions of the greatest advantage during the remaining 82% of the year. As astro-traders, we can use Mercury retrograde periods to do the things that can give us an extra edge in our market activities when Mercury is in direct motion.

When Mercury is retrograde we inevitably confront a variety of communications challenges. We can also experience an impact on travel, with interruptions, inconvenient obstacles, or unexpected delays complicating our ability to get from one place to another. When Mercury is retrograde equipment can malfunction more than usual, with computers breaking down, copy machines failing to function properly, and internet connections getting lost.

Important documents that are signed when Mercury is retrograde, such as leases, contracts, and commercial agreements, often fail to work out as anticipated, and sometimes contain errors that escape our attention, but that would have been glaring under other circumstances. The caveat here is always to take the extra time to read the fine print in any contract that needs to be signed while Mercury is in retrograde motion. If we have to execute agreements while Mercury is retrograde then we certainly can choose to do so, but only after we have gone over the paperwork four or five times, had it checked out by an attorney, and done whatever else is necessary to add an extra margin of certainty and safety to the transaction.

With Mercury retrograde there are obstacles that occur both internally and externally, in our own consciousness and in the world around us. They can impact our personal ability to keep our heads straight in dealing with other people, and because of the necessary redundancy required for handling Mercury retrograde periods properly, it often takes us a great deal more time and effort to get less done than we might otherwise expect.

Mercury retrograde is also strongly associated with challenges in trade and commercial activity. That is one of the reasons we pay particular attention to Mercury retrograde cycles in the markets. But a Mercury retrograde period can influence the behavior of the markets in other ways as well. Not only does Mercury retrograde impact commercial activity itself; it can also influence global affairs and the potential for international tensions. These are the kinds of events that can impact war and peace issues, international trade, expectations relating to the availability of critical raw materials, and other fundamentals which can influence market behavior. While we may not need to understand everything that's going on in the world completely in order to be effective in the markets, when Mercury goes into retrograde motion it gives us a clear signal that we need to pay closer attention to geopolitical affairs.

Educational and cultural activities are also impacted by Mercury retrograde periods, so we may need to make allowances in those areas as well. Whether we are trying to make plans, start projects, create projections, or are simply making an effort to push things forward, we typically have to contend with skewed results when Mercury is in retrograde motion.

Relationships at both a personal level and a professional level also come under pressure and can suffer substantially when Mercury is in retrograde motion. There are more misunderstandings and more miscommunication, and there is a strong tendency to generate more hard feelings than usual. Because that's the case, we may find that our personal levels of emotional balance and self-confidence also tend to suffer when Mercury is retrograde, and this kind of disturbance can impinge on our ability to move effortlessly through normal daily transactions.

This effect is especially important when we are actively trading in the markets. If as traders we are second-guessing ourselves or are getting confused about market directions, or if we are simply not completely at ease in the trading environment, our results are likely to suffer. We will, of course, feel the Mercury impact financially in those contexts.

One of the things that's particularly interesting about the Mercury retrograde phenomenon is that its effects can manifest in a surprising variety of ways. In some cases we can experience the Mercury retrograde impact quite directly and rapidly; in other instances the results take place more slowly and tangentially. At still other times we can see recurring effects of actions taken while Mercury is retrograde, with the recurrences plugging in to future Mercury retrograde cycles. As a way of illustrating this kind of Mercury retrograde influence, here's an example of my own decision-making process during a Mercury retrograde period.

A Sobering Lesson

It was one of my most memorable Mercury retrograde experiences; it occurred a couple of decades ago when I got a late-afternoon phone call from my father. He had decided to trade cars, he told me, and was at that moment at an automobile dealership which had offered him a wonderful deal on his next motor vehicle acquisition. In his negotiations with the car dealer there was an option on the table which would give him a generous trade-in allowance for the car he was currently driving, a fairly new Peugeot sedan with substantially less than 50,000 miles on the odometer.

But, my dad informed me, he had remembered that the car that I was then driving was literally on its last legs, barely providing me with basic transportation, and very much in need of replacement. So, my father said, if I would be willing to purchase his nearly-new Peugeot for a sum that was somewhat less than the trade-in allowance he was being offered, he was willing to make that happen and renegotiate his pending deal, making up the price difference out of his pocket in order to put me behind the wheel of a more serviceable vehicle.

There was only one catch. Time was of the essence, my father insisted, and the whole proposition had to go into effect that same day if it was to be accomplished at all. It was a take-it-or-leave-it offer.

I glanced at my astrological calendar, and saw, as I was already well aware, that Mercury was in retrograde motion at the time. Remembering the textbook warnings about making important purchases with Mercury retrograde I hesitated, about to decline his generous offer. But then I had second thoughts.

I did in fact need a new car. The offer of the Peugeot was an upgrade that far exceeded my previous expectations about coming up with a replacement vehicle. And after all, I reasoned, this was a car that my father had purchased new and then taken good care of, with documented records of all the regular maintenance that had been required.

It was clear to me that this was an extraordinary opportunity. I knew that Mercury was retrograde, but if I couldn't trust my own father in a situation like this, then who could I trust?

I gritted my teeth, made a quick decision, and agreed to meet my father within the hour take take care of the necessary paperwork. Several hours later I was ensconced behind the wheel of my nearly-new Peugeot, opening the moon-roof and breathing the fresh air as I observed the radiant Moon itself on my drive home in the darkness.

The Peugeot gave me a great deal of delight. I enjoyed riding along in comfort and loved the welcome contrast it provided to the noisy rides I had tolerated in the rickety clunker that my new car had replaced. I was pleased by the reactions of my friends and colleagues, who were effusive in their admiration of the fact that I was now driving a much classier car than I had been accustomed to.

Everything went smoothly for the next several months, and I soon banished all memories of the apprehensions I had originally felt about negotiating an important purchase while Mercury was retrograde.

But then something happened. The air conditioner on my almost-new Peugeot stopped functioning.

I took it in for repair at a shop run by a reliable and trustworthy mechanic, a Romanian who specialized in keeping European cars going. He did a diagnosis, and told me what it would take to get the cooling system running again. It was a more costly repair than I was really prepared to handle at the time, but I decided to bite the bullet and go ahead with it. And while the car was in the shop, I realized that Mercury was retrograde once again.

I managed to make ends meet while taking care of this unanticipated expense, and once again forgot about the Mercury retrograde dynamic as I plunged back into my exhilaration at driving a really nice car. This high state of ecstasy persisted for a few more months as I drove around, running errands and going to appointments, taking great pride in the fine vehicle that I had been blessed with. But just like clockwork, Mercury went retrograde again, and once again my Peugeot was in the shop for major repairs.

It didn't take too many more iterations of this cycle for me to comprehend the dilemma that I had unwittingly embraced. Every time Mercury went retrograde, my classy new vehicle suffered some expensive debilitation. After five or six of these episodes, I made the tardy but inevitable decision to part company with my prized Peugeot. I was still on speaking terms with my father, and we never discussed the Mercury retrograde factor in my purchase of the car, but I knew in no uncertain terms that I needed to pay attention to astrological dynamics in spite of my desire to honor the bonds of blood and paternal generosity.

It was a difficult and sobering lesson, to say the least. It certainly demonstrated the validity of a major astrological caveat – never buy a vehicle when Mercury is retrograde, no matter how much you know about the car and how trustworthy the source may be. But it was also important to me individually because it marked the time when I made a personal commitment to become a professional astrologer. After all, based on my own somewhat painful personal experience, I had learned that astrology really works!

I mention this personal incident not just because is is an example of the strange and potentially disastrous effects that can occur with Mercury retrograde, but also because it illustrates some key principles about the Mercury retrograde phenomenon that we can transfer to our experiences as astro-traders. To begin with, it focuses on a critical notion which we need to keep in mind if we are going to be effective in dealing with Mercury retrograde periods in the markets – when Mercury is retrograde, we need to be especially cautious about trying to find exceptions to the rules.

That's what I was doing when I made the decision to purchase the car while Mercury was retrograde, even though I knew that this particular Mercury phenomenon was supposed to have an effect on contracts and transportation. When Mercury is in retrograde motion, we sometimes look for all kinds of justifications and rationalizations for ignoring our trading rules, and if we succumb to that seduction we can experience devastating results.

Whether we are simply second-guessing ourselves in our market analysis, or whether we are taking trading positions that are too large or ignoring market signals that are telling us to get out of a trade or to adjust our stops, we are unnecessarily increasing our risk. If we feel that we can profitably allow ourselves an exception to our trading rules while Mercury is in retrograde motion, we are typically making a very big mistake.

A Business Disaster

In one sense, that desire to find exceptions to the rules is what Ford Motor Company was experiencing in 1957, when it announced that it was introducing a new line of automobiles.

Throughout the summer months of that year, Ford ran an advertising campaign based on mystery and intrigue. Rather than following the industry norm of promoting the great new features and benefits to be found in their upcoming product introduction, Ford chose instead to try to build consumer buzz by hinting that something really big was on the way, without explicitly revealing what it was.

Ford's magazine ads showed blurred pictures of an unidentifiable car speeding by, announcing that "Lately, some mysterious automobiles have been seen on the roads."

When the new cars were shipped to Ford dealerships across the country, they were all covered by tarps on the transport trucks, so that no one could see what they really looked like.

The Ford dealers were all sworn to absolute secrecy, with the promise that they would not in any way reveal the new line of cars until the actual day of the product launch.

That date was proclaimed in advance as E-Day, short for Edsel Day – September 4, 1957. At the appointed time on E-Day, all the Ford dealers in America simultaneously unveiled four models of the new Edsels to a curious public in a coordinated launch of grand proportions.

The Edsel definitely stood out from other automobiles. It was a big, fancy car with dramatic fins in the back and one truly distinguishing feature – a strange oval-shaped grill mounted vertically on the front of the vehicle.

The immediate response was that the car looked weird! One automotive commentator quipped that the Edsel looked like an Oldsmobile sucking a lemon, while another countered that it really bore more resemblance to a Pontiac pushing a toilet seat.

Nevertheless, the Edsel created quite a stir. A telegram sent to Ford corporate headquarters in the early morning hours of September 5, 1957, from L. F. Jarrett, the owner of Ford dealership Jarrett Motors in Albany, New York, testified to this fact. Addressed to N.

K. Vanderzee, the Assistant General Sales Manager of the Edsel Division at Ford Motor Company in Dearborn, Michigan, the telegram read:

> EDSEL SHOWING BEST EXPERIENCED IN PAST 30 YEARS. MORE THAN 4,800 PEOPLE IN ATTENDANCE. CARS PARKED DOUBLE FOR THREE CITY BLOCKS. TEN SALESMEN UNABLE TO PROPERLY HANDLE CROWDS. LITERATURE EXHAUSTED BY TWELVE NOON. HAVE DELIVERED FROM STOCK TWO CITATIONS, TWO PACERS, ONE CORSAIR, ONE BERMUDA. ENTIRE ORGANIZATION MOST ENTHUSIASTIC BUT COMPLETELY EXHAUSTED. EXCELLENT PROSPECT OF WRITING FIFTEEN ORDERS NEXT FEW DAYS.

By all outward appearances, the Edsel introduction was a smashing success. But what Mr. Jarrett did not understand was the real set of numbers that the company had in mind. On E-Day he had sold a total of six new Edsels, but that outstanding sales day didn't measure up to the company's expectations.

The Ford Motor Company had become so convinced in advance that it had an absolute winner with the Edsel that it not only released four different models of the new car; it created an entirely new division of the company exclusively to manufacture and distribute the Edsel, spending vast amounts of money in the process.

But the big expenses weren't going to be a problem. The company's number crunchers had come up with an astonishing sales projection – each dealership would sell this wildly popular new car at an average rate of four units of each of the four models per day. With 12,000 Ford dealerships across the country selling 16 cars every day, the sales projections were astronomical.

L. F. Jarrett at Jarrett Motors in Albany, a seasoned veteran in the car business, was overwhelmingly enthusiastic about having sold six units on the opening day, when the crowds were backed up for blocks hoping just to get a glimpse of the new mystery car, and he optimistically figured that he could probably sell 15 more cars during the next several days. He was very happy with those numbers, but the company hadn't told him what its sales expectations actually were.

Sure enough, the horoscope for that historic product launch on September 4, 1957 had Mercury in retrograde motion at 21°51' Virgo. In examining this horoscope, however, we

Edsel Introduction
Natal Chart
Sep 4 1957, Wed
09:00 EST +5:00
Detroit, MI
42°N19'53" 083°W02'45"
Geocentric
Tropical
Koch
True Node

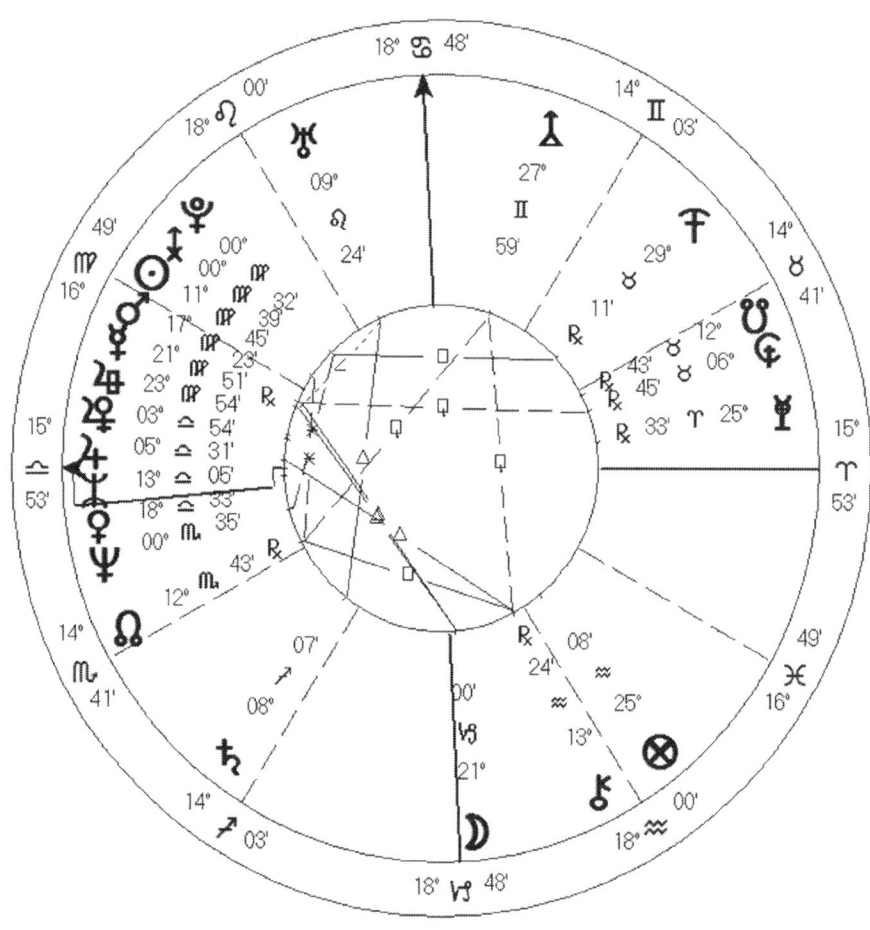

not only note the position of retrograde Mercury, but also the position of Saturn, which was at 8°07' Sagittarius at the time. As it turned out, this Saturn position was to become especially significant in the story of the Edsel.

There continued to be strong publicity for the Edsel during the first few days following its introduction, but sales soon began to lag.

It didn't take long for it become apparent that nobody really liked the weird new car, and very few people were actually willing to buy one of the strange-looking gas guzzlers, especially since Ford's competitors were introducing smaller, more fuel-efficient models.

Ford brought out its new 1959 line of Edsels in September, 1958, and the sales numbers were still tepid. Even though Ford's publicity department put out the word proclaiming the outstanding success of the original Edsel models, the public apparently wasn't convinced.

Another year went by; in September 1959 the 1960 Edsels were unveiled, and Ford's advertising included games and puzzles which encouraged prospective buyers to guess

End of the Edsel
Natal Chart
Nov 19 1959, Thu
09:00 EST +5:00
Detroit, MI
42°N19'53" 083°W02'45"
Geocentric
Tropical
Koch
True Node

what great new features the latest models were going to have. But that was to be the end of the line for the Edsel.

On January 27, 1960 a letter went out from Divisional Sales Managers of the Ford Motor Company to Ford dealers across the country, explaining that anyone who had purchased a 1960 Edsel prior to November 19, 1959 could get a $300 rebate on their Edsel if they wanted to trade it in a for a different Ford car. The company instituted a certificate program with its dealers to provide the rebates on the trade-in, because as of November 19, 1959 Ford had decided to cut its losses and stop all future production of the Edsel. The company had lost more than $400 million on the Edsel debacle, roughly equivalent to $3 billion in today's currency.

What's noteworthy here is that on November 19, 1959, when the Edsel was discontinued, transiting Mercury, once again in retrograde motion, had moved to conjoin the position of Saturn in the E-Day horoscope for the Edsel introduction. Mercury had crossed that Saturn point before that time, but the first time it did so in retrograde motion was on the day the Edsel died.

Flash Crash

While the Edsel story is a sad tale of a large-scale business disaster under the influence of Mercury retrograde, it is certainly not the only time that this planetary phenomenon has had a noticeable impact on business activities. A more recent example that directly relates to the markets was the case of BATS.

That acronym originally stood for Better Alternative Trading System. The firm, operating simply as BATS, provided computer processing for stock market transactions, and originally met with big success, growing to the point where it was handling approximately 11% of all market transactions through its clearinghouse operation.

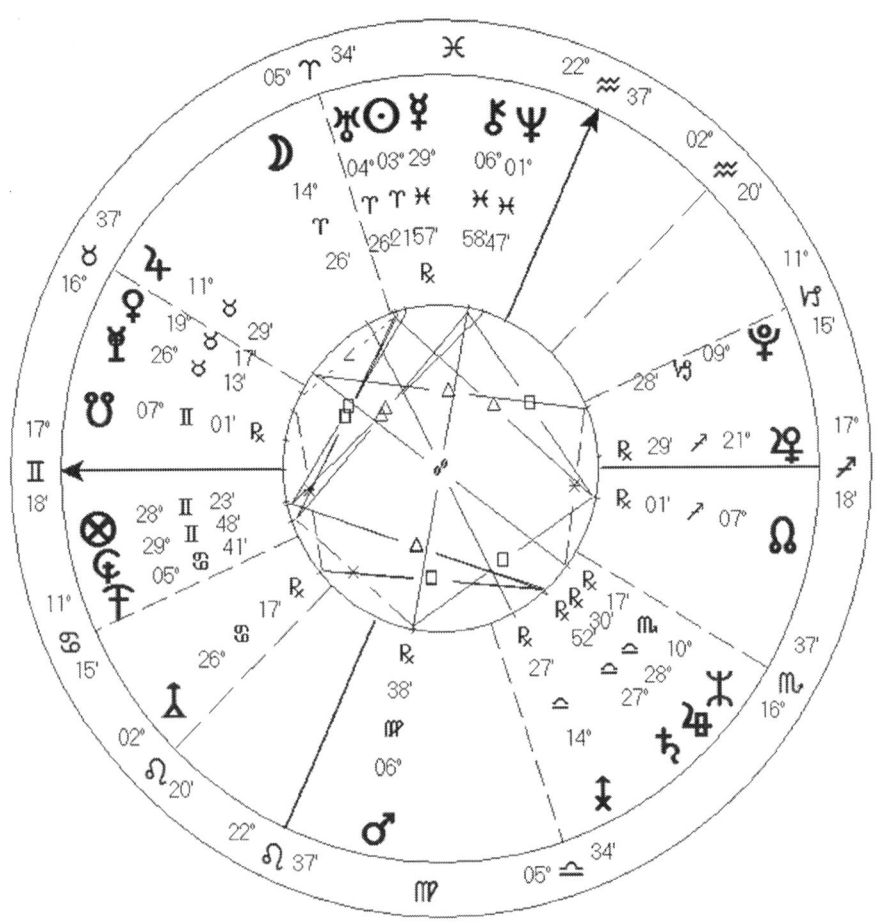

Based on its success, BATS decided to have an Initial Public Offering, putting shares of its stock on the market on March 23, 2012. The shares were first made available at 10:30 a.m. that day, with Mercury retrograde. This is a particularly interesting horoscope because at the time of the IPO, Mercury was at 29°57' Pisces. Just minutes prior to the opening bell that day, transiting Mercury moved backwards over the 0° Aries point in the zodiac; Mercury had been moving retrograde through Aries prior to that, and at virtually the exact time of the BATS IPO it crossed this key cardinal point in the zodiac. From an astrological perspective this is an extremely important zodiac point, but in this case it's particularly noteworthy because of the broad influence of the role that BATS plays in processing market transactions.

The BATS IPO began with great fanfare, but about 15 minutes later some strange things began to happen with the flow of trade transactions. Erroneous trades began to go across the wires.

The stock of Apple Computer (AAPL) had been trading at $598 a share that morning, but within a matter of seconds Apple shares plunged from that price range and were being exchanged at just a little bit above $540 a share, with the company suddenly experiencing a 9% drop in value for no apparent reason.

Something very unusual was going indeed on. In fact, the computer servers being run by BATS itself, a firm which managed computerized trade transactions as its business and which had just launched its IPO based on its outstanding record of reliable performance, were massively malfunctioning.

For some unexplained reason, the BATS computers were garbling the trade data for every company whose trading symbol began with the letters A or B. So BATS had no choice but to shut down its own trading system on the day of its IPO. That event triggered what became known as the BATS Flash Crash at 10:57 a.m.

At 12:15 that afternoon, BATS announced that it was withdrawing the IPO. The BATS stock had originally been priced by the offering agents at approximately $15 per share, but at this point on March 23 the asking price had fallen to two one-hundredths of a cent per share, which meant that you could buy 5,000 shares of BATS stock for one dollar.

The BATS disaster certainly illustrates the power of Mercury retrograde in the markets. But it is an especially strong example because of Mercury's alignment with the 0° Aries point, triggering the full force of the cardinal axis.

More importantly, the stock for Apple Computer has an especially strong relationship to the cardinal axis, as is revealed by a quick look at Apple's First-Trade horoscope on the 90-degree dial.

Without going into too much detail, simply note that the dial's pointer is aligned with the Aries point, while all of the horizontal lines across the dial perpendicular to the Aries point

AAPL
New York, NY
Dec 12 1980
10:00:00 AM EST

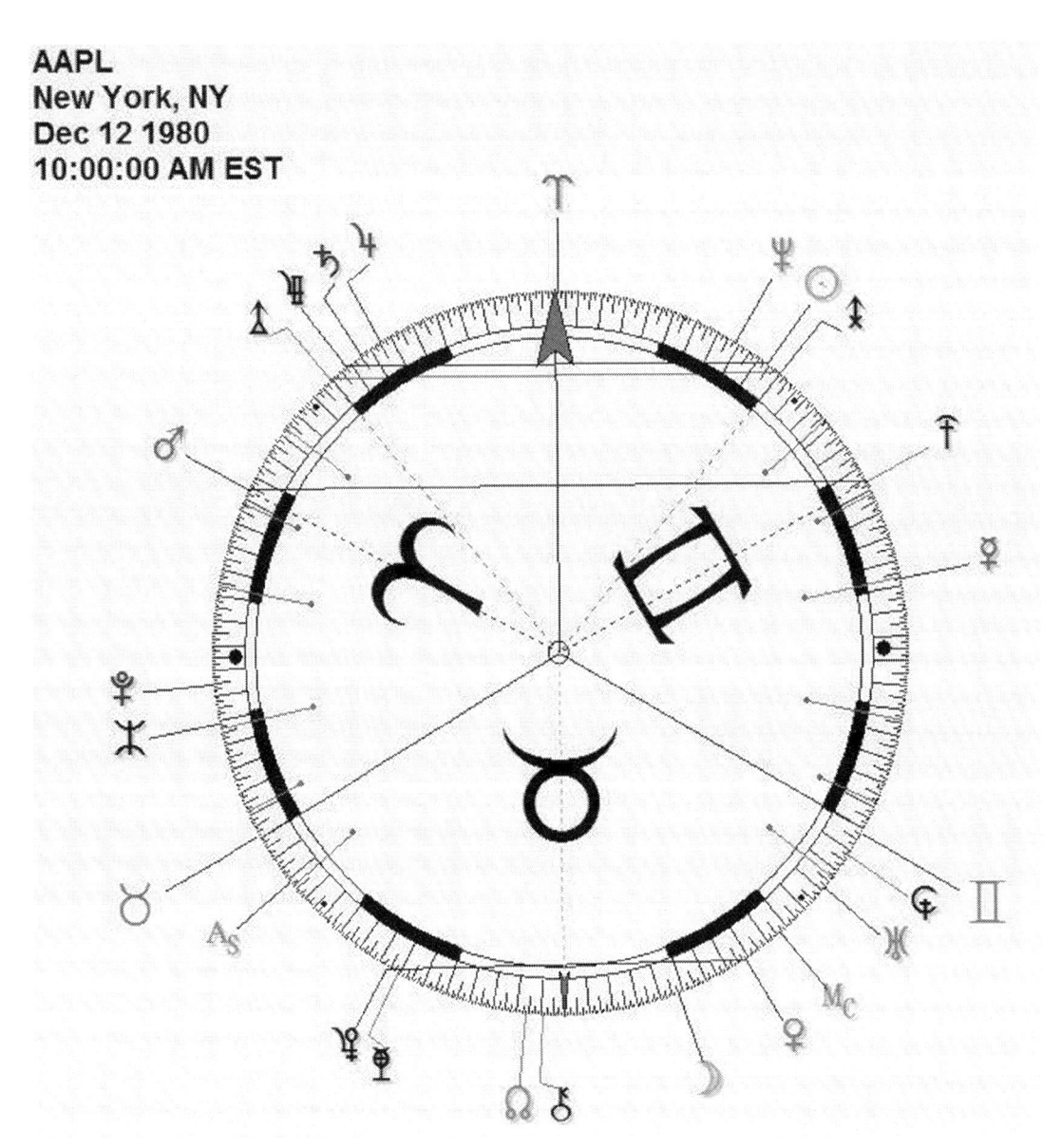

axis identify midpoint structures that connect planets in the chart with the cardinal axis.

That's one of the reasons that Apple is such a powerful company – the cardinal axis signifies strong connections on a global scale, and Apple clearly has a global influence. So when the BATS Flash Crash was triggered by Mercury hitting the 0° Aries point, the impact on Apple was especially severe. In fact, it was the big drop in the price of Apple's stock itself that initially caught the attention of traders when the BATS computers began to malfunction, alerting them to the fact that something was wrong with the overall order flow.

Retrograde Strategies

As astro-traders, our aim is to be able to move past the possibilities of being victimized by Mercury retrograde distortions, so that we can use this part of the Mercury cycle creatively and productively. As we pursue that goal, we need to deal with the Mercury retrograde phenomenon from two different perspectives – an internal one and an external one.

With the internal component, we are concerned with our own consciousness, with what's going on inside our heads and the effects of our own thoughts as we go through the Mercury retrograde experience. The external component is simply the realm of phenomena that we experience outside ourselves, in the markets or in the world at large. In order to deal with Mercury retrograde periods profitably, we need to take both perspectives into consideration.

The Internal Component

We can gain a much richer appreciation of the inner component if we use what might be called a practical esoteric approach, one that combines esoteric understanding from the ancient wisdom with pragmatic skills and strategies that can help us function more effectively in the contemporary world. The basic idea in this perspective is that if we really want to understand what Mercury retrograde is doing in our lives and with our finances, or if we want to be more effective with our trading while Mercury is retrograde, then we need to begin with a clear understanding of who we are as human beings.

The esoteric notion is that one of our defining characteristics as human beings is that we each have multiple visible and invisible bodies which are intimately and intricately interconnected, with the functions and characteristics of each of our bodies informing and vitalizing the others. As we more fully understand those connections, we can gain greater insights into the real way that are responding to a variety of circumstances, including the times when Mercury is retrograde.

At the grossest, most obvious level, we as human beings have a physical body. It includes an auric field, an energy body that surrounds the concrete observable form of the body that's made of bone, muscles, organs, and skin. This energy body plays a key role in many alternative healing modalities, and can be dramatically revealed with Kirlian photography. But it's really a part of the physical body itself.

Beyond the physical body we also have an emotional body. This typically extends beyond the bounds of the physical body, surrounding the physical body and creating a unique type of energy field as it does so. Since it's not itself physically observable, the best way to comprehend the emotional body is by observing its influence instead. For example, if we walk into a room where two people have just had a violent argument, we can sense an uneasy feeling in the room, even if the participants in the argument are now sitting quietly when we come into the room. The remnants of the angry energy are still swirling around in the room, and we can feel the unsettled state of affairs immediately. When that happens, we are actually connecting with the residual turbulence of the individuals' emotional bodies, which is giving us information that's not being revealed by the physical bodies at the time.

We also have a mental body that extends a bit beyond our emotional bodies. It is a subtle articulation of our capacity for thought, including both concrete thought, which gives us the ability to relate to specific people, places and things; and abstract thought, which gives us the ability to relate to numbers, arcane mathematical concepts, and the impulses of inspiration and intuition.

Beyond the limits of the mental body there is the realm of spirit, and depending on our individual spiritual evolution and the spiritual disciplines we engage in, we also have capacities for connecting with that realm. Our spiritual body extends far beyond the sphere of the physical body; it is what gives us a sense of a higher purpose and allows us to experience personal connections with the cosmos.

Although this is a simplified description of the esoteric understanding of human beings, it's useful because it gives us a frame of reference for considering the internal perspective in getting the best from our Mercury retrograde experiences. Within that frame of reference, we can develop some important postulates about Mercury retrograde and its effects, and gain some insights that can help us master ourselves as traders.

First of all, we can conclude that Mercury retrograde periods have some sort of spiritual purpose, if only because they give us challenges and life lessons that can strengthen our spiritual fortitude. Ultimately, however, spiritual understanding is a highly personal matter, so the best approach to the spiritual function of Mercury retrograde is most likely an agnostic one. In other words, if Mercury retrograde periods have a spiritual purpose, we may not be able to figure out exactly what that purpose is, and we can essentially be content with our lack of specific knowledge. We can simply go through our Mercury retrograde experiences to the best of our ability, trusting that they aid us spiritually in some way.

While maintaining spiritual balance is one of the most powerful strategies for enhancing personal effectiveness in the markets, in the context of our focus on Mercury what is even more important for us as astro-traders to understand is the key role played by the mental body. It is through our mental bodies that Mercury retrograde periods make their biggest impact on our lives and on our trading.

But the ultimate impact of retrograde Mercury is a dynamic process that doesn't stop with the mental body. Although Mercury directly affects the mental body, the mental body doesn't operate in isolation; it is connected on the one hand to the spiritual body, and on the other hand to the emotional body, and those connections hold the key to our personal experience of Mercury retrograde periods as viewed from the internal perspective.

If our livelihood or lifestyle has spirituality as its central focus, Mercury retrograde periods tend to amplify our spiritual practice and development. When Mercury is retrograde we can spend more time in prayer and meditation, or in following other spiritual disciplines compatible with our chosen spiritual path. Under those circumstances Mercury going retrograde can hardly be seen as a negative experience; it may actually be something that we welcome instead.

But most of us don't lead monastic lives, so we don't get much opportunity to take advantage of the potential spiritual connections that are offered us during a Mercury retrograde period.

Especially if we are active traders, we are typically much more focused on the world of commerce and communication, on issues and advocacy in public or private arenas, and on the endless stream of transactions in the mundane realm. We're engaged with fluctuations in market trends, with economic forecasts, and with issues relevant to our personal and financial security. And because that external engagement will in many cases pull us away from a spiritual focus, the Mercury retrograde energy tends to move instead from our mental body into our emotional body.

That's where the potential problems begin for us as astro-traders. Trading is primarily a mental body activity, and if we allow ourselves to be drawn into a stronger connection with the emotional body when Mercury is retrograde the mental influences can contribute to emotional imbalances.

It is in our emotional bodies that we are the most likely to experience frustrations and suffering. In extreme cases the thought forms which have moved from the mental body into the emotional body will trigger such strong responses that they are transferred to the physical body as well, manifesting as illness or fatigue.

In any event, an imbalanced emotional state will act consistently and reliably to restrict the flow of money in our lives, and with the emotional echoes and repercussions that usually accompany a cash flow inhibition we can start to become more anxious or even fearful.

Fear, of course, is one of the emotional engines that drives the action in the markets, with greed being the other prime emotional mover. If we are personally balanced in our ability to deal with fear and greed, we are much more likely to tune into the messages of the markets more precisely, and to enjoy the fruits of our trading efforts.

When Mercury is retrograde, however, it is typically far more difficult to keep the interplay of fear and greed in balance. That's when we are more likely to make foolish or ill-informed financial choices, and to make costly trading mistakes.

The key point for us to keep in mind as we consider the internal component of our Mercury retrograde experiences is that while we can encounter the effects of Mercury retrograde in all our bodies and at all levels of our being, the primary point of access for Mercury is through our mental body. Mercury is, after all, mainly connected with the functions of the mind, and so its energy is specifically directed at this part of our being. Even though this makes the mental body more vulnerable when Mercury is retrograde, it also gives us a hint about some effective strategies for managing the inner component of our encounters with Mercury in retrograde motion.

Particularly in our trading, if we want to keep our emotional bodies in balance, we need to engage the mental component rather than trying to connect directly with the emotions themselves. Ultimately all of our emotions have mental roots, so if we pay proper attention to our mental bodies, our emotional bodies are much more likely to take care of themselves and stay balanced and resilient, whether or not they feel any direct effect from the current activities of the mental body.

In practical terms, we can affect our mental bodies directly and voluntarily simply by choosing what we think. Our mental bodies are unique in that they can respond to the conscious choices that we make.

We may not be able to choose the hormone levels or heart rate in the physical body, and we may not be able to control the spontaneous feelings of fear or disgust that pump through our emotional bodies when we unexpectedly confront threatening or unpleasant circumstances. But simply by choosing our thoughts we can begin to regulate our mental activity, and when our mental bodies are functioning properly we are much more likely to get positive results in every other part of our experience.

That connection with the mental body is the core understanding behind the use of affirmations in the New Thought movement. It is the secret to the success of a variety of meditative practices. It is the basis of therapeutic and self-empowerment disciplines like Neuro-Linguistic Programming and Energetic Life Balancing.

But regardless of the specific approach that we take to the process of thinking or of the particular mental methodology that we employ, the conclusion is the same: in the markets or in other areas of our lives, we can change the results we get by altering what we think and how we think about it. If we're not happy with what we're feeling in any situation, or with the results we're getting in our trading, it's ultimately the mental dynamic that's at fault.

As Dr. Michael Ryce put it so succinctly in his book *Why Is This Happening To Me ... AGAIN?!*, "If you keep thinking what you've always thought, you'll keep getting what you've always got."

This understanding is especially important when Mercury is retrograde, since those particular occasions give us unique opportunities to interrupt the patterns in our lives, choosing different thoughts and different results.

The External Component

But even though the internal dimension provides a major arena for Mercury retrograde to make its influence felt in our lives and in our trading, there is an external component as well, in the world outside our skin.

As I learned when I purchased my Mercury retrograde Peugeot, things do sometimes go wrong, and there does seem to be an uncanny connection between Mercury retrograde periods and a variety of breakdowns, especially when transportation or communication are concerned. So if we are going to develop really effective strategies for dealing with Mercury retrogrades in the context of our trading, we would do well to take this external component into consideration.

Based on the mythological depiction of Mercury as a messenger and on continuing observation of the Mercury retrograde phenomenon, it's perhaps easiest to see the influence that Mercury can have on the communications process.

Even so, we face a challenge when we try to define exactly what communication is, since it always seems to have subjective dimensions as well as objective ones. I may feel that I know what communication is all about, but you may not agree with me, especially if you feel that I'm not communicating effectively with you to start with! And if we can't come up with an unequivocal and measurable understanding of communication itself, what hope can we possibly have of comprehending and measuring the impact of Mercury retrograde periods on the communications process from an objective point of view?

While a satisfactory definition of communication may be elusive, a good starting point is the mathematical model of communication proposed by Claude Shannon and Warren Weaver in 1948. Their classic model breaks down communication into its simplest components.

According to this model, the two key participants in any communication are the sender and the receiver, with the sender sending a message or signal along a channel and the receiver getting it on the other end. But if the flow along the communications channel only

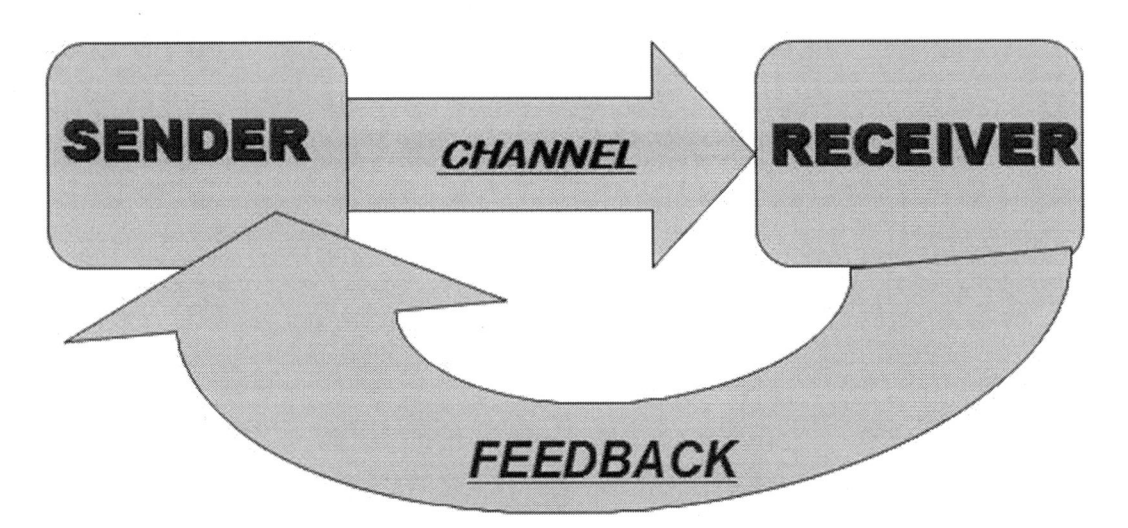

[Diagram: SENDER → CHANNEL → RECEIVER, with a FEEDBACK arrow looping back from receiver to sender.]

goes in one direction, from the sender to the receiver, we can't be sure that the message is really going through. That's why Shannon and Weaver added a reverse channel, a feedback loop, to their model, to allow for confirming signals to travel in the opposite direction, from the receiver back to the sender.

While Shannon and Weaver's mathematical model of communication in this most basic form certainly helps to simplify and clarify our understanding of processes that may otherwise seem too complex, our initial diagram of the model lacks one feature that Shannon and Weaver included in their work more than 60 years ago: the element of noise.

The addition of this feature made the Shannon/Weaver communications model much more robust, because it could now describe situations in which communications broke down, as well as instances in which the desired connections and information flow were being achieved.

"Noise" was the technical term that they used to describe any and all factors which could interrupt or distort the communications process. We ordinarily use that word to describe certain kinds of sounds which may have unpleasant qualities and which interfere with peace and quiet or which make it difficult for us to hear other, more desirable sounds.

But for Claude Shannon and Warren Weaver, noise was anything that caused a disconnection anywhere within the complete communications loop in their model, either along the sender/receiver channel or along the feedback channel. With this definition, noise may or may not be auditory; while it may come in the form of unpleasant sounds, it can also be an interruption of visual content, a burst of electronic static that scrambles a wi-fi connection, or anything else that keeps message signals from flowing freely along a communications channel.

NOISE

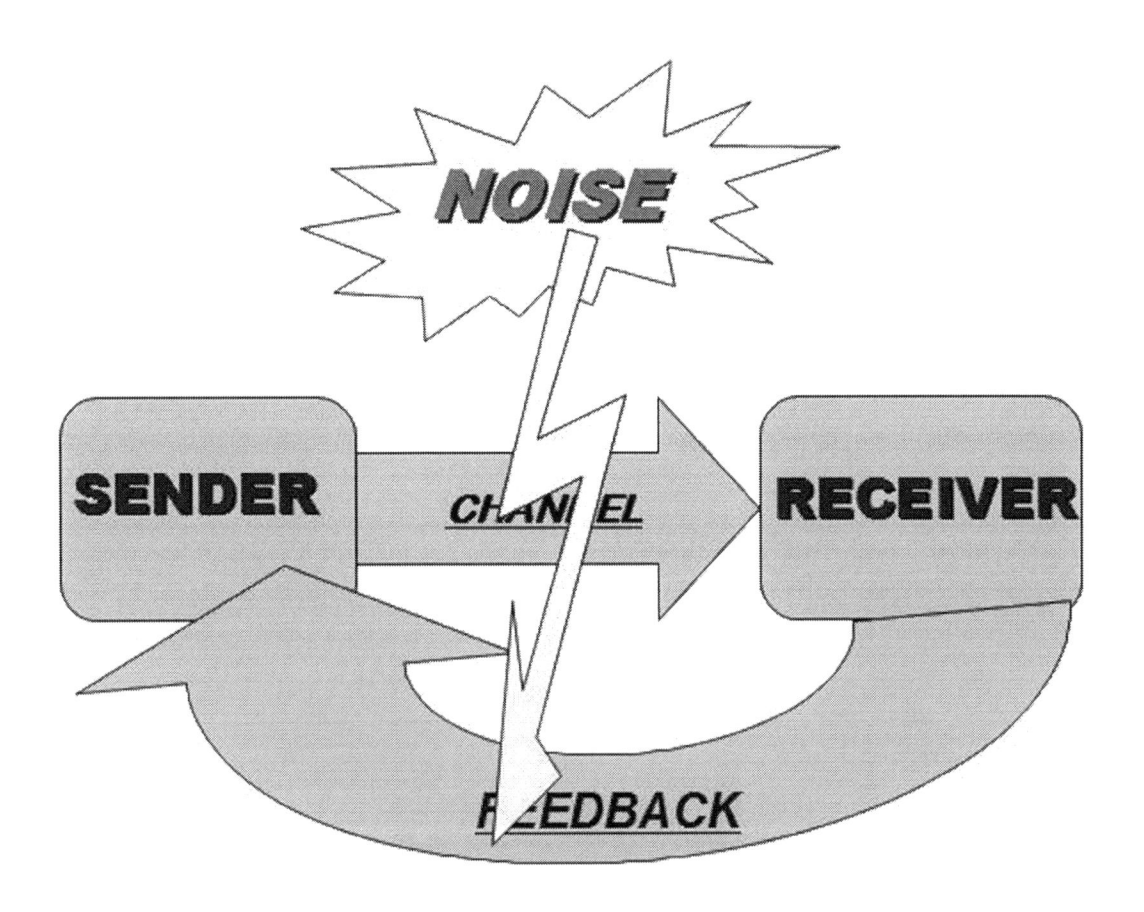

SENDER → CHANNEL → **RECEIVER**

FEEDBACK

It is precisely that broader definition of noise, presented within the context of a simple functional model of communication, that gives us an objective way of codifying the role that Mercury can play when it is in retrograde motion.

Mercury retrograde increases the amount of noise in any communications system, whether we are dealing with a flow of electronic data or with face-to-face interactions between articulate human beings. With a Mercury retrograde period in effect, we can anticipate breakdowns in the main channel of communication, distortions in the feedback loop, and the expenditure of a lot of ancillary energy without there necessarily being any additional results to show for the extra effort.

Needless to say, the introduction of Mercury retrograde noise into the daily market mix of bid/ask spread quotations and order flows can complicate things considerably for any would-be trader – the BATS IPO example gives us a good idea of just how extreme the disruption can actually become.

But because the Shannon and Weaver communications model allows us to identify the role that retrograde Mercury is playing so clearly, we are also able to suggest some specific strategies for coping with the external component in the Mercury retrograde experience.

After all, when noise disrupts any communications system, there are only a limited number of courses of action that we can pursue if we want to change what's going on – we can weaken or eliminate the noise or the source of the noise, we can strengthen or otherwise modify the message signals that are being transmitted, or we can add redundancy to the system by opening up additional channels to allow for a greater likelihood that messages in the system can be accurately sent and received.

To be effective when Mercury is retrograde, then, our task is to open up more channels of communication as we increase the amount and frequency of the feedback in the systems we are using.

In practical terms for us as traders, this can mean creating additional brokerage accounts, so that if one of our connections to the market fails we can communicate orders through an alternative process. It also suggests the wisdom of bringing some redundancy into our ways of monitoring the markets, so that we're not dependent on a single data source, and of connecting with our data sources more frequently to verify and fine-tune the impressions we are getting about the tenor and trend of the markets we are observing.

A Synthetic Approach

Ultimately, however, our most effective strategy for active participation in trading while Mercury is retrograde is to craft an approach which combines the internal and external components of the Mercury retrograde experience. Rather than trying to figure out whether Mercury retrograde distortions are taking place because of our own lack of vigilance about our mental processes, or because of extra noise impacting the objective systems of communication that we rely upon, it's much better if we become proactive and take care of both the internal and external components simultaneously.

While Mercury is retrograde, we can look for improved outcomes in our trading and in our lives if we maintain the kind of mental discipline that obliges us to be very careful with our thoughts, our language, and our attitudes, making sure that they are aligned in ways that can allow us to receive and transmit information clearly and effortlessly. Whether we are using affirmations, self-hypnosis, advanced meditation techniques, or some other method for maintaining that mental balance and alignment, we need to make our mental management practices and spiritual disciplines an especially high priority while Mercury is retrograde.

At the same time, we can add to our effectiveness even more if we take aggressive and practical steps to open up new communications channels and to increase the information flow and feedback we are getting while Mercury is retrograde. Ideally these mechanisms should be in place whether Mercury is retrograde or not, putting us in a position of simply having to tick off boxes on a checklist whenever a Mercury retrograde period begins. But even if we wait until Mercury goes retrograde before adding more redundancies to our trading operations, it's still worth doing.

An 18% Game Plan

As we've noted earlier, the 18% of each year that Mercury is retrograde gives us some unique opportunities to strengthen our advantages as astro-traders. While we can certainly benefit from giving attention to the internal and external components that we've just reviewed, there are even more specific Mercury retrograde strategies that we can pursue profitably whenever the messenger of the gods starts back-pedaling. While they are mainly concerned with the external component of our engagement with Mercury retrograde, they also have implications for the inner component as well. We'll look at each of them from the astro-trading perspective, but in most cases the general underlying principles behind each strategy can be applied in other parts of our lives as well.

Re-Energize

First of all, we want to re-energize ourselves when Mercury is going retrograde. Ideally this is something that we should do before the retrograde period starts. Because we can anticipate Mercury retrograde periods well ahead of time, and because we are knowledgeable about the obstacles and complications that we may encounter while Mercury is retrograde, we want to be sure that we are in a peak energy state before the retrograde period begins.

As Vince Lombardi once observed, "Fatigue makes cowards of us all." So if we don't have an optimum personal energy level, if we're too tired to accomplish anything, or if we're not dedicating all our physical and internal resources toward the discipline of successful trading, we will be missing out on an opportunity to use the Mercury retrograde time most effectively. But we can expect to collect big dividends if we make sure to gather our resources, to recharge our physical and psychological batteies, and to re-energize ourselves in every other possible way before Mercury's retrograde station, which marks the time that the Mercury retrograde period begins.

Refocus and Regroup

Our second Mercury retrograde strategy is to refocus and regroup. We begin by taking a look at what our specific goals are, both in our short-term trading and in terms of our longer-range personal and financial objectives. What do we hope to accomplish while Mercury is retrograde, and how do those plans fit in with our bigger objectives? Do the goals we have previously set still make sense for us under the current circumstances? If the conditions around us have changed in significant ways, we may need to reconsider our goals.

It's never a good idea to put our energy into directions that aren't congruent with where we really want to go, but if that's what we're doing while Mercury is retrograde, we compound the disadvantage. But if we are still dedicated to the goals we have previously set for ourselves, and if we know that persistent incremental actions in pursuit of those goals will ultimately give us the results we want, we can approach the Mercury retrograde period more confidently, recognizing that our progress may be a little slower than we would like, but understanding that a little extra effort and an extra dose of patience will pay off for us in the end.

Revisit

When Mercury is retrograde we have an opportunity to revisit previous experiences. We can go back and take a fresh look at what we've done before in our encounters with the markets. As we do so, we can explore what has worked well for us in the past. This is especially appropriate when Mercury is retrograde; rather than trying to launch new projects or to come up with innovative new trading ideas, we can focus instead on the things we have done in the past that have produced profitable results for us.

If we discover a particular trading strategy that has worked well previously but that has more recently been neglected, we can try it again when Mercury is retrograde, knowing that it's a safe time for us to revisit that approach, because we won't be pushing the envelope in an effort to stretch our capabilities beyond their normal limits.

Review

We've already noted the importance of careful review when we're dealing with contracts and negotiations during a Mercury retrograde period. That's also an appropriate caveat when we're involved in trading. When we enter a brokerage order online, for example, it's all too easy with Mercury retrograde to get a little careless and click the mouse to confirm our order, erroneously assuming that the numbers on our computer screen accurately reflect our real intentions for the trade, only to discover a moment later that we've purchased 10,000 shares instead of 100 shares, or that we have taken a long position when we meant to sell short. Taking a little extra time to review our trading actions and decisions carefully can save us a lot of grief when Mercury is retrograde.

Research

As W. D. Gann so accurately observed, "Money comes through knowledge." As a trader Gann was quite attuned to astrological cycles, and he was one of the most successful traders of the first half of the Twentieth Century. He was quite clear as well that there are certain times when a trader should step away from the market altogether and refrain from active trading. He followed that rule himself, knowing that when there were particular astrological transits to his natal horoscope his probability of success in the markets was greatly diminished.

But even though W. D. Gann didn't trade during those times, he didn't stop working altogether. Instead, he used those times to expand his research into market patterns and astrological phenomena. He was actively engaged in reading and study, and in exploring ever-deeper levels of the long-term cycles in the markets, but he wasn't acutally putting his money at risk. Mercury retrograde periods offer us a perfect opportunity to emulate Gann's behavior. We can do our research while backing off from active astro-trading, using the time to collect new data and to become better prepared for decisive action once Mercury has resumed direct motion.

Revise

What do we need to change in our trading behavior? When Mercury is retrograde, we may want to revise our trading systems and strategies, but if we make that choice we always need to do so in the context of a rigorous examination of the data that we've accumulated about our previous performance in the markets. We don't make revisions without having all the necessary data in hand, or without reviewing it meticulously.

If we are employing this particular strategy while Mercury is in retrograde motion, we need to determine whether or not something has been successful in the past and then thoroughly back-test any possible revisions before we decide to tweak our trading methodologies. If we are conscientious and systematic in making revisions, a Mercury retrograde period can be a good time to make adjustments that can enhance our effectiveness as astro-traders.

Repair

Mercury retrograde periods also offer us a chance to repair the elements in our trading program that aren't functioning as they should. We may need to deal with a malfunctioning computer monitor, or we may need to clean up some glitches in our database of First-Trade horoscopes. If we've been putting off getting things fixed, we have an excellent opportunity to remedy the situation when Mercury is retrograde.

While we may not want to implement all of these strategies each time that Mercury goes into retrograde motion, they do serve as a reminder that we need not feel helpless when Mercury is retrograde. There are productive things we can do that will help us move forward in our progress toward astro-trading success, even if we encounter some obstacle along the way. And, if we employ any of these specific Mercury retrograde strategies at the appropriate time, we are also taking very practical steps toward keeping the channels of communication open and assuring reliable feedback from our market experiences, reducing the potential impact of the Mercury retrograde noise as we do so.

If we modify our trading activities to take full advantage of the opportunities that Mercury retrograde periods offer us, we can be more confident that we are mastering ourselves as traders as we simultaneously move toward mastery of the markets and of our trades.

The Empirical Advantage

There are, however, additional factors that we need to consider when we deal with Mercury retrograde and the markets. While we know that we as traders will meet challenges and opportunities during this part of the Mercury cycle, it's also useful to look at the behavior of the markets themselves when this phenomenon is in effect.

Although we can speculate about generic Mercury retrograde effects in the markets, using astrological symbolism to invent hypotheses about how stocks and commodities will behave when Mercury is retrograde, that kind of approach ultimately has little real value. It doesn't give us the kind of confidence we need to incorporate astrological principles and perspectives into our real-world trading, and it burdens us with unnecessary and often inaccurate preconceptions as we consider risking our money in the markets.

A much more useful approach is to examine historical market data, looking for patterns that have occurred in association with Mercury retrograde periods. While past market performance is never a guarantee of future market behavior or results, we can at least be reasonably certain that if the Mercury retrograde phenomenon has not had an appreciable effect on a particular stock or futures contract in the past, it's not likely to do so in the future.

With that premise in mind, our team at Financial Cycles Weekly has launched an intensive study of major market indices, precious metals, international markets, and blue chip stocks, assembling all the historical data that we could get our hands on and then backtesting it to see what trends and patterns might reveal themselves.

In some cases, the results were quite surprising. As we examined the data, we found a number of examples where there was a clear and strong correlation between price movements and the Mercury retrograde phenomenon. But that kind of correlation was not evident in every case. In fact, some other stocks and indices essentially seemed to be impervious to the effects of Mercury retrograde.

Even so, we discovered that it's useful to identify the effects of Mercury retrograde, whether there's a clear price movement or whether there seems to be no obvious effect at all. With this information in hand, we can reach well-informed opinions about where there are good trading opportunities and where there are trades that are bet avoided. In every case, we can be much more confident in deciding whether or not to take active trading positions while Mercury is retrograde.

In the chapters that follow you'll find a summary of that research. As you study those results, pay particular attention to the differences in the unique responses of each stock or index. Then, if you do decide to use the Mercury retrograde phenomenon in your own trading, be sure to add your own back-testing to the mix. It is only when you have personally encountered the Mercury retrograde effect for yourself that you will have the confidence it takes to profit from this unique astro-trading advantage.

Mercury Cycles and Market Indices

As we consider the ways in which major stock market indices from around the world respond to Mercury retrograde cycles, one thing becomes obvious almost immediately: the markets don't resonate with Mercury in uniform ways!

Each market does in fact have its own unique characteristics, its own trading pace, and its own intrinsic style and rhythm of communication. Although Mercury has a common role in connecting with the basic elements of trading and commerce no matter what the venue is, its actions are nevertheless modified by the circumstances it encounters, producing nuances that are reflected in each market's individual response to Mercury stations and other Mercury phenomena.

In particular, as we examine the impact of Mercury retrograde periods on market indices, we can readily see that this astrological event has a strong impact on some markets, and a much weaker effect on others. In like manner, the Mercury retrograde effect seems to be fairly short-lived in some markets, but in others the response lasts much longer.

With that in mind, we've back-tested the response of a variety of markets to Mercury retrograde periods. In doing so, we've measured that response in three different time frames.

To begin with, we've measured the price movement each market exhibits during the period between the retrograde station and the direct station, which is the basic context of each Mercury retrograde period and the time that has traditionally been considered problematical.

Next we've measured the price response during the period beginning with the Mercury retrograde station, and ending with the time following the direct station when Mercury returns to the same degree of the zodiac at which it has originally gone retrograde, its "retrograde return".

Then we've looked at the price action solely during this final slice of the Mercury retrograde phenomenon, starting with the time of Mercury's direct station and ending with the time of its retrograde.

Since previous research by Bill Meridian has shown that certain Mercury phenomena can have markedly different effects when they occur in different signs of the zodiac, we've also looked at the price behavior of the indices in our study through the filter of zodiac triplicities — the division of the zodiac signs by element, with three signs in each element. Based on this system, the Fire signs are Aries, Leo, and Sagittarius; the Earth signs are Taurus, Virgo, and Capricorn; the Air signs are Gemini, Libra, and Aquarius; and the Water signs are Cancer, Scorpio and Pisces.

In each case we've based the selection of triplicity on the zodiacal position of Mercury at the retrograde station, and have measured changes in price one day after the retrograde station, 14 days after the retrograde station, and seven days after the direct station.

In all of our examples the time frame for the back-testing was based simply on the amount of historical market data that was available at the time of our research. But because Mercury retrograde cycles repeat with such frequency, even a relatively short time span, with market data going back just a few years, can give us a sufficient number of Mercury retrograde periods for us to get a good idea of the way that a particular index responds to this planetary phenomenon.

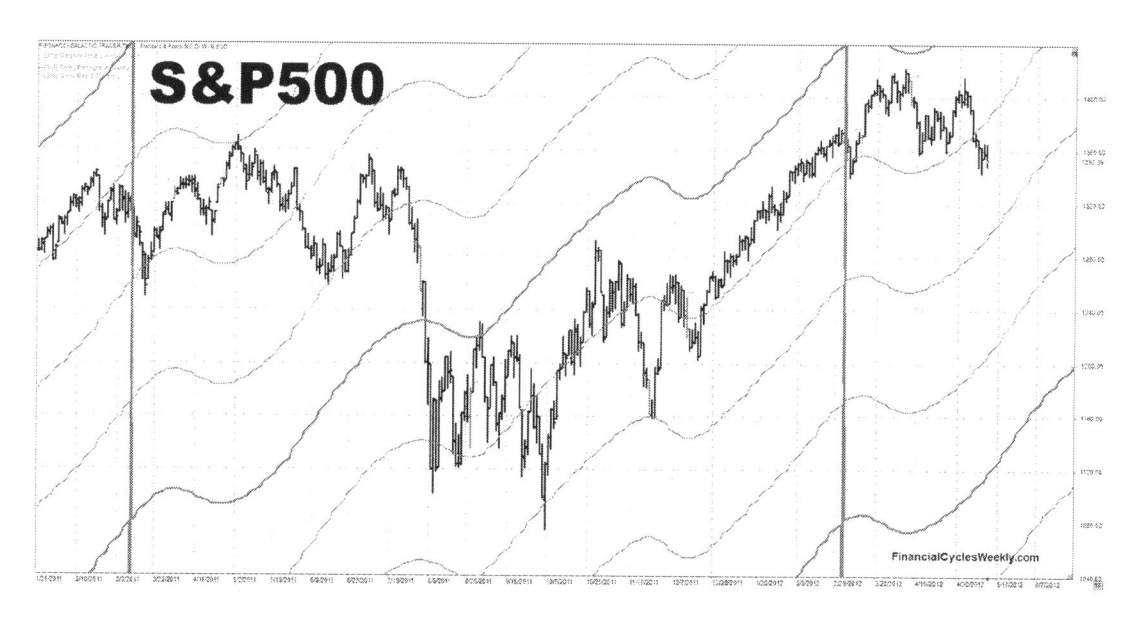

Standard & Poors 500 Index:
Back-Tested Historical Mercury Retrograde Performance

All Mercury Retrograde Periods

Retrograde Station to Direct Station	Average % Change	0.39%
Retrograde Station to Retrograde Return	Average % Change	0.46%
Direct Station to Retrograde Return	Average % Change	0.07%

Mercury Going Retrograde in Fire Signs

1 Day after Retrograde Station	Likelihood of Higher Prices	49.0%
14 Days after Retrograde Station	Likelihood of Higher Prices	63.3%
7 Days after Direct Station	Likelihood of Higher Prices	62.7%

Mercury Going Retrograde in Earth Signs

1 Day after Retrograde Station	Likelihood of Higher Prices	57.7%
14 Days after Retrograde Station	Likelihood of Higher Prices	61.5%
7 Days after Direct Station	Likelihood of Higher Prices	54.9%

Mercury Going Retrograde in Air Signs

1 Day after Retrograde Station	Likelihood of Higher Prices	53.1%
14 Days after Retrograde Station	Likelihood of Higher Prices	55.1%
7 Days after Direct Station	Likelihood of Higher Prices	53.2%

Mercury Going Retrograde in Water Signs

1 Day after Retrograde Station	Likelihood of Higher Prices	50.0%
14 Days after Retrograde Station	Likelihood of Higher Prices	45.5%
7 Days after Direct Station	Likelihood of Higher Prices	55.6%

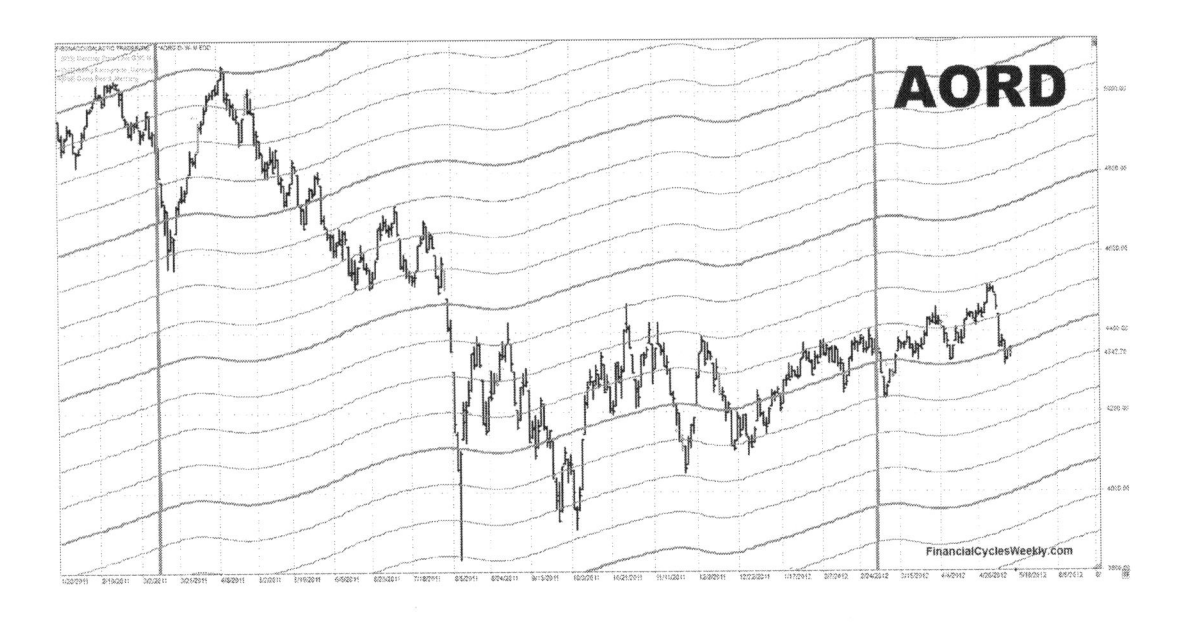

Austrailian All Ordinaries:
Back-Tested Historical Mercury Retrograde Performance

All Mercury Retrograde Periods

Retrograde Station to Direct Station	Average % Change	-0.72%
Retrograde Station to Retrograde Return	Average % Change	-0.78%
Direct Station to Retrograde Return	Average % Change	-0.05%

Mercury Going Retrograde in Fire Signs

1 Day after Retrograde Station	Likelihood of Higher Prices	62.5%
14 Days after Retrograde Station	Likelihood of Higher Prices	73.9%
7 Days after Direct Station	Likelihood of Higher Prices	52.2%

Mercury Going Retrograde in Earth Signs

1 Day after Retrograde Station	Likelihood of Higher Prices	47.8%
14 Days after Retrograde Station	Likelihood of Higher Prices	47.8%
7 Days after Direct Station	Likelihood of Higher Prices	39.1%

Mercury Going Retrograde in Air Signs

1 Day after Retrograde Station	Likelihood of Higher Prices	63.6%
14 Days after Retrograde Station	Likelihood of Higher Prices	36.4%
7 Days after Direct Station	Likelihood of Higher Prices	61.9%

Mercury Going Retrograde in Water Signs

1 Day after Retrograde Station	Likelihood of Higher Prices	63.2%
14 Days after Retrograde Station	Likelihood of Higher Prices	57.9%
7 Days after Direct Station	Likelihood of Higher Prices	65.0%

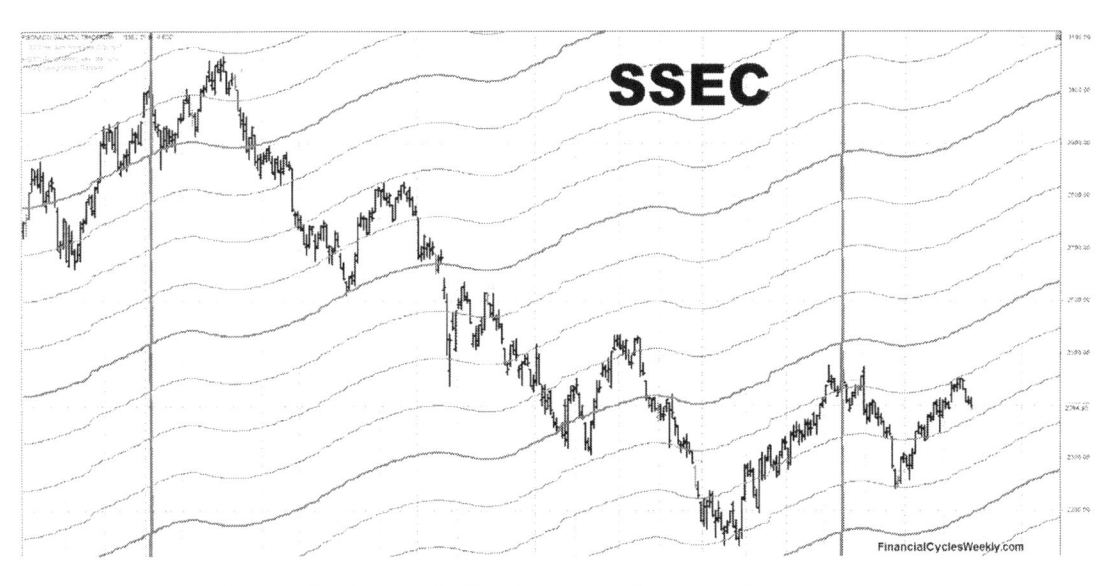

Shanghai Stock Exchange Composite Index: Back-Tested Historical Mercury Retrograde Performance

All Mercury Retrograde Periods

Retrograde Station to Direct Station	Average % Change	-1.56%
Retrograde Station to Retrograde Return	Average % Change	-1.50%
Direct Station to Retrograde Return	Average % Change	0.07%

Mercury Going Retrograde in Fire Signs

1 Day after Retrograde Station	Likelihood of Higher Prices	28.6%
14 Days after Retrograde Station	Likelihood of Higher Prices	61.5%
7 Days after Direct Station	Likelihood of Higher Prices	35.7%

Mercury Going Retrograde in Earth Signs

1 Day after Retrograde Station	Likelihood of Higher Prices	53.8%
14 Days after Retrograde Station	Likelihood of Higher Prices	69.2%
7 Days after Direct Station	Likelihood of Higher Prices	50.0%

Mercury Going Retrograde in Air Signs

1 Day after Retrograde Station	Likelihood of Higher Prices	54.5%
14 Days after Retrograde Station	Likelihood of Higher Prices	45.5%
7 Days after Direct Station	Likelihood of Higher Prices	50.0%

Mercury Going Retrograde in Water Signs

1 Day after Retrograde Station	Likelihood of Higher Prices	88.9%
14 Days after Retrograde Station	Likelihood of Higher Prices	33.3%
7 Days after Direct Station	Likelihood of Higher Prices	60.0%

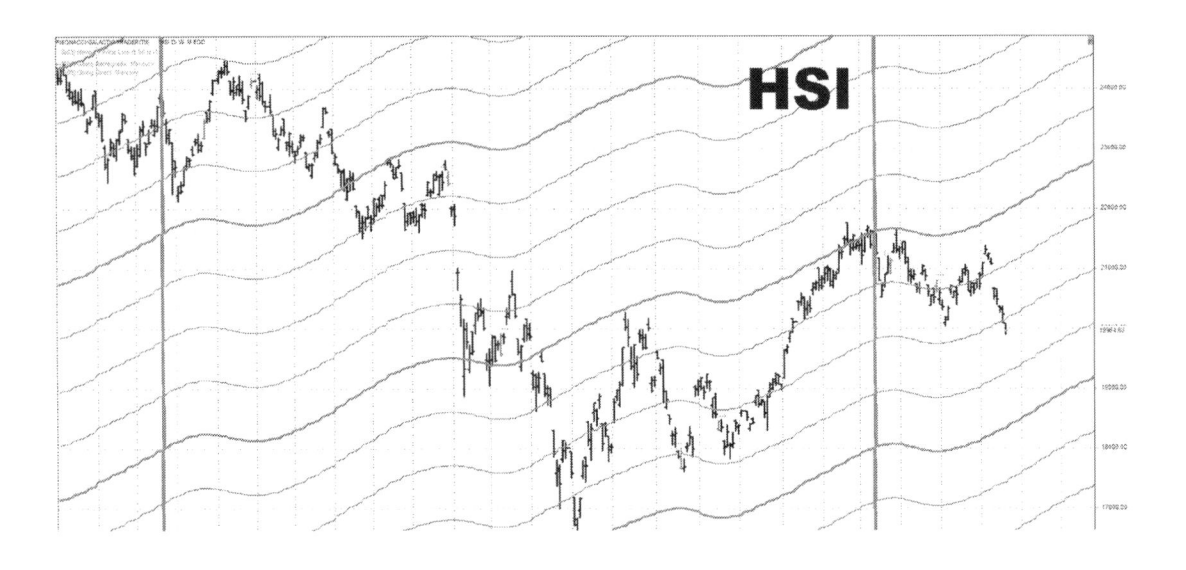

Hong Kong Hang Seng Index:
Back-Tested Historical Mercury Retrograde Performance

All Mercury Retrograde Periods

Retrograde Station to Direct Station	Average % Change	-2.06%
Retrograde Station to Retrograde Return	Average % Change	-2.30%
Direct Station to Retrograde Return	Average % Change	-0.32%

Mercury Going Retrograde in Fire Signs

1 Day after Retrograde Station	Likelihood of Higher Prices	47.4%
14 Days after Retrograde Station	Likelihood of Higher Prices	38.9%
7 Days after Direct Station	Likelihood of Higher Prices	55.0%

Mercury Going Retrograde in Earth Signs

1 Day after Retrograde Station	Likelihood of Higher Prices	52.4%
14 Days after Retrograde Station	Likelihood of Higher Prices	47.6%
7 Days after Direct Station	Likelihood of Higher Prices	59.1%

Mercury Going Retrograde in Air Signs

1 Day after Retrograde Station	Likelihood of Higher Prices	59.1%
14 Days after Retrograde Station	Likelihood of Higher Prices	54.5%
7 Days after Direct Station	Likelihood of Higher Prices	42.9%

Mercury Going Retrograde in Water Signs

1 Day after Retrograde Station	Likelihood of Higher Prices	44.4%
14 Days after Retrograde Station	Likelihood of Higher Prices	50.0%
7 Days after Direct Station	Likelihood of Higher Prices	68.8%

Bombay Stock Exchange SENSEX:
Back-Tested Historical Mercury Retrograde Performance

All Mercury Retrograde Periods

Retrograde Station to Direct Station	Average % Change	-0.17%
Retrograde Station to Retrograde Return	Average % Change	-2.33%
Direct Station to Retrograde Return	Average % Change	-2.02%

Mercury Going Retrograde in Fire Signs

1 Day after Retrograde Station	Likelihood of Higher Prices	78.6%
14 Days after Retrograde Station	Likelihood of Higher Prices	61.5%
7 Days after Direct Station	Likelihood of Higher Prices	50.0%

Mercury Going Retrograde in Earth Signs

1 Day after Retrograde Station	Likelihood of Higher Prices	46.2%
14 Days after Retrograde Station	Likelihood of Higher Prices	53.8%
7 Days after Direct Station	Likelihood of Higher Prices	58.3%

Mercury Going Retrograde in Air Signs

1 Day after Retrograde Station	Likelihood of Higher Prices	45.5%
14 Days after Retrograde Station	Likelihood of Higher Prices	27.3%
7 Days after Direct Station	Likelihood of Higher Prices	30.0%

Mercury Going Retrograde in Water Signs

1 Day after Retrograde Station	Likelihood of Higher Prices	44.4%
14 Days after Retrograde Station	Likelihood of Higher Prices	77.8%
7 Days after Direct Station	Likelihood of Higher Prices	60.0%

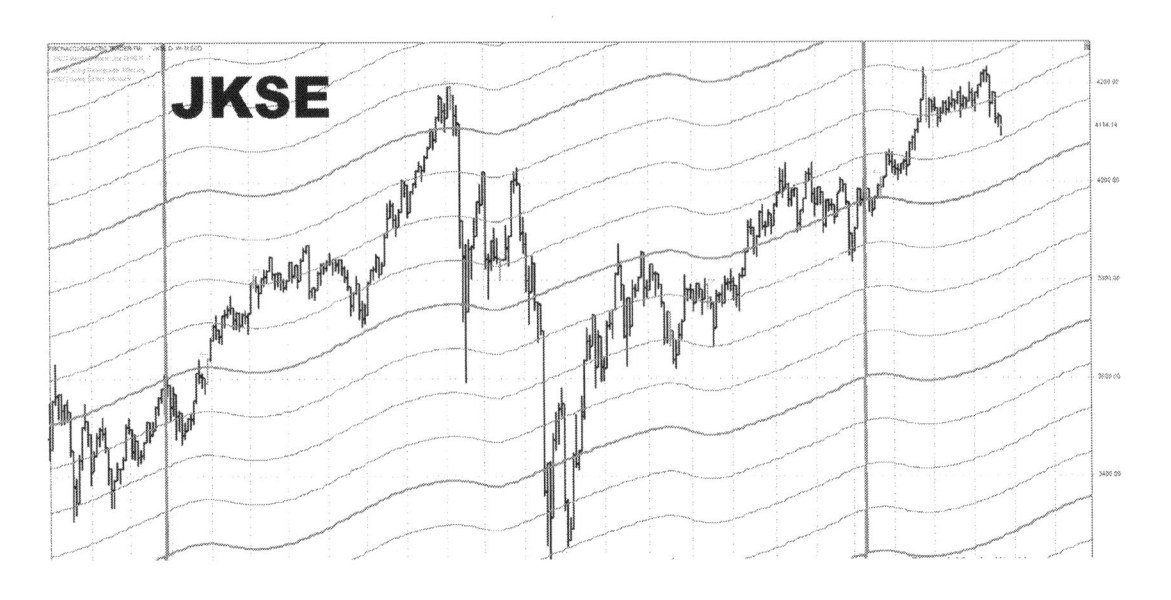

Jakarta Composite Index:
Back-Tested Historical Mercury Retrograde Performance

All Mercury Retrograde Periods

Retrograde Station to Direct Station	Average % Change	-0.21%
Retrograde Station to Retrograde Return	Average % Change	-2.06%
Direct Station to Retrograde Return	Average % Change	-1.44%

Mercury Going Retrograde in Fire Signs

1 Day after Retrograde Station	Likelihood of Higher Prices	64.3%
14 Days after Retrograde Station	Likelihood of Higher Prices	38.5%
7 Days after Direct Station	Likelihood of Higher Prices	57.1%

Mercury Going Retrograde in Earth Signs

1 Day after Retrograde Station	Likelihood of Higher Prices	30.8%
14 Days after Retrograde Station	Likelihood of Higher Prices	53.8%
7 Days after Direct Station	Likelihood of Higher Prices	58.3%

Mercury Going Retrograde in Air Signs

1 Day after Retrograde Station	Likelihood of Higher Prices	45.5%
14 Days after Retrograde Station	Likelihood of Higher Prices	54.5%
7 Days after Direct Station	Likelihood of Higher Prices	50.0%

Mercury Going Retrograde in Water Signs

1 Day after Retrograde Station	Likelihood of Higher Prices	66.7%
14 Days after Retrograde Station	Likelihood of Higher Prices	55.6%
7 Days after Direct Station	Likelihood of Higher Prices	70.0%

Bursa Malaysia Kuala Lumpur Stock Exchange Composite: Back-Tested Historical Mercury Retrograde Performance

All Mercury Retrograde Periods

Retrograde Station to Direct Station	Average % Change	-1.19%
Retrograde Station to Retrograde Return	Average % Change	-1.97%
Direct Station to Retrograde Return	Average % Change	-0.80%

Mercury Going Retrograde in Fire Signs

1 Day after Retrograde Station	Likelihood of Higher Prices	50.0%
14 Days after Retrograde Station	Likelihood of Higher Prices	38.5%
7 Days after Direct Station	Likelihood of Higher Prices	66.7%

Mercury Going Retrograde in Earth Signs

1 Day after Retrograde Station	Likelihood of Higher Prices	37.5%
14 Days after Retrograde Station	Likelihood of Higher Prices	43.8%
7 Days after Direct Station	Likelihood of Higher Prices	50.0%

Mercury Going Retrograde in Air Signs

1 Day after Retrograde Station	Likelihood of Higher Prices	62.5%
14 Days after Retrograde Station	Likelihood of Higher Prices	56.3%
7 Days after Direct Station	Likelihood of Higher Prices	12.5%

Mercury Going Retrograde in Water Signs

1 Day after Retrograde Station	Likelihood of Higher Prices	47.1%
14 Days after Retrograde Station	Likelihood of Higher Prices	25.0%
7 Days after Direct Station	Likelihood of Higher Prices	80.0%

Tokyo NIKKEI 225:
Back-Tested Historical Mercury Retrograde Performance

All Mercury Retrograde Periods

Retrograde Station to Direct Station	Average % Change	-1.07%
Retrograde Station to Retrograde Return	Average % Change	-1.80%
Direct Station to Retrograde Return	Average % Change	-0.71%

Mercury Going Retrograde in Fire Signs

1 Day after Retrograde Station	Likelihood of Higher Prices	45.8%
14 Days after Retrograde Station	Likelihood of Higher Prices	43.5%
7 Days after Direct Station	Likelihood of Higher Prices	54.2%

Mercury Going Retrograde in Earth Signs

1 Day after Retrograde Station	Likelihood of Higher Prices	45.8%
14 Days after Retrograde Station	Likelihood of Higher Prices	45.8%
7 Days after Direct Station	Likelihood of Higher Prices	54.2%

Mercury Going Retrograde in Air Signs

1 Day after Retrograde Station	Likelihood of Higher Prices	54.5%
14 Days after Retrograde Station	Likelihood of Higher Prices	59.1%
7 Days after Direct Station	Likelihood of Higher Prices	42.9%

Mercury Going Retrograde in Water Signs

1 Day after Retrograde Station	Likelihood of Higher Prices	36.8%
14 Days after Retrograde Station	Likelihood of Higher Prices	52.6%
7 Days after Direct Station	Likelihood of Higher Prices	65.0%

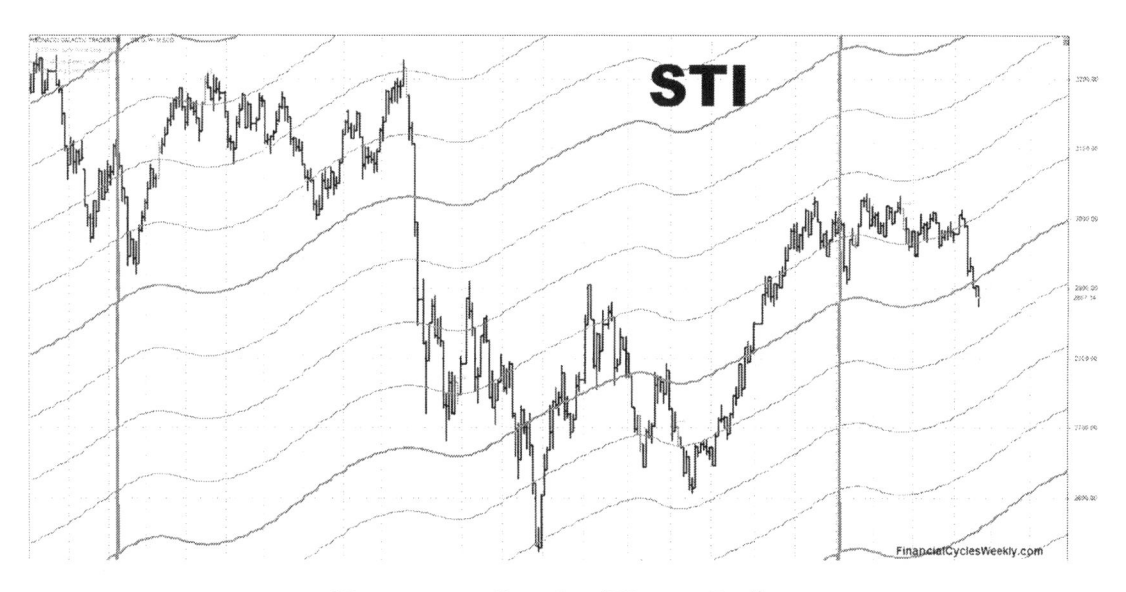

Singapore Straits Times Index:
Back-Tested Historical Mercury Retrograde Performance

All Mercury Retrograde Periods

Retrograde Station to Direct Station	Average % Change	-0.32%
Retrograde Station to Retrograde Return	Average % Change	-1.69%
Direct Station to Retrograde Return	Average % Change	-1.25%

Mercury Going Retrograde in Fire Signs

1 Day after Retrograde Station	Likelihood of Higher Prices	47.4%
14 Days after Retrograde Station	Likelihood of Higher Prices	44.4%
7 Days after Direct Station	Likelihood of Higher Prices	45.0%

Mercury Going Retrograde in Earth Signs

1 Day after Retrograde Station	Likelihood of Higher Prices	38.1%
14 Days after Retrograde Station	Likelihood of Higher Prices	42.9%
7 Days after Direct Station	Likelihood of Higher Prices	50.0%

Mercury Going Retrograde in Air Signs

1 Day after Retrograde Station	Likelihood of Higher Prices	72.7%
14 Days after Retrograde Station	Likelihood of Higher Prices	54.5%
7 Days after Direct Station	Likelihood of Higher Prices	26.3%

Mercury Going Retrograde in Water Signs

1 Day after Retrograde Station	Likelihood of Higher Prices	66.7%
14 Days after Retrograde Station	Likelihood of Higher Prices	40.0%
7 Days after Direct Station	Likelihood of Higher Prices	66.7%

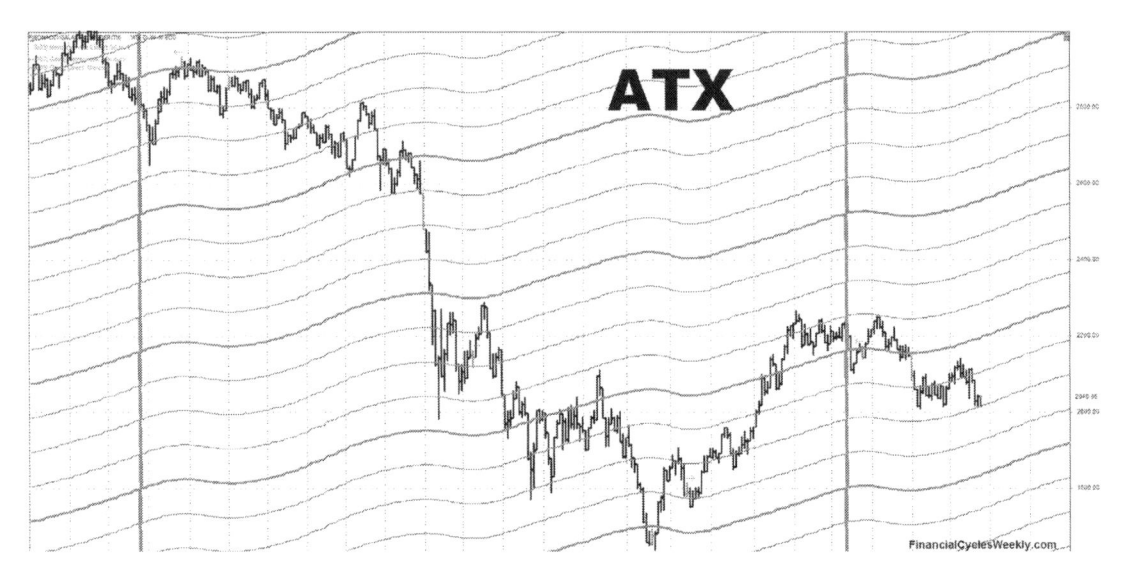

Vienna Stock Exchange Austrian Traded Index: Back-Tested Historical Mercury Retrograde Performance

All Mercury Retrograde Periods

Retrograde Station to Direct Station	Average % Change	-0.66%
Retrograde Station to Retrograde Return	Average % Change	-1.89%
Direct Station to Retrograde Return	Average % Change	-1.05%

Mercury Going Retrograde in Fire Signs

1 Day after Retrograde Station	Likelihood of Higher Prices	42.9%
14 Days after Retrograde Station	Likelihood of Higher Prices	46.2%
7 Days after Direct Station	Likelihood of Higher Prices	46.7%

Mercury Going Retrograde in Earth Signs

1 Day after Retrograde Station	Likelihood of Higher Prices	43.8%
14 Days after Retrograde Station	Likelihood of Higher Prices	68.8%
7 Days after Direct Station	Likelihood of Higher Prices	62.5%

Mercury Going Retrograde in Air Signs

1 Day after Retrograde Station	Likelihood of Higher Prices	50.0%
14 Days after Retrograde Station	Likelihood of Higher Prices	43.8%
7 Days after Direct Station	Likelihood of Higher Prices	31.3%

Mercury Going Retrograde in Water Signs

1 Day after Retrograde Station	Likelihood of Higher Prices	60.0%
14 Days after Retrograde Station	Likelihood of Higher Prices	33.3%
7 Days after Direct Station	Likelihood of Higher Prices	71.4%

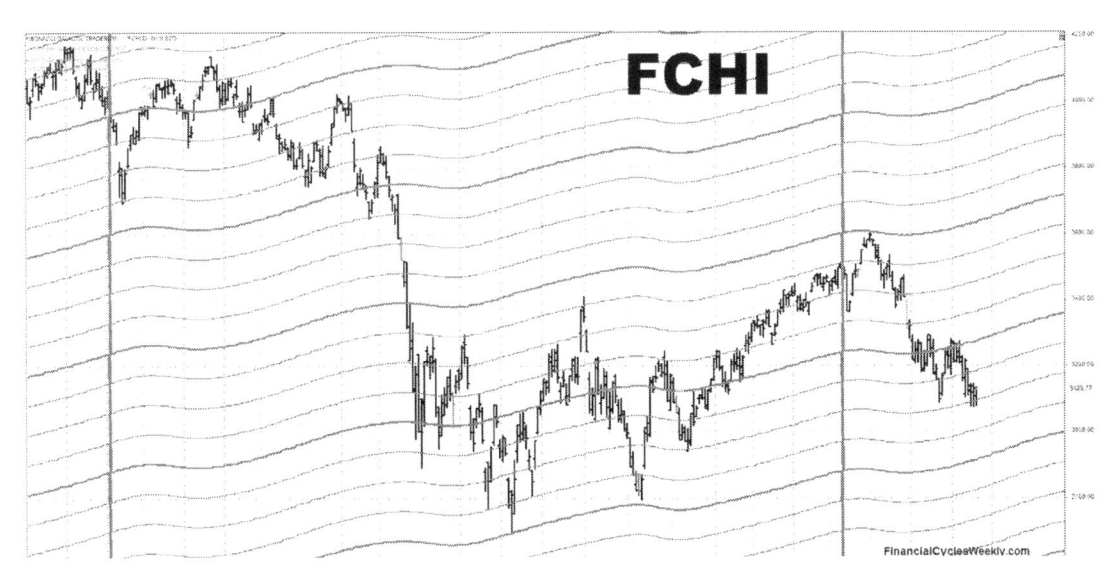

Paris Bourse CAC 40:
Back-Tested Historical Mercury Retrograde Performance

All Mercury Retrograde Periods

Retrograde Station to Direct Station	Average % Change	-1.30%
Retrograde Station to Retrograde Return	Average % Change	-1.41%
Direct Station to Retrograde Return	Average % Change	-0.10%

Mercury Going Retrograde in Fire Signs

1 Day after Retrograde Station	Likelihood of Higher Prices	63.2%
14 Days after Retrograde Station	Likelihood of Higher Prices	44.4%
7 Days after Direct Station	Likelihood of Higher Prices	50.0%

Mercury Going Retrograde in Earth Signs

1 Day after Retrograde Station	Likelihood of Higher Prices	60.0%
14 Days after Retrograde Station	Likelihood of Higher Prices	65.0%
7 Days after Direct Station	Likelihood of Higher Prices	61.1%

Mercury Going Retrograde in Air Signs

1 Day after Retrograde Station	Likelihood of Higher Prices	56.3%
14 Days after Retrograde Station	Likelihood of Higher Prices	37.5%
7 Days after Direct Station	Likelihood of Higher Prices	31.3%

Mercury Going Retrograde in Water Signs

1 Day after Retrograde Station	Likelihood of Higher Prices	40.0%
14 Days after Retrograde Station	Likelihood of Higher Prices	46.7%
7 Days after Direct Station	Likelihood of Higher Prices	80.00%

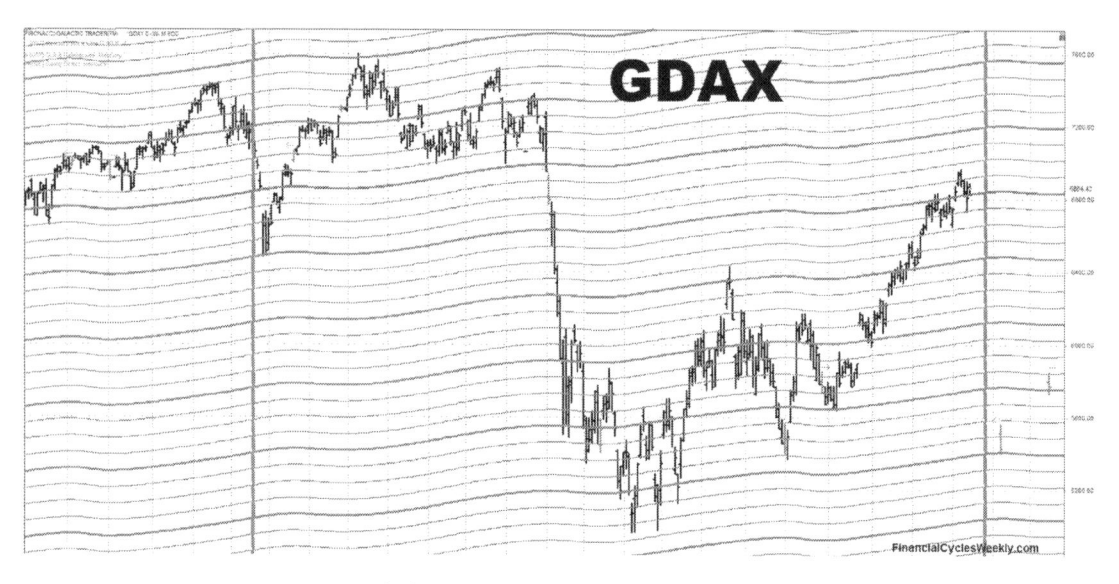

Frankfurt Stock Exchange DAX:
Back-Tested Historical Mercury Retrograde Performance

All Mercury Retrograde Periods

Retrograde Station to Direct Station	Average % Change	-1.74%
Retrograde Station to Retrograde Return	Average % Change	-2.80%
Direct Station to Retrograde Return	Average % Change	-1.10%

Mercury Going Retrograde in Fire Signs

1 Day after Retrograde Station	Likelihood of Higher Prices	37.5%
14 Days after Retrograde Station	Likelihood of Higher Prices	85.7%
7 Days after Direct Station	Likelihood of Higher Prices	50.0%

Mercury Going Retrograde in Earth Signs

1 Day after Retrograde Station	Likelihood of Higher Prices	54.5%
14 Days after Retrograde Station	Likelihood of Higher Prices	81.8%
7 Days after Direct Station	Likelihood of Higher Prices	54.5%

Mercury Going Retrograde in Air Signs

1 Day after Retrograde Station	Likelihood of Higher Prices	72.7%
14 Days after Retrograde Station	Likelihood of Higher Prices	27.3%
7 Days after Direct Station	Likelihood of Higher Prices	20.0%

Mercury Going Retrograde in Water Signs

1 Day after Retrograde Station	Likelihood of Higher Prices	55.6%
14 Days after Retrograde Station	Likelihood of Higher Prices	55.6%
7 Days after Direct Station	Likelihood of Higher Prices	57.1%

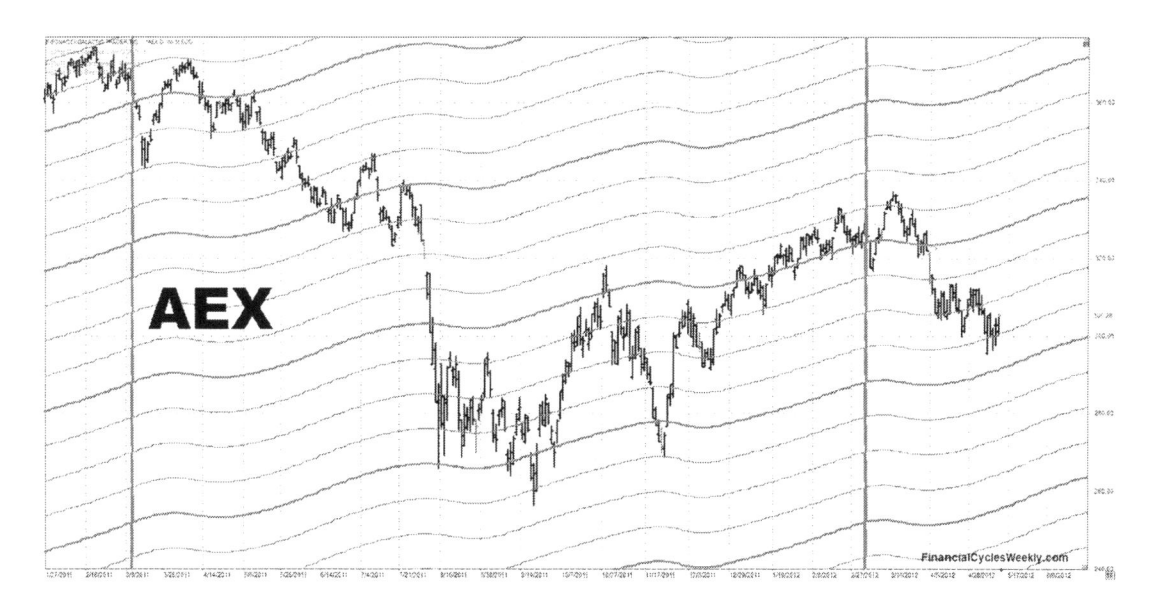

Amsterdam Exchange Index:
Back-Tested Historical Mercury Retrograde Performance

All Mercury Retrograde Periods

Retrograde Station to Direct Station	Average % Change	-1.27%
Retrograde Station to Retrograde Return	Average % Change	-1.49%
Direct Station to Retrograde Return	Average % Change	-0.17%

Mercury Going Retrograde in Fire Signs

1 Day after Retrograde Station	Likelihood of Higher Prices	53.3%
14 Days after Retrograde Station	Likelihood of Higher Prices	42.9%
7 Days after Direct Station	Likelihood of Higher Prices	60.0%

Mercury Going Retrograde in Earth Signs

1 Day after Retrograde Station	Likelihood of Higher Prices	56.3%
14 Days after Retrograde Station	Likelihood of Higher Prices	75.0%
7 Days after Direct Station	Likelihood of Higher Prices	62.5%

Mercury Going Retrograde in Air Signs

1 Day after Retrograde Station	Likelihood of Higher Prices	68.8%
14 Days after Retrograde Station	Likelihood of Higher Prices	50.0%
7 Days after Direct Station	Likelihood of Higher Prices	37.5%

Mercury Going Retrograde in Water Signs

1 Day after Retrograde Station	Likelihood of Higher Prices	33.3%
14 Days after Retrograde Station	Likelihood of Higher Prices	46.7%
7 Days after Direct Station	Likelihood of Higher Prices	57.1%

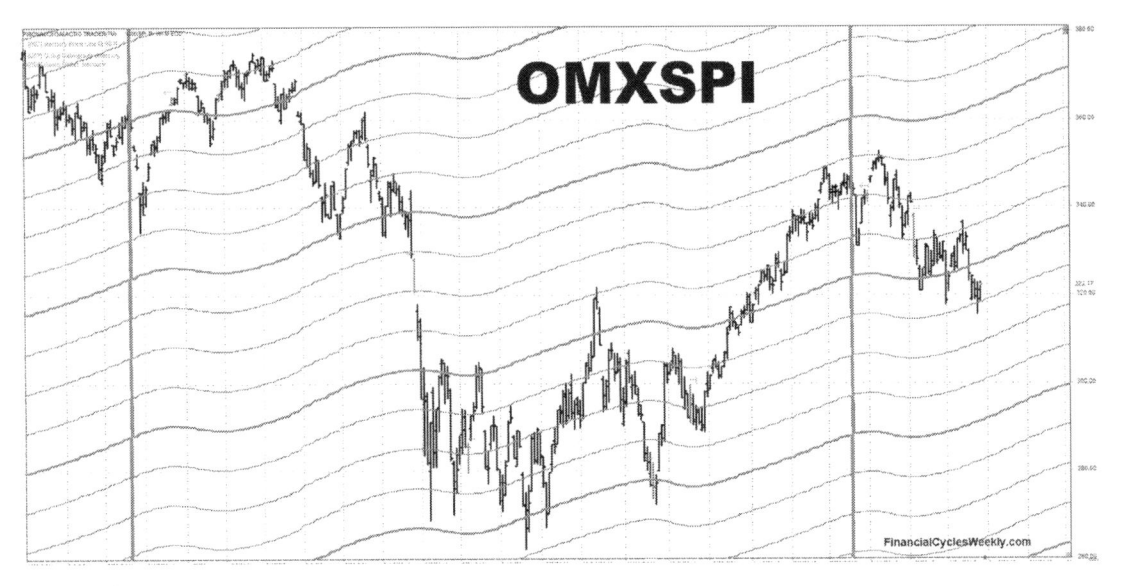

OMX Stockholm PI:
Back-Tested Historical Mercury Retrograde Performance

All Mercury Retrograde Periods

Retrograde Station to Direct Station	Average % Change	-2.13%
Retrograde Station to Retrograde Return	Average % Change	-2.97%
Direct Station to Retrograde Return	Average % Change	-0.80%

Mercury Going Retrograde in Fire Signs

1 Day after Retrograde Station	Likelihood of Higher Prices	50.0%
14 Days after Retrograde Station	Likelihood of Higher Prices	57.1%
7 Days after Direct Station	Likelihood of Higher Prices	60.0%

Mercury Going Retrograde in Earth Signs

1 Day after Retrograde Station	Likelihood of Higher Prices	45.5%
14 Days after Retrograde Station	Likelihood of Higher Prices	81.8%
7 Days after Direct Station	Likelihood of Higher Prices	45.5%

Mercury Going Retrograde in Air Signs

1 Day after Retrograde Station	Likelihood of Higher Prices	45.5%
14 Days after Retrograde Station	Likelihood of Higher Prices	18.2%
7 Days after Direct Station	Likelihood of Higher Prices	22.2%

Mercury Going Retrograde in Water Signs

1 Day after Retrograde Station	Likelihood of Higher Prices	50.0%
14 Days after Retrograde Station	Likelihood of Higher Prices	33.3%
7 Days after Direct Station	Likelihood of Higher Prices	60.0%

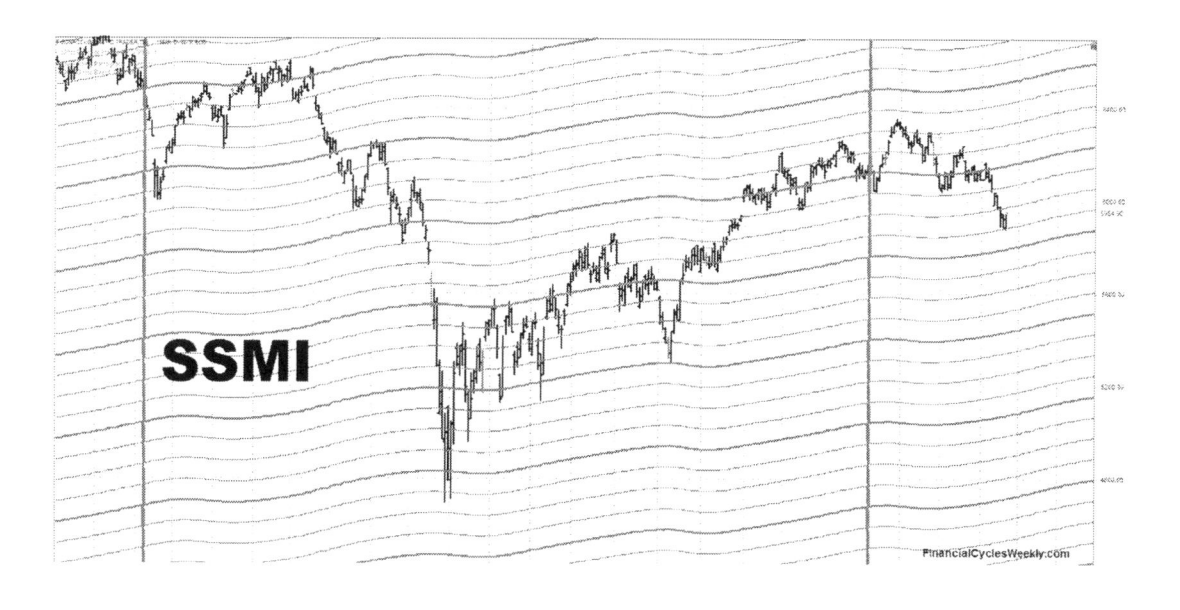

Switzerland Swiss 20 Market Index: Back-Tested Historical Mercury Retrograde Performance

All Mercury Retrograde Periods

Retrograde Station to Direct Station	Average % Change	-0.68%
Retrograde Station to Retrograde Return	Average % Change	-0.81%
Direct Station to Retrograde Return	Average % Change	-0.09%

Mercury Going Retrograde in Fire Signs

1 Day after Retrograde Station	Likelihood of Higher Prices	52.6%
14 Days after Retrograde Station	Likelihood of Higher Prices	55.6%
7 Days after Direct Station	Likelihood of Higher Prices	45.0%

Mercury Going Retrograde in Earth Signs

1 Day after Retrograde Station	Likelihood of Higher Prices	38.9%
14 Days after Retrograde Station	Likelihood of Higher Prices	61.1%
7 Days after Direct Station	Likelihood of Higher Prices	50.0%

Mercury Going Retrograde in Air Signs

1 Day after Retrograde Station	Likelihood of Higher Prices	56.3%
14 Days after Retrograde Station	Likelihood of Higher Prices	43.8%
7 Days after Direct Station	Likelihood of Higher Prices	37.5%

Mercury Going Retrograde in Water Signs

1 Day after Retrograde Station	Likelihood of Higher Prices	46.7%
14 Days after Retrograde Station	Likelihood of Higher Prices	46.7%
7 Days after Direct Station	Likelihood of Higher Prices	73.3%

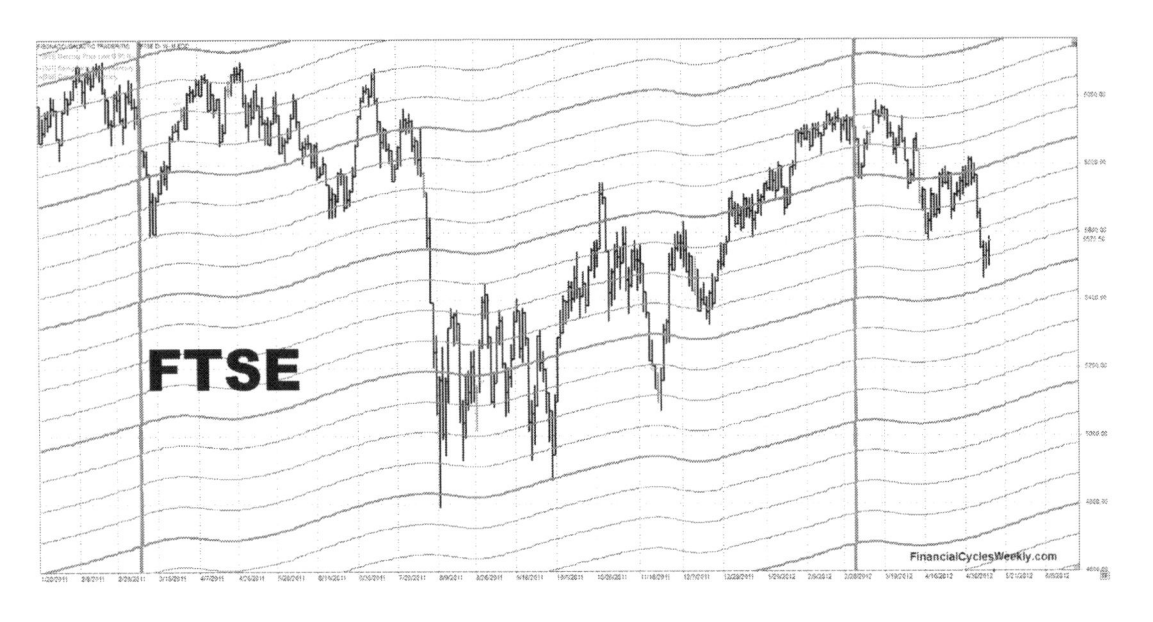

London FTSE 100:
Back-Tested Historical Mercury Retrograde Performance

All Mercury Retrograde Periods

Retrograde Station to Direct Station	Average % Change	-0.54%
Retrograde Station to Retrograde Return	Average % Change	-0.57%
Direct Station to Retrograde Return	Average % Change	-0.03%

Mercury Going Retrograde in Fire Signs

1 Day after Retrograde Station	Likelihood of Higher Prices	66.7%
14 Days after Retrograde Station	Likelihood of Higher Prices	52.2%
7 Days after Direct Station	Likelihood of Higher Prices	58.3%

Mercury Going Retrograde in Earth Signs

1 Day after Retrograde Station	Likelihood of Higher Prices	41.7%
14 Days after Retrograde Station	Likelihood of Higher Prices	66.7%
7 Days after Direct Station	Likelihood of Higher Prices	52.2%

Mercury Going Retrograde in Air Signs

1 Day after Retrograde Station	Likelihood of Higher Prices	40.9%
14 Days after Retrograde Station	Likelihood of Higher Prices	54.5%
7 Days after Direct Station	Likelihood of Higher Prices	23.8%

Mercury Going Retrograde in Water Signs

1 Day after Retrograde Station	Likelihood of Higher Prices	42.1%
14 Days after Retrograde Station	Likelihood of Higher Prices	52.6%
7 Days after Direct Station	Likelihood of Higher Prices	50.0%

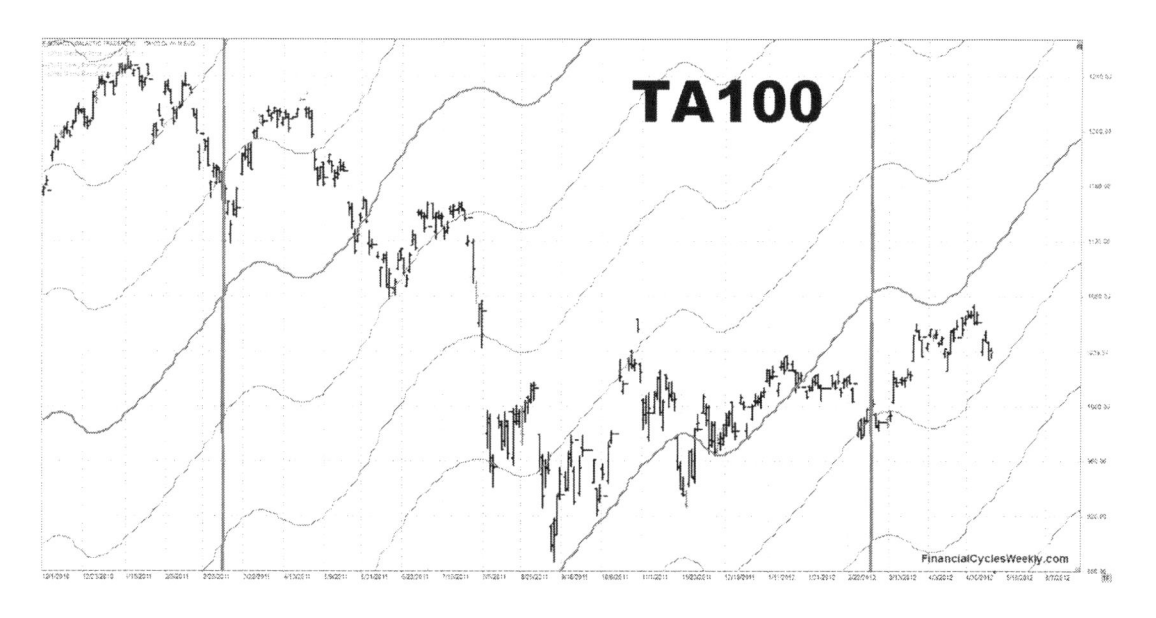

Tel Aviv TA-100 Index:
Back-Tested Historical Mercury Retrograde Performance

All Mercury Retrograde Periods

Retrograde Station to Direct Station	Average % Change	0.21%
Retrograde Station to Retrograde Return	Average % Change	-1.10%
Direct Station to Retrograde Return	Average % Change	-1.24%

Mercury Going Retrograde in Fire Signs

1 Day after Retrograde Station	Likelihood of Higher Prices	50.0%
14 Days after Retrograde Station	Likelihood of Higher Prices	61.5%
7 Days after Direct Station	Likelihood of Higher Prices	42.9%

Mercury Going Retrograde in Earth Signs

1 Day after Retrograde Station	Likelihood of Higher Prices	23.1%
14 Days after Retrograde Station	Likelihood of Higher Prices	53.8%
7 Days after Direct Station	Likelihood of Higher Prices	58.3%

Mercury Going Retrograde in Air Signs

1 Day after Retrograde Station	Likelihood of Higher Prices	72.7%
14 Days after Retrograde Station	Likelihood of Higher Prices	36.4%
7 Days after Direct Station	Likelihood of Higher Prices	20.0%

Mercury Going Retrograde in Water Signs

1 Day after Retrograde Station	Likelihood of Higher Prices	55.6%
14 Days after Retrograde Station	Likelihood of Higher Prices	66.7%
7 Days after Direct Station	Likelihood of Higher Prices	50.0%

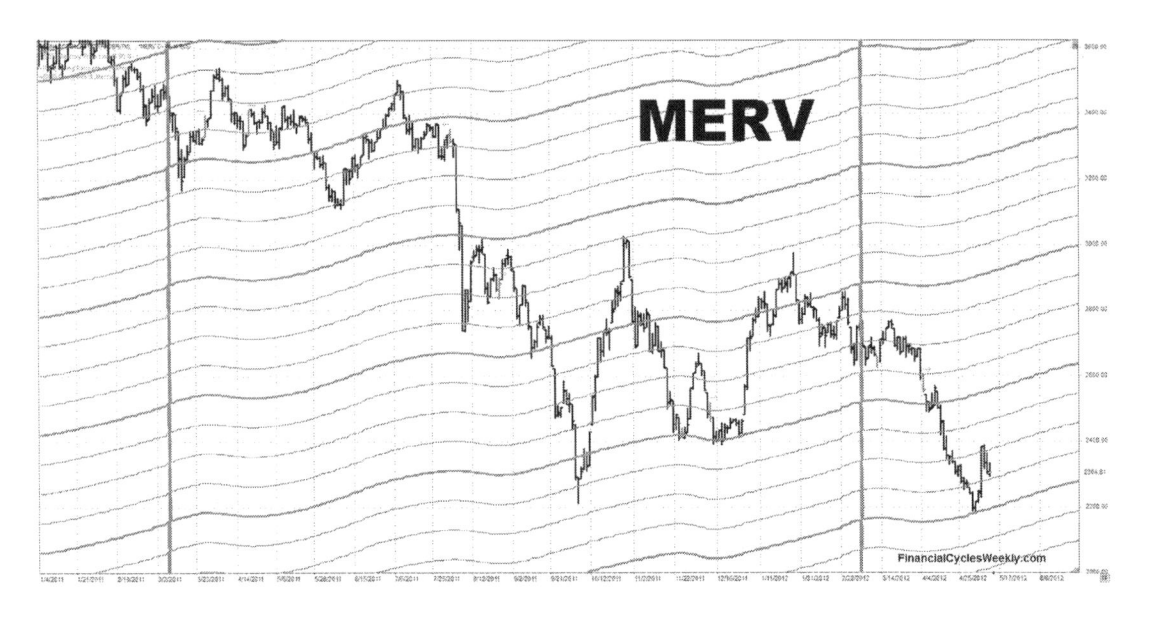

MERVAL Buenos Aires Index:
Back-Tested Historical Mercury Retrograde Performance

All Mercury Retrograde Periods

Retrograde Station to Direct Station	Average % Change	-2.17%
Retrograde Station to Retrograde Return	Average % Change	-4.14%
Direct Station to Retrograde Return	Average % Change	-1.55%

Mercury Going Retrograde in Fire Signs

1 Day after Retrograde Station	Likelihood of Higher Prices	63.4%
14 Days after Retrograde Station	Likelihood of Higher Prices	50.0%
7 Days after Direct Station	Likelihood of Higher Prices	60.0%

Mercury Going Retrograde in Earth Signs

1 Day after Retrograde Station	Likelihood of Higher Prices	60.0%
14 Days after Retrograde Station	Likelihood of Higher Prices	46.7%
7 Days after Direct Station	Likelihood of Higher Prices	53.8%

Mercury Going Retrograde in Air Signs

1 Day after Retrograde Station	Likelihood of Higher Prices	63.6%
14 Days after Retrograde Station	Likelihood of Higher Prices	45.5%
7 Days after Direct Station	Likelihood of Higher Prices	40.0%

Mercury Going Retrograde in Water Signs

1 Day after Retrograde Station	Likelihood of Higher Prices	66.7%
14 Days after Retrograde Station	Likelihood of Higher Prices	77.8%
7 Days after Direct Station	Likelihood of Higher Prices	70.0%

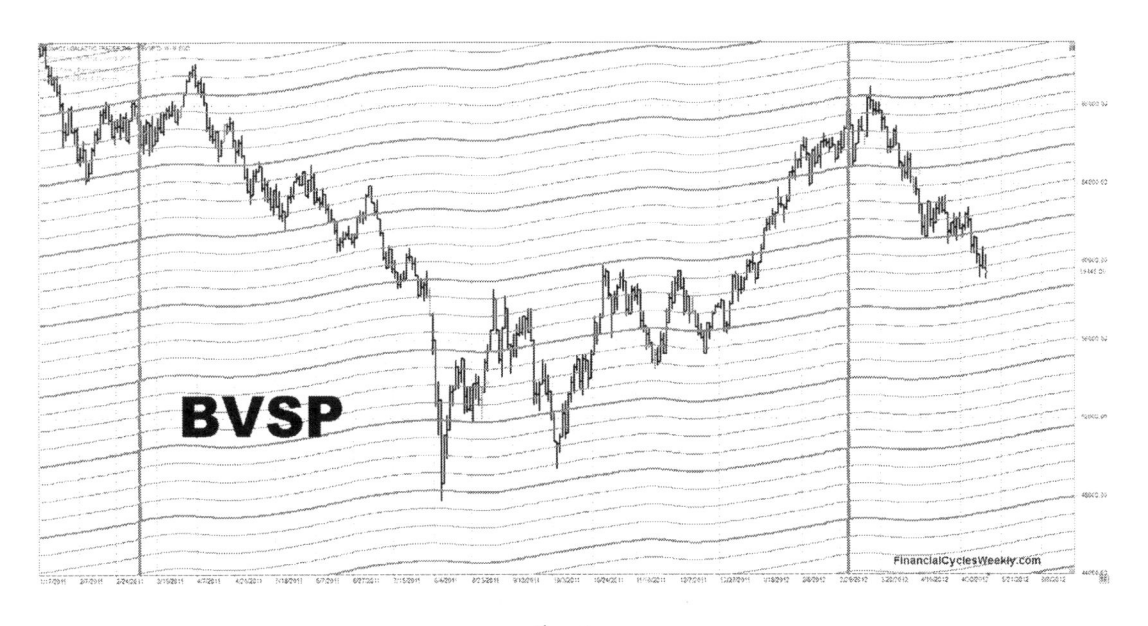

São Paolo Índice Bovespa:
Back-Tested Historical Mercury Retrograde Performance

All Mercury Retrograde Periods

Retrograde Station to Direct Station	Average % Change	-0.24%
Retrograde Station to Retrograde Return	Average % Change	-1.95%
Direct Station to Retrograde Return	Average % Change	-1.13%

Mercury Going Retrograde in Fire Signs

1 Day after Retrograde Station	Likelihood of Higher Prices	50.0%
14 Days after Retrograde Station	Likelihood of Higher Prices	50.0%
7 Days after Direct Station	Likelihood of Higher Prices	46.7%

Mercury Going Retrograde in Earth Signs

1 Day after Retrograde Station	Likelihood of Higher Prices	56.3%
14 Days after Retrograde Station	Likelihood of Higher Prices	62.5%
7 Days after Direct Station	Likelihood of Higher Prices	62.5%

Mercury Going Retrograde in Air Signs

1 Day after Retrograde Station	Likelihood of Higher Prices	68.8%
14 Days after Retrograde Station	Likelihood of Higher Prices	43.8%
7 Days after Direct Station	Likelihood of Higher Prices	43.8%

Mercury Going Retrograde in Water Signs

1 Day after Retrograde Station	Likelihood of Higher Prices	35.7%
14 Days after Retrograde Station	Likelihood of Higher Prices	50.0%
7 Days after Direct Station	Likelihood of Higher Prices	83.3%

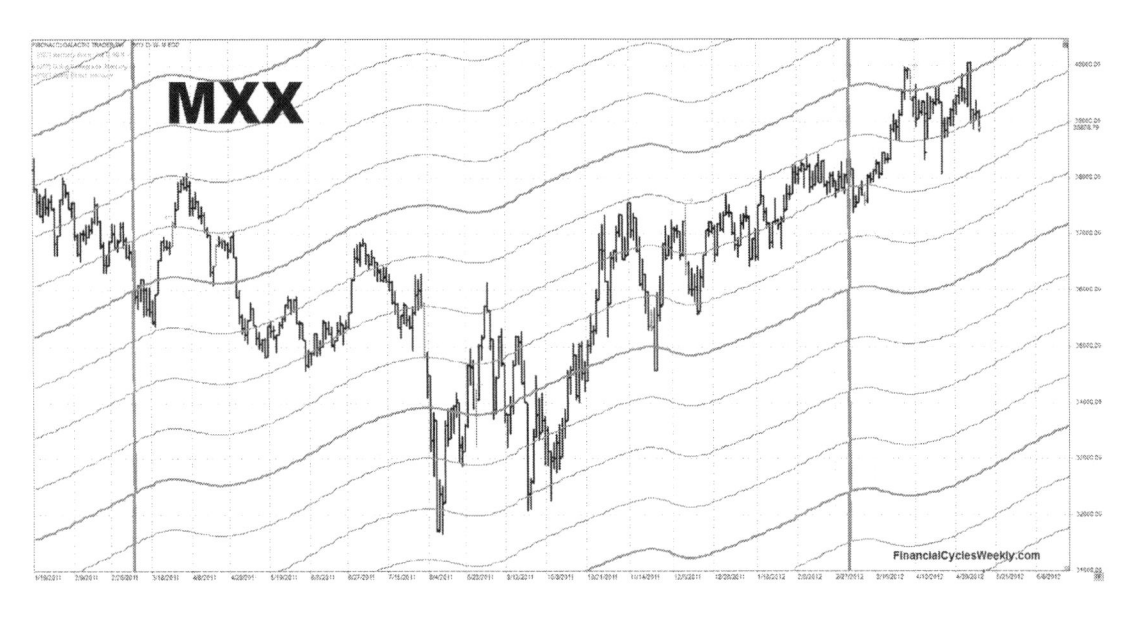

Mexican Stock Exchange Mexican Bolsa IPC Index:
Back-Tested Historical Mercury Retrograde Performance

All Mercury Retrograde Periods

Retrograde Station to Direct Station	Average % Change	-0.92%
Retrograde Station to Retrograde Return	Average % Change	-1.83%
Direct Station to Retrograde Return	Average % Change	-0.76%

Mercury Going Retrograde in Fire Signs

1 Day after Retrograde Station	Likelihood of Higher Prices	66.7%
14 Days after Retrograde Station	Likelihood of Higher Prices	55.6%
7 Days after Direct Station	Likelihood of Higher Prices	58.8%

Mercury Going Retrograde in Earth Signs

1 Day after Retrograde Station	Likelihood of Higher Prices	62.5%
14 Days after Retrograde Station	Likelihood of Higher Prices	62.5%
7 Days after Direct Station	Likelihood of Higher Prices	50.0%

Mercury Going Retrograde in Air Signs

1 Day after Retrograde Station	Likelihood of Higher Prices	56.3%
14 Days after Retrograde Station	Likelihood of Higher Prices	43.8%
7 Days after Direct Station	Likelihood of Higher Prices	50.0%

Mercury Going Retrograde in Water Signs

1 Day after Retrograde Station	Likelihood of Higher Prices	53.3%
14 Days after Retrograde Station	Likelihood of Higher Prices	46.7%
7 Days after Direct Station	Likelihood of Higher Prices	80.0%

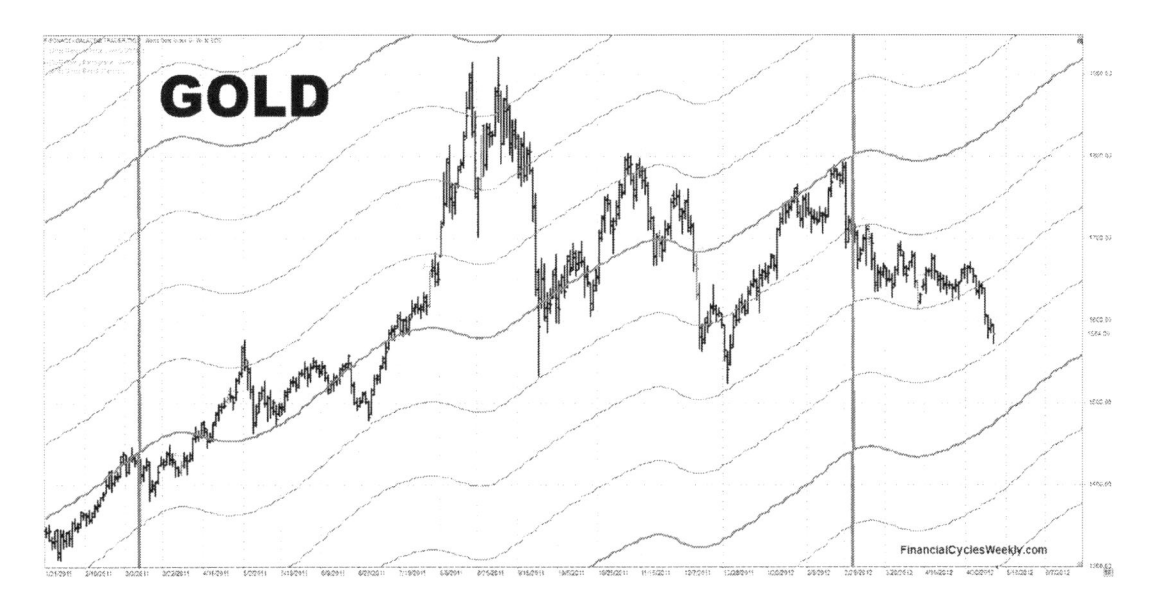

Gold:
Back-Tested Historical Mercury Retrograde Performance

All Mercury Retrograde Periods

Retrograde Station to Direct Station	Average % Change	-0.16%
Retrograde Station to Retrograde Return	Average % Change	0.12%
Direct Station to Retrograde Return	Average % Change	0.28%

Mercury Going Retrograde in Fire Signs

1 Day after Retrograde Station	Likelihood of Higher Prices	54.5%
14 Days after Retrograde Station	Likelihood of Higher Prices	47.8%
7 Days after Direct Station	Likelihood of Higher Prices	64.0%

Mercury Going Retrograde in Earth Signs

1 Day after Retrograde Station	Likelihood of Higher Prices	55.2%
14 Days after Retrograde Station	Likelihood of Higher Prices	62.1%
7 Days after Direct Station	Likelihood of Higher Prices	44.0%

Mercury Going Retrograde in Air Signs

1 Day after Retrograde Station	Likelihood of Higher Prices	38.5%
14 Days after Retrograde Station	Likelihood of Higher Prices	44.0%
7 Days after Direct Station	Likelihood of Higher Prices	38.5%

Mercury Going Retrograde in Water Signs

1 Day after Retrograde Station	Likelihood of Higher Prices	41.7%
14 Days after Retrograde Station	Likelihood of Higher Prices	40.9%
7 Days after Direct Station	Likelihood of Higher Prices	61.9%

Silver:
Back-Tested Historical Mercury Retrograde Performance

All Mercury Retrograde Periods

Retrograde Station to Direct Station	Average % Change	-1.50%
Retrograde Station to Retrograde Return	Average % Change	-1.94%
Direct Station to Retrograde Return	Average % Change	-0.37%

Mercury Going Retrograde in Fire Signs

1 Day after Retrograde Station	Likelihood of Higher Prices	46.4%
14 Days after Retrograde Station	Likelihood of Higher Prices	57.1%
7 Days after Direct Station	Likelihood of Higher Prices	37.9%

Mercury Going Retrograde in Earth Signs

1 Day after Retrograde Station	Likelihood of Higher Prices	60.6%
14 Days after Retrograde Station	Likelihood of Higher Prices	46.9%
7 Days after Direct Station	Likelihood of Higher Prices	54.8%

Mercury Going Retrograde in Air Signs

1 Day after Retrograde Station	Likelihood of Higher Prices	41.9%
14 Days after Retrograde Station	Likelihood of Higher Prices	41.9%
7 Days after Direct Station	Likelihood of Higher Prices	40.6%

Mercury Going Retrograde in Water Signs

1 Day after Retrograde Station	Likelihood of Higher Prices	51.7%
14 Days after Retrograde Station	Likelihood of Higher Prices	38.5%
7 Days after Direct Station	Likelihood of Higher Prices	65.2%

Mercury Retrograde Periods & the Dow 30 Stocks

The 30 stocks that make up the Dow Jones Industrial Average provide us with an ideal laboratory for studying the impact of Mercury Retrograde periods on individual equities. They are, after all, very well-known and widely-traded issues, with well-documented trading histories. Because that's the case, it's a fairly straightforward process to examine the prices of these stocks before, during, and after the times when Mercury has been in retrograde motion in the past.

Even more importantly, however, an examination of the Dow 30 stocks gives us a sampling that's broad enough to demonstrate unequivocally one important principle: not all stock issues respond the Mercury Retrograde periods in the same way. As we compare the responses of these issues to the influence of Mercury, we learn something about the differences in the "personalities" of the 30 stocks— some of them react quite dramatically when Mercury goes into retrograde motion, while others reserve their strongest responses for the Mercury direct stations. And there are some stocks that are inexplicably much more lethargic in their reactions to Mercury Retrograde periods, in spite of the fact that these same stocks may have a general history of definitive market action, with clear trends and price swings that have made them attractive as trading candidates on a fairly consistent basis.

But there's one other factor that we have to take into consideration here as well. When we look at market indices we are primarily concerned with price histories and the overall behavior of a group of factors in the markets. In such cases, we may or may not have specific horoscopes that become a part of our analysis. When we examine the trading history of the Standard & Poors 500 Index, for example, we may want to take a look at the horoscope for the New York Stock Exchange, but that inception chart for the New York Stock Exchange is not the sole factor that drives the price action in the S&P. In fact, there is only a tenuous relationship at best between the exchange and the market index, since one is an institution and a venue for trading while the other is a reflection of an aggregate of specific trading activities that fluctuates over time.

On the other hand, when we look at an individual stock, whether or not it happens to be part of the Dow Jones Industrial Average, we have a specific horoscope we can examine with an intrinsic relationship to the trading of the stock itself— the First-Trade horoscope. The First-Trade horoscope is exactly what the name implies: a chart that is calculated for the time of the opening bell on the date when the stock was first publicly traded on the exchange. This is typically not the date of the Initial Public Offering, since IPO shares are normally pre-subscribed in large blocks through exclusive institutional offerings by underwriting firms and are generally not available to the broader public on the open market on the IPO date itself.

Nor is a First-Trade chart an attempt to time precisely the exact moment in the course of a trading day when shares of an issue first changed hands and moved across the ticker. Instead, by creating a horoscope for the opening of the exchange on the day that the stock was first available for purchase by the general public, we have an active symbolic representation of the stock itself. In taking this approach we are following the lead of George Bayer, who noted that the time of the opening bell indicates the moment when a stock is first available for trading, and it is thus the true beginning of its trading career. This system of timing First-Trade horoscopes by the opening bell has been further popularized by Bill Meridian in several editions of his fine book *Planetary Stock Trading*, which is an invaluable resource for anyone who is looking for a sensible, well-organized approach to engaging in the equities markets with the astro-trading advantage.

While a First-Trade horoscope may in some ways actually be descriptive of the underlying company whose shares are being traded, and while it may share some commonality with other significant horoscopes connected with the company (such as a horoscope for the date of incorporation or for the opening of a corporate headquarters building), the real role of the First-Trade chart is to give us insights into the trading potential and responsive dynamics of the stock rather than the company. The structures, patterns, harmonics, and sensitive points in the First-Trade chart can give us important clues in understanding the guiding dynamics of the stock's trading activity, and when we examine key turning points or major trend accelerations in the trading history of a stock we typically expect to see some fairly clear correlations with the First-Trade horoscope, either by transit, secondary progression (direct or converse), or solar arc direction.

The angles of the First-Trade horoscope (Ascendant, Descendant, Midheaven, and Nadir) are particularly important, as are the Sun and the True North Node of the Moon. In working with a First-Trade chart, we give extra attention to transits to these sensitive points, even as we simultaneously strive to see the First-Trade horoscope as a whole. (There are some interesting correlations here with the Personal Points in the Uranian System approach to symmetrical astrology, but they would lead us into a digression that's far beyond the scope and focus of this book.) When we see transits applying to the angles in a First-Trade horoscope, particularly transits by Jupiter or Saturn, we typically have an important indication that opportunities for potentially profitable trades are on the way. Based on those indications, we can add fundamental and technical analysis to our observations and further refine our understanding of the astrological dynamics at work before making a final decision about the advisability of entering a particular trade.

Above all, an examination of a First-Trade horoscope can give us a quick but comprehensive look at combinations of internal forces that can drive the price of a stock in active trading, especially when well-defined chart patterns, planetary pictures, or dominant planets are astrologically activated. While there is ultimately no suitable substitute for patient observation of the rhythms and nuances of the price action of the stock itself during its trading history, the overview and insights that the First-Trade horoscope provides offer us a significant advantage in our analysis. The First-Trade chart isn't meant to replace technical analysis of price trends, but when it's added to the mix we can gain the kind of confirmation that can enhance our confidence in the markets and make our efforts as astro-traders much more profitable and enjoyable.

It is in that context, then, that we examine the role that Mercury plays in the First-Trade horoscope, as well as the role played by transiting Mercury, particularly during the times that Mercury goes into retrograde motion, resumes direct motion, and finally returns to the point of its retrograde station.

While Mercury is rarely the most important single factor in a First-Trade horoscope, it is nevertheless crucial for us to understand the particular role that it plays in any given First-Trade chart. Mercury is, after all, a key indicator of communication and commercial activity, so it always plays some part in the energetic expressions that make a stock unique. Trading itself is about communication and commerce, and without understanding the action of Mercury in the First-Trade chart we can't hope to comprehend the true potential that a particular offers us as a candidate for trading. Our examination of Mercury in the First-Trade horoscope may reveal intrinsic chart structures of powerful significance in clarifying the core ways that a stock behaves in the market, or it may simply add a subtle refinement to our comprehension of the ways that the stock is likely to behave under particular circumstances. In either case, Mercury has a clear potential for opening up more profitable opportunities and for fine-tuning our analytical assumptions and market timing.

As we look at Mercury in a First-Trade horoscope, there are some key questions and considerations we need to keep in mind. Is First-Trade Mercury direct or retrograde? Is it Prometheus or Epimetheus? How fast is it moving? Does it play a role in important chart patterns or planetary pictures? What planetary aspects is it applying to or separating from? Is it essentially dignified, or is it debilitated? Is it involved in a mutual reception?

These are, of course, the normal sort of questions that any competent astrologer asks in examining the role of any planet in any horoscope, so they will be a matter of routine for any financial astrologer or astro-trader. But when we use them to review the role of Mercury in a First-Trade chart, they are especially important.

When we look at the role of transiting Mercury, however, we move from conventional astrological analysis and step into empirical research. By examining the historical trading action that has taken place during particular Mercury transits in the past, we can back-test our hypotheses about the effects of those transits, and we can get vital information that's grounded in verifiable data instead of symbolic speculation.

That's exactly the kind of work behind this analysis of Mercury Retrograde cycles and the thirty stocks in the Dow Jones Industrial Average. By compiling and studying actual price data for each of the stocks, we've been able to reach some conclusions about the unique ways in which they each respond to specific transiting Mercury phenomena. The focus here is not just on the times when Mercury is retrograde; instead, we've looked at the entire Mercury retrograde cycle, examining what happens to the price of each stock from the time of the retrograde station to the direct station (the "retrograde phase"), and from the time of the direct station to the retrograde return (the "direct phase"). In doing so, we've also compared the price action with Mercury retrograde stations in each of the zodiac signs, commenting on the most significant differences and summarizing the price responses by zodiacal element.

As you study the data for each of these stocks, you'll soon see that each stock has its own unique characteristics in the way that it responds to Mercury retrograde transits. By comparing these back-testing results with the timing of future Mercury retrograde periods, you may come up with some profitable trading ideas. And along the way, you'll also get acquainted with a model you can use in analyzing any stock for which you have a First-Trade chart and a suitable amount of historical price data.

Dow 30 Stocks by First-Trade Mercury Placement in Zodiac Signs

Aries	JPM
Taurus	AXP, GE, HD, MRK
Gemini	AA, BAC, DD, HPQ, KFT, TRV
Cancer	VZ
Leo	INTC, MCD, WMT
Virgo	KO, JNJ, UTX
Libra	BA, CVX, PG
Scorpio	
Sagittarius	CAT, DIS
Capricorn	MMM, PFE
Aquarius	T, CSCO, IBM
Pisces	XOM, MSFT

20% in Fire Signs
30% in Earth Signs
40% in Air Signs
10% in Water Signs

23.3% in Cardinal Signs
33.3% in Fixed Signs
43.3% in Mutable Signs

Dow 30 Stocks with First-Trade Mercury Prometheus Direct
AA, MMM, AXP, T, CSCO, KO, GE, INTC, IBM, JNJ, JPM, MRK, WMT

Dow 30 Stocks with First-Trade Mercury Prometheus Retrograde
XOM, PFE

Dow 30 Stocks with First-Trade Mercury Epimetheus Direct
BA, BAC, CAT, DD, HPQ, MCD, PG, TRV, UTX, DIS

Dow 30 Stocks with First-Trade Mercury Epimetheus Retrograde
CVX, HD, KFT, MSFT, VZ

3M Company

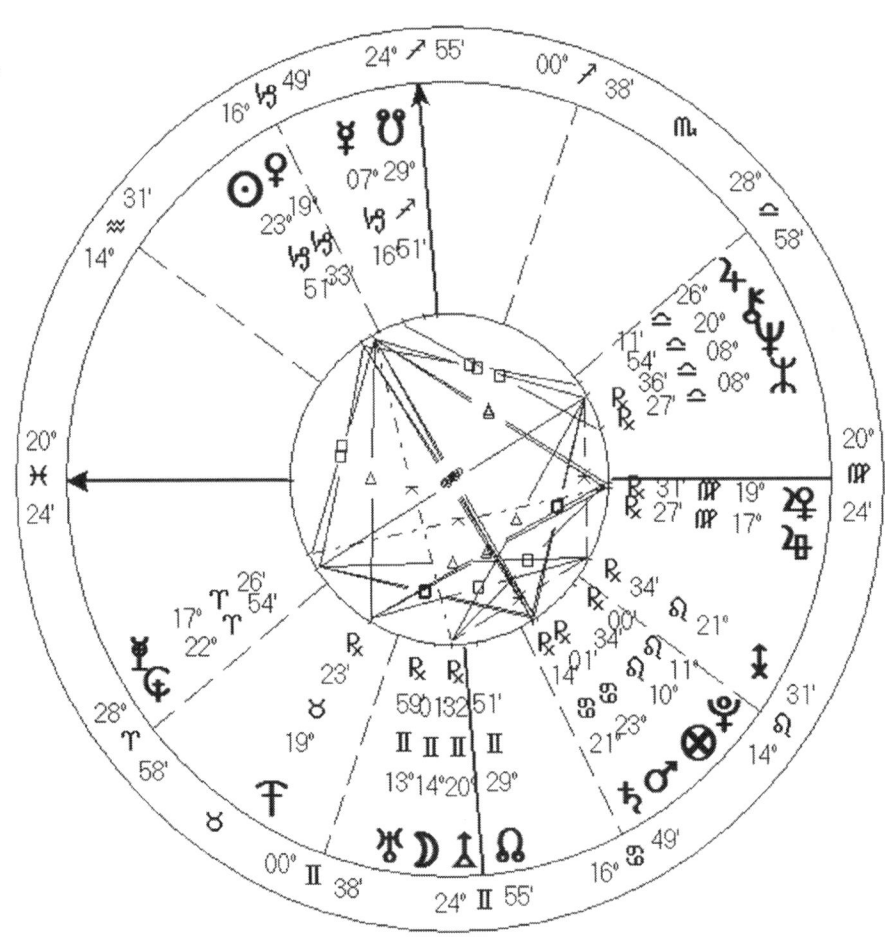

MMM
Natal Chart
Jan 14 1946, Mon
10:00 EST +5:00
New York, NY
40°N42'51" 074°W00'23"
Geocentric
Tropical
Koch
True Node

The MMM First-Trade horoscope has Mercury Prometheus Direct in Capricorn.

Secondary progressed First-Trade Mercury went into retrograde motion on March 14, 2007. It will return to direct motion on June 9, 2030.

MMM shows some of its greatest price volatility when Mercury goes retrograde in water signs, especially with Mercury retrograde in Cancer, which can pull prices down sharply while Mercury is retrograde and than rally after Mercury resumes direct motion. Mercury retrograde in Aquarius has been particularly bullish for MMM, with the strongest price advances coming after the direct station.

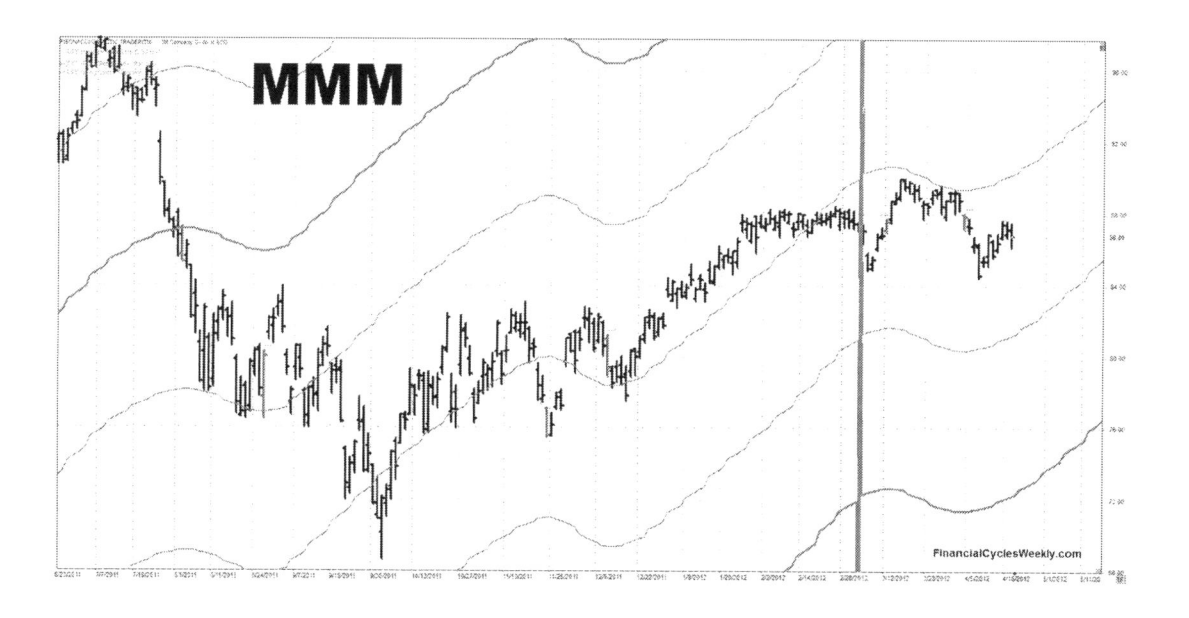

Back-Tested Historical Mercury Retrograde Performance

All Mercury Retrograde Periods

Retrograde Station to Direct Station	Average % Change	0.05%
Retrograde Station to Retrograde Return	Average % Change	-0.17%
Direct Station to Retrograde Return	Average % Change	-0.25%

Mercury Going Retrograde in Fire Signs

1 Day after Retrograde Station	Likelihood of Higher Prices	39.4%
14 Days after Retrograde Station	Likelihood of Higher Prices	48.5%
7 Days after Direct Station	Likelihood of Higher Prices	42.9%

Mercury Going Retrograde in Earth Signs

1 Day after Retrograde Station	Likelihood of Higher Prices	51.4%
14 Days after Retrograde Station	Likelihood of Higher Prices	60.0%
7 Days after Direct Station	Likelihood of Higher Prices	38.2%

Mercury Going Retrograde in Air Signs

1 Day after Retrograde Station	Likelihood of Higher Prices	59.4%
14 Days after Retrograde Station	Likelihood of Higher Prices	56.3%
7 Days after Direct Station	Likelihood of Higher Prices	53.1%

Mercury Going Retrograde in Water Signs

1 Day after Retrograde Station	Likelihood of Higher Prices	58.6%
14 Days after Retrograde Station	Likelihood of Higher Prices	48.3%
7 Days after Direct Station	Likelihood of Higher Prices	46.7%

Alcoa, Inc.

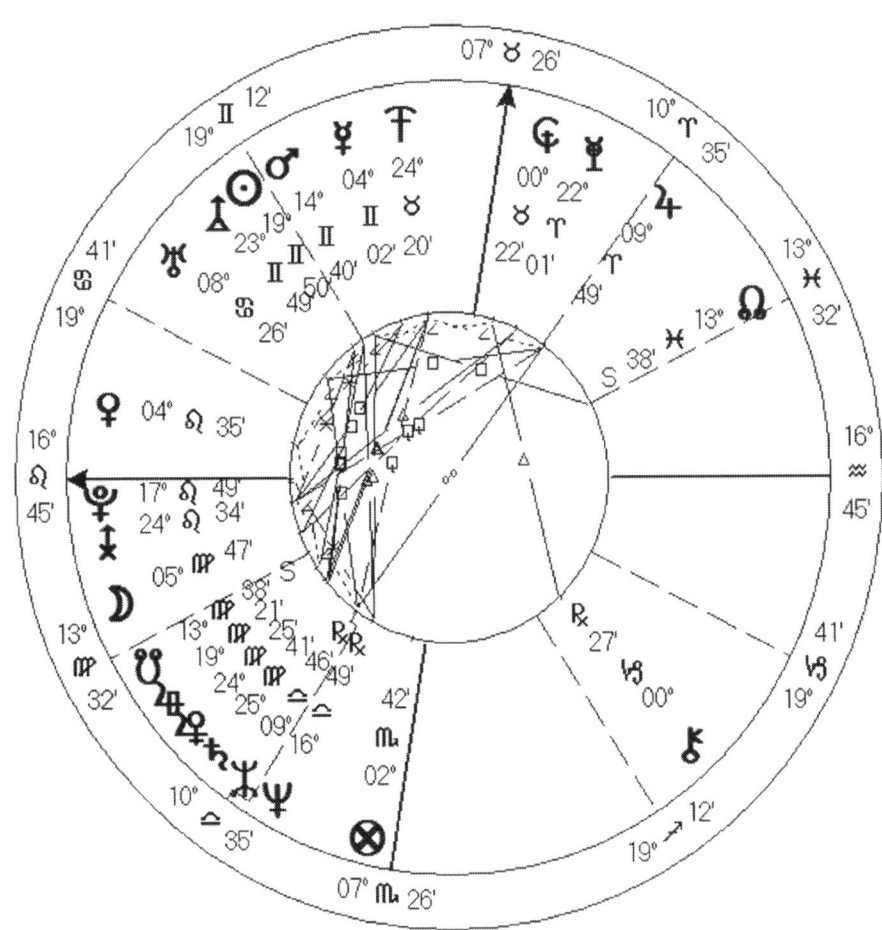

The AA First-Trade horoscope has Mercury Prometheus Direct in Gemini.

Secondary progressed First-Trade Mercury will go into retrograde motion on June 18, 2018. It will return to direct motion on September 15, 2041.

AA exhibits some of its greatest bullishness when Mercury goes retrograde in Cancer or in Aquarius, with particularly strong upward price moves following the direct station in both cases. Mercury going retrograde in either Leo or Pisces will typically create more bearish price action for AA, especially prior to the direct stations.

Back-Tested Historical Mercury Retrograde Performance

All Mercury Retrograde Periods

Retrograde Station to Direct Station	Average % Change	-1.37%
Retrograde Station to Retrograde Return	Average % Change	-1.42%
Direct Station to Retrograde Return	Average % Change	-0.04%

Mercury Going Retrograde in Fire Signs

1 Day after Retrograde Station	Likelihood of Higher Prices	44.7%
14 Days after Retrograde Station	Likelihood of Higher Prices	47.4%
7 Days after Direct Station	Likelihood of Higher Prices	56.4%

Mercury Going Retrograde in Earth Signs

1 Day after Retrograde Station	Likelihood of Higher Prices	62.5%
14 Days after Retrograde Station	Likelihood of Higher Prices	55.0%
7 Days after Direct Station	Likelihood of Higher Prices	51.2%

Mercury Going Retrograde in Air Signs

1 Day after Retrograde Station	Likelihood of Higher Prices	50.0%
14 Days after Retrograde Station	Likelihood of Higher Prices	47.5%
7 Days after Direct Station	Likelihood of Higher Prices	56.4%

Mercury Going Retrograde in Water Signs

1 Day after Retrograde Station	Likelihood of Higher Prices	54.3%
14 Days after Retrograde Station	Likelihood of Higher Prices	37.1%
7 Days after Direct Station	Likelihood of Higher Prices	68.6%

American Express Company

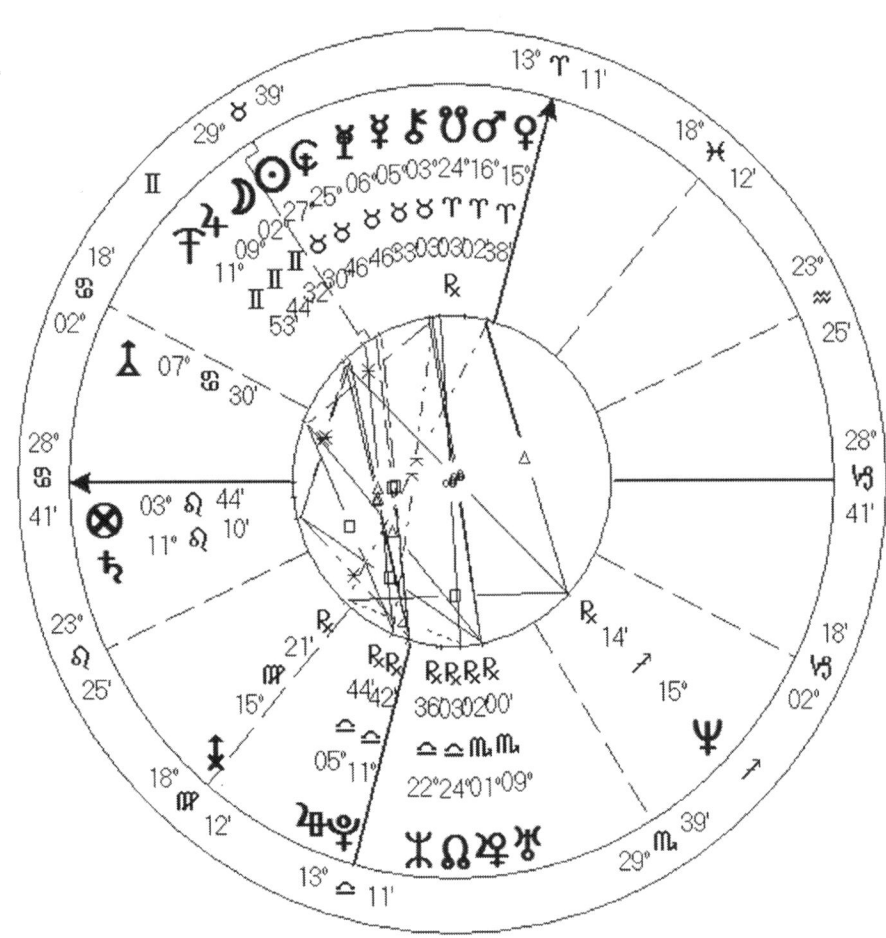

AXP
Natal Chart
May 18 1977, Wed
10:00 EDT +4:00
New York, NY
40°N42'51" 074°W00'23"
Geocentric
Tropical
Koch
True Node

The AXP First-Trade horoscope has Mercury Prometheus Direct in Taurus.

Secondary progressed First-Trade Mercury will go into retrograde motion on May 22, 2073. It will return to direct motion on June 2, 2096.

Mercury going retrograde in either Taurus or Leo generates particularly strong bearish tendencies for AXP, with declining prices both before and after the direct stations. Mercury going retrograde in Sagittarius is much more positive for AXP, however, with prices generally rising except for a brief pull-back right at the time of the direct station. Mercury going retrograde in Scorpio is also generally positive for this stock, but the greatest likelihood of higher prices then comes after the direct station.

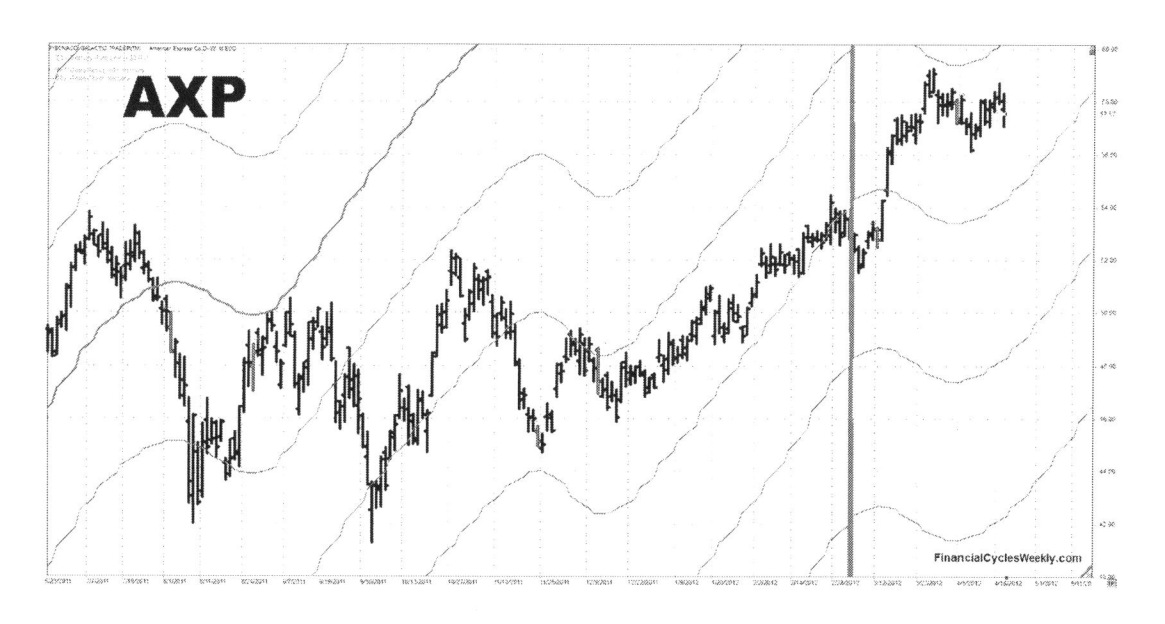

Back-Tested Historical Mercury Retrograde Performance

All Mercury Retrograde Periods

Retrograde Station to Direct Station	Average % Change	-1.04%
Retrograde Station to Retrograde Return	Average % Change	-1.38%
Direct Station to Retrograde Return	Average % Change	-0.33%

Mercury Going Retrograde in Fire Signs

1 Day after Retrograde Station	Likelihood of Higher Prices	50.0%
14 Days after Retrograde Station	Likelihood of Higher Prices	71.4%
7 Days after Direct Station	Likelihood of Higher Prices	48.3%

Mercury Going Retrograde in Earth Signs

1 Day after Retrograde Station	Likelihood of Higher Prices	51.7%
14 Days after Retrograde Station	Likelihood of Higher Prices	44.8%
7 Days after Direct Station	Likelihood of Higher Prices	40.7%

Mercury Going Retrograde in Air Signs

1 Day after Retrograde Station	Likelihood of Higher Prices	57.7%
14 Days after Retrograde Station	Likelihood of Higher Prices	46.2%
7 Days after Direct Station	Likelihood of Higher Prices	44.4%

Mercury Going Retrograde in Water Signs

1 Day after Retrograde Station	Likelihood of Higher Prices	62.5%
14 Days after Retrograde Station	Likelihood of Higher Prices	25.0%
7 Days after Direct Station	Likelihood of Higher Prices	64.0%

AT&T, Inc.

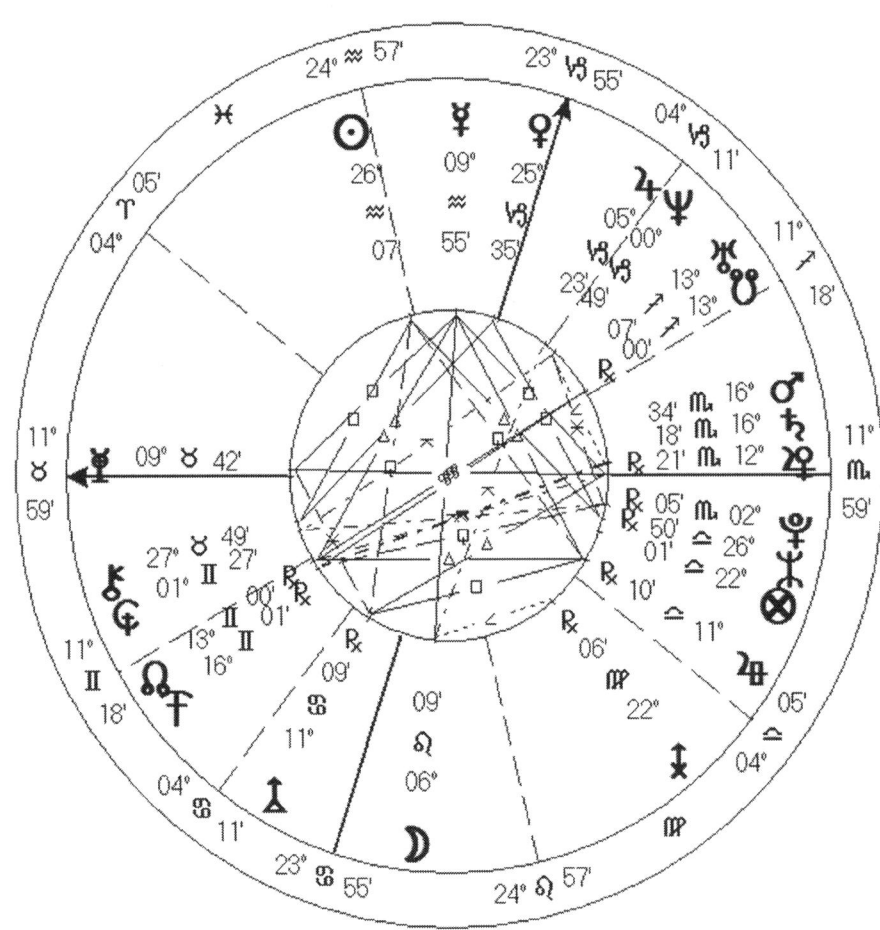

The T First-Trade horoscope has Mercury Prometheus Direct in Aquarius.

Secondary progressed First-Trade Mercury will go into retrograde motion on May 7, 2040. It will return to direct motion on January 31, 2064.

This stock has demonstrated positive price trends during Mercury retrograde periods in several zodiac signs. When Mercury goes retrograde in Gemini, the bullishness is particularly strong prior to the direct station. When Mercury goes retrograde in Scorpio, look for higher prices during the retrograde phase, and even stronger bullishness following the direct station. Retrograde stations in Sagittarius also generate bullish trends, with the greatest strength prior to the direct station. But there's typically a good bit of weakness for this stock when Mercury goes retrograde in Pisces, especially just before the direct station.

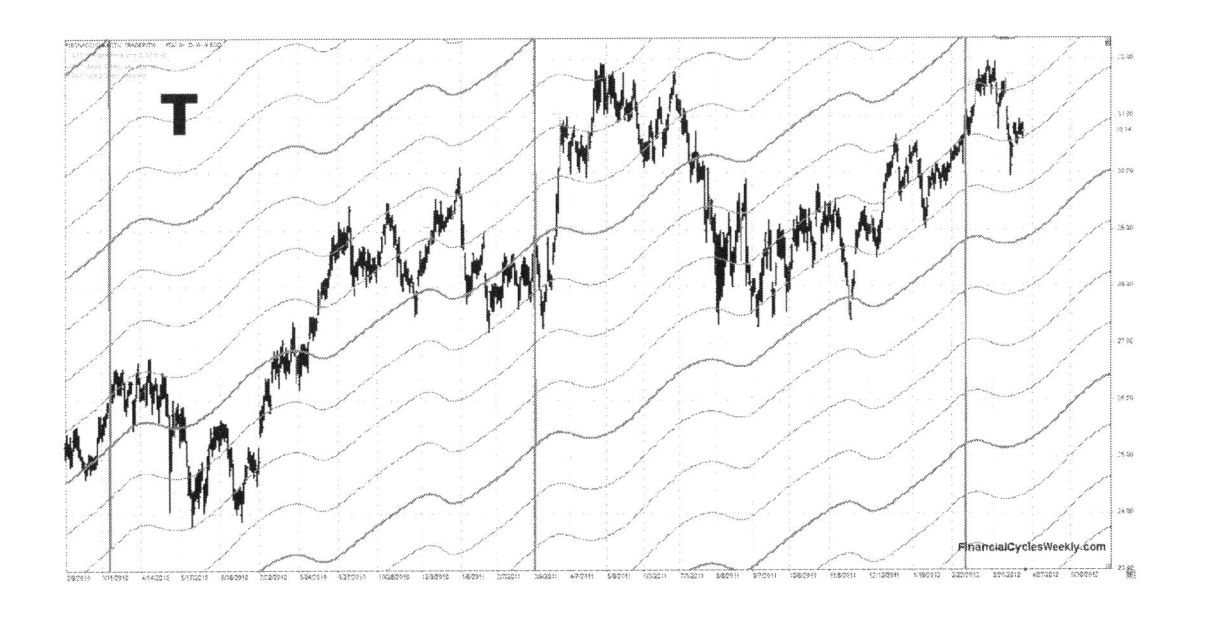

Back-Tested Historical Mercury Retrograde Performance

All Mercury Retrograde Periods

Retrograde Station to Direct Station	Average % Change	0.01%
Retrograde Station to Retrograde Return	Average % Change	0.08%
Direct Station to Retrograde Return	Average % Change	0.08%

Mercury Going Retrograde in Fire Signs

1 Day after Retrograde Station	Likelihood of Higher Prices	52.2%
14 Days after Retrograde Station	Likelihood of Higher Prices	60.9%
7 Days after Direct Station	Likelihood of Higher Prices	52.2%

Mercury Going Retrograde in Earth Signs

1 Day after Retrograde Station	Likelihood of Higher Prices	59.1%
14 Days after Retrograde Station	Likelihood of Higher Prices	63.6%
7 Days after Direct Station	Likelihood of Higher Prices	63.6%

Mercury Going Retrograde in Air Signs

1 Day after Retrograde Station	Likelihood of Higher Prices	54.5%
14 Days after Retrograde Station	Likelihood of Higher Prices	59.1%
7 Days after Direct Station	Likelihood of Higher Prices	38.1%

Mercury Going Retrograde in Water Signs

1 Day after Retrograde Station	Likelihood of Higher Prices	66.7%
14 Days after Retrograde Station	Likelihood of Higher Prices	44.4%
7 Days after Direct Station	Likelihood of Higher Prices	55.0%

Bank of America Corporation

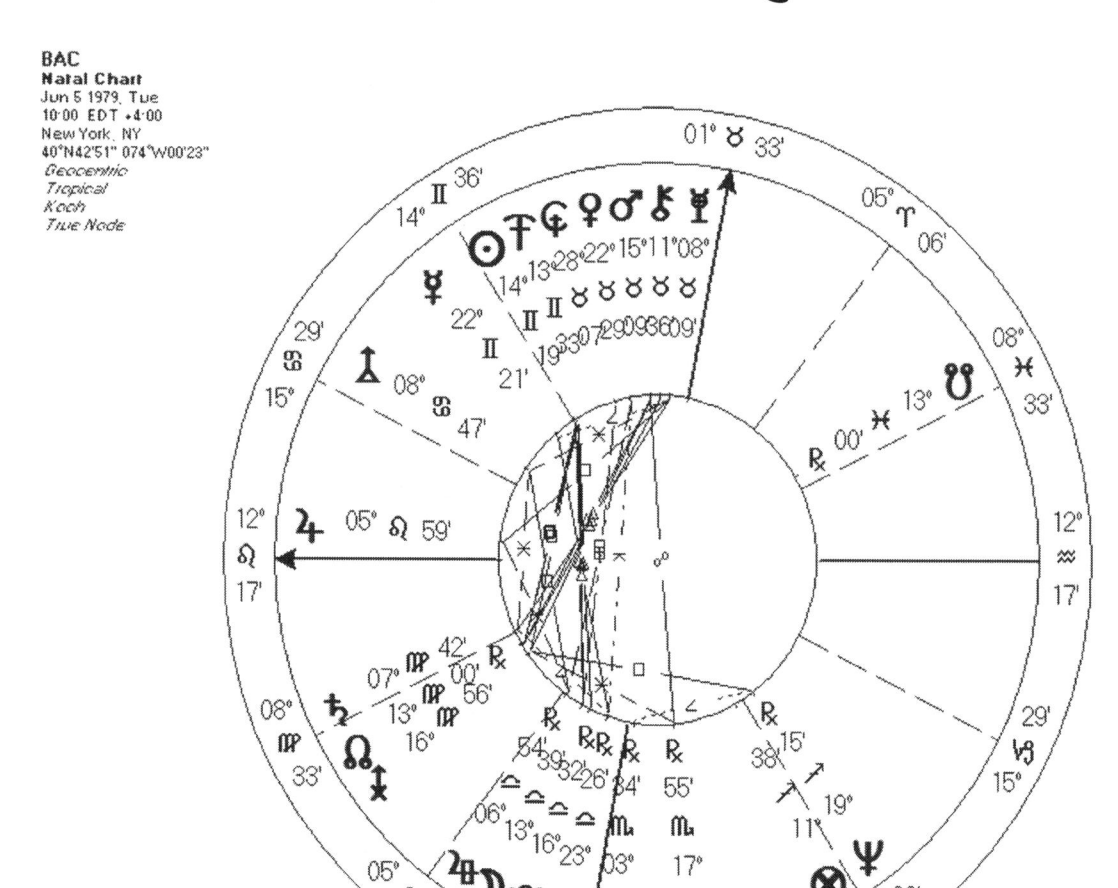

The BAC First-Trade horoscope has Mercury Epimetheus Direct in Gemini.

Secondary progressed First-Trade Mercury will go into retrograde motion on October 14, 2021. It will return to direct motion on November 26, 2045.

BAC shows some of its greatest price volatility when Mercury goes retrograde in Taurus, with prices rising solidly during the retrograde phase and then declining sharply after the direct station. That same effect occurs with Mercury retrogrades in Libra, but the sell-offs after the direct station tend to be even more severe. On the other hand, BAC tends to be bullish when Mercury goes retrograde in Sagittarius or Pisces, with rising prices during both the retrograde and direct phases.

Back-Tested Historical Mercury Retrograde Performance

All Mercury Retrograde Periods

Retrograde Station to Direct Station	Average % Change	-2.95%
Retrograde Station to Retrograde Return	Average % Change	-5.39%
Direct Station to Retrograde Return	Average % Change	-1.57%

Mercury Going Retrograde in Fire Signs

1 Day after Retrograde Station	Likelihood of Higher Prices	52.6%
14 Days after Retrograde Station	Likelihood of Higher Prices	52.6%
7 Days after Direct Station	Likelihood of Higher Prices	50.0%

Mercury Going Retrograde in Earth Signs

1 Day after Retrograde Station	Likelihood of Higher Prices	66.7%
14 Days after Retrograde Station	Likelihood of Higher Prices	61.9%
7 Days after Direct Station	Likelihood of Higher Prices	40.9%

Mercury Going Retrograde in Air Signs

1 Day after Retrograde Station	Likelihood of Higher Prices	68.2%
14 Days after Retrograde Station	Likelihood of Higher Prices	63.6%
7 Days after Direct Station	Likelihood of Higher Prices	42.9%

Mercury Going Retrograde in Water Signs

1 Day after Retrograde Station	Likelihood of Higher Prices	38.9%
14 Days after Retrograde Station	Likelihood of Higher Prices	44.4%
7 Days after Direct Station	Likelihood of Higher Prices	61.1%

The Boeing Company

BA
Natal Chart
Sep 4 1935, Wed
10:00 EDT +4:00
New York, NY
40°N42'51" 074°W00'23"
Geocentric
Tropical
Koch
True Node

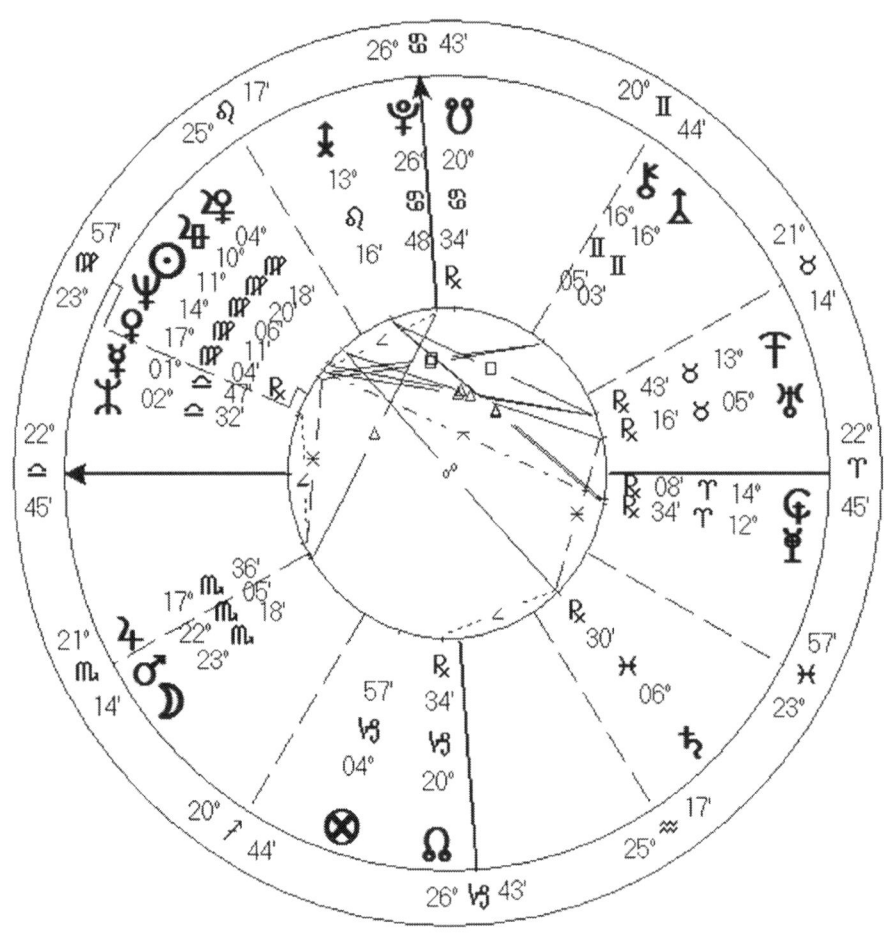

The BA First-Trade horoscope has Mercury Epimetheus Direct in Libra.

Secondary progressed First-Trade Mercury went into retrograde motion on April 3, 1967, and resumed direct motion on April 6, 1988. Secondary progressed First-Trade Mercury will go retrograde again on February 19, 2076. It will return to direct motion on March 3, 2097.

BA demonstrates its greatest price volatility when Mercury goes retrograde in either Virgo or Aquarius. In each case, the price of the stock tends to rise during the retrograde phase, and then goes into a bearish trend following the direct station.

Back-Tested Historical Mercury Retrograde Performance

All Mercury Retrograde Periods

Retrograde Station to Direct Station	Average % Change	0.76%
Retrograde Station to Retrograde Return	Average % Change	0.39%
Direct Station to Retrograde Return	Average % Change	-0.34%

Mercury Going Retrograde in Fire Signs

1 Day after Retrograde Station	Likelihood of Higher Prices	47.4%
14 Days after Retrograde Station	Likelihood of Higher Prices	63.3%
7 Days after Direct Station	Likelihood of Higher Prices	71.8%

Mercury Going Retrograde in Earth Signs

1 Day after Retrograde Station	Likelihood of Higher Prices	57.5%
14 Days after Retrograde Station	Likelihood of Higher Prices	65.0%
7 Days after Direct Station	Likelihood of Higher Prices	48.8%

Mercury Going Retrograde in Air Signs

1 Day after Retrograde Station	Likelihood of Higher Prices	52.5%
14 Days after Retrograde Station	Likelihood of Higher Prices	60.0%
7 Days after Direct Station	Likelihood of Higher Prices	33.3%

Mercury Going Retrograde in Water Signs

1 Day after Retrograde Station	Likelihood of Higher Prices	51.4%
14 Days after Retrograde Station	Likelihood of Higher Prices	40.0%
7 Days after Direct Station	Likelihood of Higher Prices	60.0%

Caterpillar Inc.

CAT
Natal Chart
Dec 2 1929, Mon
10:00 EST +5:00
New York, NY
40°N42'51" 074°W00'23"
Geocentric
Tropical
Koch
True Node

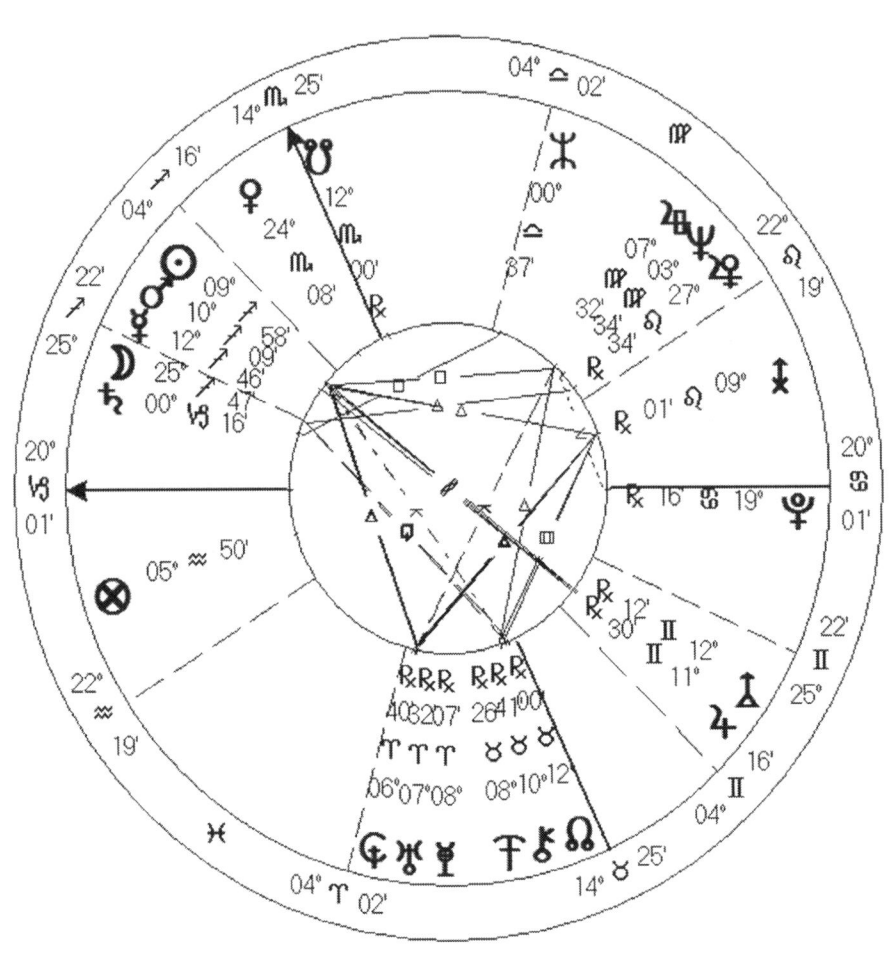

The CAT First-Trade horoscope has Mercury Epimetheus Direct in Sagittarius.

The CAT secondary progressed First-Trade Mercury went into retrograde motion on May 15, 1971, and resumed direct motion on January 12, 1992. Secondary progressed First-Trade Mercury will go retrograde again on March 22, 2087. It will return to direct motion on January 26, 2111.

When Mercury goes retrograde in Libra, CAT tends to sell off during the retrograde phase, but after the direct station the price action is decidedly bullish. That's also the case when Mercury goes retrograde in Pisces. When Mercury goes retrograde in Sagittarius, however, the opposite effect typically prevails, with rising prices during the retrograde phase and declining prices after the direct station.

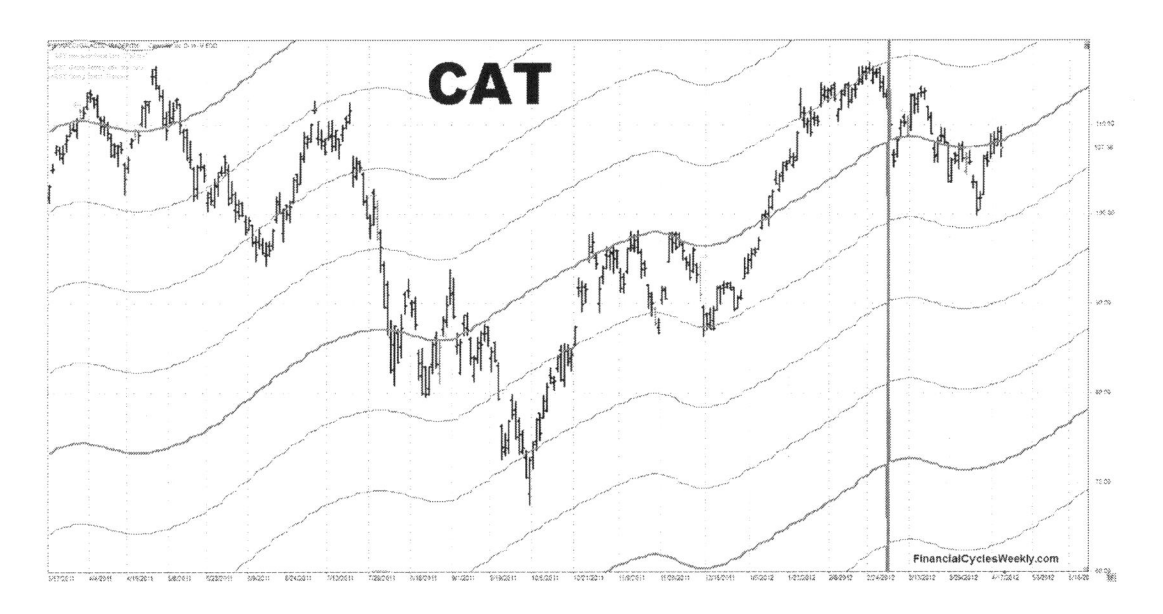

Back-Tested Historical Mercury Retrograde Performance

All Mercury Retrograde Periods

Retrograde Station to Direct Station	Average % Change	0.44%
Retrograde Station to Retrograde Return	Average % Change	0.12%
Direct Station to Retrograde Return	Average % Change	-0.16%

Mercury Going Retrograde in Fire Signs

1 Day after Retrograde Station	Likelihood of Higher Prices	57.9%
14 Days after Retrograde Station	Likelihood of Higher Prices	65.8%
7 Days after Direct Station	Likelihood of Higher Prices	48.7%

Mercury Going Retrograde in Earth Signs

1 Day after Retrograde Station	Likelihood of Higher Prices	60.0%
14 Days after Retrograde Station	Likelihood of Higher Prices	57.5%
7 Days after Direct Station	Likelihood of Higher Prices	48.8%

Mercury Going Retrograde in Air Signs

1 Day after Retrograde Station	Likelihood of Higher Prices	47.5%
14 Days after Retrograde Station	Likelihood of Higher Prices	47.5%
7 Days after Direct Station	Likelihood of Higher Prices	46.2%

Mercury Going Retrograde in Water Signs

1 Day after Retrograde Station	Likelihood of Higher Prices	58.6%
14 Days after Retrograde Station	Likelihood of Higher Prices	48.3%
7 Days after Direct Station	Likelihood of Higher Prices	46.7%

Chevron Corporation

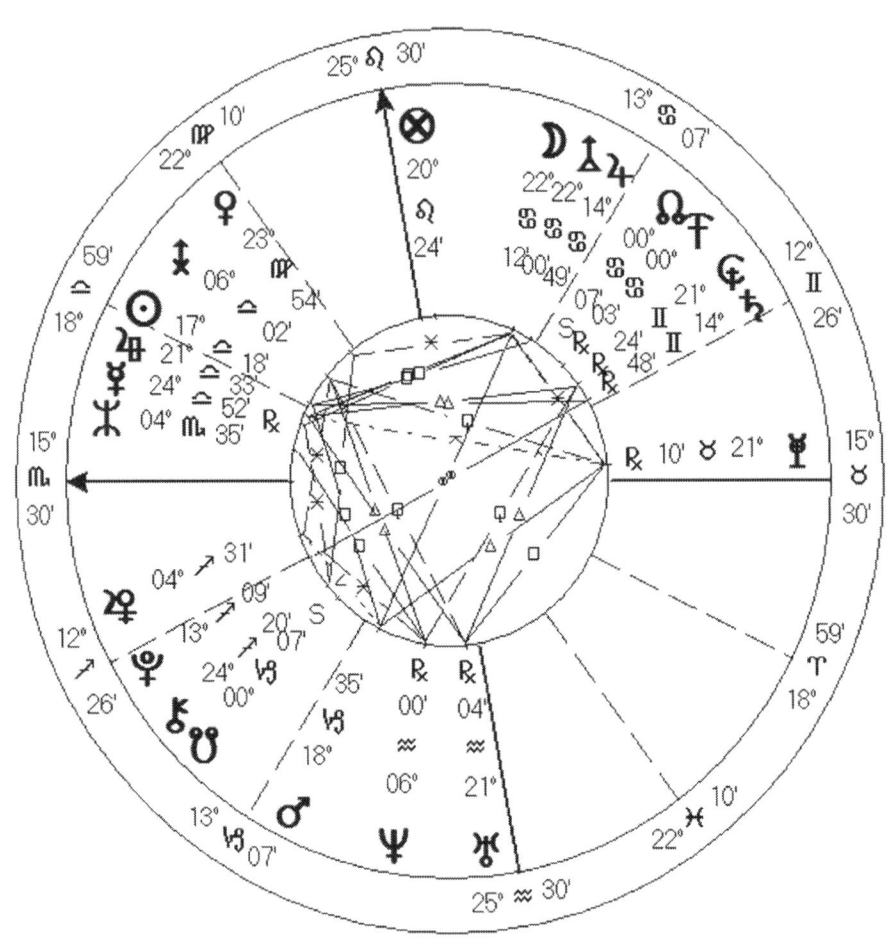

The CVX First-Trade horoscope has Mercury Epimetheus Retrograde in Libra.

Secondary progressed First-Trade Mercury will begin direct motion on March 24, 2014.

In spite of some initial weakness right at the retrograde station, the times when Mercury goes retrograde in Aries or in Pisces are decidedly bullish for CVX, with the biggest price increases after the direct station. Mercury going retrograde in Virgo is also bullish. When Mercury goes retrograde in Cancer, however, the trend tends to be bearish, with the biggest decline during the retrograde phase. Some of the greatest volatility for CVX comes when Mercury goes retrograde in Gemini, with solid bullishness during the retrograde phase and a sharp sell-off getting underway at the direct station.

Back-Tested Historical Mercury Retrograde Performance

All Mercury Retrograde Periods

Retrograde Station to Direct Station	Average % Change	0.35%
Retrograde Station to Retrograde Return	Average % Change	0.02%
Direct Station to Retrograde Return	Average % Change	-0.34%

Mercury Going Retrograde in Fire Signs

1 Day after Retrograde Station	Likelihood of Higher Prices	48.3%
14 Days after Retrograde Station	Likelihood of Higher Prices	62.1%
7 Days after Direct Station	Likelihood of Higher Prices	58.1%

Mercury Going Retrograde in Earth Signs

1 Day after Retrograde Station	Likelihood of Higher Prices	70.0%
14 Days after Retrograde Station	Likelihood of Higher Prices	73.3%
7 Days after Direct Station	Likelihood of Higher Prices	46.4%

Mercury Going Retrograde in Air Signs

1 Day after Retrograde Station	Likelihood of Higher Prices	50.0%
14 Days after Retrograde Station	Likelihood of Higher Prices	53.8%
7 Days after Direct Station	Likelihood of Higher Prices	51.9%

Mercury Going Retrograde in Water Signs

1 Day after Retrograde Station	Likelihood of Higher Prices	45.8%
14 Days after Retrograde Station	Likelihood of Higher Prices	37.5%
7 Days after Direct Station	Likelihood of Higher Prices	60.0%

Cisco Systems, Inc.

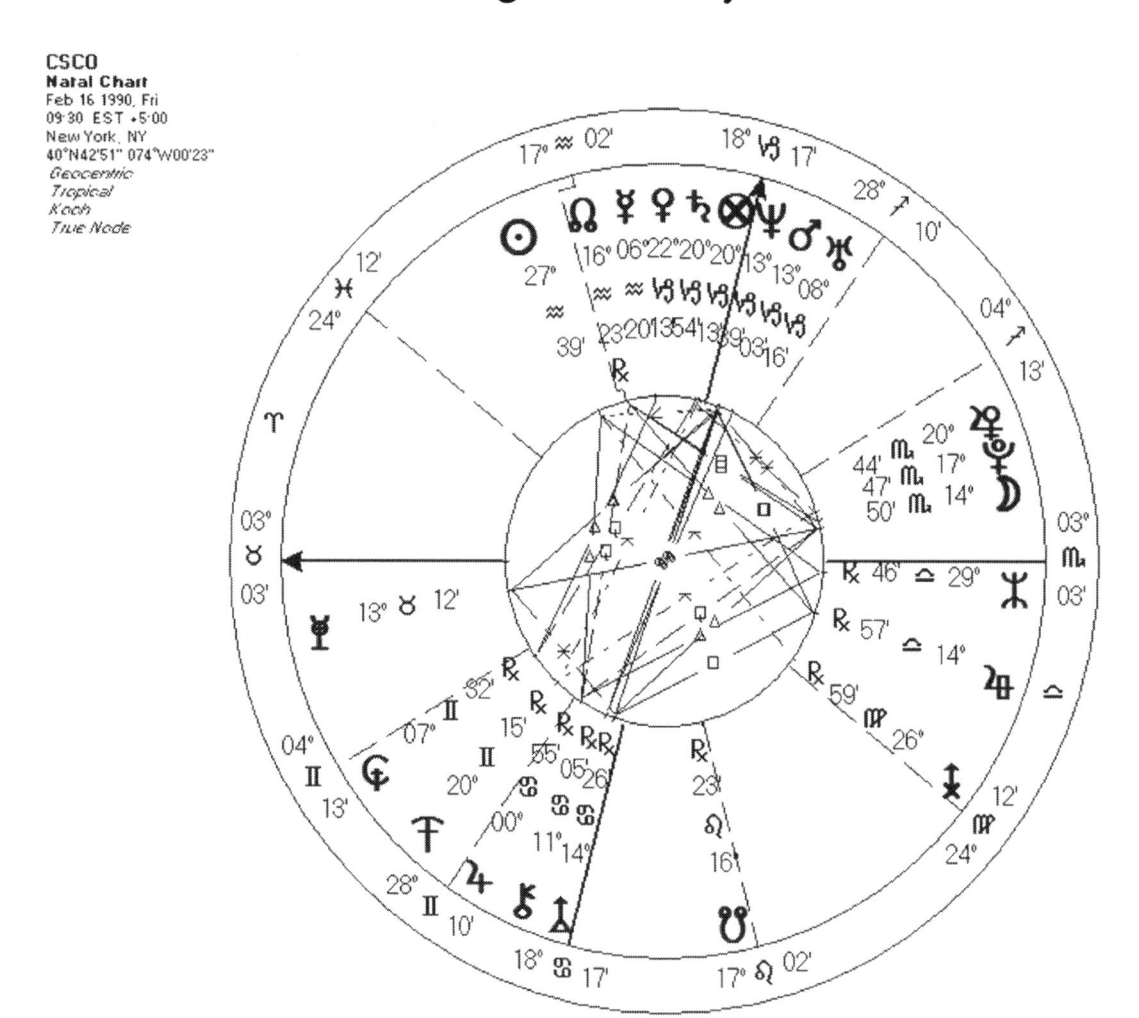

CSCO
Natal Chart
Feb 16 1990, Fri
09:30 EST +5:00
New York, NY
40°N42'51" 074°W00'23"
Geocentric
Tropical
Koch
True Node

The CSCO First-Trade horoscope has Mercury Prometheus Direct in Aquarius.

Secondary progressed First-Trade Mercury will begin retrograde motion on October 23, 2055. It will return to direct motion on August 10, 2079.

When Mercury goes retrograde in Taurus CSCO is bullish during the retrograde phase and through the direct station, but begins to sell off about a week after Mercury goes direct. When Mercury goes retrograde in Sagittarius, however, CSCO is very bullish during both the retrograde and direct phases. With Mercury going retrograde in Virgo CSCO builds up some positive momentum during the retrograde phase, but turns moderately bearish after the direct staion.

Back-Tested Historical Mercury Retrograde Performance

All Mercury Retrograde Periods

Retrograde Station to Direct Station	Average % Change	1.62%
Retrograde Station to Retrograde Return	Average % Change	1.39%
Direct Station to Retrograde Return	Average % Change	-0.02%

Mercury Going Retrograde in Fire Signs

1 Day after Retrograde Station	Likelihood of Higher Prices	38.9%
14 Days after Retrograde Station	Likelihood of Higher Prices	66.7%
7 Days after Direct Station	Likelihood of Higher Prices	55.0%

Mercury Going Retrograde in Earth Signs

1 Day after Retrograde Station	Likelihood of Higher Prices	55.0%
14 Days after Retrograde Station	Likelihood of Higher Prices	70.0%
7 Days after Direct Station	Likelihood of Higher Prices	44.4%

Mercury Going Retrograde in Air Signs

1 Day after Retrograde Station	Likelihood of Higher Prices	37.5%
14 Days after Retrograde Station	Likelihood of Higher Prices	43.8%
7 Days after Direct Station	Likelihood of Higher Prices	50.0%

Mercury Going Retrograde in Water Signs

1 Day after Retrograde Station	Likelihood of Higher Prices	64.3%
14 Days after Retrograde Station	Likelihood of Higher Prices	64.3%
7 Days after Direct Station	Likelihood of Higher Prices	53.3%

The Coca-Cola Company

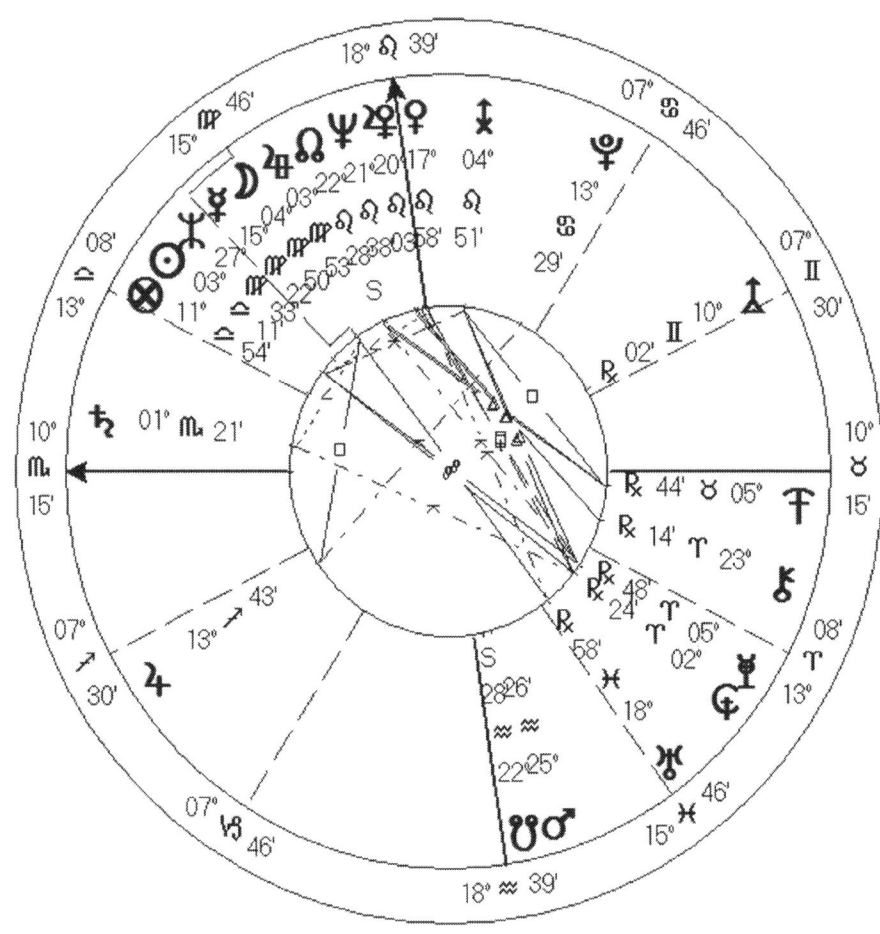

KO
Natal Chart
Sep 26 1924, Fri
10:00 EDT +4:00
New York, NY
40°N42'51" 074°W00'23"
Geocentric
Tropical
Koch
True Node

The KO First-Trade horoscope has Mercury Prometheus Direct in Virgo.

Secondary progressed First-Trade Mercury went into retrograde motion on March 12, 2007. It will return to direct motion on February 16, 2027.

When Mercury goes retrograde in Virgo KO is generally bearish during the retrograde phase, but then turns moderately bearish after the direct station. When Mercury goes retrograde in Scorpio KO tends to be somewhat bearish during the retrograde phase, but becomes moderately bullish following the direct station. With Mercury going retrogrde in Sagittarius, KO is even more strongly bullish during the retrograde phase, but the price of the stock tends to move sharpy lower at the direct station.

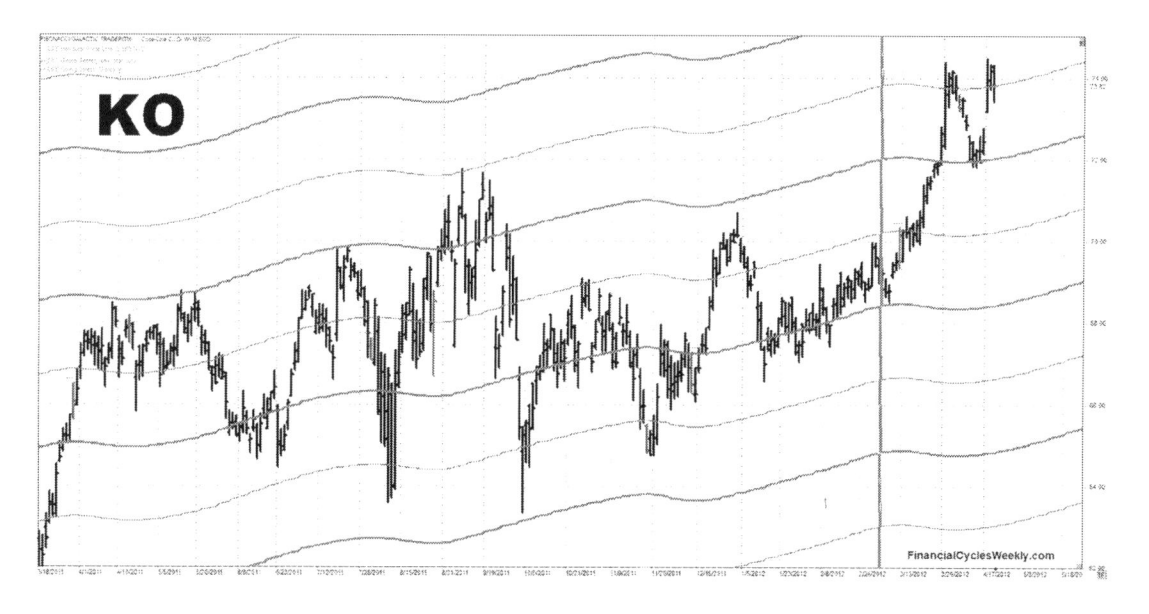

Back-Tested Historical Mercury Retrograde Performance

All Mercury Retrograde Periods

Retrograde Station to Direct Station	Average % Change	0.75%
Retrograde Station to Retrograde Return	Average % Change	0.77%
Direct Station to Retrograde Return	Average % Change	-0.00%

Mercury Going Retrograde in Fire Signs

1 Day after Retrograde Station	Likelihood of Higher Prices	52.6%
14 Days after Retrograde Station	Likelihood of Higher Prices	71.1%
7 Days after Direct Station	Likelihood of Higher Prices	51.3%

Mercury Going Retrograde in Earth Signs

1 Day after Retrograde Station	Likelihood of Higher Prices	55.0%
14 Days after Retrograde Station	Likelihood of Higher Prices	55.0%
7 Days after Direct Station	Likelihood of Higher Prices	46.3%

Mercury Going Retrograde in Air Signs

1 Day after Retrograde Station	Likelihood of Higher Prices	50.0%
14 Days after Retrograde Station	Likelihood of Higher Prices	57.5%
7 Days after Direct Station	Likelihood of Higher Prices	51.3%

Mercury Going Retrograde in Water Signs

1 Day after Retrograde Station	Likelihood of Higher Prices	51.4%
14 Days after Retrograde Station	Likelihood of Higher Prices	45.7%
7 Days after Direct Station	Likelihood of Higher Prices	42.9%

E. I. du Pont de Nemours & Company

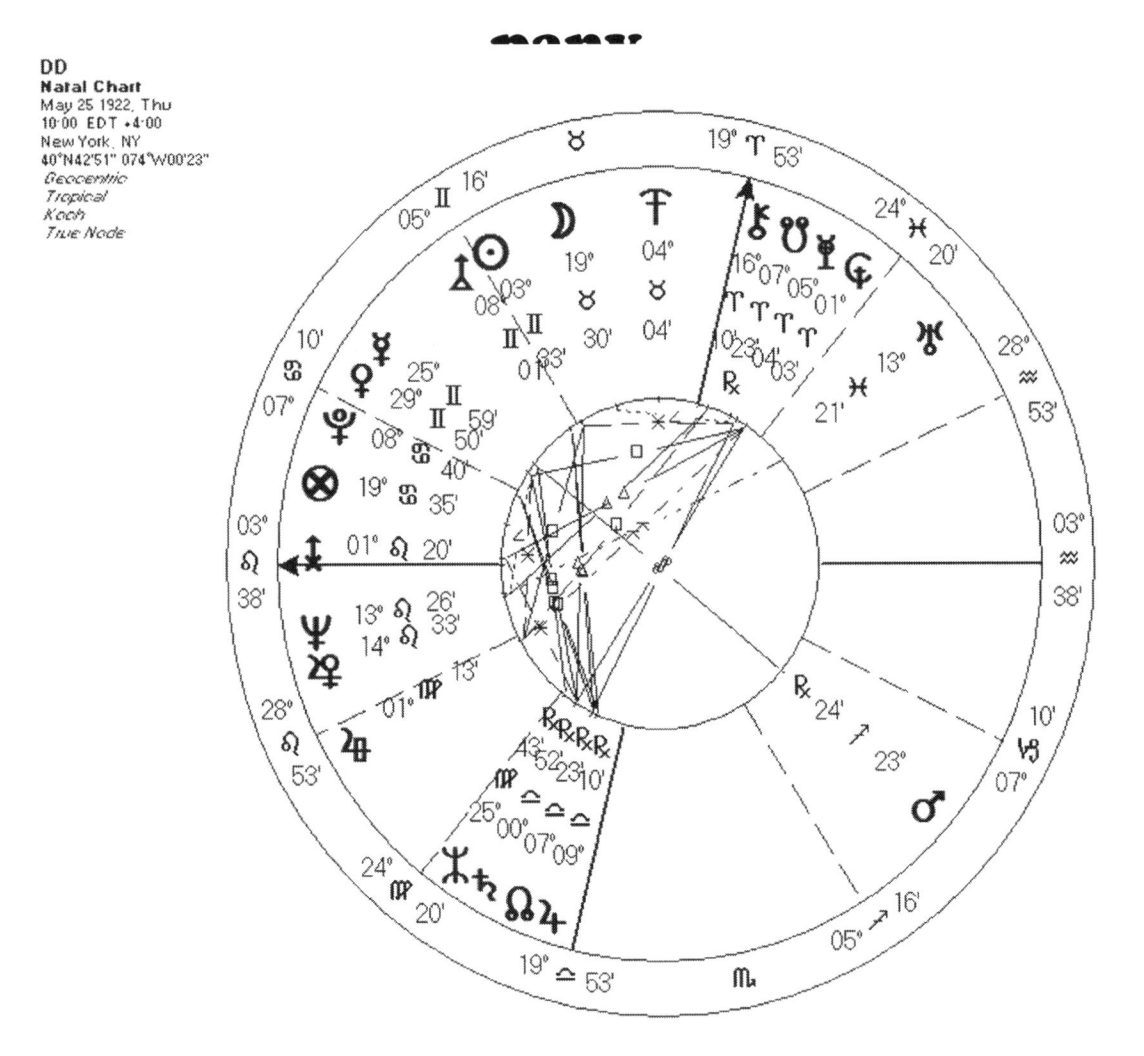

DD
Natal Chart
May 25 1922, Thu
10:00 EDT +4:00
New York, NY
40°N42'51" 074°W00'23"
Geocentric
Tropical
Koch
True Node

The DD First-Trade horoscope has Mercury Epimetheus Direct in Gemini.

Secondary progressed First-Trade Mercury went into retrograde motion on October 3, 1933, and resumed direct motion on October 15, 1957. Secondary progressed First-Trade Mercury will go retrograde again on January 26, 2053. It will return to direct motion on March 13, 2074.

DD shows some of its greatest price volatility when Mercury goes retrograde in Taurus, with rising prices during the retrograde phase and declining prices after the direct station. That's also the case when Mercury goes retrograde in Cancer, with a slightly stronger push to the downside after the direct station, and when Mercury goes retrograde in Capricorn, when DD shows even more bullishness during the retrograde phase before backing off after the direct station.

Back-Tested Historical Mercury Retrograde Performance

All Mercury Retrograde Periods

Retrograde Station to Direct Station	Average % Change	0.06%
Retrograde Station to Retrograde Return	Average % Change	-0.79%
Direct Station to Retrograde Return	Average % Change	-0.84%

Mercury Going Retrograde in Fire Signs

1 Day after Retrograde Station	Likelihood of Higher Prices	47.4%
14 Days after Retrograde Station	Likelihood of Higher Prices	50.0%
7 Days after Direct Station	Likelihood of Higher Prices	51.3%

Mercury Going Retrograde in Earth Signs

1 Day after Retrograde Station	Likelihood of Higher Prices	60.0%
14 Days after Retrograde Station	Likelihood of Higher Prices	62.5%
7 Days after Direct Station	Likelihood of Higher Prices	39.0%

Mercury Going Retrograde in Air Signs

1 Day after Retrograde Station	Likelihood of Higher Prices	60.0%
14 Days after Retrograde Station	Likelihood of Higher Prices	42.5%
7 Days after Direct Station	Likelihood of Higher Prices	51.3%

Mercury Going Retrograde in Water Signs

1 Day after Retrograde Station	Likelihood of Higher Prices	62.9%
14 Days after Retrograde Station	Likelihood of Higher Prices	40.0%
7 Days after Direct Station	Likelihood of Higher Prices	42.9%

Exxon Mobile Corporation

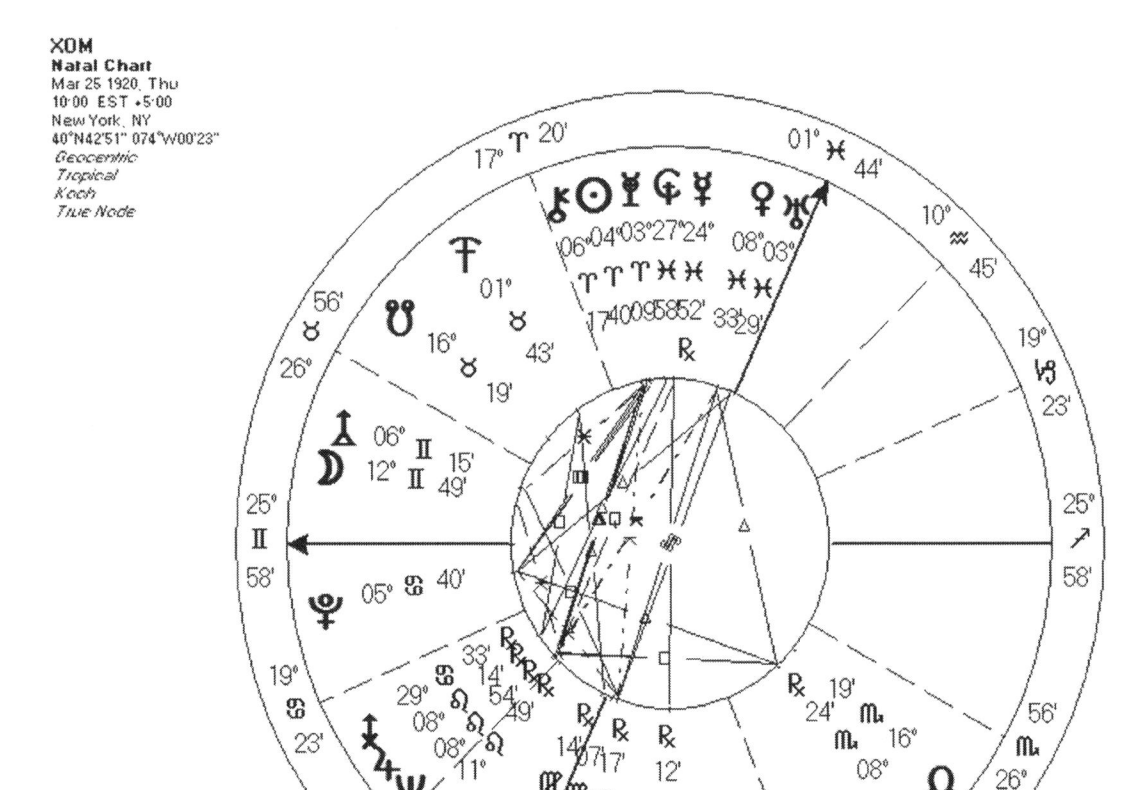

The XOM First-Trade horoscope has Mercury Prometheus Retrograde in Pisces.

Secondary progressed First-Trade Mercury went into direct motion on July 19, 1928. Secondary progressed First-Trade Mercury will go retrograde again on March 11, 2030. It will then return to direct motion on May 3, 2054.

XOM typically starts out bullish when Mercury goes retrograde in Cancer, but as the retrograde phase continues the stock begins to sell off, with the bullish tendency resuming after the direct station. When Mercury goes retrograde in Leo, XOM exhibits bearishness during the retrograde phase, but then becomes increasingly bullish after the direct station. The opposite trend occurs when Mercury goes retrograde in Capricorn, with a strong rally during the retrograde phase and a sharp decline after the direct station.

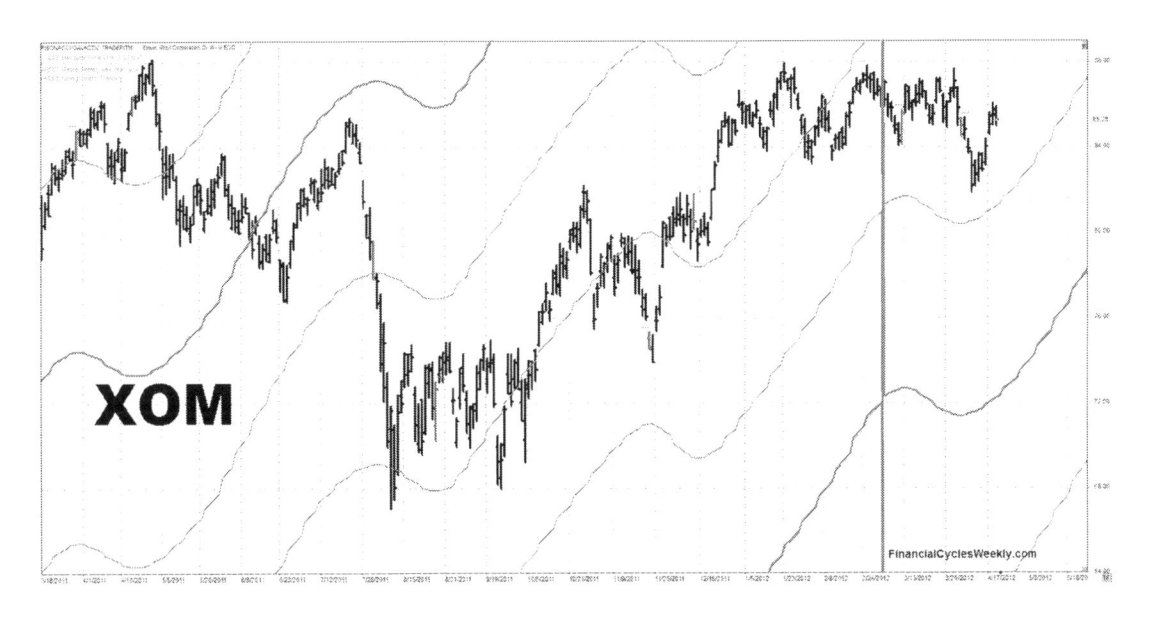

Back-Tested Historical Mercury Retrograde Performance

All Mercury Retrograde Periods

Retrograde Station to Direct Station	Average % Change	0.56%
Retrograde Station to Retrograde Return	Average % Change	0.58%
Direct Station to Retrograde Return	Average % Change	-0.01%

Mercury Going Retrograde in Fire Signs

1 Day after Retrograde Station	Likelihood of Higher Prices	51.5%
14 Days after Retrograde Station	Likelihood of Higher Prices	54.5%
7 Days after Direct Station	Likelihood of Higher Prices	60.0%

Mercury Going Retrograde in Earth Signs

1 Day after Retrograde Station	Likelihood of Higher Prices	65.7%
14 Days after Retrograde Station	Likelihood of Higher Prices	60.0%
7 Days after Direct Station	Likelihood of Higher Prices	44.1%

Mercury Going Retrograde in Air Signs

1 Day after Retrograde Station	Likelihood of Higher Prices	56.3%
14 Days after Retrograde Station	Likelihood of Higher Prices	53.1%
7 Days after Direct Station	Likelihood of Higher Prices	50.0%

Mercury Going Retrograde in Water Signs

1 Day after Retrograde Station	Likelihood of Higher Prices	55.2%
14 Days after Retrograde Station	Likelihood of Higher Prices	37.9%
7 Days after Direct Station	Likelihood of Higher Prices	53.3%

General Electric Company

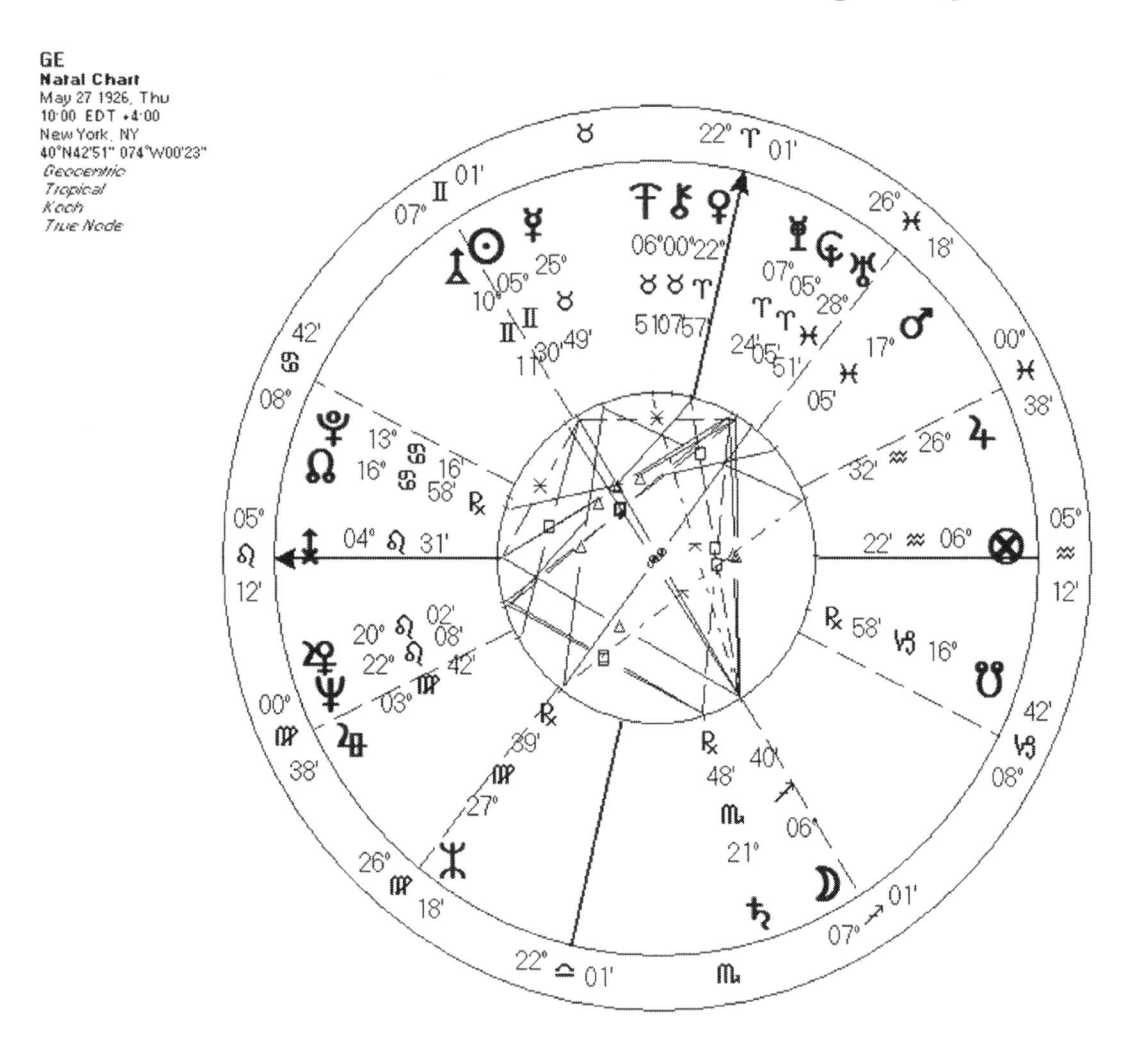

The GE First-Trade horoscope has Mercury Prometheus Direct in Taurus.

Secondary progressed First-Trade Mercury went into retrograde motion on July 12, 1984, and resumed direct motion on July 9, 2008. Secondary progressed First-Trade Mercury will go retrograde again on June 14, 2098. It will return to direct motion on April 16, 2118.

GE exhibits high price volatility when Mercury goes retrograde in Scorpio, with declining prices during the retrograde phase and bullishness after the direct station, and when Mercury goes retrograde in Capricorn, with rising prices during the retrograde phase and bearishness after the direct station. GE is most consistently bullish when Mercury goes retrograde in Virgo, with rising prices for the stock both during the retrograde phase and after the direct station.

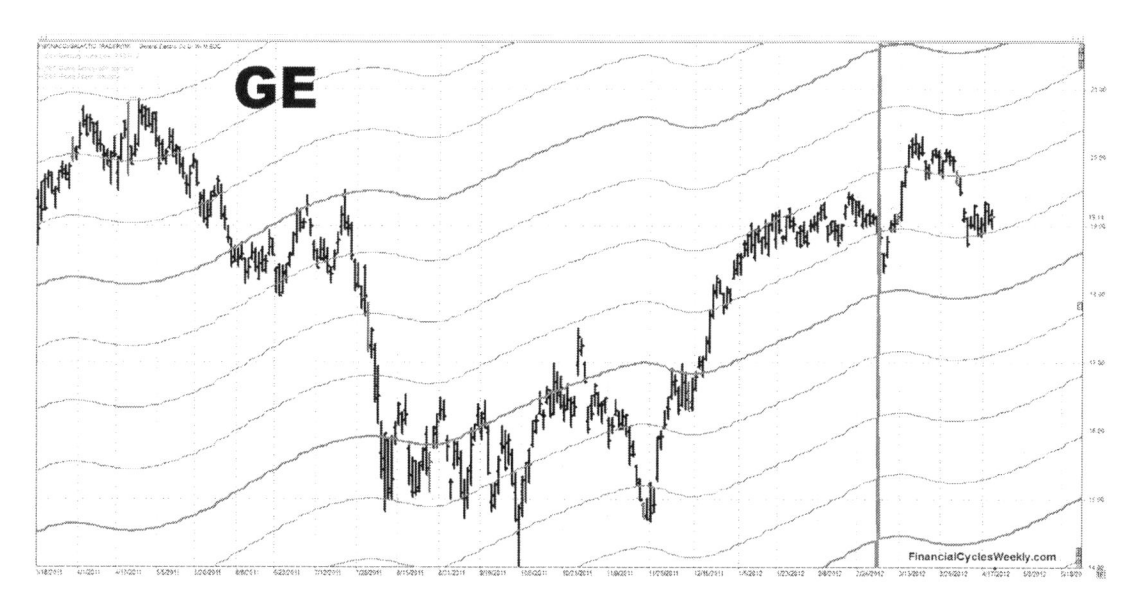

Back-Tested Historical Mercury Retrograde Performance

All Mercury Retrograde Periods

Retrograde Station to Direct Station	Average % Change	0.71%
Retrograde Station to Retrograde Return	Average % Change	0.65%
Direct Station to Retrograde Return	Average % Change	0.02%

Mercury Going Retrograde in Fire Signs

1 Day after Retrograde Station	Likelihood of Higher Prices	55.3%
14 Days after Retrograde Station	Likelihood of Higher Prices	60.5%
7 Days after Direct Station	Likelihood of Higher Prices	61.5%

Mercury Going Retrograde in Earth Signs

1 Day after Retrograde Station	Likelihood of Higher Prices	55.0%
14 Days after Retrograde Station	Likelihood of Higher Prices	60.0%
7 Days after Direct Station	Likelihood of Higher Prices	48.8%

Mercury Going Retrograde in Air Signs

1 Day after Retrograde Station	Likelihood of Higher Prices	52.5%
14 Days after Retrograde Station	Likelihood of Higher Prices	52.5%
7 Days after Direct Station	Likelihood of Higher Prices	35.9%

Mercury Going Retrograde in Water Signs

1 Day after Retrograde Station	Likelihood of Higher Prices	45.7%
14 Days after Retrograde Station	Likelihood of Higher Prices	48.6%
7 Days after Direct Station	Likelihood of Higher Prices	60.0%

Hewlett-Packard Company

HPQ
Natal Chart
May 6 2002, Mon
09:30 EDT +4:00
New York, NY
40°N42'51" 074°W00'23"
Geocentric
Tropical
Koch
True Node

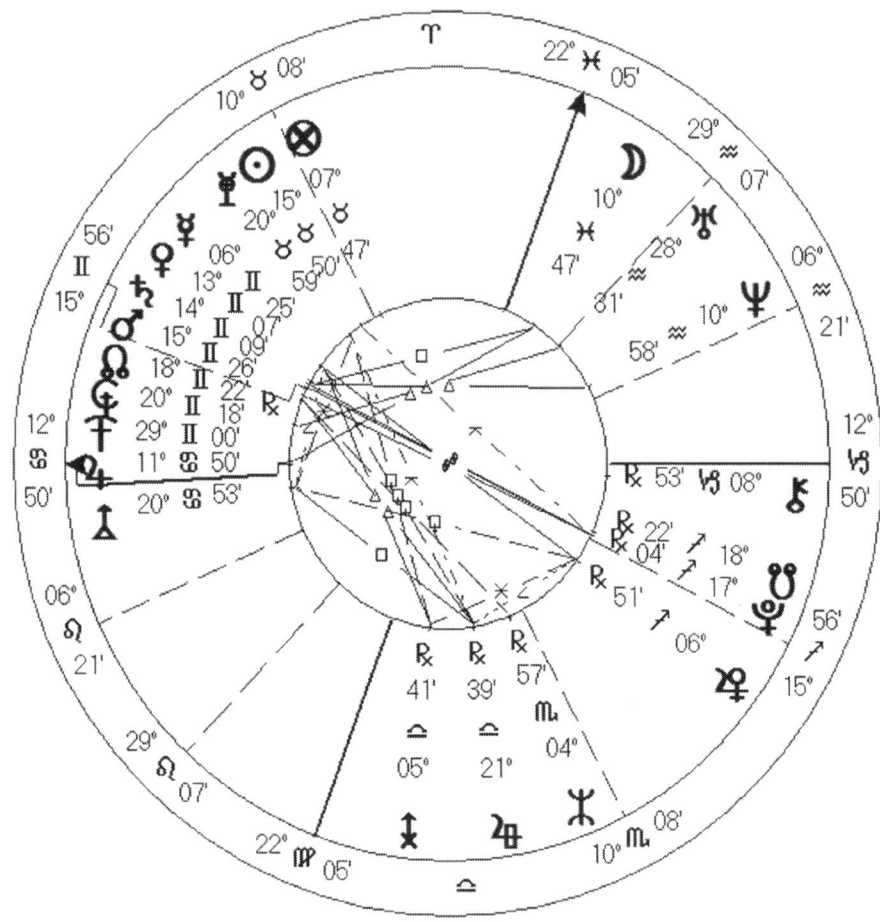

The HPQ First-Trade horoscope has Mercury Epimetheus Direct in Gemini.

Secondary progressed First-Trade Mercury went into retrograde motion on July 26, 2011. It will return to direct motion on June 1, 2035.

HPQ shows its greatest price volatility when Mercury goes retrograde in Capricorn, with modestly rising prices during the retrograde phase and a price decline following the direct station. HPQ prices also rise during the retrograde phase when Mercury goes retrograde in Aries, with falling prices after the direct station. The trend for HPQ tends to be more consistently bullish throughout the periods when Mercury goes retrograde in Scorpio or Sagittarius.

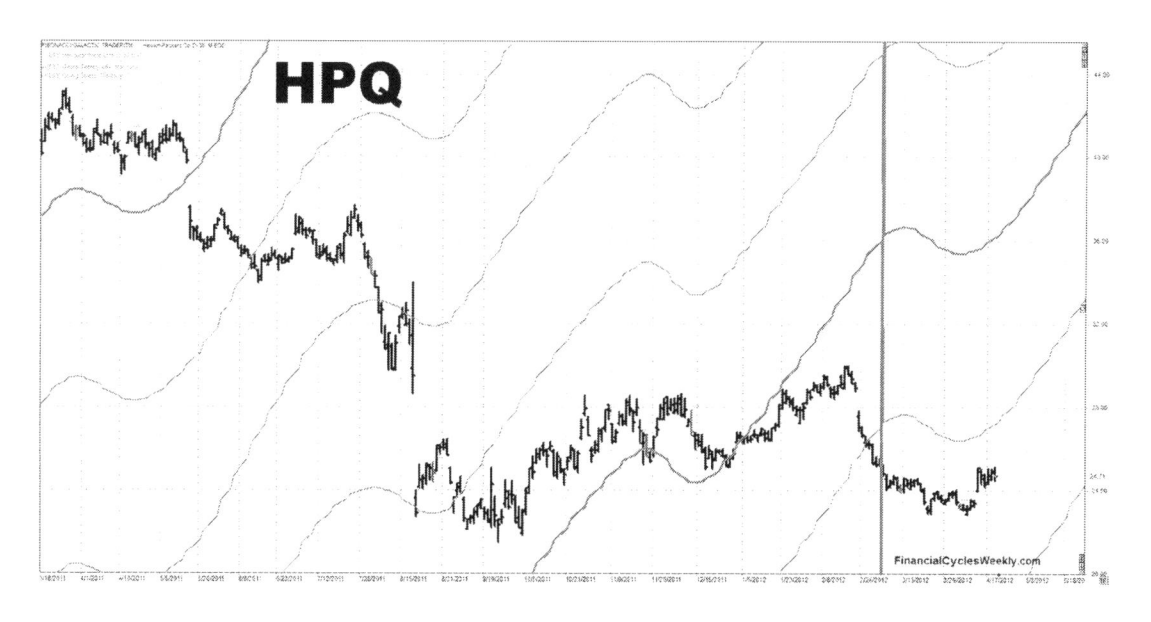

Back-Tested Historical Mercury Retrograde Performance

All Mercury Retrograde Periods

Retrograde Station to Direct Station	Average % Change	0.24%
Retrograde Station to Retrograde Return	Average % Change	0.27%
Direct Station to Retrograde Return	Average % Change	0.01%

Mercury Going Retrograde in Fire Signs

1 Day after Retrograde Station	Likelihood of Higher Prices	52.6%
14 Days after Retrograde Station	Likelihood of Higher Prices	73.7%
7 Days after Direct Station	Likelihood of Higher Prices	51.3%

Mercury Going Retrograde in Earth Signs

1 Day after Retrograde Station	Likelihood of Higher Prices	50.0%
14 Days after Retrograde Station	Likelihood of Higher Prices	42.5%
7 Days after Direct Station	Likelihood of Higher Prices	48.8%

Mercury Going Retrograde in Air Signs

1 Day after Retrograde Station	Likelihood of Higher Prices	45.0%
14 Days after Retrograde Station	Likelihood of Higher Prices	50.0%
7 Days after Direct Station	Likelihood of Higher Prices	56.4%

Mercury Going Retrograde in Water Signs

1 Day after Retrograde Station	Likelihood of Higher Prices	48.6%
14 Days after Retrograde Station	Likelihood of Higher Prices	51.4%
7 Days after Direct Station	Likelihood of Higher Prices	48.6%

The Home Depot Inc.

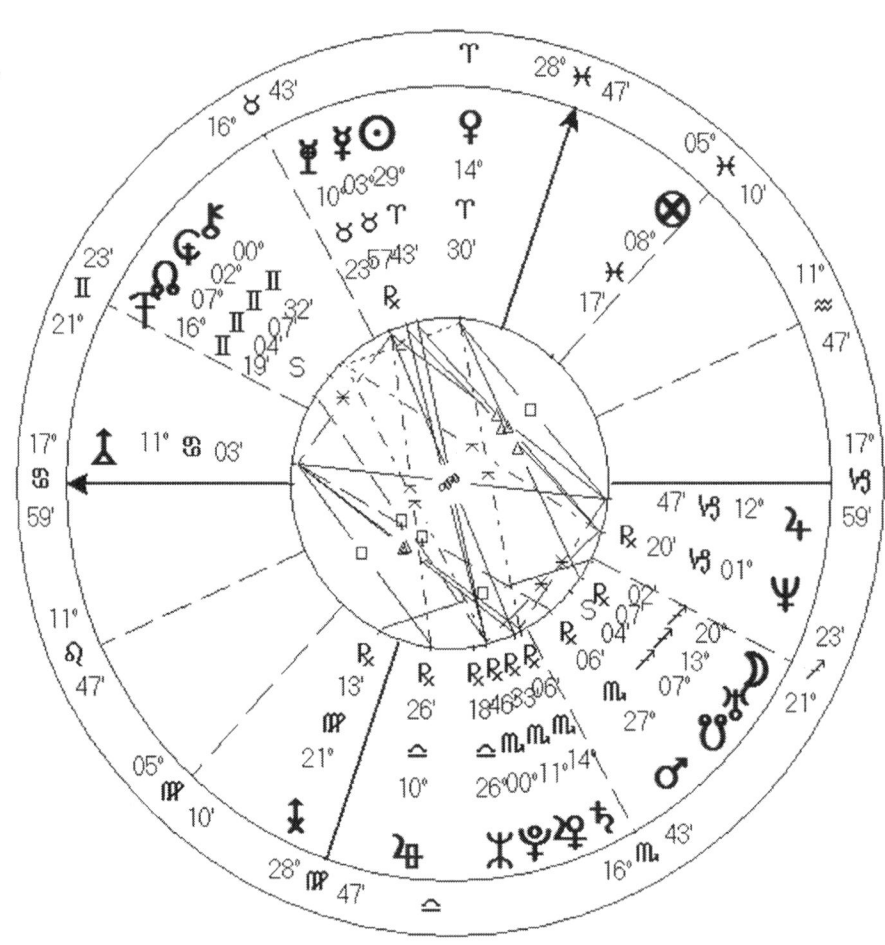

The HD First-Trade horoscope has Mercury Epimetheus Retrograde in Taurus.

Secondary progressed First-Trade Mercury went into direct motion on April 5, 2000. Secondary progressed First-Trade Mercury will go retrograde again on June 28, 2101. It will return to direct motion on November 3, 2124.

HD has shown some of its weakest price action when Mercury goes retrograde in Pisces, with declining prices both during the retrograde phase and after the direct station. HD tends to be bullish when Mercury goes retrograde in Taurus, Virgo, or Sagittarius.

Back-Tested Historical Mercury Retrograde Performance

All Mercury Retrograde Periods

Retrograde Station to Direct Station	Average % Change	0.29%
Retrograde Station to Retrograde Return	Average % Change	0.95%
Direct Station to Retrograde Return	Average % Change	0.58%

Mercury Going Retrograde in Fire Signs

1 Day after Retrograde Station	Likelihood of Higher Prices	56.5%
14 Days after Retrograde Station	Likelihood of Higher Prices	56.5%
7 Days after Direct Station	Likelihood of Higher Prices	47.8%

Mercury Going Retrograde in Earth Signs

1 Day after Retrograde Station	Likelihood of Higher Prices	61.9%
14 Days after Retrograde Station	Likelihood of Higher Prices	61.9%
7 Days after Direct Station	Likelihood of Higher Prices	59.1%

Mercury Going Retrograde in Air Signs

1 Day after Retrograde Station	Likelihood of Higher Prices	54.5%
14 Days after Retrograde Station	Likelihood of Higher Prices	49.1%
7 Days after Direct Station	Likelihood of Higher Prices	42.9%

Mercury Going Retrograde in Water Signs

1 Day after Retrograde Station	Likelihood of Higher Prices	50.0%
14 Days after Retrograde Station	Likelihood of Higher Prices	50.0%
7 Days after Direct Station	Likelihood of Higher Prices	75.0%

Intel Corporation

INTC
Natal Chart
Aug 7 1981, Fri
10:00 EDT +4:00
New York, NY
40°N42'51" 074°W00'23"
Geocentric
Tropical
Koch
True Node

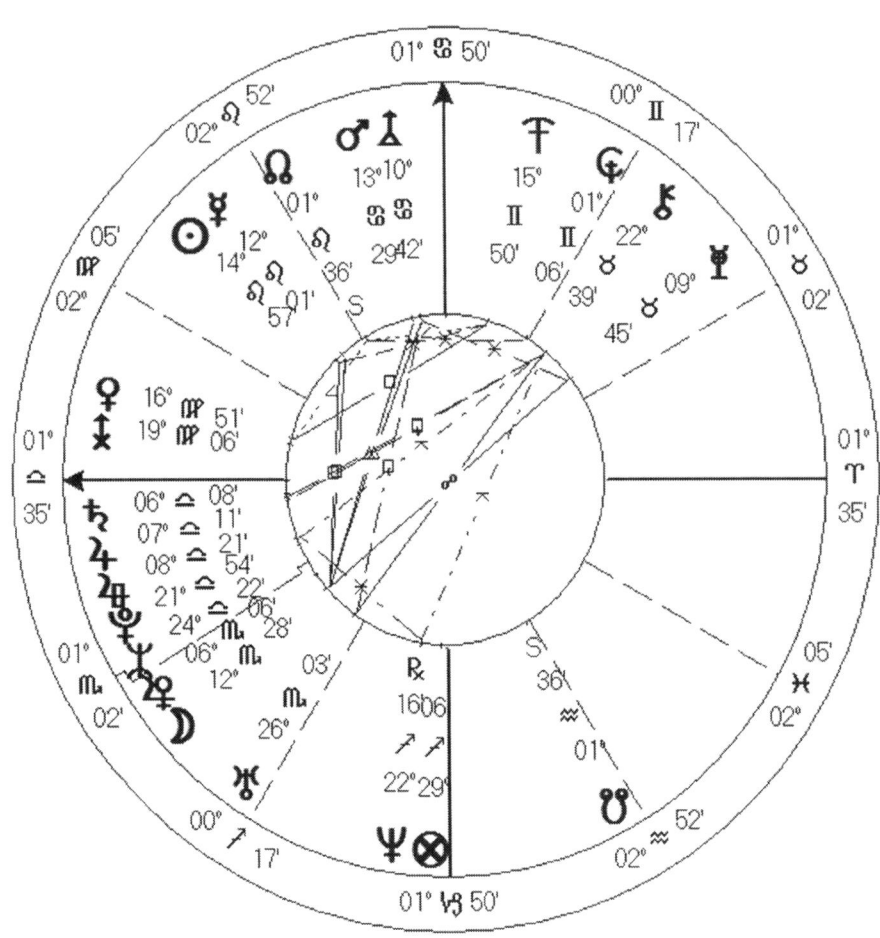

The INTC First-Trade horoscope has Mercury Prometheus Direct in Leo.

Secondary progressed First-Trade Mercury will go into retrograde motion on May 26, 2041. It will return to direct motion on May 25, 2062.

INTC shows some of its greatest price volatility when Mercury goes retrograde in Leo, with moderately rising prices during the retrograde phase and a price decline beginning soon after the direct station. That's also the case when Mercury goes retrograde in Virgo, with sharply declining prices during the retrograde phase and a solid up-trend after the direct station, and when Mercury goes retrograde in Capricorn, with strong bullishness during the retrogrde phase and a price pull-back after the direct station. When Mercury goes retrograde in Scorpio INTC responds with a bearish trend throughout the retrograde and direct phases.

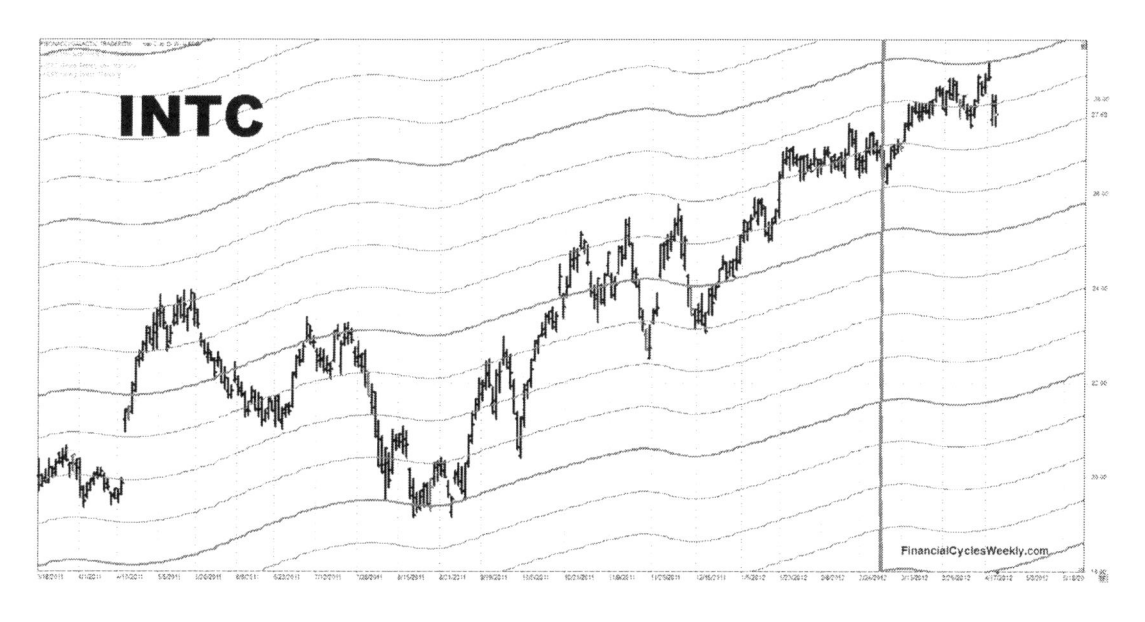

Back-Tested Historical Mercury Retrograde Performance

All Mercury Retrograde Periods

Retrograde Station to Direct Station	Average % Change	0.60%
Retrograde Station to Retrograde Return	Average % Change	0.99%
Direct Station to Retrograde Return	Average % Change	0.54%

Mercury Going Retrograde in Fire Signs

1 Day after Retrograde Station	Likelihood of Higher Prices	61.1%
14 Days after Retrograde Station	Likelihood of Higher Prices	50.0%
7 Days after Direct Station	Likelihood of Higher Prices	45.0%

Mercury Going Retrograde in Earth Signs

1 Day after Retrograde Station	Likelihood of Higher Prices	57.1%
14 Days after Retrograde Station	Likelihood of Higher Prices	52.4%
7 Days after Direct Station	Likelihood of Higher Prices	59.1%

Mercury Going Retrograde in Air Signs

1 Day after Retrograde Station	Likelihood of Higher Prices	50.0%
14 Days after Retrograde Station	Likelihood of Higher Prices	50.0%
7 Days after Direct Station	Likelihood of Higher Prices	42.9%

Mercury Going Retrograde in Water Signs

1 Day after Retrograde Station	Likelihood of Higher Prices	55.6%
14 Days after Retrograde Station	Likelihood of Higher Prices	50.0%
7 Days after Direct Station	Likelihood of Higher Prices	61.1%

International Business Machines

IBM
Natal Chart
Feb 14 1924, Thu
09:30 EST +5:00
New York, New York
40°N42'51" 074°W00'23"
Geocentric
Tropical
Koch
True Node

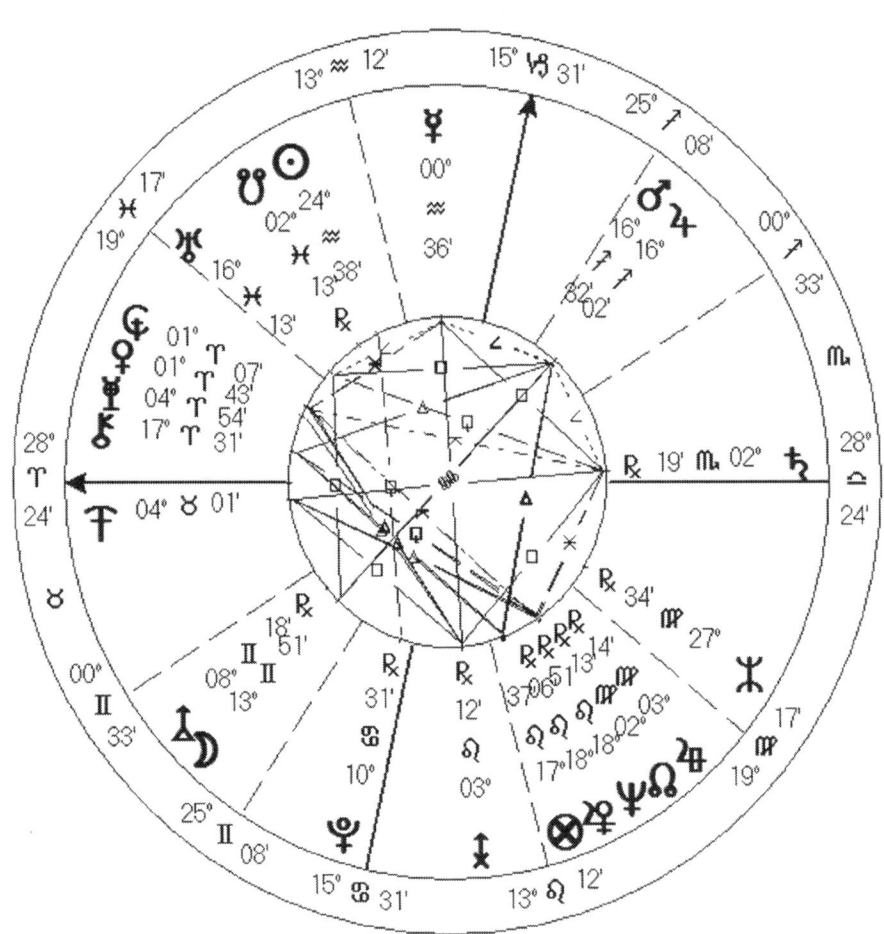

The IBM First-Trade horoscope has Mercury Prometheus Direct in Aquarius.

The IBM secondary progressed First-Trade Mercury went into retrograde motion on September 13, 1996. It will return to direct motion on July 12, 2020.

IBM dispays its greatest price volatility when Mercury goes retrograde in Libra, with rising prices for the stock during the retrograde phase and increasing selling pressure after the direct station.

Back-Tested Historical Mercury Retrograde Performance

All Mercury Retrograde Periods

Retrograde Station to Direct Station	Average % Change	0.26%
Retrograde Station to Retrograde Return	Average % Change	0.09%
Direct Station to Retrograde Return	Average % Change	-0.21%

Mercury Going Retrograde in Fire Signs

1 Day after Retrograde Station	Likelihood of Higher Prices	47.4%
14 Days after Retrograde Station	Likelihood of Higher Prices	52.6%
7 Days after Direct Station	Likelihood of Higher Prices	46.2%

Mercury Going Retrograde in Earth Signs

1 Day after Retrograde Station	Likelihood of Higher Prices	55.0%
14 Days after Retrograde Station	Likelihood of Higher Prices	57.5%
7 Days after Direct Station	Likelihood of Higher Prices	51.2%

Mercury Going Retrograde in Air Signs

1 Day after Retrograde Station	Likelihood of Higher Prices	50.0%
14 Days after Retrograde Station	Likelihood of Higher Prices	62.5%
7 Days after Direct Station	Likelihood of Higher Prices	41.0%

Mercury Going Retrograde in Water Signs

1 Day after Retrograde Station	Likelihood of Higher Prices	45.7%
14 Days after Retrograde Station	Likelihood of Higher Prices	42.9%
7 Days after Direct Station	Likelihood of Higher Prices	51.4%

Johnson & Jonhson

JNJ
Natal Chart
Sep 25 1944, Mon
10:00 EWT +4:00
New York, NY
40°N42'51" 074°W00'23"
Geocentric
Tropical
Koch
True Node

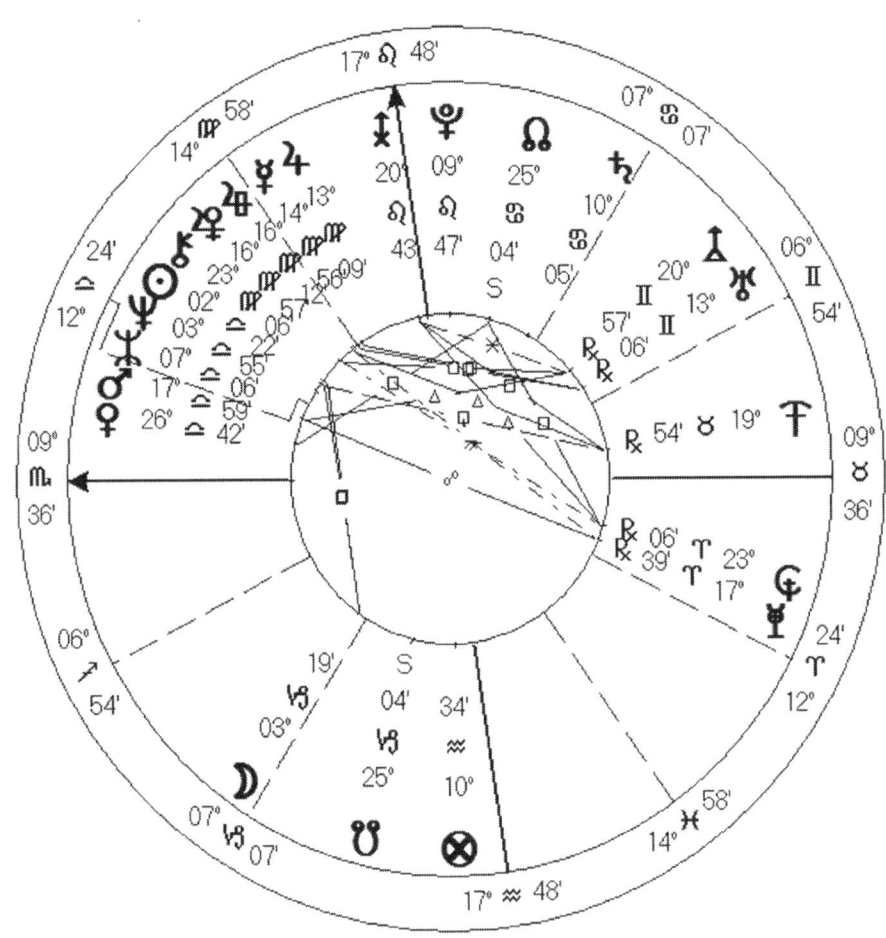

The JNJ First-Trade horoscope has Mercury Prometheus Direct in Virgo.

Secondary progressed First-Trade Mercury will go into retrograde motion on October 28, 2023. It will return to direct motion on September 6, 2043.

JNJ shows some of its greatest price volatility when Mercury goes retrograde in Gemini, Cancer, or Capricorn. When Mercury goes retrograde in Gemini or Capricorn, JNJ typically experiences rising prices during the retrograde phase, followed by a price decline after the direct station. When Mercury goes retrograde in Cancer, the opposite pattern predominates, with declining prices during the retrograde phase and a move to the upside toward the end of time line.

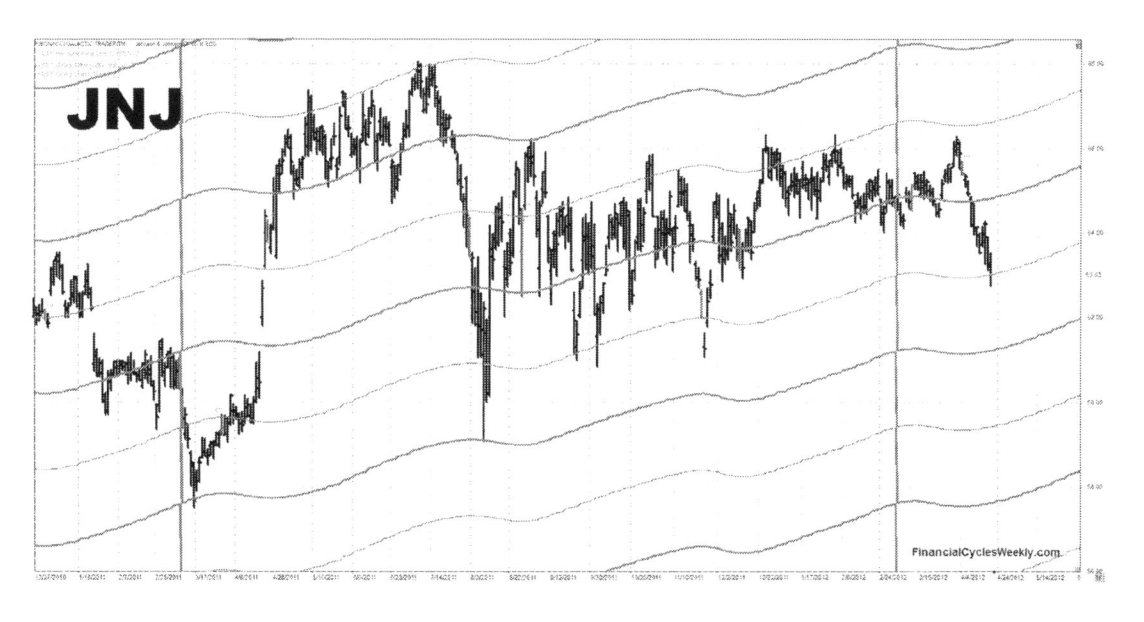

Back-Tested Historical Mercury Retrograde Performance

All Mercury Retrograde Periods

Retrograde Station to Direct Station	Average % Change	1.37%
Retrograde Station to Retrograde Return	Average % Change	1.32%
Direct Station to Retrograde Return	Average % Change	-0.00%

Mercury Going Retrograde in Fire Signs

1 Day after Retrograde Station	Likelihood of Higher Prices	51.5%
14 Days after Retrograde Station	Likelihood of Higher Prices	66.7%
7 Days after Direct Station	Likelihood of Higher Prices	62.9%

Mercury Going Retrograde in Earth Signs

1 Day after Retrograde Station	Likelihood of Higher Prices	57.1%
14 Days after Retrograde Station	Likelihood of Higher Prices	71.4%
7 Days after Direct Station	Likelihood of Higher Prices	47.1%

Mercury Going Retrograde in Air Signs

1 Day after Retrograde Station	Likelihood of Higher Prices	43.8%
14 Days after Retrograde Station	Likelihood of Higher Prices	65.6%
7 Days after Direct Station	Likelihood of Higher Prices	50.0%

Mercury Going Retrograde in Water Signs

1 Day after Retrograde Station	Likelihood of Higher Prices	58.6%
14 Days after Retrograde Station	Likelihood of Higher Prices	44.8%
7 Days after Direct Station	Likelihood of Higher Prices	56.7%

JPMorgan Chase and Company

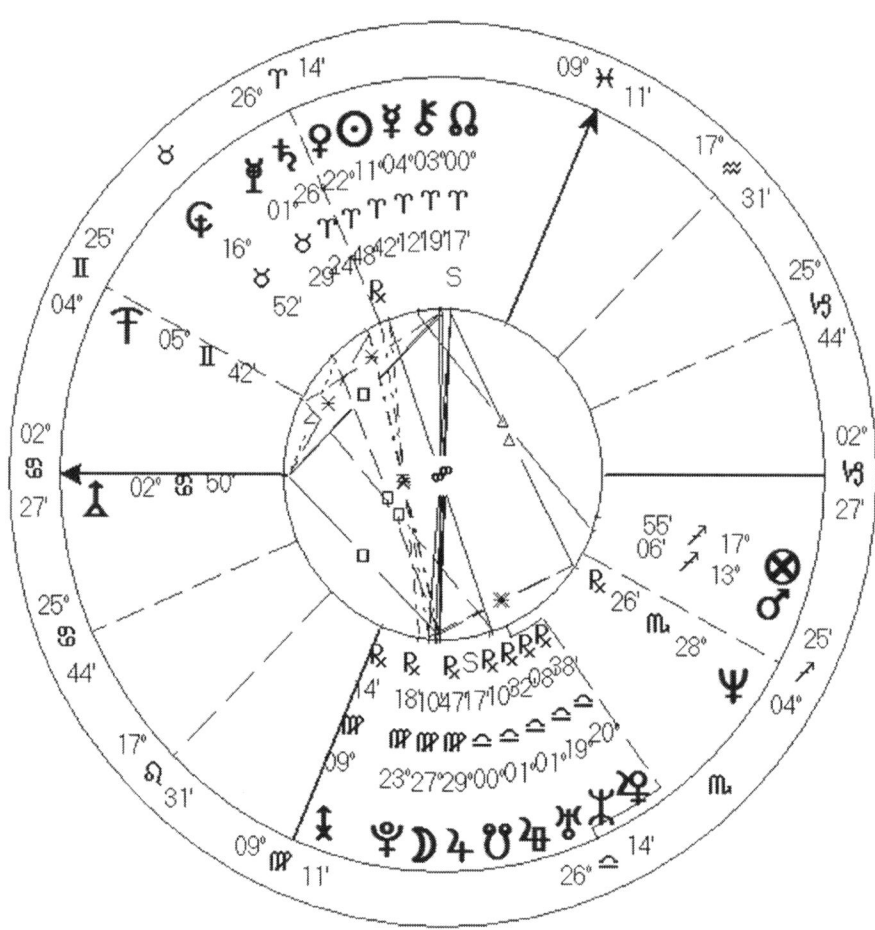

The JPM First-Trade horoscope has Mercury Prometheus Direct in Aries.

Secondary progressed First-Trade Mercury will go into retrograde motion on June 2, 2015. It will return to direct motion on April 13, 2039.

The greatest price volatility for JPM takes place when Mercury goes retrograde in Virgo, Scorpio, or Aquarius. In each case bullish tendencies during the retrograde phase are replaced with a declining price trend after the direct station. Mercury going retrograde in Libra is more uniformly bearish for JPM, while Mercury going retrograde in Sagittarius creates a bullish trend more consistently.

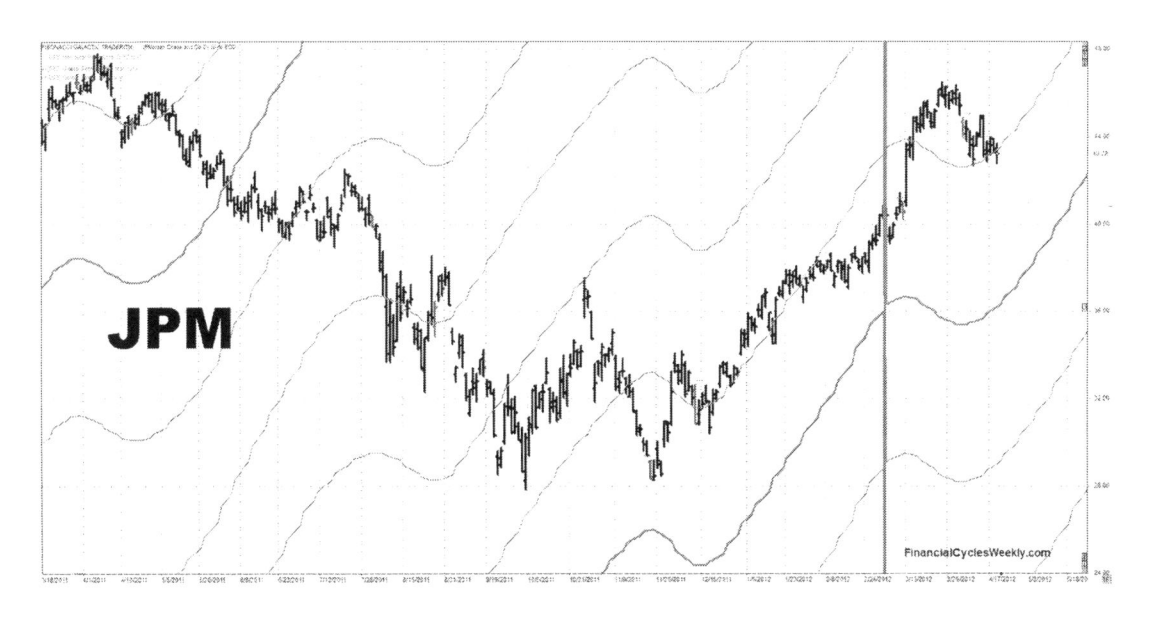

Back-Tested Historical Mercury Retrograde Performance

All Mercury Retrograde Periods

Retrograde Station to Direct Station	Average % Change	-0.82%
Retrograde Station to Retrograde Return	Average % Change	-2.54%
Direct Station to Retrograde Return	Average % Change	-1.71%

Mercury Going Retrograde in Fire Signs

1 Day after Retrograde Station	Likelihood of Higher Prices	56.5%
14 Days after Retrograde Station	Likelihood of Higher Prices	52.2%
7 Days after Direct Station	Likelihood of Higher Prices	54.2%

Mercury Going Retrograde in Earth Signs

1 Day after Retrograde Station	Likelihood of Higher Prices	65.2%
14 Days after Retrograde Station	Likelihood of Higher Prices	56.5%
7 Days after Direct Station	Likelihood of Higher Prices	36.4%

Mercury Going Retrograde in Air Signs

1 Day after Retrograde Station	Likelihood of Higher Prices	50.0%
14 Days after Retrograde Station	Likelihood of Higher Prices	50.0%
7 Days after Direct Station	Likelihood of Higher Prices	38.1%

Mercury Going Retrograde in Water Signs

1 Day after Retrograde Station	Likelihood of Higher Prices	72.2%
14 Days after Retrograde Station	Likelihood of Higher Prices	44.4%
7 Days after Direct Station	Likelihood of Higher Prices	45.0%

Kraft Foods Inc.

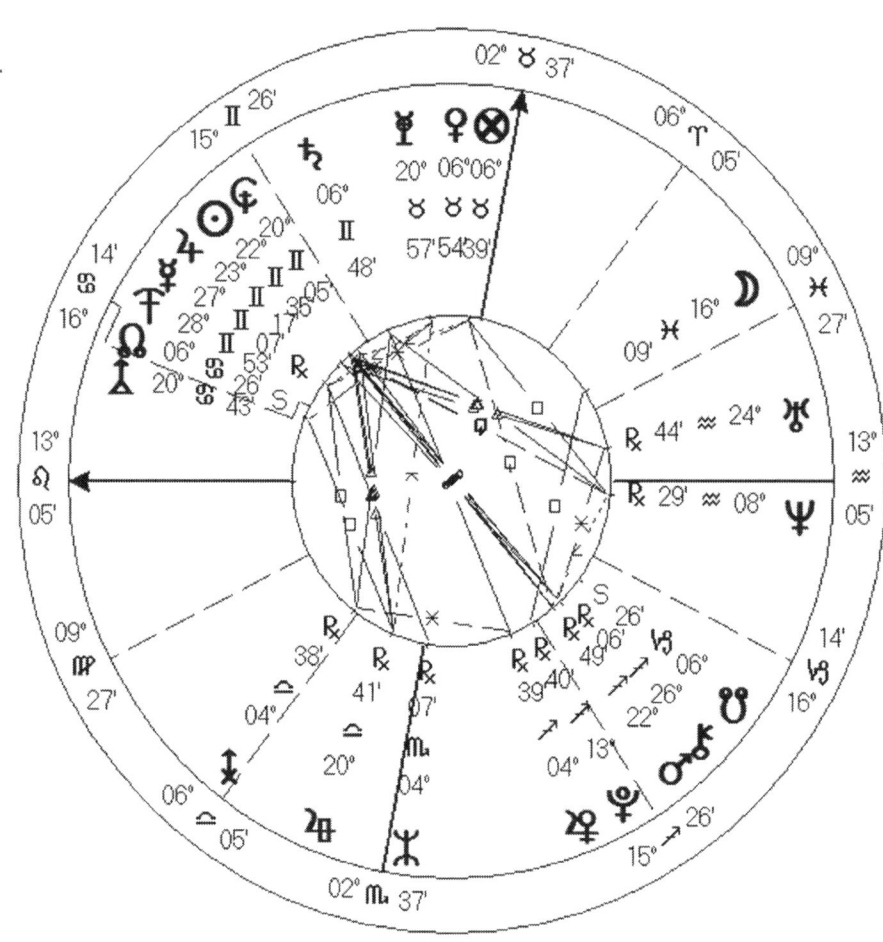

The KFT First-Trade horoscope has Mercury Epimetheus Retrograde in Gemini.

Secondary progressed First-Trade Mercury will go into direct motion on February 17, 2016.

KFT shows some of its greatest price volatility when Mercury goes retrograde in Leo. The stock shows solid bearishness during the retrograde phase, and then prices tend to rise rather dramatically once Mercury resumes direct motion. Overall, KFT reacts quite strongly to Mercury retrograde periods: Mercury going retrograde in Virgo is bullish for the stock, but KFT typically declines in price when Mercury goes retrograde in Libra, Scorpio, Capricorn, or Pisces.

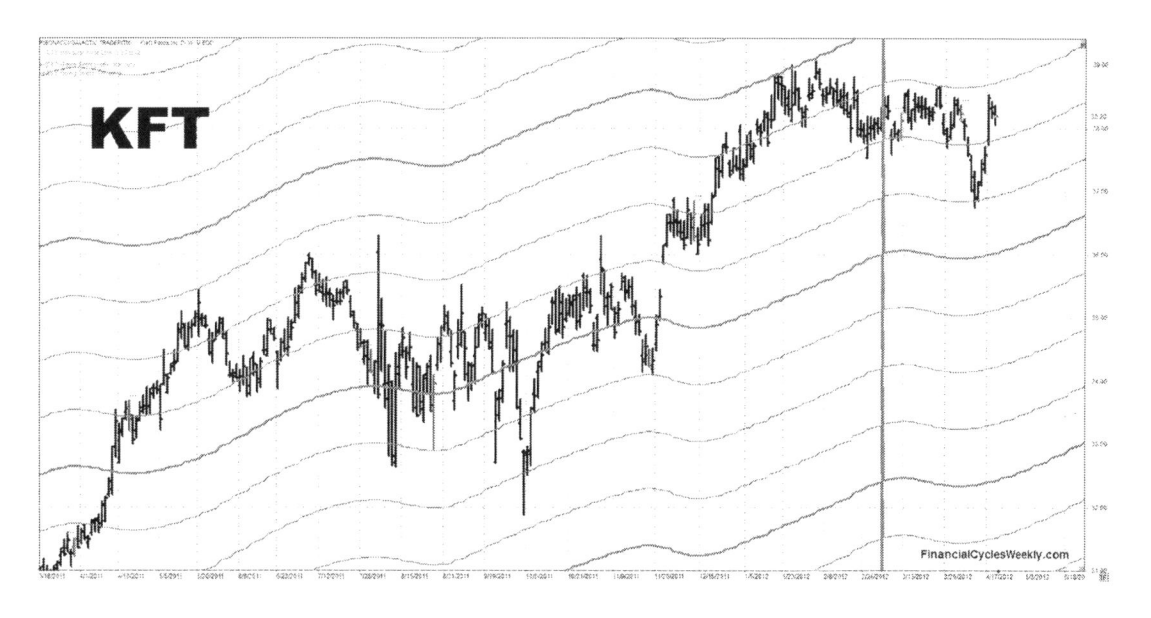

Back-Tested Historical Mercury Retrograde Performance

All Mercury Retrograde Periods

Retrograde Station to Direct Station	Average % Change	0.50%
Retrograde Station to Retrograde Return	Average % Change	-0.78%
Direct Station to Retrograde Return	Average % Change	-1.33%

Mercury Going Retrograde in Fire Signs

1 Day after Retrograde Station	Likelihood of Higher Prices	42.9%
14 Days after Retrograde Station	Likelihood of Higher Prices	71.4%
7 Days after Direct Station	Likelihood of Higher Prices	50.0%

Mercury Going Retrograde in Earth Signs

1 Day after Retrograde Station	Likelihood of Higher Prices	36.4%
14 Days after Retrograde Station	Likelihood of Higher Prices	72.7%
7 Days after Direct Station	Likelihood of Higher Prices	45.5%

Mercury Going Retrograde in Air Signs

1 Day after Retrograde Station	Likelihood of Higher Prices	50.0%
14 Days after Retrograde Station	Likelihood of Higher Prices	30.0%
7 Days after Direct Station	Likelihood of Higher Prices	50.0%

Mercury Going Retrograde in Water Signs

1 Day after Retrograde Station	Likelihood of Higher Prices	20.0%
14 Days after Retrograde Station	Likelihood of Higher Prices	20.0%
7 Days after Direct Station	Likelihood of Higher Prices	40.0%

McDonald's Corporation

MCD
Natal Chart
Jul 5 1966, Tue
10:00 EDT +4:00
New York, NY
40°N42'51" 074°W00'23"
Geocentric
Tropical
Koch
True Node

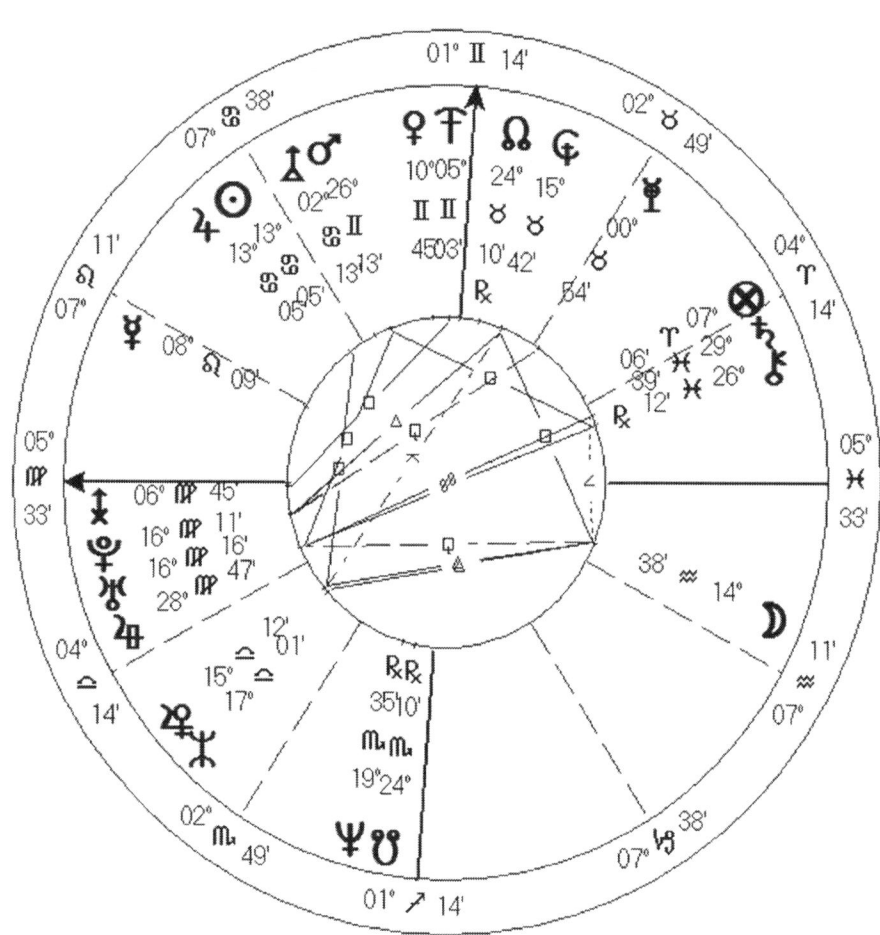

The MCD First-Trade horoscope has Mercury Epimetheus Direct in Leo.

Secondary progressed First-Trade Mercury went into retrograde motion on October 8, 1975, returning to direct motion on November 29, 1999. The MCD secondary progressed Mercury will next go retrograde on September 2, 2090. It will return to direct motion on September 1, 2110.

MCD shows some of its greatest price volatility when Mercury goes retrograde in Gemini, Leo, Sagittarius, or Aquarius. When Mercury goes retrograde in Gemini or Aquarius, the stock is bullish during the retrograde phase and sells off after the direct station; when Mercury goes retrograde in Leo or Sagittarius, MCD is bearish during the retrograde phase but picks up a positive price trend after the direct station.

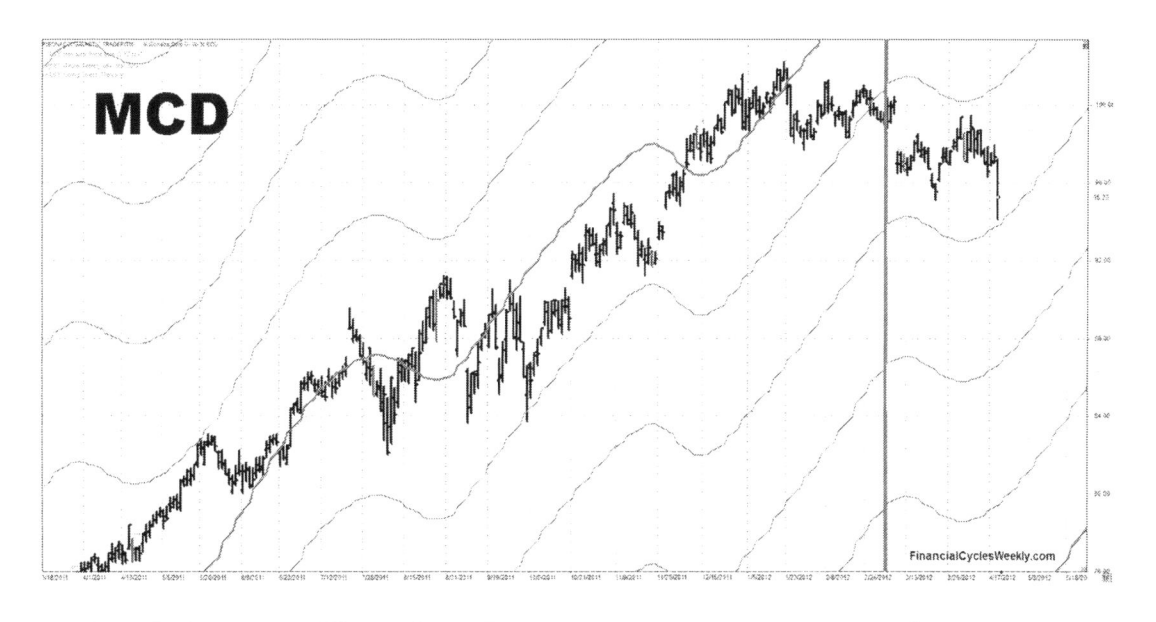

Back-Tested Historical Mercury Retrograde Performance

All Mercury Retrograde Periods

Retrograde Station to Direct Station	Average % Change	0.63%
Retrograde Station to Retrograde Return	Average % Change	1.06%
Direct Station to Retrograde Return	Average % Change	0.31%

Mercury Going Retrograde in Fire Signs

1 Day after Retrograde Station	Likelihood of Higher Prices	54.5%
14 Days after Retrograde Station	Likelihood of Higher Prices	66.7%
7 Days after Direct Station	Likelihood of Higher Prices	42.9%

Mercury Going Retrograde in Earth Signs

1 Day after Retrograde Station	Likelihood of Higher Prices	54.3%
14 Days after Retrograde Station	Likelihood of Higher Prices	54.3%
7 Days after Direct Station	Likelihood of Higher Prices	35.3%

Mercury Going Retrograde in Air Signs

1 Day after Retrograde Station	Likelihood of Higher Prices	75.0%
14 Days after Retrograde Station	Likelihood of Higher Prices	68.8%
7 Days after Direct Station	Likelihood of Higher Prices	46.9%

Mercury Going Retrograde in Water Signs

1 Day after Retrograde Station	Likelihood of Higher Prices	55.2%
14 Days after Retrograde Station	Likelihood of Higher Prices	44.8%
7 Days after Direct Station	Likelihood of Higher Prices	56.7%

Merck & Company Inc.

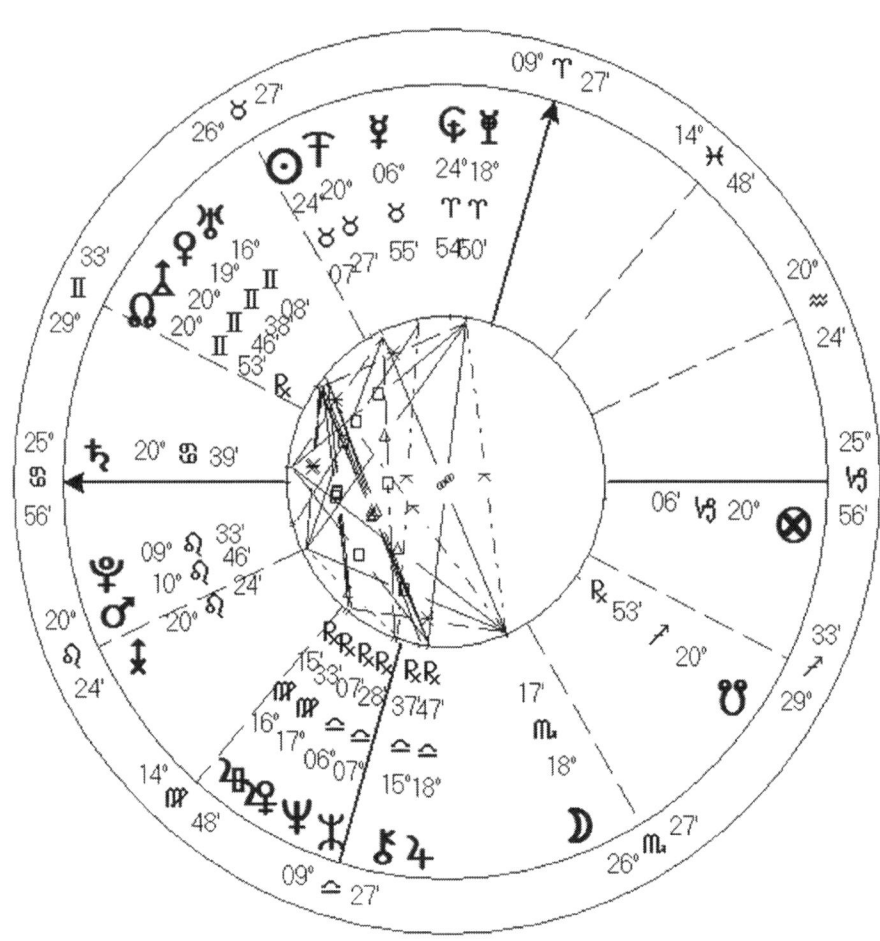

MRK
Event Chart
May 15 1946, Wed
10:00 EDT +4:00
New York, NY
40°N42'51" 074°W00'23"
Geocentric
Tropical
Koch
True Node

The MRK First-Trade horoscope has Mercury Prometheus Direct in Taurus.

Secondary progressed First-Trade Mercury went into retrograde motion on July 29, 2011. It will return to direct motion on August 30, 2035.

Mercury going retrograde in Taurus has been consistently bearish for this stock, with declining prices during both the retrograde and direct phases. MRK shows some of its greatest price volatility when Mercury goes retrograde in Gemini, Leo, or Libra: when Mercury goes retrograde in Gemini or Libra, MRK is bullish during the retrograde phase but sells off after the direct station; when Mercury goes retrograde in Leo bearishness during the retrograde phase is replaced by rising prices after the direct station.

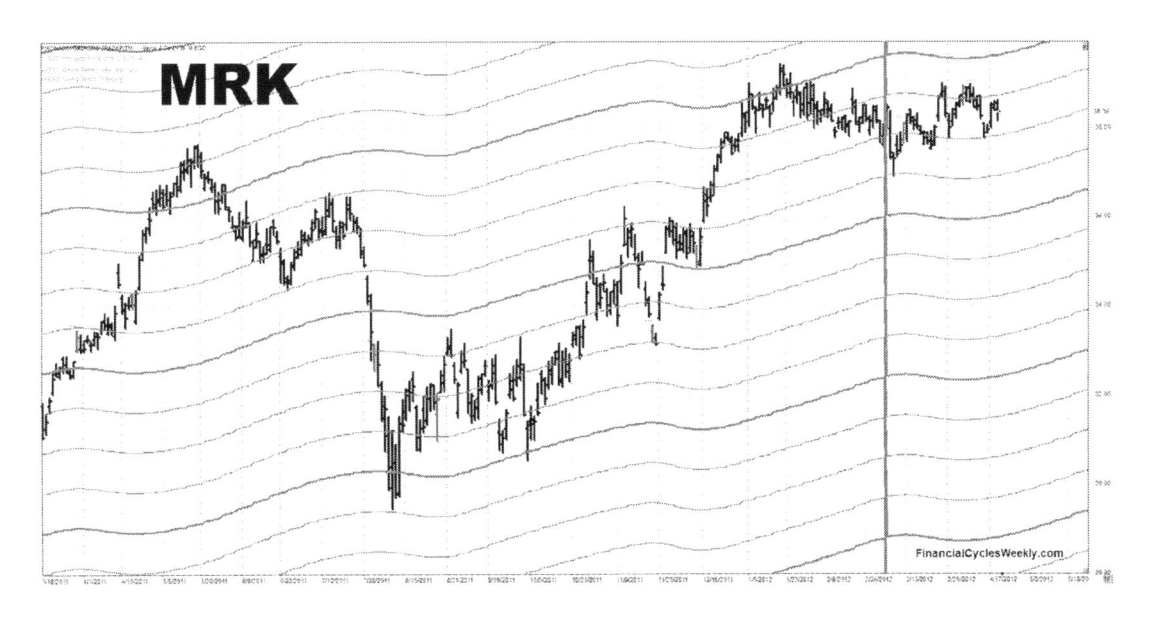

Back-Tested Historical Mercury Retrograde Performance

All Mercury Retrograde Periods

Retrograde Station to Direct Station	Average % Change	1.05%
Retrograde Station to Retrograde Return	Average % Change	0.93%
Direct Station to Retrograde Return	Average % Change	-0.14%

Mercury Going Retrograde in Fire Signs

1 Day after Retrograde Station	Likelihood of Higher Prices	63.6%
14 Days after Retrograde Station	Likelihood of Higher Prices	69.7%
7 Days after Direct Station	Likelihood of Higher Prices	68.6%

Mercury Going Retrograde in Earth Signs

1 Day after Retrograde Station	Likelihood of Higher Prices	28.6%
14 Days after Retrograde Station	Likelihood of Higher Prices	57.1%
7 Days after Direct Station	Likelihood of Higher Prices	41.2%

Mercury Going Retrograde in Air Signs

1 Day after Retrograde Station	Likelihood of Higher Prices	65.6%
14 Days after Retrograde Station	Likelihood of Higher Prices	65.6%
7 Days after Direct Station	Likelihood of Higher Prices	50.0%

Mercury Going Retrograde in Water Signs

1 Day after Retrograde Station	Likelihood of Higher Prices	51.7%
14 Days after Retrograde Station	Likelihood of Higher Prices	51.7%
7 Days after Direct Station	Likelihood of Higher Prices	43.3%

Microsoft Corporation

MSFT
Natal Chart
Mar 13 1986, Thu
09:30 EST +5:00
New York, New York
40°N42'51" 074°W00'23"
Geocentric
Tropical
Koch
True Node

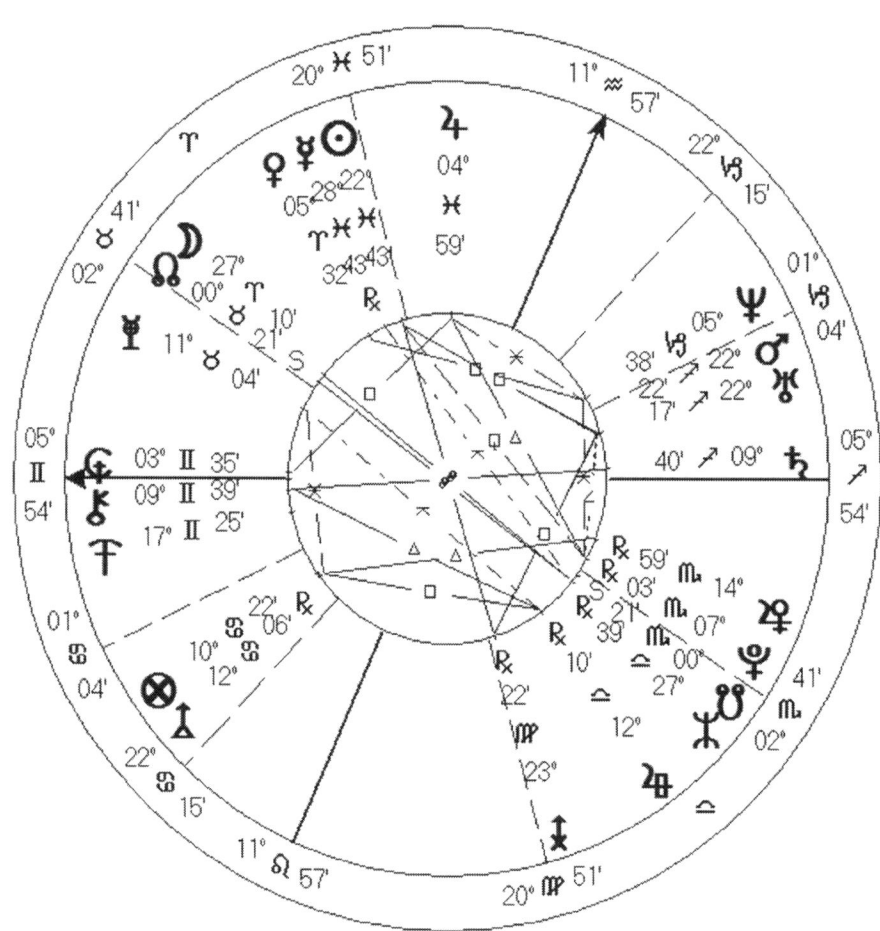

The MSFT First-Trade horoscope has Mercury Epimetheus Retrograde in Pisces.

Secondary progressed First-Trade Mercury went into direct motion on December 15, 2002.

MSFT shows some of its greatest price volatility when Mercury goes retrograde in Virgo or Aquarius. When Mercury goes retrograde in Virgo, bullishness during the retrograde phase turns bearish after the direct station. When Mercury goes retrograde in Aquarius, declining prices during the retrograde phase turn decidedly bullish after the direct station. When Mercury goes retrograde in Leo, MSFT exhibits bearish tendencies through both the retrograde and direct phases.

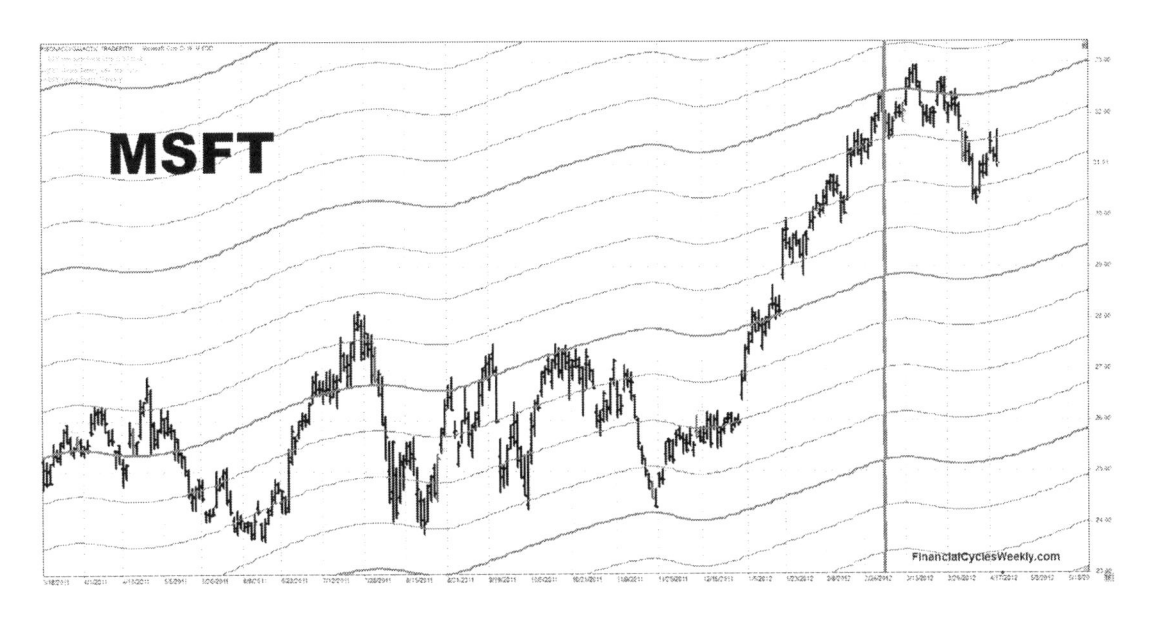

Back-Tested Historical Mercury Retrograde Performance

All Mercury Retrograde Periods

Retrograde Station to Direct Station	Average % Change	1.60%
Retrograde Station to Retrograde Return	Average % Change	2.19%
Direct Station to Retrograde Return	Average % Change	0.68%

Mercury Going Retrograde in Fire Signs

1 Day after Retrograde Station	Likelihood of Higher Prices	47.4%
14 Days after Retrograde Station	Likelihood of Higher Prices	63.2%
7 Days after Direct Station	Likelihood of Higher Prices	45.0%

Mercury Going Retrograde in Earth Signs

1 Day after Retrograde Station	Likelihood of Higher Prices	81.0%
14 Days after Retrograde Station	Likelihood of Higher Prices	66.7%
7 Days after Direct Station	Likelihood of Higher Prices	54.5%

Mercury Going Retrograde in Air Signs

1 Day after Retrograde Station	Likelihood of Higher Prices	54.5%
14 Days after Retrograde Station	Likelihood of Higher Prices	40.9%
7 Days after Direct Station	Likelihood of Higher Prices	47.6%

Mercury Going Retrograde in Water Signs

1 Day after Retrograde Station	Likelihood of Higher Prices	61.1%
14 Days after Retrograde Station	Likelihood of Higher Prices	55.6%
7 Days after Direct Station	Likelihood of Higher Prices	52.6%

Pfizer Inc.

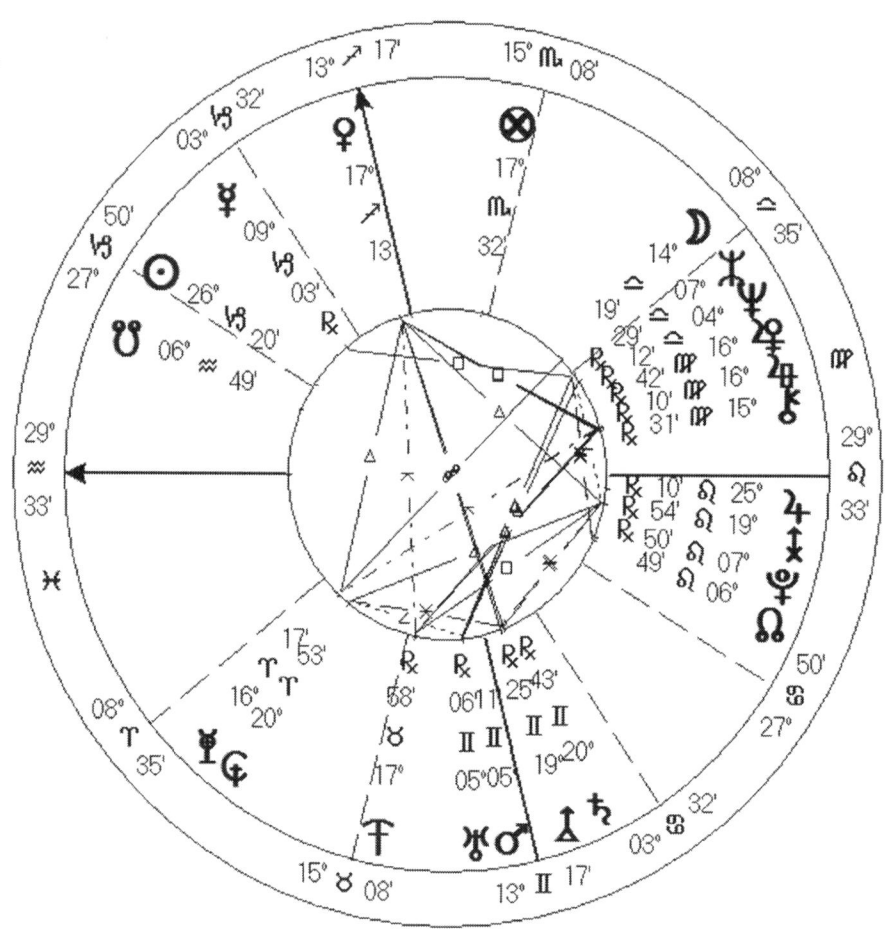

PFE
Natal Chart
Jan 17 1944, Mon
10:00 EWT +4:00
New York, NY
40°N42'51" 074°W00'23"
Geocentric
Tropical
Koch
True Node

The PFE First-Trade horoscope has Mercury Prometheus Retrograde in Capricorn.

Secondary progressed First-Trade Mercury went into direct motion on June 8, 1946. The PFE secondary progressed First-Trade Mercury will go into retrograde motion again on June 26, 2039. It will return to direct motion on April 12, 2063.

PFE exhibits some of its greatest price volatility when Mercury goes retrograde in Gemini. Bullish tendencies during the retrograde phase have become increasingly bearish after the direct station. The trading action in PFE has been more consistently bullish when Mercury goes retrograde in Aries or Virgo. When Mercury goes retrograde in Pisces, however, this stock typically has decidedly bearish tendencies throughout both the retrograde and direct phases.

Back-Tested Historical Mercury Retrograde Performance

All Mercury Retrograde Periods

Retrograde Station to Direct Station	Average % Change	1.14%
Retrograde Station to Retrograde Return	Average % Change	0.51%
Direct Station to Retrograde Return	Average % Change	-0.61%

Mercury Going Retrograde in Fire Signs

1 Day after Retrograde Station	Likelihood of Higher Prices	52.2%
14 Days after Retrograde Station	Likelihood of Higher Prices	56.5%
7 Days after Direct Station	Likelihood of Higher Prices	75.0%

Mercury Going Retrograde in Earth Signs

1 Day after Retrograde Station	Likelihood of Higher Prices	56.0%
14 Days after Retrograde Station	Likelihood of Higher Prices	60.0%
7 Days after Direct Station	Likelihood of Higher Prices	52.0%

Mercury Going Retrograde in Air Signs

1 Day after Retrograde Station	Likelihood of Higher Prices	69.2%
14 Days after Retrograde Station	Likelihood of Higher Prices	53.8%
7 Days after Direct Station	Likelihood of Higher Prices	45.8%

Mercury Going Retrograde in Water Signs

1 Day after Retrograde Station	Likelihood of Higher Prices	38.9%
14 Days after Retrograde Station	Likelihood of Higher Prices	33.3%
7 Days after Direct Station	Likelihood of Higher Prices	50.0%

Procter & Gamble Company

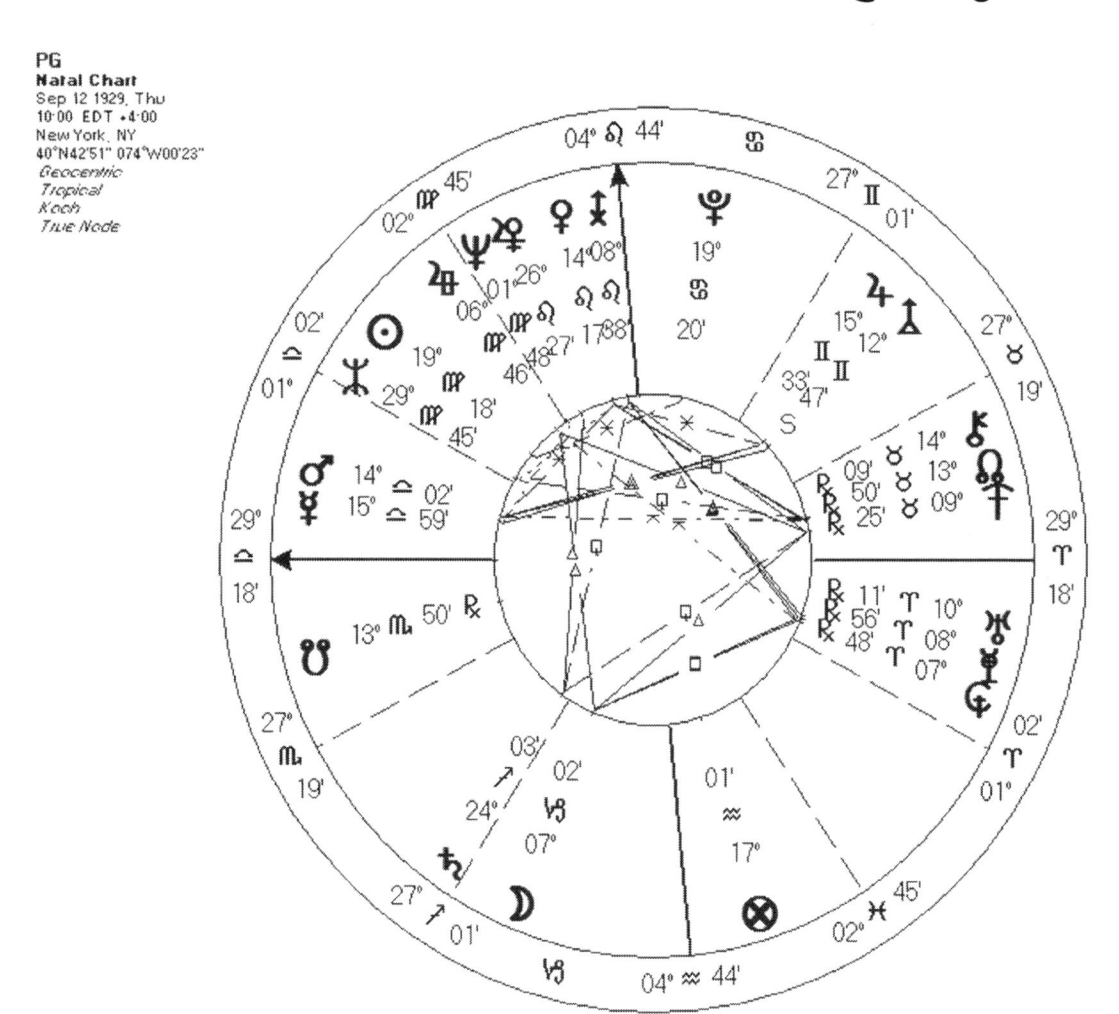

PG
Natal Chart
Sep 12 1929, Thu
10:00 EDT +4:00
New York, NY
40°N42'51" 074°W00'23"
Geocentric
Tropical
Koch
True Node

The PG First-Trade horoscope has Mercury Epimetheus Direct in Libra.

Secondary progressed First-Trade Mercury went into retrograde motion on November 18, 1942, returning to direct motion on May 1, 1964. The PG secondary progressed First-Trade Mercury will go retrograde again on March 8, 2052. It will then return to direct motion on November 6, 2072.

Historically PG has shown some of its greatest price volatility when Mercury goes retrograde in Gemini. When that happens the stock tends to be bullish during the retrograde phase, but then sells off after the direct station.

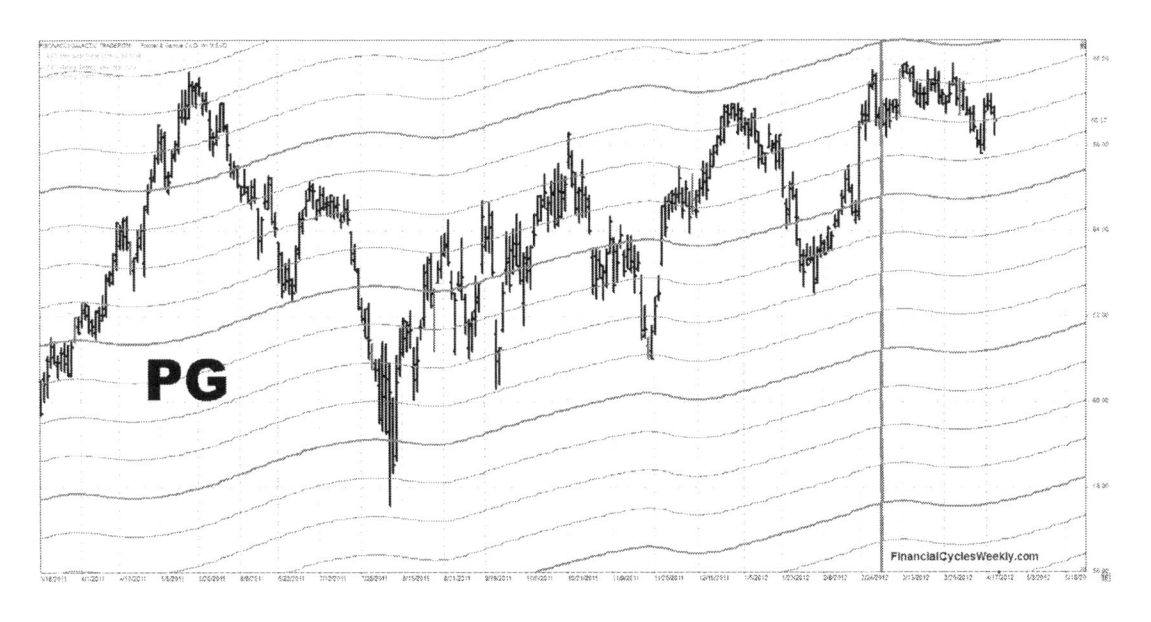

Back-Tested Historical Mercury Retrograde Performance

All Mercury Retrograde Periods

Retrograde Station to Direct Station	Average % Change	0.89%
Retrograde Station to Retrograde Return	Average % Change	1.14%
Direct Station to Retrograde Return	Average % Change	0.25%

Mercury Going Retrograde in Fire Signs

1 Day after Retrograde Station	Likelihood of Higher Prices	45.5%
14 Days after Retrograde Station	Likelihood of Higher Prices	60.6%
7 Days after Direct Station	Likelihood of Higher Prices	54.3%

Mercury Going Retrograde in Earth Signs

1 Day after Retrograde Station	Likelihood of Higher Prices	48.6%
14 Days after Retrograde Station	Likelihood of Higher Prices	60.0%
7 Days after Direct Station	Likelihood of Higher Prices	41.2%

Mercury Going Retrograde in Air Signs

1 Day after Retrograde Station	Likelihood of Higher Prices	53.1%
14 Days after Retrograde Station	Likelihood of Higher Prices	56.3%
7 Days after Direct Station	Likelihood of Higher Prices	65.6%

Mercury Going Retrograde in Water Signs

1 Day after Retrograde Station	Likelihood of Higher Prices	72.4%
14 Days after Retrograde Station	Likelihood of Higher Prices	41.4%
7 Days after Direct Station	Likelihood of Higher Prices	43.3%

Travelers Companies Inc.

TRV
Natal Chart
May 11 1988, Wed
09:30 EDT +4:00
New York, NY
40°N42'51" 074°W00'23"
Geocentric
Tropical
Koch
True Node

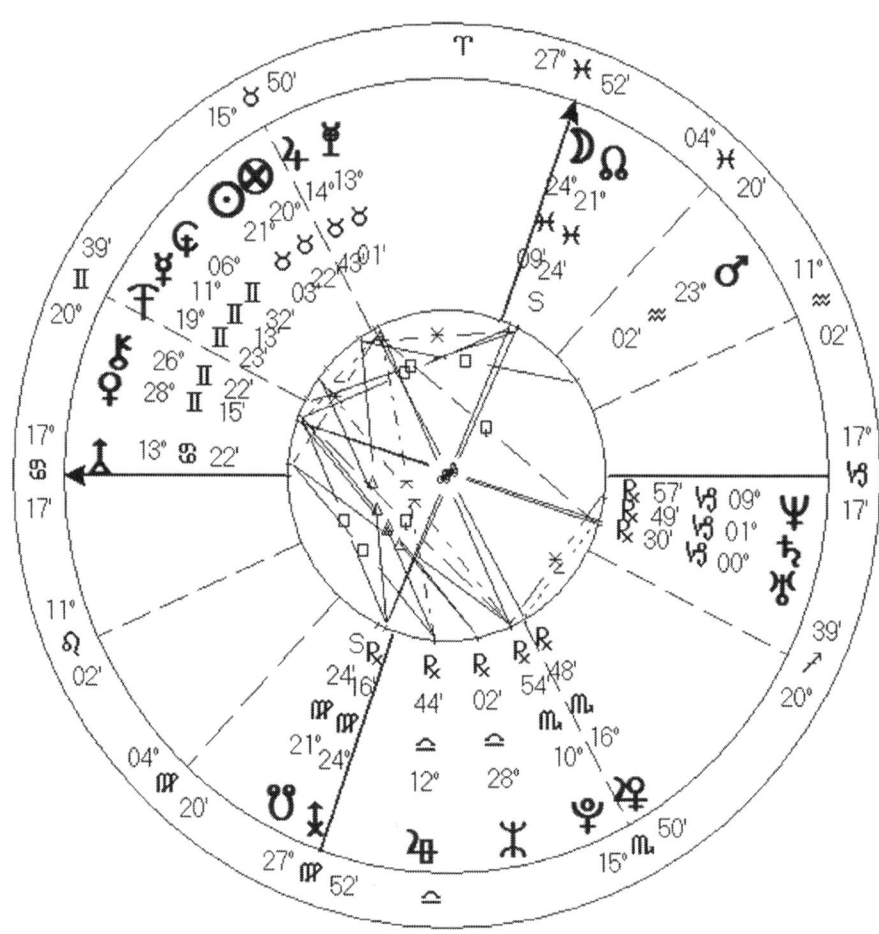

The TRV First-Trade horoscope has Mercury Epimetheus Direct in Gemini.

Secondary progressed First-Trade Mercury went into retrograde motion on September 28, 2008. It will return to direct motion on September 27, 2032.

TRV shows some of its greatest price volatility when Mercury goes retrograde in Gemini. Trading in the stock tends to be bullish during the retrograde phase, but when Mercury goes back to direct motion TRV takes on a slightly bearish bias which intensifies in the weeks following the direct station.

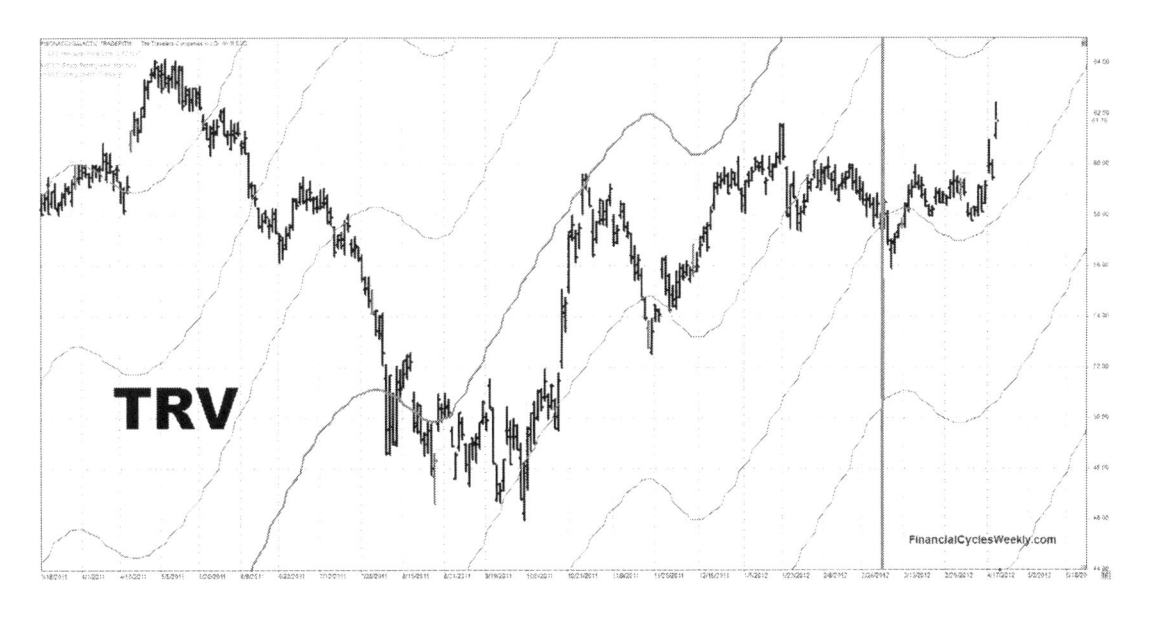

Back-Tested Historical Mercury Retrograde Performance

All Mercury Retrograde Periods

Retrograde Station to Direct Station	Average % Change	-0.41%
Retrograde Station to Retrograde Return	Average % Change	0.07%
Direct Station to Retrograde Return	Average % Change	0.39%

Mercury Going Retrograde in Fire Signs

1 Day after Retrograde Station	Likelihood of Higher Prices	44.4%
14 Days after Retrograde Station	Likelihood of Higher Prices	61.1%
7 Days after Direct Station	Likelihood of Higher Prices	55.0%

Mercury Going Retrograde in Earth Signs

1 Day after Retrograde Station	Likelihood of Higher Prices	38.1%
14 Days after Retrograde Station	Likelihood of Higher Prices	52.4%
7 Days after Direct Station	Likelihood of Higher Prices	68.2%

Mercury Going Retrograde in Air Signs

1 Day after Retrograde Station	Likelihood of Higher Prices	59.1%
14 Days after Retrograde Station	Likelihood of Higher Prices	59.1%
7 Days after Direct Station	Likelihood of Higher Prices	47.6%

Mercury Going Retrograde in Water Signs

1 Day after Retrograde Station	Likelihood of Higher Prices	61.1%
14 Days after Retrograde Station	Likelihood of Higher Prices	44.4%
7 Days after Direct Station	Likelihood of Higher Prices	50.0%

United Technologies Corporation

UTX
Natal Chart
Sep 5 1934, Wed
10:00 EDT +4:00
New York, NY
40°N42'51" 074°W00'23"
Geocentric
Tropical
Koch
True Node

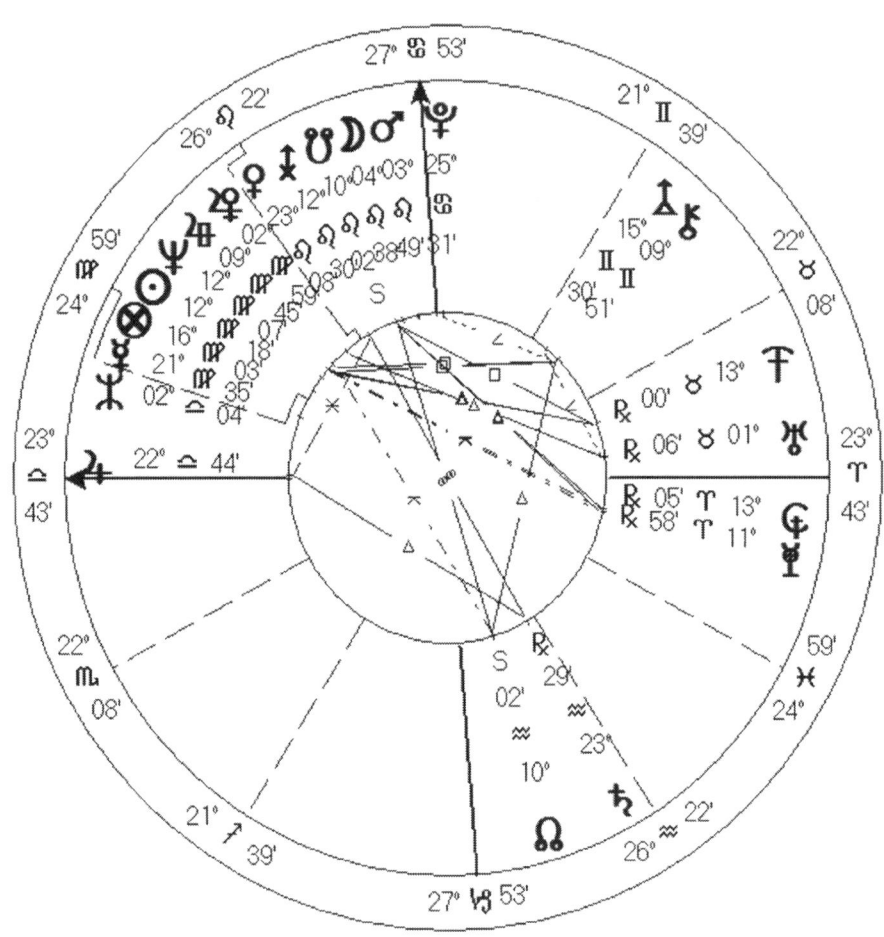

The UTX First-Trade horoscope has Mercury Epimetheus Direct in Virgo.

Secondary progressed First-Trade Mercury went into retrograde motion on December 16, 1981, resuming direct motion on May 5, 2002. The UTX secondary progressed First-Trade Mercury will again go retrograde on May 26, 2090. It will then return to direct motion on February 28, 2112.

UTX tends to display some of its greatest price volatility when Mercury goes retrograde in Virgo. It typically increases in price throughout the retrograde phase, but then shows a decidedly bearish bias following the direct station.

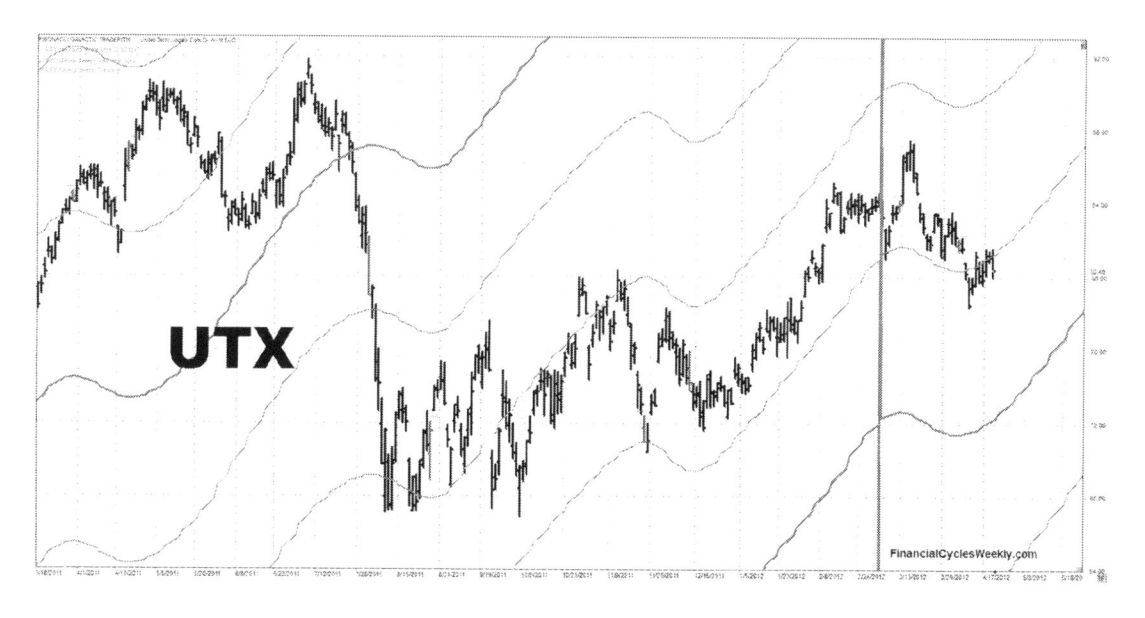

Back-Tested Historical Mercury Retrograde Performance

All Mercury Retrograde Periods

Retrograde Station to Direct Station	Average % Change	0.20%
Retrograde Station to Retrograde Return	Average % Change	-0.09%
Direct Station to Retrograde Return	Average % Change	-0.24%

Mercury Going Retrograde in Fire Signs

1 Day after Retrograde Station	Likelihood of Higher Prices	57.6%
14 Days after Retrograde Station	Likelihood of Higher Prices	51.5%
7 Days after Direct Station	Likelihood of Higher Prices	51.4%

Mercury Going Retrograde in Earth Signs

1 Day after Retrograde Station	Likelihood of Higher Prices	51.4%
14 Days after Retrograde Station	Likelihood of Higher Prices	62.9%
7 Days after Direct Station	Likelihood of Higher Prices	47.1%

Mercury Going Retrograde in Air Signs

1 Day after Retrograde Station	Likelihood of Higher Prices	50.0%
14 Days after Retrograde Station	Likelihood of Higher Prices	50.0%
7 Days after Direct Station	Likelihood of Higher Prices	53.1%

Mercury Going Retrograde in Water Signs

1 Day after Retrograde Station	Likelihood of Higher Prices	48.3%
14 Days after Retrograde Station	Likelihood of Higher Prices	44.8%
7 Days after Direct Station	Likelihood of Higher Prices	53.3%

Verizon Communications Inc.

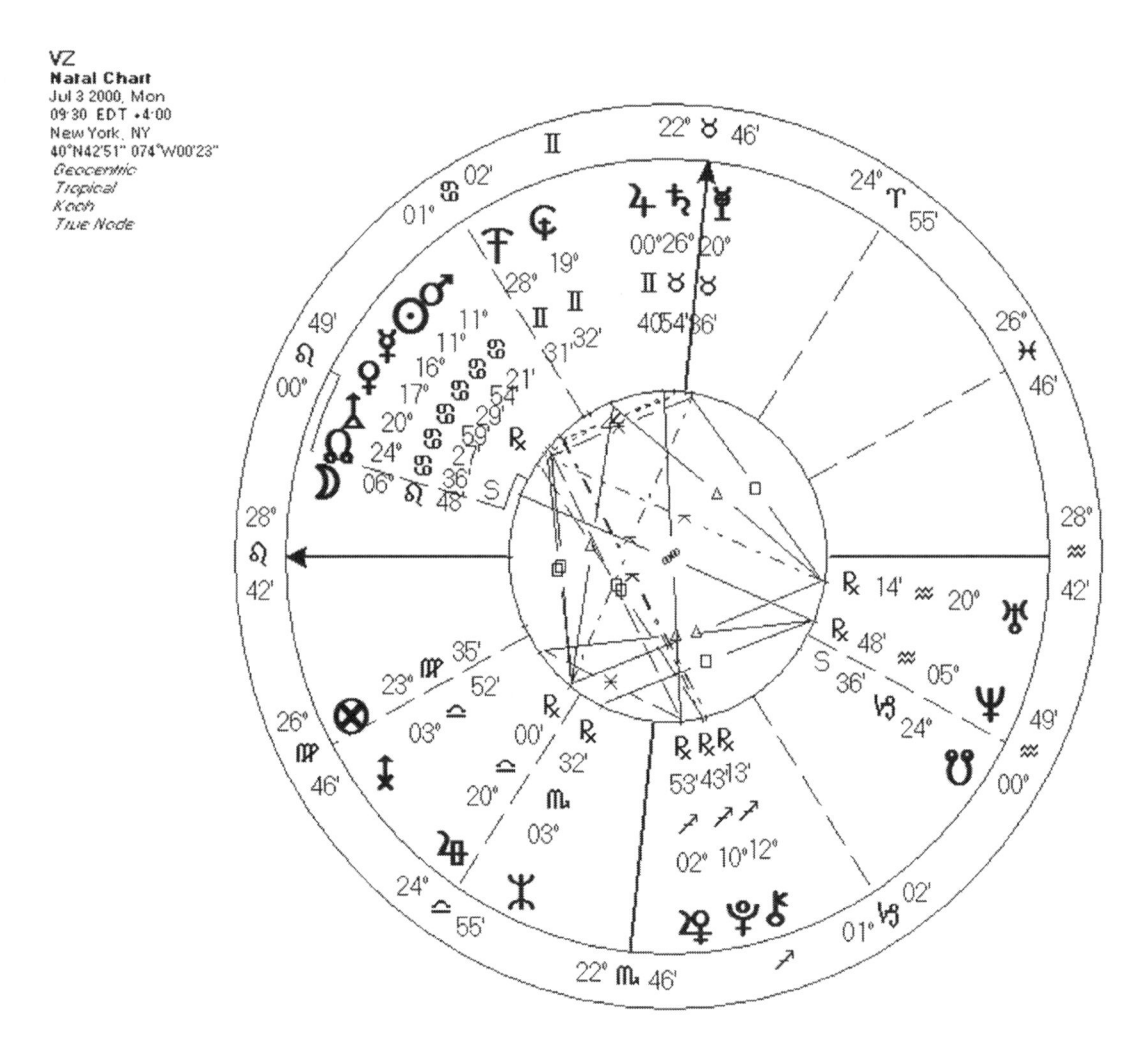

The VZ First-Trade horoscope has Mercury Epimetheus Retrograde in Cancer.

Secondary progressed First-Trade Mercury will go into direct motion on July 1, 2014.

The trading action for VZ tends to be solidly bullish when Mercury goes retrograde in Capricorn, with rising prices for the stock during both the retrograde phase and the direct phase. VZ shows some of its greatest price volatility when Mercury goes retrograde in Aries or Gemini. When Mercury goes retrograde in Aries, the stock typically sells off during the retrograde phase, but then slowly picks up more bullish characteristics after the direct station. When Mercury goes retrograde in Gemini, however, the price of VZ usually goes up during the retrograde phase but then slowly reverses to the downside following the direct station.

Back-Tested Historical Mercury Retrograde Performance

All Mercury Retrograde Periods

Retrograde Station to Direct Station	Average % Change	-1.10%
Retrograde Station to Retrograde Return	Average % Change	-0.08%
Direct Station to Retrograde Return	Average % Change	0.05%

Mercury Going Retrograde in Fire Signs

1 Day after Retrograde Station	Likelihood of Higher Prices	34.8%
14 Days after Retrograde Station	Likelihood of Higher Prices	47.8%
7 Days after Direct Station	Likelihood of Higher Prices	58.3%

Mercury Going Retrograde in Earth Signs

1 Day after Retrograde Station	Likelihood of Higher Prices	54.2%
14 Days after Retrograde Station	Likelihood of Higher Prices	62.5%
7 Days after Direct Station	Likelihood of Higher Prices	68.2%

Mercury Going Retrograde in Air Signs

1 Day after Retrograde Station	Likelihood of Higher Prices	50.0%
14 Days after Retrograde Station	Likelihood of Higher Prices	50.0%
7 Days after Direct Station	Likelihood of Higher Prices	47.6%

Mercury Going Retrograde in Water Signs

1 Day after Retrograde Station	Likelihood of Higher Prices	38.9%
14 Days after Retrograde Station	Likelihood of Higher Prices	38.9%
7 Days after Direct Station	Likelihood of Higher Prices	50.0%

Wal-Mart Stores Inc.

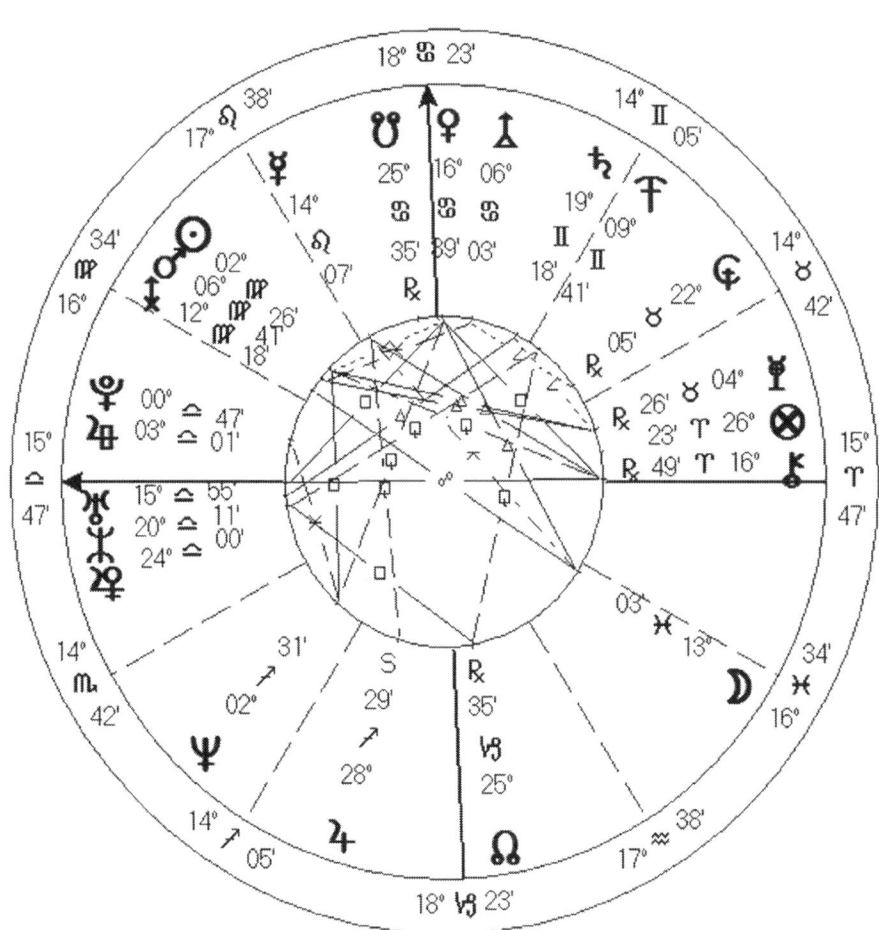

The WMT First-Trade horoscope has Mercury Prometheus Direct in Leo.

Secondary progressed First-Trade Mercury will go into retrograde motion on December 1, 2054. It will return to direct motion on September 30, 2074.

The trading patterns for WMT during Mercury Retrograde periods are fairly inconsistent, with the stock typically failing to resolve itself into clearly defined trends. When Mercury goes retrograde in Libra, however, WMT is typically bearish throughout the entire period, with falling prices during both the retrograde and direct phases.

Back-Tested Historical Mercury Retrograde Performance

All Mercury Retrograde Periods

Retrograde Station to Direct Station	Average % Change	0.97%
Retrograde Station to Retrograde Return	Average % Change	1.50%
Direct Station to Retrograde Return	Average % Change	0.56%

Mercury Going Retrograde in Fire Signs

1 Day after Retrograde Station	Likelihood of Higher Prices	60.0%
14 Days after Retrograde Station	Likelihood of Higher Prices	63.3%
7 Days after Direct Station	Likelihood of Higher Prices	55.2%

Mercury Going Retrograde in Earth Signs

1 Day after Retrograde Station	Likelihood of Higher Prices	53.3%
14 Days after Retrograde Station	Likelihood of Higher Prices	53.3%
7 Days after Direct Station	Likelihood of Higher Prices	48.4%

Mercury Going Retrograde in Air Signs

1 Day after Retrograde Station	Likelihood of Higher Prices	56.3%
14 Days after Retrograde Station	Likelihood of Higher Prices	62.5%
7 Days after Direct Station	Likelihood of Higher Prices	50.0%

Mercury Going Retrograde in Water Signs

1 Day after Retrograde Station	Likelihood of Higher Prices	58.6%
14 Days after Retrograde Station	Likelihood of Higher Prices	44.8%
7 Days after Direct Station	Likelihood of Higher Prices	60.0%

The Walt Disney Company

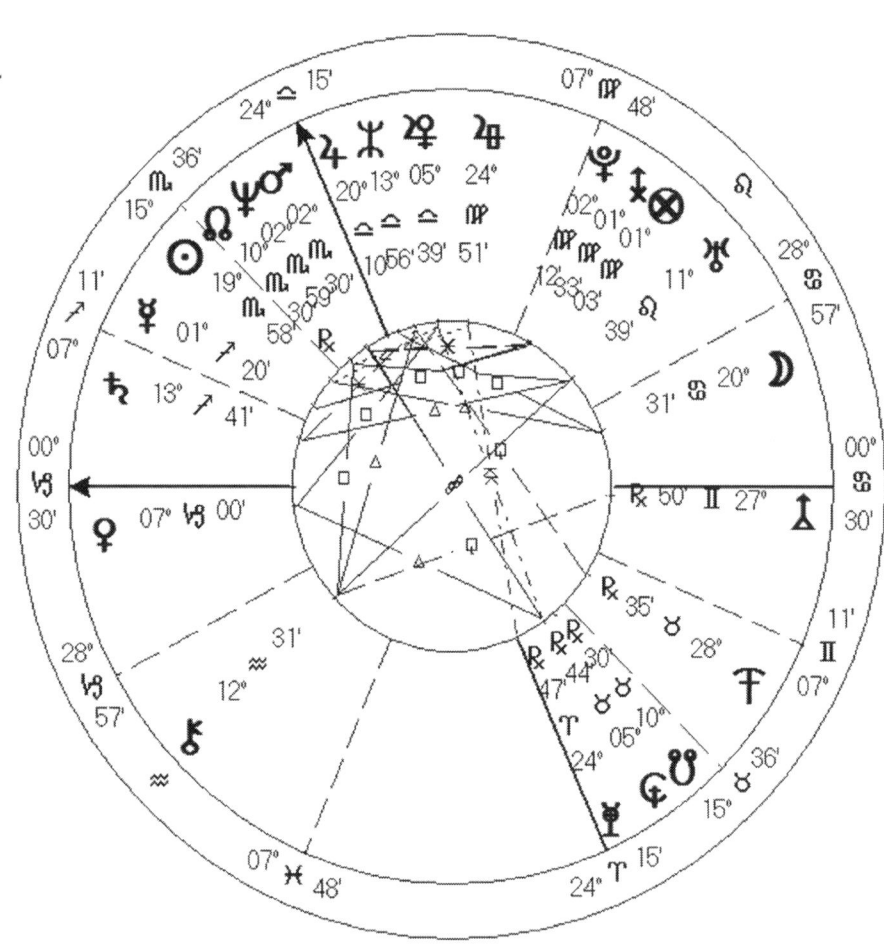

DIS
Natal Chart
Nov 12 1957, Tue
10:00 EST +5:00
New York, NY
40°N42'51" 074°W00'23"
Geocentric
Tropical
Koch
True Node

The DIS First-Trade horoscope has Mercury Epimetheus Direct in Sagittarius.

Secondary progressed First-Trade Mercury went into retrograde motion on September 14, 1991. It retu;rned to direct motion on August 7, 2011.

DIS shows some of its greatest price volatility when Mercury goes retrograde in Leo or Scorpio. DIS typically has a short-term bearish reaction with a retrograde station in Leo, but moves into bullishness just before and after the direct station, only to become very bearish after that. There's a similar pattern with the Scorpio retrograde, but the bearishness resumes just prior to the direct station. This stock is also bearish when Mercury goes retrograde in Cancer or Libra, and is generally bullish with retrogrades in Sagittarius or Pisces, except for pull-backs around the direct stations.

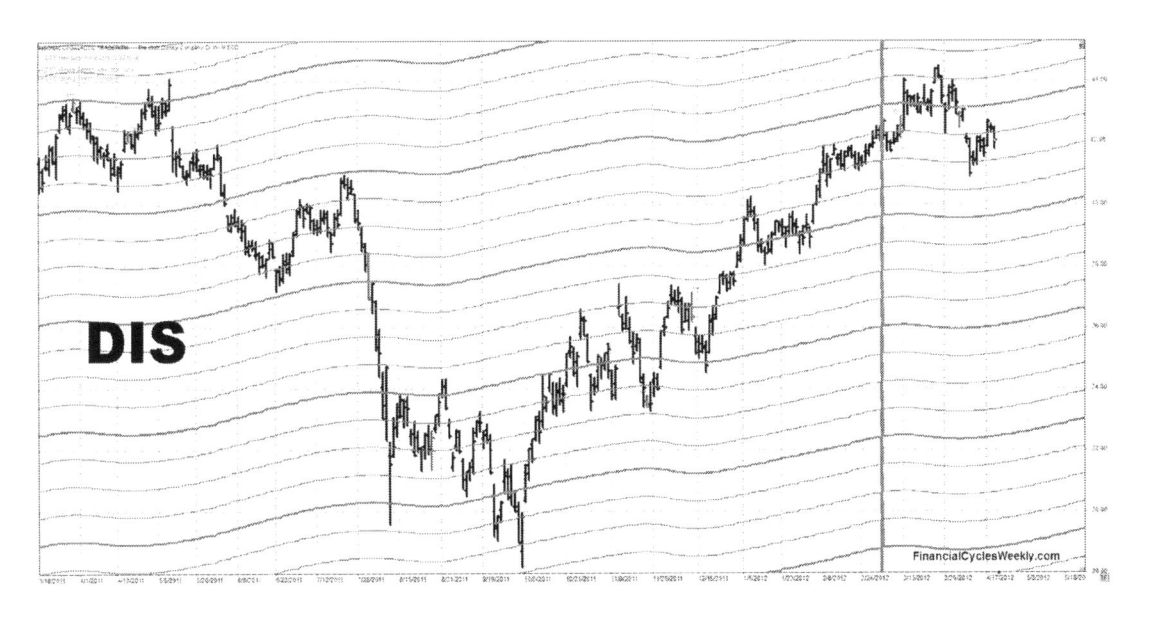

Back-Tested Historical Mercury Retrograde Performance

All Mercury Retrograde Periods

Retrograde Station to Direct Station	Average % Change	0.59%
Retrograde Station to Retrograde Return	Average % Change	0.55%
Direct Station to Retrograde Return	Average % Change	0.04%

Mercury Going Retrograde in Fire Signs

1 Day after Retrograde Station	Likelihood of Higher Prices	44.7%
14 Days after Retrograde Station	Likelihood of Higher Prices	65.8%
7 Days after Direct Station	Likelihood of Higher Prices	43.6%

Mercury Going Retrograde in Earth Signs

1 Day after Retrograde Station	Likelihood of Higher Prices	37.5%
14 Days after Retrograde Station	Likelihood of Higher Prices	57.5%
7 Days after Direct Station	Likelihood of Higher Prices	51.2%

Mercury Going Retrograde in Air Signs

1 Day after Retrograde Station	Likelihood of Higher Prices	42.5%
14 Days after Retrograde Station	Likelihood of Higher Prices	52.5%
7 Days after Direct Station	Likelihood of Higher Prices	43.6%

Mercury Going Retrograde in Water Signs

1 Day after Retrograde Station	Likelihood of Higher Prices	45.7%
14 Days after Retrograde Station	Likelihood of Higher Prices	54.3%
7 Days after Direct Station	Likelihood of Higher Prices	45.7%

Emerald Tablet Trades

We began our study of Mercury in the markets in this book with some background information on Mercury's role in mythology and the esoteric tradition. Our aim in doing so was to acknowledge the fact that there's much more to astro-trading than improving our forecasting by back-testing the correlations of planetary cycles to market movements and fine-tuning our timing by coordinating our trades with current planetary dynamics.

But the esoteric lore associated with Mercury is more than just a means of enriching our perspectives and of adding a salutary dose of humility to our approach to the cosmic patterns that are revealed in the markets. It's not only a way of adding the power of whole-brain thinking to our astro-trading efforts. It also offers us some very pragmatic guidelines that we can apply to our trading quite profitably.

The Emerald Tablet offers us a good example. When we first read the text of this arcane document, we may be inspired by the language and the poetry. We may be intrigued by its associations with the ancient world. Or we may just be confused. But if we study the Emerald Tablet from a more literal point of view, we can discover some specific ideas that can help us identify unique trading opportunities.

As we've already noted, this text was held in very high regard by alchemists throughout the ages. The alchemists, of course, focused most of their attention on transmuting base substances into gold. And as the Emerald Tablet itself states, the text is all about "the work of the Sun".

In both the alchemical and astrological traditions, the Sun and gold were considered equivalent. Gold was the specific metal of the Sun, and anyone seeking gold was in reality performing "the work of the Sun". Most of today's astro-traders don't actually spend much time stoking fires in alchemical furnaces, but like the alchemists of previous centuries they have a golden opportunity. In today's economic context gold can be acquired as the physical metal, or as a trade in futures, options, or ETFs. Each approach offers its own unique advantages and carries its own unique risks, but in every case trading in gold today is just as much "the work of the Sun" as the labors of the alchemists were in the ancient world.

So what advice can this ancient wisdom provide for us if we're trading gold? As the Emerald Tablet informs us, when we perform the work of the Sun we need to pay attention to the fact that "that which is above is like that which is below, and that which is below

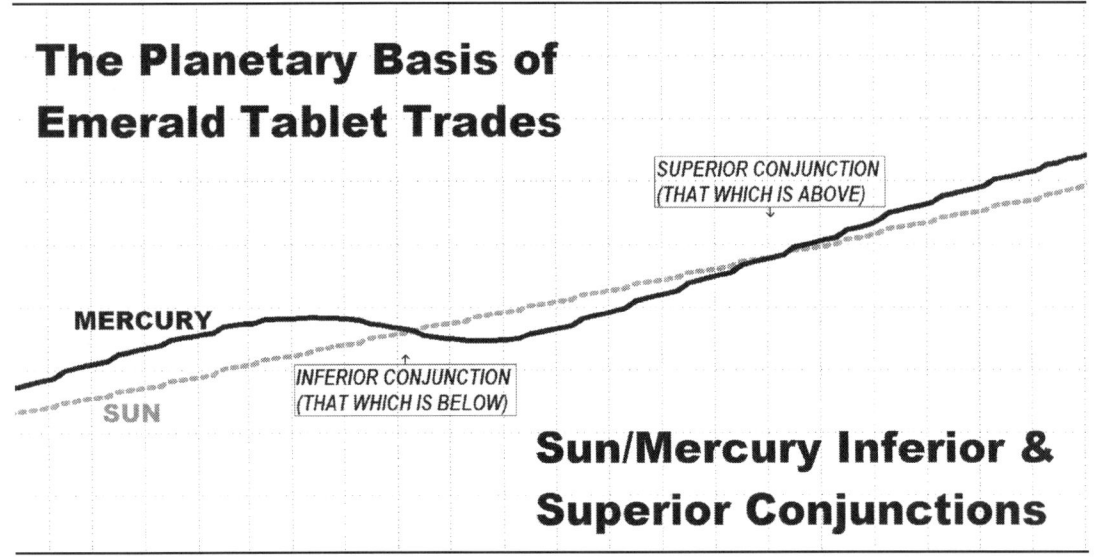

The Planetary Basis of Emerald Tablet Trades

SUPERIOR CONJUNCTION (THAT WHICH IS ABOVE)

MERCURY

INFERIOR CONJUNCTION (THAT WHICH IS BELOW)

SUN

Sun/Mercury Inferior & Superior Conjunctions

is like that which is above." In other words, we can discover potentially profitable trading opportunities when we examine gold at the times of the superior and inferior conjunctions of Mercury and the Sun.

The most obvious correlation is in the price of gold. In many cases, we will find that the price of gold at the time of an inferior conjunction is repeated at the time of the next superior conjunction, regardless of what happens to the price in the interim. This little bit of knowledge can help us take potentially profitable positions in the yellow metal, because it increases the likelihood that our trade will reach a particular price target at a specific time in the future.

In applying this technique, however, we don't try to match the inferior-conjunction price exactly. We aren't concerned with timing the Sun/Mercury conjunctions to the minute, especially since they sometimes occur outside the range of normal trading hours. Instead we look at the daily price range of gold on the trading day nearest the inferior conjunction, and then look for the price range on the day nearest the superior conjunction to overlap, but not necessarily duplicate, that price range. When we find a notable divergence from these price ranges during the interim period, we have a opportunity to enter a trade-- the greater the divergence is, the more potential profits the trade will offer us.

To help clarify this concept a little more, here are a few examples of this Emerald Tablet trading technique in action. In order to provide a uniform data source for the various illustrations featured here, the charts are based on daily price bars for the World Gold Index (XGLD), the Deutsche Bank AG exchange-traded fund indexed to the price of the physical metal.

September 27 2002

The price of Gold had been moving up since shortly after the Mercury retrograde station on September 13, 2002, but just before the Sun/Mercury inferior conjunction Gold sold off for a couple of trading sessions. The inferior conjunction itself brought a trading day with the price of Gold ranging from a low of 319.00 to a high of 321.20, with the session ending at 319.70.

Trading in Gold stayed fairly congested for more than a week after the inferior conjunction, but the price soon began to lose ground, taking Gold to a low of 309.10 on October 24, 2002. After that Gold moved into an uptrend until the Sun/Mercury superior conjunction.

The superior conjunction came on November 13, 2002, with the day's trading forming a bearish outside bar that put an abrupt end to a three-week rally. On the date of the superior conjunction Gold traded between a low of 317.00 and a high of 325.40, finishing the session at 318.90, less than a point lower than its closing price at the inferior conjunction.

July 18 2006

When the Sun/Mercury inferior conjunction occurred on July 18, 2006, Gold had just hit an important trading top at 676.10. Trading on July 18 took Gold sharply lower, falling from an intraday high of 654.50 to a low of 626.50 and a close at 631.60.

Gold found a bottom at 601.60 on July 24, 2006, moved back to a high at 656.23 on August 2, 2006, and then sold off into more congested trading and a low of 606.70 on August 29, 2006.

It was two days later, on August 31, 2006, that there was a superior Sun/Mercury conjunction, with Gold trading between 618.80 and 627.20 and closing at 626.70, back in the same price range that had been defined by the inferior station five weeks earlier.

November 8 2006

Trading in Gold had just moved into a period of congestion when there was a Sun/Mercury inferior conjunction on November 8, 2006. That trading day saw a low for Gold at 612.80 and a high at 626.10. The closing price for the day's trading was 615.60.

After the inferior conjunction, the trading action resolved itself into a modest wave down, with Gold finding a short-term bottom at 614.20 on November 17, 2006. From that point a solid uptrend was in place until December 1, 2006, with Gold hitting an intraday high of 649.80.

A more sustained downward move brought Gold to a low of 611.40 on December 18, 2006, but a rebound rally during the next couple of weeks brought the yellow metal back to a trading high of 645.00 on January 3, 2007. A lower close that day at 626.80 pushed Gold back down, with trading at the superior conjunction on January 5, 2007 ranging from a low of 601.60 to a high of 626.20. That was just one-tenth of a point away from the high from the inferior conjunction; Gold closed that day at 607.12.

May 18 2009

Gold had been in a two-week uptrend prior to the Sun/Mercury inferior conjunction on May 18, 2009, which saw the metal trade between a low of 915.20 and a high of 934.10, with a daily close at 921.70.

The uptrend continued until June 3, 2009, when Gold hit an intraday high of 992.10. The trend reversed at that point, however, sending Gold prices lower until the metal found support in the price zone defined by the Sun/Mercury inferior conjunction.

On July 13, 2009, as the superior conjunction took place, Gold traded between a low of 907.40 and a high of 923.40, with a daily close at 920.80

January 4 2010

The trading range for Gold on January 4, 2010, with the Sun/Mercury inferior conjunction, brought a low of 1093.90 and a high of 1124.60, with a daily close at 1121.80.

The Gold Index climbed to a high of 1163.00 on January 11, 2010, and dropped to a low of 1044.50 on February 5, 2010. This was followed by a rally up to 1145.80 on March 3, 2010.

While that rally high took Gold well above the price range that accompanied the inferior conjunction on January 4, the Emerald Tablet correlation held up nicely in this particular case, pulling the price of Gold back down in the days prior to the Sun/Mercury superior conjunction. When that conjunction came on March 12, 2010, Gold's trading range had returned to the inferior conjunction zone, with a low of 1097.30, a high of 1119.50, and a daily close of 1102.00.

December 2, 2011

When Mercury and the Sun met in an inferior conjunction on December 2, 2011 the daily trading range for the Gold Index was 1741.70 to 1767.10, with a close at 1751.30.

Following the conjunction Gold spent the rest of December in selling mode, hitting an intraday low of 1523.90 on December 29, 2011. After that, though, the yellow metal rallied again. The trading day at the superior conjunction, February 7, 2012, saw a price range which returned to the levels of the inferior conjunction, with an intraday low of 1712.60, a high of 1752.60, and a close at 1748.40.

Note especially the size of the price swings in this example. An astro-trader entering a long position following Gold's greatest negative excursion in December would have been in a position to collect a 14.7% profit holding Gold until the superior conjunction and selling at that point.

Trading Opportunities

While these example charts clearly demonstrate the power and precision of the Emerald Tablet trading approach, it's important to keep a few key notions in mind. After all, the Emerald Tablet system is certainly not the Holy Grail of astro-trading, guaranteeing infallible profits in any market under any circumstances.

First of all, remember that this trading technique has only been tested with "the work of the Sun" in trading Gold. While it may have validity with other markets as well, that applicability hasn't been tested or verified. If you'd like to try it with different trading opportunities, go right ahead. Just be sure to back-test it thoroughly with the market you are considering trading; don't put money at risk with this technique unless you're comfortable with the probabilities of success that back-testing reveals.

Secondly, the Emerald Tablet technique, like any other trading system, doesn't generate accurate signals 100% of the time. No system does. That's why it's vital to stay highly focused on disciplined money management if you're trading with the Emerald Tablet approach. If you are managing your risk appropriately with well-structured stop loss orders or hedging positions, you're certain to find this "work of the Sun" much more rewarding.

Finally, keep in mind the fact that the Emerald Tablet technique can only be applied on a limited basis. It's structured in the recurring patterns of inferior and superior conjunctions of Mercury with the Sun, and there are typically only three superior conjunctions during the course of a year. This is definitely not an everyday, bread-and-butter technique for frequent trading, but it does offer regular opportunities which are worth keeping an eye on.

Use the listing that follows to identify opportunities for Emerald Tablet trades. It lists the date and time of day for each conjunction, as well as the position in the zodiac where the conjunction takes place. The dates and times are calculated for Greenwich Mean Time throughout.

Mercury/Sun Conjunctions

Date	Time	Position	Type
Feb 7 2012	09:02:28	17°Aq59'	Superior Conjunction
Mar 21 2012	19:20:31	01°Ar34'	Inferior Conjunction
May 27 2012	12:19:19	06°Ge34'	Superior Conjunction
Jul 28 2012	20:57:15	06°Le07'	Inferior Conjunction
Sep 10 2012	13:43:47	18°Vi12'	Superior Conjunction
Nov 17 2012	15:46:37	25°Sc42'	Inferior Conjunction

Jan 18 2013	08:56:10	28°Cp26'	Superior Conjunction
Mar 4 2013	12:58:01	14°Pi06'	Inferior Conjunction
May 11 2013	22:09:57	21°Ta19'	Superior Conjunction
Jul 9 2013	19:41:07	17°Cn42'	Inferior Conjunction
Aug 24 2013	21:56:02	01°Vi50'	Superior Conjunction
Nov 1 2013	20:19:17	09°Sc34'	Inferior Conjunction
Dec 29 2013	06:27:28	07°Cp41'	Superior Conjunction
Feb 15 2014	20:21:34	27°Aq04'	Inferior Conjunction
Apr 26 2014	04:27:14	05°Ta49'	Superior Conjunction
Jun 19 2014	23:50:12	28°Ge34'	Inferior Conjunction
Aug 8 2014	17:21:01	16°Le03'	Superior Conjunction
Oct 16 2014	21:39:46	23°Li24'	Inferior Conjunction
Dec 8 2014	09:51:10	16°Sg13'	Superior Conjunction
Jan 30 2015	13:45:15	10°Aq20'	Inferior Conjunction
Apr 10 2015	05:00:06	19°Ar58'	Superior Conjunction
May 30 2015	17:55:46	08°Ge58'	Inferior Conjunction
Jul 23 2015	20:23:30	00°Le37'	Superior Conjunction
Sep 30 2015	15:38:02	07°Li07'	Inferior Conjunction
Nov 17 2015	14:52:54	24°Sc55'	Superior Conjunction
Jan 14 2016	14:04:33	23°Cp49'	Inferior Conjunction
Mar 23 2016	20:10:54	03°Ar37'	Superior Conjunction
May 9 2016	16:12:02	19°Ta25'	Inferior Conjunction
Jul 7 2016	04:23:47	15°Cn27'	Superior Conjunction
Sep 13 2016	00:39:58	20°Vi37'	Inferior Conjunction
Oct 27 2016	17:16:21	04°Sc40'	Superior Conjunction
Dec 28 2016	18:47:16	07°Cp28'	Inferior Conjunction
Mar 7 2017	00:28:39	16°Pi37'	Superior Conjunction
Apr 20 2017	06:53:59	00°Ta20'	Inferior Conjunction
Jun 21 2017	15:14:01	00°Cn23'	Superior Conjunction
Aug 26 2017	21:42:08	03°Vi47'	Inferior Conjunction
Oct 8 2017	21:53:31	15°Li45'	Superior Conjunction
Dec 13 2017	01:48:34	21°Sg14'	Inferior Conjunction
Feb 17 2018	12:27:09	28°Aq47'	Superior Conjunction
Apr 1 2018	18:52:54	11°Ar56'	Inferior Conjunction
Jun 6 2018	03:01:40	15°Ge20'	Superior Conjunction

Aug 9 2018	03:05:50	16°Le27'	Inferior Conjunction
Sep 21 2018	02:51:55	28°Vi02'	Superior Conjunction
Nov 27 2018	09:14:46	05°Sg03'	Inferior Conjunction
Jan 30 2019	02:51:33	09°Aq54'	Superior Conjunction
Mar 15 2019	01:47:24	24°Pi11'	Inferior Conjunction
May 21 2019	14:06:44	00°Ge12'	Superior Conjunction
Jul 21 2019	13:33:51	28°Cn28'	Inferior Conjunction
Sep 4 2019	02:39:59	11°Vi15'	Superior Conjunction
Nov 11 2019	15:21:35	18°Sc55'	Inferior Conjunction
Jan 10 2020	15:19:15	19°Cp49'	Superior Conjunction
Feb 26 2020	01:44:36	06°Pi55'	Inferior Conjunction
May 4 2020	22:41:21	14°Ta52'	Superior Conjunction
Jul 1 2020	03:52:28	09°Cn44'	Inferior Conjunction
Aug 17 2020	16:07:10	25°Le09'	Superior Conjunction
Oct 25 2020	18:22:57	02°Sc47'	Inferior Conjunction
Dec 20 2020	03:25:34	28°Sg42'	Superior Conjunction
Feb 8 2021	13:47:41	20°Aq01'	Inferior Conjunction
Apr 19 2021	01:49:21	29°Ar14'	Superior Conjunction
Jun 11 2021	01:12:43	20°Ge21'	Inferior Conjunction
Aug 1 2021	14:07:21	09°Le32'	Superior Conjunction
Oct 9 2021	16:18:03	16°Li35'	Inferior Conjunction
Nov 29 2021	04:39:14	07°Sg10'	Superior Conjunction
Jan 23 2022	10:27:56	03°Aq22'	Inferior Conjunction
Apr 2 2022	23:10:36	13°Ar11'	Superior Conjunction
May 21 2022	19:17:47	00°Ge43'	Inferior Conjunction
Jul 16 2022	19:37:28	24°Cn15'	Superior Conjunction
Sep 23 2022	06:49:40	00°Li14'	Inferior Conjunction
Nov 8 2022	16:42:33	16°Sc15'	Superior Conjunction
Jan 7 2023	12:56:45	16°Cp56'	Inferior Conjunction
Mar 17 2023	10:44:23	26°Pi34'	Superior Conjunction
May 1 2023	23:27:22	11°Ta19'	Inferior Conjunction
Jul 1 2023	05:05:30	09°Cn08'	Superior Conjunction
Sep 6 2023	11:08:54	13°Vi36'	Inferior Conjunction
Oct 20 2023	05:37:48	26°Li34'	Superior Conjunction
Dec 22 2023	18:53:47	00°Cp39'	Inferior Conjunction

Feb 28 2024	08:42:37	09°Pi14'	Superior Conjunction
Apr 11 2024	23:02:41	22°Ar32'	Inferior Conjunction
Jun 14 2024	16:32:17	24°Ge06'	Superior Conjunction
Aug 19 2024	01:57:48	26°Le35'	Inferior Conjunction
Sep 30 2024	21:09:06	08°Li11'	Superior Conjunction
Dec 6 2024	02:17:33	14°Sg27'	Inferior Conjunction
Feb 9 2025	12:07:49	20°Aq59'	Superior Conjunction
Mar 24 2025	19:48:04	04°Ar24'	Inferior Conjunction
May 30 2025	04:12:29	09°Ge01'	Superior Conjunction
Jul 31 2025	23:41:01	09°Le00'	Inferior Conjunction
Sep 13 2025	10:51:30	20°Vi54'	Superior Conjunction
Nov 20 2025	09:22:58	28°Sc18'	Inferior Conjunction
Jan 21 2026	15:48:35	01°Aq36'	Superior Conjunction
Mar 7 2026	11:01:25	16°Pi52'	Inferior Conjunction
May 14 2026	14:24:05	23°Ta48'	Superior Conjunction
Jul 13 2026	01:25:28	20°Cn42'	Inferior Conjunction
Aug 27 2026	17:03:29	04°Vi26'	Superior Conjunction
Nov 4 2026	14:24:01	12°Sc10'	Inferior Conjunction
Jan 1 2027	17:07:11	11°Cp02'	Superior Conjunction
Feb 18 2027	16:38:43	29°Aq47'	Inferior Conjunction
Apr 28 2027	21:21:33	08°Ta21'	Superior Conjunction
Jun 23 2027	07:59:15	01°Cn39'	Inferior Conjunction
Aug 11 2027	11:01:53	18°Le34'	Superior Conjunction
Oct 19 2027	15:30:20	26°Li01'	Inferior Conjunction
Dec 11 2027	22:16:24	19°Sg38'	Superior Conjunction
Feb 2 2028	08:46:55	13°Aq01'	Inferior Conjunction
Apr 11 2028	22:55:37	22°Ar34'	Superior Conjunction
Jun 2 2028	02:45:51	12°Ge06'	Inferior Conjunction
Jul 25 2028	13:07:09	03°Le06'	Superior Conjunction
Oct 2 2028	10:37:08	09°Li45'	Inferior Conjunction
Nov 20 2028	01:39:44	28°Sc15'	Superior Conjunction
Jan 16 2029	08:16:08	26°Cp29'	Inferior Conjunction
Mar 26 2029	16:33:35	06°Ar18'	Superior Conjunction
May 12 2029	23:26:57	22°Ta30'	Inferior Conjunction
Jul 9 2029	20:31:16	17°Cn54'	Superior Conjunction

Sep 15 2029	21:10:31	23°Vi18'	Inferior Conjunction
Oct 30 2029	23:13:23	07°Sc49'	Superior Conjunction
Dec 31 2029	12:27:43	10°Cp06'	Inferior Conjunction
Mar 9 2030	22:54:01	19°Pi24'	Superior Conjunction
Apr 23 2030	11:14:00	03°Ta21'	Inferior Conjunction
Jun 24 2030	07:04:10	02°Cn50'	Superior Conjunction
Aug 29 2030	20:10:11	06°Vi32'	Inferior Conjunction
Oct 11 2030	23:47:10	18°Li42'	Superior Conjunction
Dec 15 2030	19:13:44	23°Sg51'	Inferior Conjunction
Feb 20 2031	13:35:49	01°Pi42'	Superior Conjunction
Apr 4 2031	20:01:29	14°Ar51'	Inferior Conjunction
Jun 8 2031	18:49:21	17°Ge47'	Superior Conjunction
Aug 12 2031	04:04:11	19°Le17'	Inferior Conjunction
Sep 24 2031	01:26:49	00°Li49'	Superior Conjunction
Nov 30 2031	02:42:30	07°Sg40'	Inferior Conjunction
Feb 2 2032	07:31:15	13°Aq00'	Superior Conjunction
Mar 17 2032	01:10:25	27°Pi00'	Inferior Conjunction
May 23 2032	06:06:28	02°Ge40'	Superior Conjunction
Jul 23 2032	17:30:18	01°Le24'	Inferior Conjunction
Sep 5 2032	22:47:10	13°Vi54'	Superior Conjunction
Nov 13 2032	09:07:53	21°Sc32'	Inferior Conjunction
Jan 12 2033	23:56:04	23°Cp06'	Superior Conjunction
Feb 27 2033	22:59:12	09°Pi40'	Inferior Conjunction
May 7 2033	15:10:59	17°Ta22'	Superior Conjunction
Jul 4 2033	10:47:22	12°Cn47'	Inferior Conjunction
Aug 20 2033	10:32:58	27°Le43'	Superior Conjunction
Oct 28 2033	12:45:01	05°Sc24'	Inferior Conjunction
Dec 23 2033	15:08:11	02°Cp05'	Superior Conjunction
Feb 11 2034	09:28:24	22°Aq42'	Inferior Conjunction
Apr 21 2034	20:07:44	01°Ta47'	Superior Conjunction
Jun 14 2034	10:58:20	23°Ge28'	Inferior Conjunction
Aug 4 2034	08:23:26	12°Le03'	Superior Conjunction
Oct 12 2034	11:35:01	19°Li13'	Inferior Conjunction
Dec 2 2034	16:44:53	10°Sg34'	Superior Conjunction

Jan 26 2035	05:05:21	06°Aq03'	Inferior Conjunction
Apr 5 2035	18:41:04	15°Ar48'	Superior Conjunction
May 25 2035	04:44:33	03°Ge50'	Inferior Conjunction
Jul 19 2035	13:04:33	26°Cn43'	Superior Conjunction
Sep 26 2035	03:21:57	02°Li53'	Inferior Conjunction
Nov 12 2035	01:55:51	19°Sc29'	Superior Conjunction
Jan 10 2036	06:51:25	19°Cp35'	Inferior Conjunction
Mar 19 2036	07:53:57	29°Pi17'	Superior Conjunction
May 4 2036	06:33 :06	14°Ta23'	Inferior Conjunction
Jul 2 2036	22:03:12	11°Cn35'	Superior Conjunction
Sep 8 2036	09:25:18	16°Vi18'	Inferior Conjunction
Oct 22 2036	10:45:53	29°Li37'	Superior Conjunction
Dec 24 2036	12:24:30	03°Cp16'	Inferior Conjunction
Mar 2 2037	08:08:39	12°Pi04'	Superior Conjunction
Apr 15 2037	02:55:13	25°Ar29'	Inferior Conjunction
Jun 17 2037	09:17:45	26°Ge32'	Superior Conjunction
Aug 22 2037	02:27:11	29°Le21'	Inferior Conjunction
Oct 3 2037	22:33:47	11°Li03'	Superior Conjunction
Dec 8 2037	19:41:49	17°Sg03'	Inferior Conjunction
Feb 12 2038	14:39:23	23°Aq58'	Superior Conjunction
Mar 27 2038	20:40:35	07°Ar16'	Inferior Conjunction
Jun 1 2038	21:03:27	11°Ge28'	Superior Conjunction
Aug 4 2038	02:54:38	11°Le52'	Inferior Conjunction
Sep 16 2038	09:21:30	23°Vi37'	Superior Conjunction
Nov 23 2038	02:56:52	00°Sg54'	Inferior Conjunction
Jan 24 2039	22:08:51	04°Aq46'	Superior Conjunction
Mar 10 2039	09:26:51	19°Pi39'	Inferior Conjunction
May 17 2039	07:35:28	26°Ta17'	Superior Conjunction
Jul 16 2039	07:42:51	23°Cn40'	Inferior Conjunction
Aug 30 2039	13:25:36	07°Vi03'	Superior Conjunction
Nov 7 2039	08:25:24	14°Sc46'	Inferior Conjunction
Jan 5 2040	03:22:08	14°Cp22'	Superior Conjunction
Feb 21 2040	13:12:33	02°Pi30'	Inferior Conjunction
Apr 30 2040	15:09:42	10°Ta52'	Superior Conjunction
Jun 25 2040	16:52:34	04°Cn43'	Inferior Conjunction

Aug 13 2040	05:52:37	21°Le06'	Superior Conjunction
Oct 21 2040	10:15:11	28°Li37'	Inferior Conjunction
Dec 14 2040	10:38:49	23°Sg03'	Superior Conjunction
Feb 4 2041	03:58:49	15°Aq42'	Inferior Conjunction
Apr 14 2041	17:41:47	25°Ar08'	Superior Conjunction
Jun 5 2041	12:38:43	15°Ge13'	Inferior Conjunction
Jul 28 2041	06:57:22	05°Le35'	Superior Conjunction
Oct 5 2041	06:23:46	12°Li23'	Inferior Conjunction
Nov 23 2041	12:48:07	01°Sg35'	Superior Conjunction
Jan 19 2042	02:31:07	29°Cp07'	Inferior Conjunction
Mar 29 2042	12:41:43	08°Ar57'	Superior Conjunction
May 16 2042	08:03:14	25°Ta36'	Inferior Conjunction
Jul 12 2042	13:42:52	20°Cn21'	Superior Conjunction
Sep 18 2042	18:22:17	25°Vi58'	Inferior Conjunction
Nov 3 2042	06:44:03	10°Sc58'	Superior Conjunction
Jan 3 2043	06:09:12	12°Cp44'	Inferior Conjunction
Mar 12 2043	20:57:49	22°Pi10'	Superior Conjunction
Apr 26 2043	17:03:47	06°Ta22'	Inferior Conjunction
Jun 26 2043	23:54:56	05°Cn16'	Superior Conjunction
Sep 1 2043	19:15:53	09°Vi15'	Inferior Conjunction
Oct 15 2043	03:12:37	21°Li39'	Superior Conjunction
Dec 18 2043	12:39:35	26°Sg27'	Inferior Conjunction
Feb 23 2044	14:15:27	04°Pi36'	Superior Conjunction
Apr 6 2044	22:39:28	17°Ar46'	Inferior Conjunction
Jun 10 2044	11:36:59	20°Ge14'	Superior Conjunction
Aug 14 2044	05:40:07	22°Le05'	Inferior Conjunction
Sep 26 2044	01:31:11	03°Li37'	Superior Conjunction
Dec 1 2044	20:10:01	10°Sg17'	Inferior Conjunction
Feb 4 2045	11:35:39	16°Aq03'	Superior Conjunction
Mar 20 2045	00:55:37	29°Pi49'	Inferior Conjunction
May 25 2045	23:05:38	05°Ge08'	Superior Conjunction
Jul 26 2045	22:04:01	04°Le19'	Inferior Conjunction
Sep 8 2045	20:18:52	16°Vi35'	Superior Conjunction
Nov 16 2045	02:52:49	24°Sc09'	Inferior Conjunction

Jan 16 2046	08:01:03	26°Cp20'	Superior Conjunction
Mar 2 2046	20:30:33	12°Pi25'	Inferior Conjunction
May 10 2046	08:37:45	19°Ta52'	Superior Conjunction
Jul 7 2046	18:22:01	15°Cn49'	Inferior Conjunction
Aug 23 2046	06:13:05	00°Vi18'	Superior Conjunction
Oct 31 2046	07:01:42	08°Sc01'	Inferior Conjunction
Dec 27 2046	02:33:53	05°Cp28'	Superior Conjunction
Feb 14 2047	05:21:04	25°Aq25'	Inferior Conjunction
Apr 24 2047	14:16:37	04°Ta20'	Superior Conjunction
Jun 17 2047	20:33:07	26°Ge35'	Inferior Conjunction
Aug 7 2047	02:45:23	14°Le34'	Superior Conjunction
Oct 15 2047	06:41:20	21°Li50'	Inferior Conjunction
Dec 6 2047	04:58:06	13°Sg58'	Superior Conjunction
Jan 28 2048	23:49:03	08°Aq43'	Inferior Conjunction
Apr 7 2048	13:54:20	18°Ar25'	Superior Conjunction
May 27 2048	14:14:44	06°Ge58'	Inferior Conjunction
Jul 21 2048	06:33:50	29°Cn11'	Superior Conjunction
Sep 27 2048	23:40:00	05°Li32'	Inferior Conjunction
Nov 14 2048	11:41:14	22°Sc46'	Superior Conjunction
Jan 12 2049	00:49:38	22°Cp14'	Inferior Conjunction
Mar 22 2049	04:44:19	01°Ar59'	Superior Conjunction
May 7 2049	14:00:32	17°Ta27'	Inferior Conjunction
Jul 5 2049	15:03:06	14°Cn02'	Superior Conjunction
Sep 11 2049	07:22:56	19°Vi01'	Inferior Conjunction
Oct 25 2049	16:32:20	02°Sc42'	Superior Conjunction
Dec 27 2049	05:57:35	05°Cp54'	Inferior Conjunction
Mar 5 2050	07:12:31	14°Pi54'	Superior Conjunction
Apr 18 2050	07:20:00	28°Ar27'	Inferior Conjunction
Jun 20 2050	02:05:00	28°Ge59'	Superior Conjunction
Aug 25 2050	02:35:00	02°Vi07'	Inferior Conjunction
Oct 7 2050	00:30:40	13°Li57'	Superior Conjunction
Dec 11 2050	13:08:03	19°Sg40'	Inferior Conjunction

Other Mercury Trading Strategies

Although the Mercury cycles we have explored in this book offer us plenty of valuable clues that can help us identify high-probability trading opportunities, they certainly aren't the only Mercury phenomena associated with market movements. Nor do they represent all the possible strategies for using Mercury to generate bigger and more consistent profits with our astro-trading.

For example, when we are using a First-Trade horoscope as one of the components in our astro-trading analysis, we can apply all sorts of concepts and techniques employed by astrologers to that specific endeavor, much as we have done in looking at Mercury dynamics in the natal charts of traders. We can look at harmonic structures in the chart, or consider secondary progressions, converse progressions, and solar arc directions, as well as current and upcoming transits to those derivative horoscopes.

If you are well-versed in astrological methodologies there are really no limits to the experiments and hypothetical constructs you can apply to the astro-trading discipline, since market astrology always offers you the opportunity to back-test your hypotheses to find out in no uncertain terms whether your creative ideas will actually work in the markets or not. Experimentation is the doorway to new discoveries, and when we test new ideas about the astro-trading opportunities that Mercury offers us we can often get remarkable insights that can help us tune in to the nuances of potential trades in original and potentially profitable ways.

We are also fortunate as astro-traders today that we aren't the first to explore the connections between astrology and market action. Astro-trading pioneers and noteworthy researchers have gone before us, and some of them, along with market astrologers of the present day, have shared their observations about the ways that Mercury can impact market movements and play a role in setting up potentially profitable trades.

If we really want to enjoy the full advantage of Mercury's role in astro-trading, we need to take that research by others into consideration. Generally speaking, we always put ourselves at a distinct disadvantage if we ignore the efforts and experiences of others. When Mercury trading strategies are involved, however, we can easily compound that disadvantage, because we risk missing out on the information and intelligence acquired by others in ways that can make it impossible for us to profit from their experience at all.

In short, we owe it to ourselves to learn as much as we can about the ways that others have used the power of Mercury to get better results from their trading. Whenever it has been feasible, I've found it best to study primary sources and original presentations of research, and I recommend the same course of action to any astro-trader who is serious about applying advanced Mercury methodologies to a personal trading program.

In each case, however, it's important not only to read and ponder the original writings, but also to work through examples for the techniques that are being described, so that you can get a clear understanding of the processes and begin to internalize the methodologies.

Once you have done so, of course, you will want to apply your newly-learned Mercury trading techniques to contemporary market situations-- begin with back-testing using a variety of recent market data, preferably with a market you have personally traded, or at least one that you are familiar with.

To get the most reliable results, back-test the techniques with data from bull markets, from bear markets, and from markets that were moving sideways in congested trading patterns. If your back-testing demonstrates to your satisfaction that the technique you are investigating does in fact have some validity in today's markets, then you can begin to use it in your own trading.

That's really the ultimate test; when your own money is at risk, and your own emotions and prejudices are added to the mix, you can make an intelligent decision about whether or not that particular Mercury methodology deserves a more permanent place in your personal astro-trading toolbox.

With that approach in mind, here are a few contributions from other researchers and astro-traders that you may want to investigate. Each has its own merits and its own limitations, so in each case you will have to come to your own conclusions about whether or not there's a good match for you and your personal approach to astro-trading. In each case I've mentioned a particular individual solely because he or she has actively integrated Mercury dynamics into a trading strategy in one way or another.

In summarizing their work here, my goal is to help other astro-traders make better sense of the amazing variety of approaches to the markets which feature Mercury in a trading strategy. Along the way, I've tried to be candid about where I've found particularly useful insights and where I've encountered challenges, limitations, or unanswered questions, in the hope that my comments will make your own investigations a little easier and more profitable.

W. D. Gann

No book on astro-trading would be complete without mentioning the work of W. D. Gann. This master trader in stocks and commodities achieved nearly legendary status prior to his death in 1955, and in the decades since then his innovative and often mysterious work has inspired a never-ending stream of commentaries and interpretations as generations of traders have sought to comprehend and emulate his unique methodologies.

Although W. D. Gann wrote extensively about trading techniques and the behavior of the markets, he rarely mentioned astrology explicitly in his writings. "It is not my aim to explain the cause of cycles," he said. "The general public is not yet ready for it and probably would not understand or believe it if I explained it."

It's nevertheless clear to any careful student that astrology was an essential component of Gann's work. He combined his astrological knowledge with concepts and strategies from geometry, numerology, biblical studies, and the universal principles of the Law of Vibration, in many cases leaving it up to his readers to sort through his many allusions and figure out his trading methodologies for themselves. His idiosyncratic approach to mastering the markets can sometimes make it quite challenging for today's traders to apply Gann's principles to their own trading, but those who have taken the time to dig into Gann's work more deeply have typically found that it's worth the effort to do so.

In 1927 Gann presented some of his best astrological material in the form of a strange book called *The Tunnel Thru the Air or Looking Back from 1940*. On the surface it seems to be a badly-written romance novel whose hero, Robert Gordon, is a pioneering aviator, trading wizard, and ingenious inventor who almost single-handedly defends the United States against foreign invaders in a global war, all while he is striving diligently to be reunited with the love of his life, a woman who has disappeared under mysterious circumstances.

While Gann's novel does in fact mention astrology admiringly a few times in the course of the narrative, *The Tunnel Thru the Air,* at least on first reading, doesn't appear to offer much astrological substance at all. But in his foreword to the book Gann explained that it "shows the value of science, foreknowledge and preparedness," "contains a valuable secret, clothed in veiled language," and recommended that the novel be read three times.

"You will read it the first time because you are interested in the love story and for amusement," he said. "This will create a desire to read it a second time for instruction and knowledge. The second reading will unfold some of the hidden meanings and you will gain knowledge thru understanding which will stimulate an incentive to put knowledge into action. You will read it the third time because you want to make your dreams and ideals become real and find how to start knowledge into action."

He added that "When you read it the third time, a new light will dawn." The kind of insight he was talking about actually comes when you as a reader engage with The Tunnel Thru the Air at a deeper level, specifically by paying attention to every date mentioned in the narrative, no matter how inconsequential it may seem. If you calculate a horoscope for each date mentioned in the book, and then study those horoscopes with an ephemeris handy for reference, the real structure of the narrative soon begins to reveal itself – this insipid romance novel is in reality a textbook filled with examples that illustrate the power of the astro-trading dynamics with specific planetary events, most notably eclipses, major conjunctions, and planetary stations. Throughout the book these examples are connected with casual or sometimes oblique references to economic conditions, changes in market trends, or the successful stock and commodity trades that Robert Gordon uses to amass his personal fortune.

It is through a study of the horoscopes associated with the dates mentioned in *The Tunnel Thru the Air* that Gann's use of Mercury become evident. While they are certainly not the central planetary dynamic inferred in the book, Mercury actions were clearly an important feature of Robert Gordon's successful cotton trading campaign, which is described intermittently in the first half of the novel. Gordon makes his initial futures contract for 200 bales of July cotton on the date of a Sun/Mercury superior conjunction, and many of the key trading decisions and market moves mentioned in the book come on the dates of

Mercury aspects to other planets in longitude or declination, Mercury stations, or Mercury ingresses into various signs of the zodiac.

It takes a lot of hard work and patient analysis to give **The Tunnel Thru the Air** the kind of meticulous attention it deserves, but the endeavor makes a great training program for an aspiring astro-trader who really wants to internalize the impact of planetary cycles in the markets. But don't expect to study the work of W. D. Gann as a quick and easy path to astro-trading success.

George Bayer

Along with W. D. Gann, George Bayer was one of the true astro-trading masters whose ground-breaking work during the first half of the twentieth century helped to define an entire field of endeavor while demonstrating its incredible effectiveness in the world of active trading. But while W. D. Gann relied heavily on astrology in his market timing, he rarely spoke or wrote about astrology directly. Bayer, on the other hand, was much more open in giving credit to astrology as one of the key tools that he used in his successful forecasting and trading.

Even so, George Bayer was adamant in declaring that his approach to astrology was not like the lore that could be found in traditional astrology textbooks. While he used conventional methods in calculating horoscopes, he invented his own methods for interpreting charts and for applying astrological insights to the markets. In doing so, he became an innovator unlike any other. In fact, his thinking and methods were so original that they are sometimes quite challenging for today's astro-traders to comprehend, especially since his writings are riddled with digressions, obscure Biblical references, awkward analogies, and multi-lingual literary allusions. And to make matters even more difficult from our perspective today, much of what he wrote was either privately printed or distributed as mimeographed typescripts, so after seven decades much of it is long out of print and often hard to come by.

In spite of those obstacles, however, time spent studying Bayer's material is a valuable investment for any serious astro-trader. And it's of particular interest to us here that Bayer formulated an extensive list of astrologically-based rules for trading, including ones based on observations of Mercury phenomena that can't be found anywhere else in the astro-trading literature.

Although any of Bayer's publications are worth investigating, the primary source for his work with Mercury is his book **Stock and Commodity Traders' Hand-Book of Trend De-**

termination: Secrets of Forecasting Values, Especially Commodities, Including Stocks (privately published by George Bayer in Carmel, California in 1940). In that book Bayer lists 48 specific rules for trading wheat successfully. Most of the rules are based on astrological analysis, and 17 of them involve Mercury in one way or another. Indeed, Bayer refers to Mercury as "the most important planet of all."

Some of Bayer's rules demonstrate a truly remarkable understanding of the potential effects that Mercury can have on market action, as least as far as wheat futures are concerned. For example, Bayer suggests constructing a geocentric horoscope for the exact time that transiting Mercury hits either 15° Aquarius or 15° Leo in its passage through the zodiac. On that horoscope we note the precise position of each of the other planets. Then, says Bayer, "As Mercury keeps on going through the zodiac and passes the places of the other planets," the astro-trader will find that "we get changes of trend" in the price of wheat.

While a reiteration or analysis of all George Bayer's Mercury rules is beyond the scope of this current book, his original work is well worth careful study, particularly because of the way that it combines truly innovative astrological methods with solid instruction in sensible trading discipline. While Bayer focused most of his trading on the wheat market, he also traded other commodities and some stocks as well, and it may prove profitable to back-test his rules in a variety of market situations.

Jeanne Long

In her book *Universal Clock: Forecasting Time and Price in the Footsteps of W. D. Gann*, published in 1993, Jeanne Long details her efforts to understand Gann's trading tools and techniques. After learning that Gann had spent time traveling in Europe and India in pursuit of trading insights, Jeanne Long decided to retrace some of Gann's journeys, which is when she found herself in London's British Museum, where she saw 5000-year-old clay tablets from the ancient city of Ur with "cuneiform writings describing the astronomical phenomena of the time. These tablets not only gave the planetary information but also predicted the events expected to occur at the specific time. Some tablets referred to the price of wheat in relationship to the planets Mercury and the Sun. It immediately became clear to me how W. D. Gann saw this as repetition of similar conditions, repetition of cycles and even repetition of price."

This realization led her to explore Mercury cycles in modern soybean trading, where she found that the planetary correlations still apply to price patterns. In *Universal Clock* she describes a variety of astrological trading techniques; while not all of them deal with Mercury, they are important material for any serious astro-trader, making this book extremely valuable reading for anyone committed to the profitable application of astrology to the markets.

Five years prior to her publication of *Universal Clock*, Jeanne Long also wrote ***Basic Astrotech: A New Technique for Trading Commodities Using Geocosmic Energy Fields with Technical Analysis***. In this brief volume she outlines a technique for trading gold based on the heliocentric passage of Mercury through Sagittarius, a phenomenon that sets up about four specific trading opportunities each year.

Based on her observation that "When Heliocentric Mercury travels through the sign of Sagittarius, more often than not the price of Gold moves up," she sets out specific entry and exit rules for trading gold when this particular planetary transit is in effect. While this technique doesn't produce profitable trades 100 percent of the time, Jeanne Long's presentation of it in ***Basic Astrotech*** is worth studying closely because of the way that she integrates precise trading rules with Mercury dynamics.

Dr. Alan Richter

Alan Richter, Ph.D., a professional geneticist with an avocational passion for astrology and investments, conducted some highly original research into astrological correlations with market phenomena. He used both geocentric and heliocentric models in his work, and published his findings and theories in a variety of periodicals. In 1996 Carol Mull collected sixteen of Dr. Richter's articles from 1984 through 1994 and published them in a compilation, ***The Investment Astrology Articles of Dr. Alan Richter*** (CATT Books, Indianapolis, Indiana). Several pieces in that volume mention ways of incorporating Mercury into astro-analysis of the markets.

One of Alan Richter's most interesting observations is the correlation between multiple orbital cycles of Mercury with long-term market trends. In particular, he noted that six orbits of Mercury (88 days x 6 = 528 days) and eleven orbits of Mercury (88 days x 11 = 968 days) approximate major trending patterns in the markets. Although Richter focused primarily on the U.S. equities markets, he also found correlations with these Mercury cycles and Gold, Treasury Bonds, Treasury Bills, the U.S. Dollar Index, and the NIKKEI.

Other studies by Dr. Richter include an examination of Mercury/Neptune dynamics and their impact on Gold prices, and some insightful observations of key points in the cycles of heliocentric Mercury. He noted that there's a correlation between Mercury at perihelion (its closest approach to the Sun) and Mercury at aphelion (the point in its orbit when it is most distant from the Sun) and major price trends in a variety of commodities.

While Richter's work is certainly innovative, his research is geared more toward longer-term investment patterns rather than toward short-term trading. It's worth a look by today's astro-traders, however, because the culmination of long-term market movements can set up particularly powerful trading situations that can be capitalized upon with an intelligent short-term application of the astro-trading advantage.

Larry Pesavento

An expert trainer of traders and a veteran trader himself, Larry Pesavento has made a number of significant contributions to the art and science of making money in the markets, ranging from explorations of artificial intelligence and computerized market algorithms to pragmatic, down-to-earth observations on the psychology of trading, in which he demonstrates the kind of rare combination of intellectual discipline and genuine humility that every trader should strive to model in the essential task of keeping ego out of the trading equation. Along the way, he spent several years exploring the application of astrology to the markets, and although he insists that he doesn't personally aspire to become an astrologer himself, he has documented his research in several important books on astro-trading.

In one of those volumes, ***Harmonic Vibrations: A Metamorphosis from Traditional Cycle Theory to Astro-Harmonics*** (published in 1991 by Astro-Cycles in Pismo Beach, California), Larry Pesavento details his research into a phenomenon he refers to as "combust", the conjunction of Mercury and Venus. His premise is that because of the proximity of these two planets to the Sun, their conjunction creates a significant amplification of the solar energy, influencing weather patterns and impacting crop yields and commodity prices.

Based on his research and back-testing, Larry Pesavento's conclusion was that the Mercury/Venus conjunction does indeed have an impact, but that the effect of this alignment is strongest when it is combined with important lunar dynamics. He found the greatest influence in the grain and soybean markets, but this phenomenon may be worth investigating in other markets as well.

Earik Beann

In *The Handbook of Market Esoterica*, Earik Beann descusses a variety of astrological and numerological methods for market analysis and timing. Using a one-year trading chart with daily price bars for Microsoft (MSFT), he demonstrates some remarkable correspondences between price trends in the stock and a graph plotting Mercury's declination.

One of the things that's interesting about his work is that he demonstrates an important astro-trading principle: although he found that changes in price trend can have a close correspondence with changes in the Mercury declination trend, the critical thing to observe is the timing of the trend change rather than the direction of the trend itself. Thus, as Beann illustrates, there are times when the graph of Mercury's declination closely mimics the trend and direction of Microsoft, but at other times the declination graph needs to be inverted in order to see more clearly the correspondences with the price of the stock.

Earik Beann says that "most stocks do respond to Mercury's declination. What will happen is that you'll see a stock suddenly lock onto the declination, and begin to move in step with it, either following along or doing the opposite. Once that happens, the stock should stay in step for 6 months or so, and then it may fade out again. So what you need to do is track the declination, and be aware of when your stock starts locking on to it."

While this technique may have value for the astro-trader who is religiously following a particular stock over an extended period of time, it obviously has some limitations as a predictive tool, since the price trend must first be observed syncing up with Mercury's declination before the declination graph can be used to forecast upcoming prices and turning points. In other words, Mercury's declination sometimes shows a market correlation that may continue for some time once it starts to happen, but there's not necessarily any way of predicting in advance when or if that kind of correlation will actually occur at all.

Raymond Merriman

In his book *Geocosmic Correlations to Trading Cycles*, published as Volume 3 of *The Ultimate Book on Stock Market Timing*, market astrologer Raymond Merriman shares the results of his research on the impact of Mercury stations on the U.S. stock market, based on correspondences with price action in the Dow Jones Industrial Average and the S&P futures.

From his study of these market indices and Mercury retrograde cycles Merriman concludes that while traders can often anticipate market swings of about 4% near either the retrograde or direct stations, there is a much higher correspondence to significant moves in the market if traders allow an orb of 8 trading days before and after the dates of the stations when they set up timing parameters for their trades. He also comments that since traders tend to fluctuate in their decision-making process while Mercury is retrograde, it's wise to "take profits too soon" rather than to wait for turning points at conventional levels of support and resistance.

Raymond Merriman has done a massive amount of laborious research on the correlations of planetary phenomena to market trends, and his work on outer-planet cycles is valuable because it helps us identify the planetary interactions that have the greatest effect in moving the U.S. stock market. Even so, when it comes to Mercury cycles in particular, it's important to keep his research conclusions in proper perspective.

According to Merriman's work, if we are looking for a market move on the date of a Mercury station, plus or minus 8 trading days, we are in effect saying that we anticipate a significant market event on any one of 17 trading days. With five trading days in each week, this means that we are considering a time frame of roughly two-and-a-half weeks, or about 23 calendar days -- approximately the duration of an entire Mercury retrograde period. If we're looking at both the retrograde and direct stations as potential trigger points, Raymond Merriman's guidelines thus suggest that we need to be alert for Mercury effects for about 46 days each time Mercury is retrograde. My personal experience has been that using an orb that broad severely limits the usefulness of this approach as a tool for short-term market timing.

Bill Meridian

In addition to his excellent work on planetary stock trading, astrologically-based economic forecasting, and the power of eclipse paths in mundane astrology, Bill Meridian has created important models and methods for astrological market analysis. His work in that area has been featured as a vital component of several software programs for applying astrology to the markets, and it provides an essential back-testing framework for any astro-trader who hopes to succeed in using astrological dynamics intelligently and profitably.

Meridian's brief article on "The Development of Planetary Stock Market Forecasting" (available on his web site at billmeridian.com) provides a quick, easy-to-understand introduction to this important methodology. As an illustration of the technique, he uses the example of Sun/Mercury conjunctions and their impact on the stock market. As he describes his techniques in his article, one of Meridian's conclusions is that the zodiacal position of the conjunction is a key modifying factor in determining whether or not a particular Sun/Mercury conjunction sets up market conditions that can be traded reliably.

Bill Meridian is a skilled technical analyst as well as an innovative astrologer and an extremely rigorous researcher. The methods that he has developed consistently provide useful guidance for aspiring astro-traders, and I've found them extremely helpful in my own work with the markets. His discovery that Mercury phenomena can have significantly different influences when they occur in different parts of the zodiac has been particularly useful in designing some of the empirical research models that have gone into the preparation of this book.

New Directions

Although there is much valuable information that can be gained from reviewing the work of market astrologers like the ones mentioned here, our main aim in presenting their efforts in this chapter is to provide a source of inspiration. While the planetary principles governing the movements of Mercury and their correlation to the markets are universal, they can be applied to astro-trading opportunities in a remarkable variety of ways, as these examples demonstrate so plainly.

Whether you're an experienced trader or are just embarking as a newcomer to astro-trading, keep these examples in mind as you move ahead with your efforts at market mastery. As you test Mercury techniques in your own trading and experiment with new ideas in your own research and in devising your own trading systems, remember that there are others who share this journey with you. There's a lot you can learn from their investigations. And, if you take the time to examine their work with Mercury as you set new directions for yourself, you're likely to realize that embracing the astro-trading advantage can put you in some very good company along the way!

Mercury Retrograde Periods 1900 - 2100

Whether we are back-testing Mercury Retrograde effects or whether we are looking for future times that may set up advantageous trading situations, it's of course essential that we know exactly when Mercury is retrograde.

While any good astrological software can generate lists of Mercury Retrograde periods quite quickly, and while you'll also find Mercury positions and stations listed in the tables of any geocentric ephemeris, it's also helpful to have a "hard copy" listing of Mercury Retrograde periods for easy reference.

Such a listing not only helps you make a rapid determination about specific times when Mercury is retrograde; it also offers the opportunity to observe the longer-term patterns in the cycle of retrogradation as Mercury moves through signs and elements in an orderly sequence during sequential retrograde periods. When you study those patterns and begin to internalize a sense of the cosmic ebb and flow that is such a distinctive characteristic of the Mercury Retrograde cycle, you automatically gain a richer understanding of the universal order that shapes the course of human events-- and that motivates the motions of the markets as well.

With that second purpose in mind, the listing here covers two centuries, combining an attention to detail with a comprehensive perspective. The times and dates noted are all calculated for Greenwich Mean Time (UT), with no corrections for Summer Time, War Time, or Daylight Saving Time.

1900-1909

Mercury Retrograde Station	Mar 15 1900 13:21	09°Ar09' R
Mercury Direct Station	Apr 7 1900 18:50	26°Pi32' D
Mercury Retrograde Station	Jul 18 1900 12:53	15°Le15' R
Mercury Direct Station	Aug 11 1900 15:10	03°Le48' D
Mercury Retrograde Station	Nov 9 1900 23:36	06°Sg16' R
Mercury Direct Station	Nov 29 1900 21:33	20°Sc08' D
Mercury Retrograde Station	Feb 26 1901 12:18	22°Pi05' R
Mercury Direct Station	Mar 21 1901 02:30	08°Pi08' D
Mercury Retrograde Station	Jun 30 1901 02:52	25°Cn59' R
Mercury Direct Station	Jul 24 1901 08:16	15°Cn57' D
Mercury Retrograde Station	Oct 24 1901 12:09	20°Sc24' R
Mercury Direct Station	Nov 13 1901 19:42	04°Sc27' D
Mercury Retrograde Station	Feb 9 1902 22:18	05°Pi26' R
Mercury Direct Station	Mar 3 1902 18:50	20°Aq29' D
Mercury Retrograde Station	Jun 11 1902 04:41	06°Cn08' R
Mercury Direct Station	Jul 5 1902 06:25	27°Ge11' D
Mercury Retrograde Station	Oct 7 1902 19:59	04°Sc21' R
Mercury Direct Station	Oct 28 1902 18:05	18°Li44' D
Mercury Retrograde Station	Jan 24 1903 15:15	19°Aq08' R
Mercury Direct Station	Feb 14 1903 18:20	03°Aq30' D
Mercury Retrograde Station	May 22 1903 19:39	16°Ge05' R
Mercury Direct Station	Jun 15 1903 17:24	07°Ge32' D
Mercury Retrograde Station	Sep 20 1903 22:21	18°Li03' R
Mercury Direct Station	Oct 12 1903 14:39	02°Li54' D
Mercury Retrograde Station	Jan 8 1904 11:55	03°Aq04' R
Mercury Direct Station	Jan 28 1904 23:47	17°Cp01' D
Mercury Retrograde Station	May 2 1904 09:33	26°Ta24' R

Mercury Direct Station	May 26 1904 05:57	17°Ta22' D
Mercury Retrograde Station	Sep 2 1904 18:36	01°Li19' R
Mercury Direct Station	Sep 25 1904 06:46	16°Vi53' D
Mercury Retrograde Station	Dec 22 1904 09:50	17°Cp07' R
Mercury Direct Station	Jan 11 1905 10:25	00°Cp52' D
Mercury Retrograde Station	Apr 13 1905 11:34	07°Ta26' R
Mercury Direct Station	May 7 1905 05:35	27°Ar12' D
Mercury Retrograde Station	Aug 16 1905 08:22	14°Vi03' R
Mercury Direct Station	Sep 8 1905 15:01	00°Vi35' D
Mercury Retrograde Station	Dec 6 1905 06:57	01°Cp16' R
Mercury Direct Station	Dec 26 1905 01:34	14°Sg59' D
Mercury Retrograde Station	Mar 26 1906 08:03	19°Ar18' R
Mercury Direct Station	Apr 18 1906 19:32	07°Ar33' D
Mercury Retrograde Station	Jul 29 1906 14:37	26°Le03' R
Mercury Direct Station	Aug 22 1906 11:15	13°Le48' D
Mercury Retrograde Station	Nov 20 1906 01:40	15°Sg27' R
Mercury Direct Station	Dec 9 1906 20:28	29°Sc14' D
Mercury Retrograde Station	Mar 8 1907 22:19	01°Ar54' R
Mercury Direct Station	Mar 31 1907 21:51	18°Pi41' D
Mercury Retrograde Station	Jul 11 1907 11:16	07°Le14' R
Mercury Direct Station	Aug 4 1907 15:18	26°Cn24' D
Mercury Retrograde Station	Nov 3 1907 16:39	29°Sc37' R
Mercury Direct Station	Nov 23 1907 17:56	13°Sc33' D
Mercury Retrograde Station	Feb 20 1908 02:21	15°Pi02' R
Mercury Direct Station	Mar 13 1908 09:32	00°Pi37' D
Mercury Retrograde Station	Jun 21 1908 19:46	17°Cn41' R
Mercury Direct Station	Jul 16 1908 00:22	08°Cn10' D
Mercury Retrograde Station	Oct 17 1908 03:10	13°Sc41' R
Mercury Direct Station	Nov 6 1908 16:31	27°Li52' D
Mercury Retrograde Station	Feb 2 1909 15:50	28°Aq35' R
Mercury Direct Station	Feb 24 1909 04:54	13°Aq17' D
Mercury Retrograde Station	Jun 2 1909 16:02	27°Ge41' R
Mercury Direct Station	Jun 26 1909 16:24	19°Ge01' D
Mercury Retrograde Station	Sep 30 1909 08:34	27°Li33' R
Mercury Direct Station	Oct 21 1909 14:21	12°Li06' D

1910-1919

Mercury Retrograde Station	Jan 17 1910 10:52	12°Aq23' R
Mercury Direct Station	Feb 7 1910 06:52	26°Cp32' D
Mercury Retrograde Station	May 14 1910 05:30	07°Ge43' R
Mercury Direct Station	Jun 7 1910 01:49	29°Ta05' D
Mercury Retrograde Station	Sep 13 1910 08:36	11°Li06' R
Mercury Direct Station	Oct 5 1910 09:15	26°Vi13' D
Mercury Retrograde Station	Jan 1 1911 08:26	26°Cp21' R
Mercury Direct Station	Jan 21 1911 14:44	10°Cp12' D
Mercury Retrograde Station	Apr 24 1911 23:08	18°Ta19' R
Mercury Direct Station	May 18 1911 18:36	08°Ta51' D
Mercury Retrograde Station	Aug 27 1911 02:24	24°Vi09' R
Mercury Direct Station	Sep 18 1911 22:22	10°Vi06' D
Mercury Retrograde Station	Dec 16 1911 06:09	10°Cp28' R
Mercury Direct Station	Jan 5 1912 03:32	24°Sg12' D
Mercury Retrograde Station	Apr 5 1912 08:26	29°Ar44' R
Mercury Direct Station	Apr 29 1912 00:53	18°Ar52' D
Mercury Retrograde Station	Aug 8 1912 12:58	06°Vi35' R
Mercury Direct Station	Sep 1 1912 02:11	23°Le37' D
Mercury Retrograde Station	Nov 29 1912 02:15	24°Sg38' R
Mercury Direct Station	Dec 18 1912 20:24	08°Sg23' D
Mercury Retrograde Station	Mar 18 1913 12:57	11°Ar57' R
Mercury Direct Station	Apr 10 1913 20:04	29°Pi32' D
Mercury Retrograde Station	Jul 21 1913 15:03	18°Le15' R
Mercury Direct Station	Aug 14 1913 16:14	06°Le36' D
Mercury Retrograde Station	Nov 12 1913 19:28	08°Sg49' R
Mercury Direct Station	Dec 2 1913 16:25	22°Sc40' D
Mercury Retrograde Station	Mar 1 1914 09:48	24°Pi47' R
Mercury Direct Station	Mar 24 1914 02:24	11°Pi01' D
Mercury Retrograde Station	Jul 3 1914 06:58	29°Cn06' R
Mercury Direct Station	Jul 27 1914 12:10	18°Cn51' D

Mercury Retrograde Station	Oct 27 1914 08:47	22°Sc58' R
Mercury Direct Station	Nov 16 1914 14:27	06°Sc59' D
Mercury Retrograde Station	Feb 12 1915 18:23	08°Pi06' R
Mercury Direct Station	Mar 6 1915 17:41	23°Aq16' D
Mercury Retrograde Station	Jun 14 1915 10:38	09°Cn19' R
Mercury Direct Station	Jul 8 1915 13:03	00°Cn14' D
Mercury Retrograde Station	Oct 10 1915 17:22	06°Sc57' R
Mercury Direct Station	Oct 31 1915 13:00	21°Li16' D
Mercury Retrograde Station	Jan 27 1916 10:28	21°Aq46' R
Mercury Direct Station	Feb 17 1916 16:11	06°Aq11' D
Mercury Retrograde Station	May 25 1916 02:33	19°Ge15' R
Mercury Direct Station	Jun 18 1916 01:02	10°Ge43' D
Mercury Retrograde Station	Sep 22 1916 20:27	20°Li42' R
Mercury Direct Station	Oct 14 1916 10:01	05°Li28' D
Mercury Retrograde Station	Jan 10 1917 06:49	05°Aq39'
Mercury Direct Station	Jan 30 1917 20:43	19°Cp39' D
Mercury Retrograde Station	May 5 1917 15:47	29°Ta29' R
Mercury Direct Station	May 29 1917 12:11	20°Ta35' D
Mercury Retrograde Station	Sep 5 1917 17:37	04°Li03' R
Mercury Direct Station	Sep 28 1917 02:56	19°Vi30' D
Mercury Retrograde Station	Dec 25 1917 04:43	19°Cp41' R
Mercury Direct Station	Jan 14 1918 06:33	03°Cp28' D
Mercury Retrograde Station	Apr 16 1918 15:28	10°Ta24' R
Mercury Direct Station	May 10 1918 09:46	00°Ta23' D
Mercury Retrograde Station	Aug 19 1918 08:32	16°Vi53' R
Mercury Direct Station	Sep 11 1918 12:30	03°Vi14' D
Mercury Retrograde Station	Dec 9 1918 02:05	03°Cp49' R
Mercury Direct Station	Dec 28 1918 21:10	17°Sg33' D
Mercury Retrograde Station	Mar 29 1919 09:01	22°Ar10' R
Mercury Direct Station	Apr 21 1919 21:57	10°Ar39' D
Mercury Retrograde Station	Aug 1 1919 16:02	28°Le59' R
Mercury Direct Station	Aug 25 1919 10:48	6°Le33' D
Mercury Retrograde Station	Nov 22 1919 21:12	18°Sg00' R
Mercury Direct Station	Dec 12 1919 15:39	01°Sg47' D

1920-1929

Mercury Retrograde Station	Mar 10 1920 20:51	04°Ar40' R
Mercury Direct Station	Apr 2 1920 22:39	21°Pi39' D
Mercury Retrograde Station	Jul 13 1920 14:05	10°Le18' R
Mercury Direct Station	Aug 6 1920 17:37	29°Cn15' D
Mercury Retrograde Station	Nov 5 1920 12:47	02°Sg12' R
Mercury Direct Station	Nov 25 1920 12:50	16°Sc05' D
Mercury Retrograde Station	Feb 21 1921 23:12	17°Pi44' R
Mercury Direct Station	Mar 16 1921 08:55	03°Pi28' D
Mercury Retrograde Station	Jun 25 1921 00:26	20°Cn50' R
Mercury Direct Station	Jul 19 1921 05:33	11°Cn09' D
Mercury Retrograde Station	Oct 20 1921 00:00	16°Sc16' R
Mercury Direct Station	Nov 9 1921 11:17	00°Sc24' D
Mercury Retrograde Station	Feb 5 1922 11:35	01°Pi14' R
Mercury Direct Station	Feb 27 1922 03:12	16°Aq02' D
Mercury Retrograde Station	Jun 5 1922 22:38	00°Cn52' R
Mercury Direct Station	Jun 29 1922 23:28	22°Ge08' D
Mercury Retrograde Station	Oct 3 1922 06:17	00°Sc11' R
Mercury Direct Station	Oct 24 1922 09:18	14°Li40' D
Mercury Retrograde Station	Jan 20 1923 05:59	14°Aq58' R
Mercury Direct Station	Feb 10 1923 04:20	29°Cp12' D
Mercury Retrograde Station	May 17 1923 12:30	10°Ge53' R
Mercury Direct Station	Jun 10 1923 09:10	02°Ge18' D
Mercury Retrograde Station	Sep 16 1923 07:09	13°Li46' R
Mercury Direct Station	Oct 8 1923 04:47	28°Vi48' D
Mercury Retrograde Station	Jan 4 1924 03:14	28°Cp55' R
Mercury Direct Station	Jan 24 1924 11:24	12°Cp48' D
Mercury Retrograde Station	Apr 27 1924 04:27	21°Ta22' R
Mercury Direct Station	May 21 1924 00:20	12°Ta04' D
Mercury Retrograde Station	Aug 29 1924 01:50	26°Vi54' R

Mercury Direct Station	Sep 20 1924 19:03	12°Vi43' D
Mercury Retrograde Station	Dec 18 1924 01:00	13°Cp01' R
Mercury Direct Station	Jan 6 1925 23:27	26°Sg46' D
Mercury Retrograde Station	Apr 8 1925 11:02	02°Ta39' R
Mercury Direct Station	May 2 1925 04:15	22°Ar01' D
Mercury Retrograde Station	Aug 11 1925 13:27	09°Vi27' R
Mercury Direct Station	Sep 4 1925 00:33	26°Le18' D
Mercury Retrograde Station	Dec 1 1925 21:30	27°Sg11' R
Mercury Direct Station	Dec 21 1925 15:43	10°Sg55' D
Mercury Retrograde Station	Mar 21 1926 12:55	14°Ar45' R
Mercury Direct Station	Apr 13 1926 21:35	02°Ar34' D
Mercury Retrograde Station	Jul 24 1926 17:05	21°Le14' R
Mercury Direct Station	Aug 17 1926 16:54	09°Le23' D
Mercury Retrograde Station	Nov 15 1926 15:18	11°Sg23' R
Mercury Direct Station	Dec 5 1926 11:22	25°Sc11' D
Mercury Retrograde Station	Mar 4 1927 07:34	27°Pi30' R
Mercury Direct Station	Mar 27 1927 02:33	13°Pi55' D
Mercury Retrograde Station	Jul 6 1927 10:50	02°Le13' R
Mercury Direct Station	Jul 30 1927 15:42	21°Cn46' D
Mercury Retrograde Station	Oct 30 1927 05:19	25°Sc32' R
Mercury Direct Station	Nov 19 1927 09:16	09°Sc30' D
Mercury Retrograde Station	Feb 15 1928 14:35	10°Pi45' R
Mercury Direct Station	Mar 8 1928 16:44	26°Aq03' D
Mercury Retrograde Station	Jun 16 1928 16:11	12°Cn29' R
Mercury Direct Station	Jul 10 1928 19:21	03°Cn16' D
Mercury Retrograde Station	Oct 12 1928 14:32	09°Sc33' R
Mercury Direct Station	Nov 2 1928 07:52	23°Li49' D
Mercury Retrograde Station	Jan 29 1929 05:48	24°Aq22' R
Mercury Direct Station	Feb 19 1929 14:07	08°Aq53' D
Mercury Retrograde Station	May 28 1929 09:17	22°Ge26' R
Mercury Direct Station	Jun 21 1929 08:28	13°Ge52' D
Mercury Retrograde Station	Sep 25 1929 18:23	23°Li21' R
Mercury Direct Station	Oct 17 1929 05:15	08°Li03' D

1930-1939

Mercury Retrograde Station	Jan 13 1930 01:46	08°Aq13' R
Mercury Direct Station	Feb 2 1930 17:43	22°Cp17' D
Mercury Retrograde Station	May 8 1930 22:19	02°Ge35' R
Mercury Direct Station	Jun 1 1930 18:38	23°Ta48' D
Mercury Retrograde Station	Sep 8 1930 16:32	06°Li46' R
Mercury Direct Station	Sep 30 1930 22:53	22°Vi06' D
Mercury Retrograde Station	Dec 27 1930 23:38	22°Cp15' R
Mercury Direct Station	Jan 17 1931 02:52	06°Cp04' D
Mercury Retrograde Station	Apr 19 1931 19:51	13°Ta23' R
Mercury Direct Station	May 13 1931 14:32	03°Ta35' D
Mercury Retrograde Station	Aug 22 1931 08:33	19°Vi41' R
Mercury Direct Station	Sep 14 1931 09:44	05°Vi53' D
Mercury Retrograde Station	Dec 11 1931 21:11	06°Cp22' R
Mercury Direct Station	Dec 31 1931 16:55	20°Sg06'
Mercury Retrograde Station	Mar 31 1932 10:27	25°Ar02' R
Mercury Direct Station	Apr 24 1932 00:45	13°Ar45' D
Mercury Retrograde Station	Aug 3 1932 17:13	01°Vi54' R
Mercury Direct Station	Aug 27 1932 10:02	19°Le16' D
Mercury Retrograde Station	Nov 24 1932 16:40	20°Sg34' R
Mercury Direct Station	Dec 14 1932 10:54	04°Sg19' D
Mercury Retrograde Station	Mar 13 1933 19:43	07°Ar26' R
Mercury Direct Station	Apr 5 1933 23:35	24°Pi38' D
Mercury Retrograde Station	Jul 16 1933 16:37	13°Le19' R
Mercury Direct Station	Aug 9 1933 19:32	02°Le04' D
Mercury Retrograde Station	Nov 8 1933 08:47	04°Sg45' R
Mercury Direct Station	Nov 28 1933 07:41	18°Sc38' D
Mercury Retrograde Station	Feb 24 1934 20:17	20°Pi25' R
Mercury Direct Station	Mar 19 1934 08:25	06°Pi20' D
Mercury Retrograde Station	Jun 28 1934 04:57	23°Cn59' R
Mercury Direct Station	Jul 22 1934 10:21	14°Cn07' D

Mercury Retrograde Station	Oct 22 1934 20:44	18°Sc51' R
Mercury Direct Station	Nov 12 1934 05:58	02°Sc57' D
Mercury Retrograde Station	Feb 8 1935 07:25	03°Pi51' R
Mercury Direct Station	Mar 2 1935 01:37	18°Aq47' D
Mercury Retrograde Station	Jun 9 1935 05:06	04°Cn05' R
Mercury Direct Station	Jul 3 1935 06:24	25°Ge14' D
Mercury Retrograde Station	Oct 6 1935 03:53	02°Sc48' R
Mercury Direct Station	Oct 27 1935 04:11	17°Li14' D
Mercury Retrograde Station	Jan 23 1936 01:05	17°Aq35' R
Mercury Direct Station	Feb 13 1936 01:57	01°Aq53' D
Mercury Retrograde Station	May 19 1936 19:26	14°Ge02' R
Mercury Direct Station	Jun 12 1936 16:35	05°Ge29' D
Mercury Retrograde Station	Sep 18 1936 05:33	16°Li27' R
Mercury Direct Station	Oct 10 1936 00:17	01°Li23' D
Mercury Retrograde Station	Jan 5 1937 22:03	01°Aq31' R
Mercury Direct Station	Jan 26 1937 08:10	15°Cp26' D
Mercury Retrograde Station	Apr 30 1937 10:03	24°Ta26' R
Mercury Direct Station	May 24 1937 06:16	15°Ta17' D
Mercury Retrograde Station	Sep 1 1937 01:08	29°Vi40' R
Mercury Direct Station	Sep 23 1937 15:38	15°Vi20' D
Mercury Retrograde Station	Dec 20 1937 19:54	15°Cp35' R
Mercury Direct Station	Jan 9 1938 19:29	29°Sg21' D
Mercury Retrograde Station	Apr 11 1938 14:11	05°Ta36' R
Mercury Direct Station	May 5 1938 07:54	25°Ar11' D
Mercury Retrograde Station	Aug 14 1938 13:51	12°Vi18' R
Mercury Direct Station	Sep 6 1938 22:39	28°Le59' D
Mercury Retrograde Station	Dec 4 1938 16:46	29°Sg45' R
Mercury Direct Station	Dec 24 1938 11:09	13°Sg28' D
Mercury Retrograde Station	Mar 24 1939 13:17	17°Ar35' R
Mercury Direct Station	Apr 16 1939 23:26	05°Ar37' D
Mercury Retrograde Station	Jul 27 1939 18:54	24°Le12' R
Mercury Direct Station	Aug 20 1939 17:07	12°Le09' D
Mercury Retrograde Station	Nov 18 1939 11:04	13°Sg57' R
Mercury Direct Station	Dec 8 1939 06:23	27°Sc44' D

1940-1949

Mercury Retrograde Station	Mar 6 1940 05:32	00°Ar14' R
Mercury Direct Station	Mar 29 1940 02:57	16°Pi50' D
Mercury Retrograde Station	Jul 8 1940 14:17	05°Le18' R
Mercury Direct Station	Aug 1 1940 18:42	24°Cn39' D
Mercury Retrograde Station	Nov 1 1940 01:39	28°Sc06' R
Mercury Direct Station	Nov 21 1940 04:05	12°Sc04' D
Mercury Retrograde Station	Feb 17 1941 10:57	13°Pi26' R
Mercury Direct Station	Mar 11 1941 15:52	28°Aq52' D
Mercury Retrograde Station	Jun 19 1941 21:17	15°Cn39' R
Mercury Direct Station	Jul 14 1941 01:15	06°Cn17' D
Mercury Retrograde Station	Oct 15 1941 11:30	12°Sc09' R
Mercury Direct Station	Nov 5 1941 02:41	26°Li22' D
Mercury Retrograde Station	Feb 1 1942 01:16	26°Aq59' R
Mercury Direct Station	Feb 22 1942 12:08	11°Aq36' D
Mercury Retrograde Station	May 31 1942 16:03	25°Ge38' R
Mercury Direct Station	Jun 24 1942 15:54	17°Ge01' D
Mercury Retrograde Station	Sep 28 1942 16:12	25°Li59' R
Mercury Direct Station	Oct 20 1942 00:22	10°Li37' D
Mercury Retrograde Station	Jan 15 1943 20:46	10°Aq49' R
Mercury Direct Station	Feb 5 1943 14:50	24°Cp55' D
Mercury Retrograde Station	May 12 1943 05:13	05°Ge43' R
Mercury Direct Station	Jun 5 1943 01:29	27°Ta01' D
Mercury Retrograde Station	Sep 11 1943 15:23	09°Li29' R
Mercury Direct Station	Oct 3 1943 18:41	24°Vi42' D
Mercury Retrograde Station	Dec 30 1943 18:32	24°Cp49' R
Mercury Direct Station	Jan 19 1944 23:20	08°Cp39' D
Mercury Retrograde Station	Apr 22 1944 00:34	16°Ta24' R
Mercury Direct Station	May 15 1944 19:39	06°Ta47' D
Mercury Retrograde Station	Aug 24 1944 08:25	22°Vi27' R

Mercury Direct Station	Sep 16 1944 06:47	08°Vi31' D
Mercury Retrograde Station	Dec 13 1944 16:11	08°Cp56' R
Mercury Direct Station	Jan 2 1945 12:45	22°Sg39' D
Mercury Retrograde Station	Apr 3 1945 12:12	27°Ar55' R
Mercury Direct Station	Apr 27 1945 03:46	16°Ar51' D
Mercury Retrograde Station	Aug 6 1945 18:10	04°Vi47' R
Mercury Direct Station	Aug 30 1945 09:02	21°Le58' D
Mercury Retrograde Station	Nov 27 1945 12:00	23°Sg08' R
Mercury Direct Station	Dec 17 1945 06:11	06°Sg52' D
Mercury Retrograde Station	Mar 16 1946 18:55	10°Ar12' R
Mercury Direct Station	Apr 9 1946 00:38	27°Pi37' D
Mercury Retrograde Station	Jul 19 1946 18:55	16°Le20' R
Mercury Direct Station	Aug 12 1946 21:03	04°Le53' D
Mercury Retrograde Station	Nov 11 1946 04:43	07°Sg18' R
Mercury Direct Station	Dec 1 1946 02:32	21°Sc10' D
Mercury Retrograde Station	Feb 27 1947 17:35	23°Pi08' R
Mercury Direct Station	Mar 22 1947 08:05	09°Pi12' D
Mercury Retrograde Station	Jul 1 1947 09:13	27°Cn07' R
Mercury Direct Station	Jul 25 1947 14:37	17°Cn02' D
Mercury Retrograde Station	Oct 25 1947 17:25	21°Sc26' R
Mercury Direct Station	Nov 15 1947 00:40	05°Sc29' D
Mercury Retrograde Station	Feb 11 1948 03:24	06°Pi29' R
Mercury Direct Station	Mar 4 1948 00:19	21°Aq33' D
Mercury Retrograde Station	Jun 11 1948 11:15	07°Cn16' R
Mercury Direct Station	Jul 5 1948 13:04	28°Ge17' D
Mercury Retrograde Station	Oct 8 1948 01:22	05°Sc24' R
Mercury Direct Station	Oct 28 1948 23:05	19°Li47' D
Mercury Retrograde Station	Jan 24 1949 20:17	20°Aq11' R
Mercury Direct Station	Feb 14 1949 23:45	04°Aq34' D
Mercury Retrograde Station	May 23 1949 02:16	17°Ge12' R
Mercury Direct Station	Jun 16 1949 00:08	08°Ge40' D
Mercury Retrograde Station	Sep 21 1949 03:49	19°Li06' R
Mercury Direct Station	Oct 12 1949 19:44	03°Li57' D

1950-1959

Mercury Retrograde Station	Jan 8 1950 16:54	04°Aq06' R
Mercury Direct Station	Jan 29 1950 05:03	18°Cp04' D
Mercury Retrograde Station	May 3 1950 16:06	27°Ta30' R
Mercury Direct Station	May 27 1950 12:28	18°Ta30' D
Mercury Retrograde Station	Sep 4 1950 00:14	02°Li24' R
Mercury Direct Station	Sep 26 1950 11:59	17°Vi56' D
Mercury Retrograde Station	Dec 23 1950 14:48	18°Cp10' R
Mercury Direct Station	Jan 12 1951 15:34	01°Cp55' D
Mercury Retrograde Station	Apr 14 1951 17:50	08°Ta32' R
Mercury Direct Station	May 8 1951 11:50	28°Ar20' D
Mercury Retrograde Station	Aug 17 1951 14:04	15°Vi08' R
Mercury Direct Station	Sep 9 1951 20:22	01°Vi39' D
Mercury Retrograde Station	Dec 7 1951 11:57	02°Cp19' R
Mercury Direct Station	Dec 27 1951 06:38	16°Sg02' D
Mercury Retrograde Station	Mar 26 1952 13:54	20°Ar24' R
Mercury Direct Station	Apr 19 1952 01:32	08°Ar41' D
Mercury Retrograde Station	Jul 29 1952 20:31	27°Le09' R
Mercury Direct Station	Aug 22 1952 16:54	14°Le53' D
Mercury Retrograde Station	Nov 20 1952 06:43	16°Sg30' R
Mercury Direct Station	Dec 10 1952 01:28	00°Sg17' D
Mercury Retrograde Station	Mar 9 1953 03:44	02°Ar58' R
Mercury Direct Station	Apr 1 1953 03:36	19°Pi47' D
Mercury Retrograde Station	Jul 11 1953 17:25	08°Le22' R
Mercury Direct Station	Aug 4 1953 21:21	27°Cn30' D
Mercury Retrograde Station	Nov 3 1953 21:50	00°Sg40' R
Mercury Direct Station	Nov 23 1953 22:55	14°Sc36' D
Mercury Retrograde Station	Feb 20 1954 07:33	16°Pi06' R
Mercury Direct Station	Mar 14 1954 15:06	01°Pi42' D
Mercury Retrograde Station	Jun 23 1954 02:09	18°Cn49' R
Mercury Direct Station	Jul 17 1954 06:50	09°Cn17' D

Mercury Retrograde Station	Oct 18 1954 08:25	14°Sc45' R
Mercury Direct Station	Nov 7 1954 21:30	28°Li55' D
Mercury Retrograde Station	Feb 3 1955 20:55	29°Aq38' R
Mercury Direct Station	Feb 25 1955 10:17	14°Aq21' D
Mercury Retrograde Station	Jun 3 1955 22:46	28°Ge50' R
Mercury Direct Station	Jun 27 1955 23:11	20°Ge09' D
Mercury Retrograde Station	Oct 1 1955 13:58	28°Li37' R
Mercury Direct Station	Oct 22 1955 19:22	13°Li10' D
Mercury Retrograde Station	Jan 18 1956 15:52	13°Aq26' R
Mercury Direct Station	Feb 8 1956 12:10	27°Cp35' D
Mercury Retrograde Station	May 14 1956 12:12	08°Ge52' R
Mercury Direct Station	Jun 7 1956 08:34	00°Ge14' D
Mercury Retrograde Station	Sep 13 1956 14:08	12°Li10' R
Mercury Direct Station	Oct 5 1956 14:21	27°Vi16' D
Mercury Retrograde Station	Jan 1 1957 13:23	27°Cp25' R
Mercury Direct Station	Jan 21 1957 19:56	11°Cp16' D
Mercury Retrograde Station	Apr 25 1957 05:32	19°Ta26' R
Mercury Direct Station	May 19 1957 01:04	09°Ta59' D
Mercury Retrograde Station	Aug 27 1957 08:04	25°Vi14' R
Mercury Direct Station	Sep 19 1957 03:37	11°Vi10' D
Mercury Retrograde Station	Dec 16 1957 11:05	11°Cp31' R
Mercury Direct Station	Jan 5 1958 08:39	25°Sg14' D
Mercury Retrograde Station	Apr 6 1958 14:24	00°Ta49' R
Mercury Direct Station	Apr 30 1958 06:57	20°Ar00' D
Mercury Retrograde Station	Aug 9 1958 18:47	07°Vi41' R
Mercury Direct Station	Sep 2 1958 07:42	24°Le41' D
Mercury Retrograde Station	Nov 30 1958 07:16	25°Sg41' R
Mercury Direct Station	Dec 20 1958 01:27	09°Sg25' D
Mercury Retrograde Station	Mar 19 1959 18:34	13°Ar00' R
Mercury Direct Station	Apr 12 1959 01:53	00°Ar39' D
Mercury Retrograde Station	Jul 22 1959 21:02	19°Le21' R
Mercury Direct Station	Aug 15 1959 22:05	07°Le41' D
Mercury Retrograde Station	Nov 14 1959 00:37	09°Sg52' R
Mercury Direct Station	Dec 3 1959 21:25	23°Sc43' D

1960-1969

Mercury Retrograde Station	Mar 1 1960 15:10	25°Pi51' R
Mercury Direct Station	Mar 24 1960 08:05	12°Pi06' D
Mercury Retrograde Station	Jul 3 1960 13:15	00°Le14' R
Mercury Direct Station	Jul 27 1960 18:24	19°Cn58' D
Mercury Retrograde Station	Oct 27 1960 14:02	24°Sc01' R
Mercury Direct Station	Nov 16 1960 19:27	08°Sc01' D
Mercury Retrograde Station	Feb 12 1961 23:32	09°Pi09' R
Mercury Direct Station	Mar 6 1961 23:16	24°Aq21' D
Mercury Retrograde Station	Jun 14 1961 17:06	10°Cn26' R
Mercury Direct Station	Jul 8 1961 19:36	01°Cn21' D
Mercury Retrograde Station	Oct 10 1961 22:42	08°Sc00' R
Mercury Direct Station	Oct 31 1961 18:01	22°Li19' D
Mercury Retrograde Station	Jan 27 1962 15:31	22°Aq48' R
Mercury Direct Station	Feb 17 1962 21:35	07°Aq15' D
Mercury Retrograde Station	May 26 1962 09:09	20°Ge23' R
Mercury Direct Station	Jun 19 1962 07:46	11°Ge50' D
Mercury Retrograde Station	Sep 24 1962 01:53	21°Li45' R
Mercury Direct Station	Oct 15 1962 15:04	06°Li31' D
Mercury Retrograde Station	Jan 11 1963 11:47	06°Aq42' R
Mercury Direct Station	Feb 1 1963 01:58	20°Cp42' D
Mercury Retrograde Station	May 6 1963 22:30	00°Ge36' R
Mercury Direct Station	May 30 1963 18:52	21°Ta44' D
Mercury Retrograde Station	Sep 6 1963 23:09	05°Li07' R
Mercury Direct Station	Sep 29 1963 08:04	20°Vi33' D
Mercury Retrograde Station	Dec 26 1963 09:40	20°Cp43' R
Mercury Direct Station	Jan 15 1964 11:42	04°Cp29' D
Mercury Retrograde Station	Apr 16 1964 21:50	11°Ta30' R
Mercury Direct Station	May 10 1964 16:08	01°Ta31'
Mercury Retrograde Station	Aug 19 1964 14:14	17°Vi57'
Mercury Direct Station	Sep 11 1964 17:48	04°Vi18' D

Mercury Retrograde Station	Dec 9 1964 07:05	04°Cp52' R
Mercury Direct Station	Dec 29 1964 02:15	18°Sg35' D
Mercury Retrograde Station	Mar 29 1965 14:53	23°Ar14' R
Mercury Direct Station	Apr 22 1965 04:00	11°Ar45' D
Mercury Retrograde Station	Aug 1 1965 21:56	00°Vi04' R
Mercury Direct Station	Aug 25 1965 16:24	17°Le37' D
Mercury Retrograde Station	Nov 23 1965 02:16	19°Sg02' R
Mercury Direct Station	Dec 12 1965 20:40	02°Sg49' D
Mercury Retrograde Station	Mar 12 1966 02:18	05°Ar43' R
Mercury Direct Station	Apr 4 1966 04:25	22°Pi44' D
Mercury Retrograde Station	Jul 14 1966 20:14	11°Le24' R
Mercury Direct Station	Aug 7 1966 23:42	00°Le21' D
Mercury Retrograde Station	Nov 6 1966 17:55	03°Sg13' R
Mercury Direct Station	Nov 26 1966 17:49	17°Sc08' D
Mercury Retrograde Station	Feb 23 1967 04:26	18°Pi47' R
Mercury Direct Station	Mar 17 1967 14:27	04°Pi32' D
Mercury Retrograde Station	Jun 26 1967 06:51	21°Cn58' R
Mercury Direct Station	Jul 20 1967 12:01	12°Cn15' D
Mercury Retrograde Station	Oct 21 1967 05:16	17°Sc19' R
Mercury Direct Station	Nov 10 1967 16:16	01°Sc27' D
Mercury Retrograde Station	Feb 6 1968 16:40	02°Pi16' R
Mercury Direct Station	Feb 28 1968 08:36	17°Aq06' D
Mercury Retrograde Station	Jun 6 1968 05:17	02°Cn01' R
Mercury Direct Station	Jun 30 1968 06:09	23°Ge15' D
Mercury Retrograde Station	Oct 3 1968 11:40	01°Sc15' R
Mercury Direct Station	Oct 24 1968 14:17	15°Li43' D
Mercury Retrograde Station	Jan 20 1969 10:57	16°Aq02' R
Mercury Direct Station	Feb 10 1969 09:38	00°Aq15' D
Mercury Retrograde Station	May 17 1969 19:06	12°Ge00' R
Mercury Direct Station	Jun 10 1969 15:48	03°Ge25' D
Mercury Retrograde Station	Sep 16 1969 12:42	14°Li51' R
Mercury Direct Station	Oct 8 1969 09:53	29°Vi51' D

1970-1979

Mercury Retrograde Station	Jan 4 1970 08:10	29°Cp59' R
Mercury Direct Station	Jan 24 1970 16:38	13°Cp52' D
Mercury Retrograde Station	Apr 28 1970 10:51	22°Ta29' R
Mercury Direct Station	May 22 1970 06:47	13°Ta12' D
Mercury Retrograde Station	Aug 30 1970 07:28	28°Vi00' R
Mercury Direct Station	Sep 22 1970 00:18	13°Vi47' D
Mercury Retrograde Station	Dec 19 1970 05:59	14°Cp04' R
Mercury Direct Station	Jan 8 1971 04:36	27°Sg49' D
Mercury Retrograde Station	Apr 9 1971 17:11	03°Ta45' R
Mercury Direct Station	May 3 1971 10:25	23°Ar09' D
Mercury Retrograde Station	Aug 12 1971 19:14	10°Vi32' R
Mercury Direct Station	Sep 5 1971 06:03	27°Le22' D
Mercury Retrograde Station	Dec 3 1971 02:33	28°Sg14' R
Mercury Direct Station	Dec 22 1971 20:47	11°Sg58' D
Mercury Retrograde Station	Mar 21 1972 18:39	15°Ar49' R
Mercury Direct Station	Apr 14 1972 03:29	03°Ar41' D
Mercury Retrograde Station	Jul 24 1972 23:02	22°Le20' R
Mercury Direct Station	Aug 17 1972 22:38	10°Le28' D
Mercury Retrograde Station	Nov 15 1972 20:27	12°Sg26' R
Mercury Direct Station	Dec 5 1972 16:23	26°Sc14' D
Mercury Retrograde Station	Mar 4 1973 12:58	28°Pi35' R
Mercury Direct Station	Mar 27 1973 08:19	15°Pi01' D
Mercury Retrograde Station	Jul 6 1973 17:00	03°Le20' R
Mercury Direct Station	Jul 30 1973 21:47	22°Cn52' D
Mercury Retrograde Station	Oct 30 1973 10:30	26°Sc35' R
Mercury Direct Station	Nov 19 1973 14:14	10°Sc33' D
Mercury Retrograde Station	Feb 15 1974 19:45	11°Pi49' R
Mercury Direct Station	Mar 9 1974 22:16	27°Aq09' D
Mercury Retrograde Station	Jun 17 1974 22:38	13°Cn38' R
Mercury Direct Station	Jul 12 1974 01:56	04°Cn24' D

Mercury Retrograde Station	Oct 13 1974 19:48	10°Sc36' R
Mercury Direct Station	Nov 3 1974 12:51	24°Li51' D
Mercury Retrograde Station	Jan 30 1975 10:48	25°Aq26' R
Mercury Direct Station	Feb 20 1975 19:28	09°Aq58' D
Mercury Retrograde Station	May 29 1975 16:01	23°Ge35' R
Mercury Direct Station	Jun 22 1975 15:19	15°Ge01' D
Mercury Retrograde Station	Sep 26 1975 23:46	24°Li24' R
Mercury Direct Station	Oct 18 1975 10:15	09°Li05' D
Mercury Retrograde Station	Jan 14 1976 06:43	09°Aq17' R
Mercury Direct Station	Feb 3 1976 22:57	23°Cp20' D
Mercury Retrograde Station	May 9 1976 05:05	03°Ge43' R
Mercury Direct Station	Jun 2 1976 01:20	24°Ta57' D
Mercury Retrograde Station	Sep 8 1976 22:04	07°Li50' R
Mercury Direct Station	Oct 1 1976 04:00	23°Vi09' D
Mercury Retrograde Station	Dec 28 1976 04:34	23°Cp18' R
Mercury Direct Station	Jan 17 1977 08:01	07°Cp06' D
Mercury Retrograde Station	Apr 20 1977 02:09	14°Ta29' R
Mercury Direct Station	May 13 1977 20:52	04°Ta43' D
Mercury Retrograde Station	Aug 22 1977 14:19	20°Vi46' R
Mercury Direct Station	Sep 14 1977 15:04	06°Vi57' D
Mercury Retrograde Station	Dec 12 1977 02:11	07°Cp25' R
Mercury Direct Station	Dec 31 1977 22:02	21°Sg09' D
Mercury Retrograde Station	Apr 1 1978 16:18	26°Ar07' R
Mercury Direct Station	Apr 25 1978 06:48	14°Ar51' D
Mercury Retrograde Station	Aug 4 1978 23:08	02°Vi59' R
Mercury Direct Station	Aug 28 1978 15:41	20°Le21' D
Mercury Retrograde Station	Nov 25 1978 21:42	21°Sg36' R
Mercury Direct Station	Dec 15 1978 15:57	05°Sg22' D
Mercury Retrograde Station	Mar 15 1979 01:16	08°Ar30' R
Mercury Direct Station	Apr 7 1979 05:22	25°Pi44' D
Mercury Retrograde Station	Jul 17 1979 22:42	14°Le26' R
Mercury Direct Station	Aug 11 1979 01:33	03°Le10' D
Mercury Retrograde Station	Nov 9 1979 13:55	05°Sg48' R
Mercury Direct Station	Nov 29 1979 12:41	19°Sc39' D

1980-1989

Mercury Retrograde Station	Feb 26 1980 01:33	21°Pi29' R
Mercury Direct Station	Mar 19 1980 13:59	07°Pi24' D
Mercury Retrograde Station	Jun 28 1980 11:13	25°Cn07' R
Mercury Direct Station	Jul 22 1980 16:37	15°Cn12' D
Mercury Retrograde Station	Oct 23 1980 01:59	19°Sc54' R
Mercury Direct Station	Nov 12 1980 10:57	03°Sc59' D
Mercury Retrograde Station	Feb 8 1981 12:31	04°Pi55' R
Mercury Direct Station	Mar 2 1981 07:06	19°Aq51' D
Mercury Retrograde Station	Jun 9 1981 11:36	05°Cn12' R
Mercury Direct Station	Jul 3 1981 12:58	26°Ge20' D
Mercury Retrograde Station	Oct 6 1981 09:16	03°Sc51' R
Mercury Direct Station	Oct 27 1981 09:11	18°Li15' D
Mercury Retrograde Station	Jan 23 1982 06:04	18°Aq37' R
Mercury Direct Station	Feb 13 1982 07:18	02°Aq55' D
Mercury Retrograde Station	May 21 1982 02:06	15°Ge10' R
Mercury Direct Station	Jun 13 1982 23:21	06°Ge37' D
Mercury Retrograde Station	Sep 19 1982 11:03	17°Li31' R
Mercury Direct Station	Oct 11 1982 05:22	02°Li26' D
Mercury Retrograde Station	Jan 7 1983 03:00	02°Aq33' R
Mercury Direct Station	Jan 27 1983 13:26	16°Cp28' D
Mercury Retrograde Station	May 1 1983 16:37	25°Ta32' R
Mercury Direct Station	May 25 1983 12:49	16°Ta25' D
Mercury Retrograde Station	Sep 2 1983 06:42	00°Li44' R
Mercury Direct Station	Sep 24 1983 20:50	16°Vi24' D
Mercury Retrograde Station	Dec 22 1983 00:54	16°Cp37' R
Mercury Direct Station	Jan 11 1984 00:38	00°Cp24' D
Mercury Retrograde Station	Apr 11 1984 20:24	06°Ta41' R
Mercury Direct Station	May 5 1984 14:06	26°Ar18' D
Mercury Retrograde Station	Aug 14 1984 19:34	13°Vi23' R

Mercury Direct Station	Sep 7 1984 04:02	00°Vi02' D
Mercury Retrograde Station	Dec 4 1984 21:47	00°Cp47' R
Mercury Direct Station	Dec 24 1984 16:11	14°Sg31' D
Mercury Retrograde Station	Mar 24 1985 19:01	18°Ar38' R
Mercury Direct Station	Apr 17 1985 05:23	06°Ar43' D
Mercury Retrograde Station	Jul 28 1985 00:53	25°Le18' R
Mercury Direct Station	Aug 20 1985 22:48	13°Le13' D
Mercury Retrograde Station	Nov 18 1985 16:10	14°Sg59' R
Mercury Direct Station	Dec 8 1985 11:23	28°Sc46' D
Mercury Retrograde Station	Mar 7 1986 10:57	01°Ar18' R
Mercury Direct Station	Mar 30 1986 08:42	17°Pi56' D
Mercury Retrograde Station	Jul 9 1986 20:27	06°Le24' R
Mercury Direct Station	Aug 3 1986 00:48	25°Cn44' D
Mercury Retrograde Station	Nov 2 1986 06:48	29°Sc09' R
Mercury Direct Station	Nov 22 1986 09:03	13°Sc05' D
Mercury Retrograde Station	Feb 18 1987 16:08	14°Pi29' R
Mercury Direct Station	Mar 12 1987 21:23	29°Aq57' D
Mercury Retrograde Station	Jun 21 1987 03:45	16°Cn48' R
Mercury Direct Station	Jul 15 1987 07:52	07°Cn24' D
Mercury Retrograde Station	Oct 16 1987 16:46	13°Sc12' R
Mercury Direct Station	Nov 6 1987 07:40	27°Li24' D
Mercury Retrograde Station	Feb 2 1988 06:18	28°Aq02' R
Mercury Direct Station	Feb 23 1988 17:30	12°Aq41' D
Mercury Retrograde Station	May 31 1988 22:44	26°Ge46' R
Mercury Direct Station	Jun 24 1988 22:40	18°Ge09' D
Mercury Retrograde Station	Sep 28 1988 21:37	27°Li02' R
Mercury Direct Station	Oct 20 1988 05:22	11°Li39' D
Mercury Retrograde Station	Jan 16 1989 01:46	11°Aq52' R
Mercury Direct Station	Feb 5 1989 20:08	25°Cp59' D
Mercury Retrograde Station	May 12 1989 11:53	06°Ge51' R
Mercury Direct Station	Jun 5 1989 08:07	28°Ta09' D
Mercury Retrograde Station	Sep 11 1989 20:58	10°Li32' R
Mercury Direct Station	Oct 3 1989 23:48	25°Vi45' D
Mercury Retrograde Station	Dec 30 1989 23:30	25°Cp52' R

1990-1999

Mercury Direct Station	Jan 20 1990 04:32	09°Cp42' D
Mercury Retrograde Station	Apr 23 1990 06:55	17°Ta31' R
Mercury Direct Station	May 17 1990 02:02	07°Ta55' D
Mercury Retrograde Station	Aug 25 1990 14:09	23°Vi33' R
Mercury Direct Station	Sep 17 1990 12:06	09°Vi35' D
Mercury Retrograde Station	Dec 14 1990 21:09	09°Cp59' R
Mercury Direct Station	Jan 3 1991 17:52	23°Sg43' D
Mercury Retrograde Station	Apr 4 1991 18:09	29°Ar00' R
Mercury Direct Station	Apr 28 1991 09:50	17°Ar59' D
Mercury Retrograde Station	Aug 7 1991 23:58	05°Vi53' R
Mercury Direct Station	Aug 31 1991 14:35	23°Le03' D
Mercury Retrograde Station	Nov 28 1991 17:01	24°Sg10' R
Mercury Direct Station	Dec 18 1991 11:12	07°Sg54' D
Mercury Retrograde Station	Mar 17 1992 00:33	11°Ar17' R
Mercury Direct Station	Apr 9 1992 06:27	28°Pi44' D
Mercury Retrograde Station	Jul 20 1992 00:54	17°Le27' R
Mercury Direct Station	Aug 13 1992 02:54	05°Le58' D
Mercury Retrograde Station	Nov 11 1992 09:50	08°Sg22' R
Mercury Direct Station	Dec 1 1992 07:31	22°Sc13' D
Mercury Retrograde Station	Feb 27 1993 22:54	24°Pi11' R
Mercury Direct Station	Mar 22 1993 13:44	10°Pi17' D
Mercury Retrograde Station	Jul 1 1993 15:29	28°Cn15' R
Mercury Direct Station	Jul 25 1993 20:50	18°Cn09' D
Mercury Retrograde Station	Oct 25 1993 22:40	22°Sc29' R
Mercury Direct Station	Nov 15 1993 05:39	06°Sc32' D
Mercury Retrograde Station	Feb 11 1994 08:30	07°Pi33' R
Mercury Direct Station	Mar 5 1994 05:49	22°Aq38' D
Mercury Retrograde Station	Jun 12 1994 17:49	08°Cn24' R
Mercury Direct Station	Jul 6 1994 19:43	29°Ge25' D

Mercury Retrograde Station	Oct 9 1994 06:44	06°Sc28' R
Mercury Direct Station	Oct 30 1994 04:06	20°Li50' D
Mercury Retrograde Station	Jan 26 1995 01:16	21°Aq14' R
Mercury Direct Station	Feb 16 1995 05:07	05°Aq37' D
Mercury Retrograde Station	May 24 1995 09:02	18°Ge21' R
Mercury Direct Station	Jun 17 1995 06:59	09°Ge49' D
Mercury Retrograde Station	Sep 22 1995 09:15	20°Li10' R
Mercury Direct Station	Oct 14 1995 00:48	05°Li01' D
Mercury Retrograde Station	Jan 9 1996 21:52	05°Aq08' R
Mercury Direct Station	Jan 30 1996 10:17	19°Cp07' D
Mercury Retrograde Station	May 3 1996 22:40	28°Ta37' R
Mercury Direct Station	May 27 1996 19:03	19°Ta39' D
Mercury Retrograde Station	Sep 4 1996 05:48	03°Li28' R
Mercury Direct Station	Sep 26 1996 17:09	19°Vi00' D
Mercury Retrograde Station	Dec 23 1996 19:46	19°Cp12' R
Mercury Direct Station	Jan 12 1997 20:42	02°Cp59' D
Mercury Retrograde Station	Apr 15 1997 00:02	09°Ta38' R
Mercury Direct Station	May 8 1997 18:06	29°Ar28' D
Mercury Retrograde Station	Aug 17 1997 19:49	16°Vi13' R
Mercury Direct Station	Sep 10 1997 01:43	02°Vi43' D
Mercury Retrograde Station	Dec 7 1997 16:57	03°Cp21' R
Mercury Direct Station	Dec 27 1997 11:41	17°Sg03' D
Mercury Retrograde Station	Mar 27 1998 19:42	21°Ar28' R
Mercury Direct Station	Apr 20 1998 07:32	09°Ar47' D
Mercury Retrograde Station	Jul 31 1998 02:28	28°Le15' R
Mercury Direct Station	Aug 23 1998 22:36	15°Le58' D
Mercury Retrograde Station	Nov 21 1998 11:46	17°Sg33' R
Mercury Direct Station	Dec 11 1998 06:30	01°Sg19' D
Mercury Retrograde Station	Mar 10 1999 09:12	04°Ar02' R
Mercury Direct Station	Apr 2 1999 09:20	20°Pi52' D
Mercury Retrograde Station	Jul 12 1999 23:33	09°Le28' R
Mercury Direct Station	Aug 6 1999 03:27	28°Cn35' D
Mercury Retrograde Station	Nov 5 1999 03:00	01°Sg42' R
Mercury Direct Station	Nov 25 1999 03:55	15°Sc38' D

2000-2009

Mercury Retrograde Station	Feb 21 2000 12:47	17°Pi10' R
Mercury Direct Station	Mar 14 2000 20:40	02°Pi47' D
Mercury Retrograde Station	Jun 23 2000 08:32	19°Cn57' R
Mercury Direct Station	Jul 17 2000 13:21	10°Cn23' D
Mercury Retrograde Station	Oct 18 2000 13:42	15°Sc47' R
Mercury Direct Station	Nov 8 2000 02:29	29°Li57' D
Mercury Retrograde Station	Feb 4 2001 01:59	00°Pi40' R
Mercury Direct Station	Feb 25 2001 15:42	15°Aq25' D
Mercury Retrograde Station	Jun 4 2001 05:22	29°Ge57' R
Mercury Direct Station	Jun 28 2001 05:50	21°Ge16' D
Mercury Retrograde Station	Oct 1 2001 19:24	29°Li40' R
Mercury Direct Station	Oct 23 2001 00:23	14°Li13' D
Mercury Retrograde Station	Jan 18 2002 20:51	14°Aq27' R
Mercury Direct Station	Feb 8 2002 17:28	28°Cp38' D
Mercury Retrograde Station	May 15 2002 18:50	09°Ge58' R
Mercury Direct Station	Jun 8 2002 15:12	01°Ge21' D
Mercury Retrograde Station	Sep 14 2002 19:39	13°Li13' R
Mercury Direct Station	Oct 6 2002 19:26	28°Vi20' D
Mercury Retrograde Station	Jan 2 2003 18:20	28°Cp26' R
Mercury Direct Station	Jan 23 2003 01:09	12°Cp18' D
Mercury Retrograde Station	Apr 26 2003 12:00	20°Ta33' R
Mercury Direct Station	May 20 2003 07:33	11°Ta07' D
Mercury Retrograde Station	Aug 28 2003 13:42	26°Vi19' R
Mercury Direct Station	Sep 20 2003 08:53	12°Vi12' D
Mercury Retrograde Station	Dec 17 2003 16:02	12°Cp33' R
Mercury Direct Station	Jan 6 2004 13:45	26°Sg16' D
Mercury Retrograde Station	Apr 6 2004 20:28	01°Ta54' R
Mercury Direct Station	Apr 30 2004 13:06	21°Ar07' D
Mercury Retrograde Station	Aug 10 2004 00:33	08°Vi45' R

Mercury Direct Station	Sep 2 2004 13:10	25°Le44' D
Mercury Retrograde Station	Nov 30 2004 12:18	26°Sg44' R
Mercury Direct Station	Dec 20 2004 06:30	10°Sg27' D
Mercury Retrograde Station	Mar 20 2005 00:15	14°Ar05' R
Mercury Direct Station	Apr 12 2005 07:46	01°Ar45' D
Mercury Retrograde Station	Jul 23 2005 03:01	20°Le27' R
Mercury Direct Station	Aug 16 2005 03:51	08°Le45' D
Mercury Retrograde Station	Nov 14 2005 05:43	10°Sg55' R
Mercury Direct Station	Dec 4 2005 02:24	24°Sc45' D
Mercury Retrograde Station	Mar 2 2006 20:30	26°Pi54' R
Mercury Direct Station	Mar 25 2006 13:43	13°Pi11' D
Mercury Retrograde Station	Jul 4 2006 19:34	01°Le21' R
Mercury Direct Station	Jul 29 2006 00:40	21°Cn04' D
Mercury Retrograde Station	Oct 28 2006 19:17	25°Sc03' R
Mercury Direct Station	Nov 18 2006 00:26	09°Sc05' D
Mercury Retrograde Station	Feb 14 2007 04:38	10°Pi12' R
Mercury Direct Station	Mar 8 2007 04:45	25°Aq25' D
Mercury Retrograde Station	Jun 15 2007 23:41	11°Cn35' R
Mercury Direct Station	Jul 10 2007 02:16	02°Cn29' D
Mercury Retrograde Station	Oct 12 2007 04:01	09°Sc03' R
Mercury Direct Station	Nov 1 2007 22:59	23°Li22' D
Mercury Retrograde Station	Jan 28 2008 20:31	23°Aq51' R
Mercury Direct Station	Feb 19 2008 02:58	08°Aq20' D
Mercury Retrograde Station	May 26 2008 15:48	21°Ge32' R
Mercury Direct Station	Jun 19 2008 14:32	12°Ge58' D
Mercury Retrograde Station	Sep 24 2008 07:17	22°Li49' R
Mercury Direct Station	Oct 15 2008 20:06	07°Li35' D
Mercury Retrograde Station	Jan 11 2009 16:44	07°Aq44' R
Mercury Direct Station	Feb 1 2009 07:11	21°Cp45' D
Mercury Retrograde Station	May 7 2009 05:01	01°Ge44' R
Mercury Direct Station	May 31 2009 01:22	22°Ta52' D
Mercury Retrograde Station	Sep 7 2009 04:45	06°Li12' R
Mercury Direct Station	Sep 29 2009 13:14	21°Vi36' D
Mercury Retrograde Station	Dec 26 2009 14:39	21°Cp47' R

2010-2019

Mercury Direct Station	Jan 15 2010 16:52	05°Cp33' D
Mercury Retrograde Station	Apr 18 2010 04:07	12°Ta37' R
Mercury Direct Station	May 11 2010 22:27	02°Ta40' D
Mercury Retrograde Station	Aug 20 2010 19:59	19°Vi02' R
Mercury Direct Station	Sep 12 2010 23:09	05°Vi23' D
Mercury Retrograde Station	Dec 10 2010 12:05	05°Cp56' R
Mercury Direct Station	Dec 30 2010 07:21	19°Sg38' D
Mercury Retrograde Station	Mar 30 2011 20:48	24°Ar20' R
Mercury Direct Station	Apr 23 2011 10:05	12°Ar53' D
Mercury Retrograde Station	Aug 3 2011 03:51	01°Vi11' R
Mercury Direct Station	Aug 26 2011 22:04	18°Le42' D
Mercury Retrograde Station	Nov 24 2011 07:20	20°Sg06' R
Mercury Direct Station	Dec 14 2011 01:43	03°Sg52' D
Mercury Retrograde Station	Mar 12 2012 07:50	06°Ar48' R
Mercury Direct Station	Apr 4 2012 10:12	23°Pi51' D
Mercury Retrograde Station	Jul 15 2012 02:17	12°Le31' R
Mercury Direct Station	Aug 8 2012 05:41	01°Le26' D
Mercury Retrograde Station	Nov 6 2012 23:04	04°Sg16' R
Mercury Direct Station	Nov 26 2012 22:48	18°Sc11' D
Mercury Retrograde Station	Feb 23 2013 09:42	19°Pi52' R
Mercury Direct Station	Mar 17 2013 20:04	05°Pi38' D
Mercury Retrograde Station	Jun 26 2013 13:08	23°Cn06' R
Mercury Direct Station	Jul 20 2013 18:23	13°Cn22' D
Mercury Retrograde Station	Oct 21 2013 10:29	18°Sc23' R
Mercury Direct Station	Nov 10 2013 21:12	02°Sc30' D
Mercury Retrograde Station	Feb 6 2014 21:44	03°Pi18' R
Mercury Direct Station	Feb 28 2014 14:01	18°Aq09' D
Mercury Retrograde Station	Jun 7 2014 11:57	03°Cn10' R
Mercury Direct Station	Jul 1 2014 12:51	24°Ge22' D

Mercury Retrograde Station	Oct 4 2014 17:03	02°Sc18' R
Mercury Direct Station	Oct 25 2014 19:17	16°Li46' D
Mercury Retrograde Station	Jan 21 2015 15:55	17°Aq04' R
Mercury Direct Station	Feb 11 2015 14:58	01°Aq18' D
Mercury Retrograde Station	May 19 2015 01:50	13°Ge08' R
Mercury Direct Station	Jun 11 2015 22:34	04°Ge34' D
Mercury Retrograde Station	Sep 17 2015 18:10	15°Li54' R
Mercury Direct Station	Oct 9 2015 14:58	00°Li54' D
Mercury Retrograde Station	Jan 5 2016 13:06	01°Aq02' R
Mercury Direct Station	Jan 25 2016 21:50	14°Cp55' D
Mercury Retrograde Station	Apr 28 2016 17:20	23°Ta35' R
Mercury Direct Station	May 22 2016 13:20	14°Ta20' D
Mercury Retrograde Station	Aug 30 2016 13:04	29°Vi04' R
Mercury Direct Station	Sep 22 2016 05:31	14°Vi50' D
Mercury Retrograde Station	Dec 19 2016 10:56	15°Cp07' R
Mercury Direct Station	Jan 8 2017 09:43	28°Sg51' D
Mercury Retrograde Station	Apr 9 2017 23:15	04°Ta50' R
Mercury Direct Station	May 3 2017 16:33	24°Ar16' D
Mercury Retrograde Station	Aug 13 2017 01:01	11°Vi37' R
Mercury Direct Station	Sep 5 2017 11:30	28°Le25' D
Mercury Retrograde Station	Dec 3 2017 07:35	29°Sg17' R
Mercury Direct Station	Dec 23 2017 01:51	13°Sg01' D
Mercury Retrograde Station	Mar 23 2018 00:20	16°Ar53' R
Mercury Direct Station	Apr 15 2018 09:21	04°Ar46' D
Mercury Retrograde Station	Jul 26 2018 05:03	23°Le26' R
Mercury Direct Station	Aug 19 2018 04:25	11°Le32' D
Mercury Retrograde Station	Nov 17 2018 01:34	13°Sg28' R
Mercury Direct Station	Dec 6 2018 21:23	27°Sc17' D
Mercury Retrograde Station	Mar 5 2019 18:19	29°Pi38' R
Mercury Direct Station	Mar 28 2019 13:59	16°Pi05' D
Mercury Retrograde Station	Jul 7 2019 23:15	04°Le27' R
Mercury Direct Station	Aug 1 2019 03:58	23°Cn57' D
Mercury Retrograde Station	Oct 31 2019 15:42	27°Sc37' R
Mercury Direct Station	Nov 20 2019 19:12	11°Sc36' D

2020-2029

Mercury Retrograde Station	Feb 17 2020 00:55	12°Pi52' R
Mercury Direct Station	Mar 10 2020 03:49	28°Aq13' D
Mercury Retrograde Station	Jun 18 2020 05:00	14°Cn45' R
Mercury Direct Station	Jul 12 2020 08:27	05°Cn29' D
Mercury Retrograde Station	Oct 14 2020 01:06	11°Sc39' R
Mercury Direct Station	Nov 3 2020 17:50	25°Li54' D
Mercury Retrograde Station	Jan 30 2021 15:52	26°Aq28' R
Mercury Direct Station	Feb 21 2021 00:53	11°Aq02' D
Mercury Retrograde Station	May 29 2021 22:35	24°Ge42' R
Mercury Direct Station	Jun 22 2021 22:01	16°Ge08' D
Mercury Retrograde Station	Sep 27 2021 05:11	25°Li27' R
Mercury Direct Station	Oct 18 2021 15:17	10°Li08' D
Mercury Retrograde Station	Jan 14 2022 11:42	10°Aq20' R
Mercury Direct Station	Feb 4 2022 04:14	24°Cp23' D
Mercury Retrograde Station	May 10 2022 11:48	04°Ge51' R
Mercury Direct Station	Jun 3 2022 08:01	26°Ta05' D
Mercury Retrograde Station	Sep 10 2022 03:39	08°Li54' R
Mercury Direct Station	Oct 2 2022 09:08	24°Vi12' D
Mercury Retrograde Station	Dec 29 2022 09:32	24°Cp20' R
Mercury Direct Station	Jan 18 2023 13:13	08°Cp08' D
Mercury Retrograde Station	Apr 21 2023 08:36	15°Ta36' R
Mercury Direct Station	May 15 2023 03:17	05°Ta51' D
Mercury Retrograde Station	Aug 23 2023 20:00	21°Vi50' R
Mercury Direct Station	Sep 15 2023 20:22	08°Vi01' D
Mercury Retrograde Station	Dec 13 2023 07:10	08°Cp28' R
Mercury Direct Station	Jan 2 2024 03:08	22°Sg11' D
Mercury Retrograde Station	Apr 1 2024 22:15	27°Ar12' R
Mercury Direct Station	Apr 25 2024 12:55	15°Ar58 D
Mercury Retrograde Station	Aug 5 2024 04:57	04°Vi05' R

Mercury Direct Station	Aug 28 2024 21:15	21°Le25' D
Mercury Retrograde Station	Nov 26 2024 02:43	22°Sg39' R
Mercury Direct Station	Dec 15 2024 20:57	06°Sg24' D
Mercury Retrograde Station	Mar 15 2025 06:47	09°Ar34' R
Mercury Direct Station	Apr 7 2025 11:08	26°Pi49' D
Mercury Retrograde Station	Jul 18 2025 04:46	15°Le33' R
Mercury Direct Station	Aug 11 2025 07:31	04°Le15' D
Mercury Retrograde Station	Nov 9 2025 19:02	06°Sg50' R
Mercury Direct Station	Nov 29 2025 17:39	20°Sc43' D
Mercury Retrograde Station	Feb 26 2026 06:49	22°Pi33' R
Mercury Direct Station	Mar 20 2026 19:33	08°Pi30' D
Mercury Retrograde Station	Jun 29 2026 17:37	26°Cn15' R
Mercury Direct Station	Jul 23 2026 22:59	16°Cn19' D
Mercury Retrograde Station	Oct 24 2026 07:13	20°Sc58' R
Mercury Direct Station	Nov 13 2026 15:55	05°Sc02' D
Mercury Retrograde Station	Feb 9 2027 17:37	05°Pi57' R
Mercury Direct Station	Mar 3 2027 12:33	20°Aq55' D
Mercury Retrograde Station	Jun 10 2027 18:16	06°Cn21' R
Mercury Direct Station	Jul 4 2027 19:40	27°Ge28' D
Mercury Retrograde Station	Oct 7 2027 14:38	04°Sc55' R
Mercury Direct Station	Oct 28 2027 14:11	19°Li19' D
Mercury Retrograde Station	Jan 24 2028 11:03	19°Aq41' R
Mercury Direct Station	Feb 14 2028 12:38	03°Aq59' D
Mercury Retrograde Station	May 21 2028 08:44	16°Ge18' R
Mercury Direct Station	Jun 14 2028 06:07	07°Ge45' D
Mercury Retrograde Station	Sep 19 2028 16:34	18°Li35' R
Mercury Direct Station	Oct 11 2028 10:28	03°Li29' D
Mercury Retrograde Station	Jan 7 2029 07:57	03°Aq37' R
Mercury Direct Station	Jan 27 2029 18:41	17°Cp33' D
Mercury Retrograde Station	May 1 2029 23:06	26°Ta39' R
Mercury Direct Station	May 25 2029 19:21	17°Ta34' D
Mercury Retrograde Station	Sep 2 2029 12:19	01°Li49' R
Mercury Direct Station	Sep 25 2029 02:02	17°Vi28' D
Mercury Retrograde Station	Dec 22 2029 05:51	17°Cp41' R

2030-2039

Mercury Direct Station	Jan 11 2030 05:46	01°Cp27' D
Mercury Retrograde Station	Apr 13 2030 02:34	07°Ta47' R
Mercury Direct Station	May 6 2030 20:15	27°Ar26' D
Mercury Retrograde Station	Aug 16 2030 01:21	14°Vi29' R
Mercury Direct Station	Sep 8 2030 09:28	01°Vi06' D
Mercury Retrograde Station	Dec 6 2030 02:48	01°Cp50' R
Mercury Direct Station	Dec 25 2030 21:15	15°Sg34' D
Mercury Retrograde Station	Mar 26 2031 00:44	19°Ar43' R
Mercury Direct Station	Apr 18 2031 11:16	07°Ar50' D
Mercury Retrograde Station	Jul 29 2031 06:48	26°Le25' R
Mercury Direct Station	Aug 22 2031 04:29	14°Le18' D
Mercury Retrograde Station	Nov 19 2031 21:16	16°Sg02' R
Mercury Direct Station	Dec 9 2031 16:24	29°Sc49' D
Mercury Retrograde Station	Mar 7 2032 16:22	02°Ar22' R
Mercury Direct Station	Mar 30 2032 14:30	19°Pi02' D
Mercury Retrograde Station	Jul 10 2032 02:34	07°Le32' R
Mercury Direct Station	Aug 3 2032 06:53	26°Cn49' D
Mercury Retrograde Station	Nov 2 2032 11:57	00°Sg12' R
Mercury Direct Station	Nov 22 2032 14:01	14°Sc08' D
Mercury Retrograde Station	Feb 18 2033 21:21	15°Pi32' R
Mercury Direct Station	Mar 13 2033 02:58	01°Pi02' D
Mercury Retrograde Station	Jun 21 2033 10:06	17°Cn56' R
Mercury Direct Station	Jul 15 2033 14:20	08°Cn30' D
Mercury Retrograde Station	Oct 16 2033 22:04	14°Sc15' R
Mercury Direct Station	Nov 6 2033 12:40	28°Li27' D
Mercury Retrograde Station	Feb 2 2034 11:23	29°Aq06' R
Mercury Direct Station	Feb 23 2034 22:55	13°Aq45' D
Mercury Retrograde Station	Jun 2 2034 05:24	27°Ge54' R
Mercury Direct Station	Jun 26 2034 05:24	19°Ge17' D

Mercury Retrograde Station	Sep 30 2034 03:01	28°Li06' R
Mercury Direct Station	Oct 21 2034 10:23	12°Li42' D
Mercury Retrograde Station	Jan 17 2035 06:45	12°Aq55' R
Mercury Direct Station	Feb 7 2035 01:25	27°Cp02' D
Mercury Retrograde Station	May 13 2035 18:41	07°Ge58' R
Mercury Direct Station	Jun 6 2035 14:53	29°Ta18' D
Mercury Retrograde Station	Sep 13 2035 02:29	11°Li36' R
Mercury Direct Station	Oct 5 2035 04:54	26°Vi48' D
Mercury Retrograde Station	Jan 1 2036 04:25	26°Cp54' R
Mercury Direct Station	Jan 21 2036 09:43	10°Cp44' D
Mercury Retrograde Station	Apr 23 2036 13:19	18°Ta37' R
Mercury Direct Station	May 17 2036 08:30	09°Ta03' D
Mercury Retrograde Station	Aug 25 2036 19:48	24°Vi37' R
Mercury Direct Station	Sep 17 2036 17:21	10°Vi39' D
Mercury Retrograde Station	Dec 15 2036 02:07	11°Cp01' R
Mercury Direct Station	Jan 3 2037 22:58	24°Sg45' D
Mercury Retrograde Station	Apr 5 2037 00:06	00°Ta05' R
Mercury Direct Station	Apr 28 2037 15:57	19°Ar06' D
Mercury Retrograde Station	Aug 8 2037 05:46	06°Vi59' R
Mercury Direct Station	Aug 31 2037 20:08	24°Le07' D
Mercury Retrograde Station	Nov 28 2037 22:01	25°Sg12' R
Mercury Direct Station	Dec 18 2037 16:13	08°Sg57' D
Mercury Retrograde Station	Mar 18 2038 06:08	12°Ar21' R
Mercury Direct Station	Apr 10 2038 12:13	29°Pi49' D
Mercury Retrograde Station	Jul 21 2038 06:59	18°Le34' R
Mercury Direct Station	Aug 14 2038 08:50	07°Le03' D
Mercury Retrograde Station	Nov 12 2038 14:57	09°Sg24' R
Mercury Direct Station	Dec 2 2038 12:31	23°Sc14' D
Mercury Retrograde Station	Mar 1 2039 04:13	25°Pi14' R
Mercury Direct Station	Mar 23 2039 19:20	11°Pi22' D
Mercury Retrograde Station	Jul 2 2039 21:48	29°Cn22' R
Mercury Direct Station	Jul 27 2039 03:07	19°Cn15' D
Mercury Retrograde Station	Oct 27 2039 03:55	23°Sc32' R
Mercury Direct Station	Nov 16 2039 10:39	07°Sc34' D

2040-2049

Mercury Retrograde Station	Feb 12 2040 13:39	08°Pi37' R
Mercury Direct Station	Mar 5 2040 11:20	23°Aq41' D
Mercury Retrograde Station	Jun 13 2040 00:20	09°Cn31' R
Mercury Direct Station	Jul 7 2040 02:22	00°Cn32' D
Mercury Retrograde Station	Oct 9 2040 12:06	07°Sc31' R
Mercury Direct Station	Oct 30 2040 09:07	21°Li51' D
Mercury Retrograde Station	Jan 26 2041 06:15	22°Aq17' R
Mercury Direct Station	Feb 16 2041 10:28	06°Aq40' D
Mercury Retrograde Station	May 24 2041 15:39	19°Ge28' R
Mercury Direct Station	Jun 17 2041 13:42	10°Ge56' D
Mercury Retrograde Station	Sep 22 2041 14:44	21°Li14'
Mercury Direct Station	Oct 14 2041 05:52	06°Li03' D
Mercury Retrograde Station	Jan 10 2042 02:48	06°Aq11' R
Mercury Direct Station	Jan 30 2042 15:32	20°Cp10' D
Mercury Retrograde Station	May 5 2042 05:14	29°Ta44' R
Mercury Direct Station	May 29 2042 01:32	20°Ta47' D
Mercury Retrograde Station	Sep 5 2042 11:22	04°Li33' R
Mercury Direct Station	Sep 27 2042 22:19	20°Vi04' D
Mercury Retrograde Station	Dec 25 2042 00:45	20°Cp14' R
Mercury Direct Station	Jan 14 2043 01:50	04°Cp01' D
Mercury Retrograde Station	Apr 16 2043 06:18	10°Ta44' R
Mercury Direct Station	May 10 2043 00:20	00°Ta37' D
Mercury Retrograde Station	Aug 19 2043 01:34	17°Vi18' R
Mercury Direct Station	Sep 11 2043 07:05	03°Vi46' D
Mercury Retrograde Station	Dec 8 2043 21:58	04°Cp23' R
Mercury Direct Station	Dec 28 2043 16:46	18°Sg07' D
Mercury Retrograde Station	Mar 28 2044 01:32	22°Ar34' R
Mercury Direct Station	Apr 20 2044 13:35	10°Ar54' D
Mercury Retrograde Station	Jul 31 2044 08:22	29°Le21' R

Mercury Direct Station	Aug 24 2044 04:13	17°Le02' D
Mercury Retrograde Station	Nov 21 2044 16:52	18°Sg35' R
Mercury Direct Station	Dec 11 2044 11:32	02°Sg21' D
Mercury Retrograde Station	Mar 10 2045 14:43	05°Ar07' R
Mercury Direct Station	Apr 2 2045 15:10	21°Pi59' D
Mercury Retrograde Station	Jul 13 2045 05:39	10°Le35' R
Mercury Direct Station	Aug 6 2045 09:28	29°Cn40' D
Mercury Retrograde Station	Nov 5 2045 08:08	02°Sg46' R
Mercury Direct Station	Nov 25 2045 08:55	16°Sc40' D
Mercury Retrograde Station	Feb 21 2046 18:01	18°Pi13' R
Mercury Direct Station	Mar 16 2046 02:13	03°Pi52' D
Mercury Retrograde Station	Jun 24 2046 14:58	21°Cn06' R
Mercury Direct Station	Jul 18 2046 19:52	11°Cn31' D
Mercury Retrograde Station	Oct 19 2046 18:57	16°Sc50' R
Mercury Direct Station	Nov 9 2046 07:27	01°Sc00' D
Mercury Retrograde Station	Feb 5 2047 07:02	01°Pi44' R
Mercury Direct Station	Feb 26 2047 21:05	16°Aq29' D
Mercury Retrograde Station	Jun 5 2047 12:05	01°Cn07' R
Mercury Direct Station	Jun 29 2047 12:36	22°Ge24' D
Mercury Retrograde Station	Oct 3 2047 00:46	00°Sc43' R
Mercury Direct Station	Oct 24 2047 05:22	15°Li16' D
Mercury Retrograde Station	Jan 20 2048 01:48	15°Aq31' R
Mercury Direct Station	Feb 9 2048 22:45	29°Cp42' D
Mercury Retrograde Station	May 16 2048 01:32	11°Ge07' R
Mercury Direct Station	Jun 8 2048 21:57	02°Ge30' D
Mercury Retrograde Station	Sep 15 2048 01:10	14°Li17' R
Mercury Direct Station	Oct 7 2048 00:30	29°Vi23' D
Mercury Retrograde Station	Jan 2 2049 23:15	29°Cp29' R
Mercury Direct Station	Jan 23 2049 06:20	13°Cp21' D
Mercury Retrograde Station	Apr 26 2049 18:21	21°Ta39' R
Mercury Direct Station	May 20 2049 13:58	12°Ta15' D
Mercury Retrograde Station	Aug 28 2049 19:22	27°Vi24' R
Mercury Direct Station	Sep 20 2049 14:10	13°Vi16' D
Mercury Retrograde Station	Dec 17 2049 21:00	13°Cp35' R

2050-2059

Mercury Direct Station	Jan 6 2050 18:52	27°Sg20' D
Mercury Retrograde Station	Apr 8 2050 02:29	03°Ta00' R
Mercury Direct Station	May 1 2050 19:11	22°Ar15' D
Mercury Retrograde Station	Aug 11 2050 06:23	09°Vi52' R
Mercury Direct Station	Sep 3 2050 18:43	26°Le49' D
Mercury Retrograde Station	Dec 1 2050 17:20	27°Sg46' R
Mercury Direct Station	Dec 21 2050 11:33	11°Sg29' D
Mercury Retrograde Station	Mar 21 2051 05:57	15°Ar10' R
Mercury Direct Station	Apr 13 2051 13:38	02°Ar51' D
Mercury Retrograde Station	Jul 24 2051 09:03	21°Le35' R
Mercury Direct Station	Aug 17 2051 09:42	09°Le50' D
Mercury Retrograde Station	Nov 15 2051 10:51	11°Sg58' R
Mercury Direct Station	Dec 5 2051 07:25	25°Sc47' D
Mercury Retrograde Station	Mar 3 2052 01:52	27°Pi58' R
Mercury Direct Station	Mar 25 2052 19:25	14°Pi17' D
Mercury Retrograde Station	Jul 5 2052 01:46	02°Le29' R
Mercury Direct Station	Jul 29 2052 06:49	22°Cn09' D
Mercury Retrograde Station	Oct 29 2052 00:30	26°Sc06' R
Mercury Direct Station	Nov 18 2052 05:25	10°Sc07' D
Mercury Retrograde Station	Feb 14 2053 09:46	11°Pi16' R
Mercury Direct Station	Mar 8 2053 10:17	26°Aq29' D
Mercury Retrograde Station	Jun 16 2053 06:05	12°Cn42' R
Mercury Direct Station	Jul 10 2053 08:49	03°Cn34' D
Mercury Retrograde Station	Oct 12 2053 09:19	10°Sc07' R
Mercury Direct Station	Nov 2 2053 03:58	24°Li25' D
Mercury Retrograde Station	Jan 29 2054 01:31	24°Aq53' R
Mercury Direct Station	Feb 19 2054 08:20	09°Aq22' D
Mercury Retrograde Station	May 27 2054 22:32	22°Ge39' R
Mercury Direct Station	Jun 20 2054 21:19	14°Ge07' D

Mercury Retrograde Station	Sep 25 2054 12:42	23°Li53' R
Mercury Direct Station	Oct 17 2054 01:08	08°Li38' D
Mercury Retrograde Station	Jan 12 2055 21:42	08°Aq46' R
Mercury Direct Station	Feb 2 2055 12:26	22°Cp47' D
Mercury Retrograde Station	May 8 2055 11:42	02°Ge51' R
Mercury Direct Station	Jun 1 2055 07:59	24°Ta00' D
Mercury Retrograde Station	Sep 8 2055 10:18	07°Li16' R
Mercury Direct Station	Sep 30 2055 18:22	22°Vi40' D
Mercury Retrograde Station	Dec 27 2055 19:38	22°Cp48' R
Mercury Direct Station	Jan 16 2056 22:02	06°Cp36' D
Mercury Retrograde Station	Apr 18 2056 10:26	13°Ta43' R
Mercury Direct Station	May 12 2056 04:51	03°Ta47' D
Mercury Retrograde Station	Aug 21 2056 01:42	20°Vi07' R
Mercury Direct Station	Sep 13 2056 04:29	06°Vi25' D
Mercury Retrograde Station	Dec 10 2056 17:05	06°Cp57' R
Mercury Direct Station	Dec 30 2056 12:27	20°Sg39' D
Mercury Retrograde Station	Mar 31 2057 02:40	25°Ar25' R
Mercury Direct Station	Apr 23 2057 16:09	14°Ar00' D
Mercury Retrograde Station	Aug 3 2057 09:47	02°Vi17' R
Mercury Direct Station	Aug 27 2057 03:43	19°Le46' D
Mercury Retrograde Station	Nov 24 2057 12:22	21°Sg09' R
Mercury Direct Station	Dec 14 2057 06:46	04°Sg54' D
Mercury Retrograde Station	Mar 13 2058 13:20	07°Ar52' R
Mercury Direct Station	Apr 5 2058 15:58	24°Pi56' D
Mercury Retrograde Station	Jul 16 2058 08:24	13°Le39' R
Mercury Direct Station	Aug 9 2058 11:43	02°Le30' D
Mercury Retrograde Station	Nov 8 2058 04:13	05°Sg19' R
Mercury Direct Station	Nov 28 2058 03:47	19°Sc13' D
Mercury Retrograde Station	Feb 24 2059 14:57	20°Pi55' R
Mercury Direct Station	Mar 19 2059 01:37	06°Pi43' D
Mercury Retrograde Station	Jun 27 2059 19:32	24°Cn14' R
Mercury Direct Station	Jul 22 2059 00:51	14°Cn28' D
Mercury Retrograde Station	Oct 22 2059 15:44	19°Sc25' R
Mercury Direct Station	Nov 12 2059 02:09	03°Sc33' D

2060-2069

Mercury Retrograde Station	Feb 8 2060 02:48	04°Pi21' R
Mercury Direct Station	Feb 29 2060 19:25	19°Aq14' D
Mercury Retrograde Station	Jun 7 2060 18:32	04°Cn17' R
Mercury Direct Station	Jul 1 2060 19:30	25°Ge30' D
Mercury Retrograde Station	Oct 4 2060 22:28	03°Sc21' R
Mercury Direct Station	Oct 26 2060 00:18	17°Li49' D
Mercury Retrograde Station	Jan 21 2061 20:54	18°Aq06' R
Mercury Direct Station	Feb 11 2061 20:19	02°Aq22' D
Mercury Retrograde Station	May 19 2061 08:28	14°Ge15' R
Mercury Direct Station	Jun 12 2061 05:16	05°Ge41' D
Mercury Retrograde Station	Sep 17 2061 23:41	16°Li58' R
Mercury Direct Station	Oct 9 2061 20:04	01°Li58' D
Mercury Retrograde Station	Jan 5 2062 18:04	02°Aq04' R
Mercury Direct Station	Jan 26 2062 03:05	15°Cp58' D
Mercury Retrograde Station	Apr 29 2062 23:51	24°Ta42' R
Mercury Direct Station	May 23 2062 19:50	15°Ta29' D
Mercury Retrograde Station	Aug 31 2062 18:44	00°Li09' R
Mercury Direct Station	Sep 23 2062 10:49	15°Vi53' D
Mercury Retrograde Station	Dec 20 2062 15:54	16°Cp09' R
Mercury Direct Station	Jan 9 2063 14:52	29°Sg54' D
Mercury Retrograde Station	Apr 11 2063 05:24	05°Ta56' R
Mercury Direct Station	May 4 2063 22:42	25°Ar24' D
Mercury Retrograde Station	Aug 14 2063 06:46	12°Vi43' R
Mercury Direct Station	Sep 6 2063 16:56	29°Le30' D
Mercury Retrograde Station	Dec 4 2063 12:36	00°Cp20' R
Mercury Direct Station	Dec 24 2063 06:55	14°Sg03' D
Mercury Retrograde Station	Mar 23 2064 06:05	17°Ar59' R
Mercury Direct Station	Apr 15 2064 15:18	05°Ar54' D
Mercury Retrograde Station	Jul 26 2064 10:58	24°Le33' R

Mercury Direct Station	Aug 19 2064 10:07	12°Le36' D
Mercury Retrograde Station	Nov 17 2064 06:39	14°Sg31' R
Mercury Direct Station	Dec 7 2064 02:22	28°Sc20' D
Mercury Retrograde Station	Mar 5 2065 23:41	00°Ar41' R
Mercury Direct Station	Mar 28 2065 19:41	17°Pi12' D
Mercury Retrograde Station	Jul 8 2065 05:28	05°Le35' R
Mercury Direct Station	Aug 1 2065 10:06	25°Cn03' D
Mercury Retrograde Station	Oct 31 2065 20:54	28°Sc41' R
Mercury Direct Station	Nov 21 2065 00:11	12°Sc39' D
Mercury Retrograde Station	Feb 17 2066 06:02	13°Pi56' R
Mercury Direct Station	Mar 11 2066 09:20	29°Aq17' D
Mercury Retrograde Station	Jun 19 2066 11:29	15°Cn54' R
Mercury Direct Station	Jul 13 2066 15:01	06°Cn37' D
Mercury Retrograde Station	Oct 15 2066 06:22	12°Sc43' R
Mercury Direct Station	Nov 4 2066 22:49	26°Li58' D
Mercury Retrograde Station	Jan 31 2067 20:55	27°Aq31' R
Mercury Direct Station	Feb 22 2067 06:16	12°Aq06' D
Mercury Retrograde Station	May 31 2067 05:18	25°Ge51' R
Mercury Direct Station	Jun 24 2067 04:50	17°Ge16' D
Mercury Retrograde Station	Sep 28 2067 10:36	26°Li32' R
Mercury Direct Station	Oct 19 2067 20:20	11°Li12' D
Mercury Retrograde Station	Jan 15 2068 16:42	11°Aq22' R
Mercury Direct Station	Feb 5 2068 09:30	25°Cp26' D
Mercury Retrograde Station	May 10 2068 18:25	05°Ge58' R
Mercury Direct Station	Jun 3 2068 14:40	27°Ta13' D
Mercury Retrograde Station	Sep 10 2068 09:14	09°Li59' R
Mercury Direct Station	Oct 2 2068 14:17	25°Vi16' D
Mercury Retrograde Station	Dec 29 2068 14:32	25°Cp24' R
Mercury Direct Station	Jan 18 2069 18:26	09°Cp12' D
Mercury Retrograde Station	Apr 21 2069 14:56	16°Ta43' R
Mercury Direct Station	May 15 2069 09:43	06°Ta59' D
Mercury Retrograde Station	Aug 24 2069 01:44	22°Vi55' R
Mercury Direct Station	Sep 16 2069 01:41	09°Vi05' D
Mercury Retrograde Station	Dec 13 2069 12:08	09°Cp32' R

2070-2079

Mercury Direct Station	Jan 2 2070 08:14	23°Sg14' D
Mercury Retrograde Station	Apr 3 2070 04:12	28°Ar17' R
Mercury Direct Station	Apr 26 2070 18:59	17°Ar07' D
Mercury Retrograde Station	Aug 6 2070 10:50	05°Vi12' R
Mercury Direct Station	Aug 30 2070 02:51	22°Le30' D
Mercury Retrograde Station	Nov 27 2070 07:45	23°Sg42' R
Mercury Direct Station	Dec 17 2070 02:00	07°Sg27' D
Mercury Retrograde Station	Mar 16 2071 12:20	10°Ar39' R
Mercury Direct Station	Apr 8 2071 16:54	27°Pi56' D
Mercury Retrograde Station	Jul 19 2071 10:45	16°Le41' R
Mercury Direct Station	Aug 12 2071 13:26	05°Le20' D
Mercury Retrograde Station	Nov 11 2071 00:10	07°Sg53' R
Mercury Direct Station	Nov 30 2071 22:37	21°Sc46' D
Mercury Retrograde Station	Feb 27 2072 12:07	23°Pi37' R
Mercury Direct Station	Mar 21 2072 01:11	09°Pi35' D
Mercury Retrograde Station	Jun 29 2072 23:54	27°Cn22' R
Mercury Direct Station	Jul 24 2072 05:19	17°Cn25' D
Mercury Retrograde Station	Oct 24 2072 12:28	22°Sc01' R
Mercury Direct Station	Nov 13 2072 20:52	06°Sc05' D
Mercury Retrograde Station	Feb 9 2073 22:43	07°Pi00' R
Mercury Direct Station	Mar 3 2073 18:02	21°Aq59' D
Mercury Retrograde Station	Jun 11 2073 00:54	07°Cn28' R
Mercury Direct Station	Jul 5 2073 02:19	28°Ge35' D
Mercury Retrograde Station	Oct 7 2073 20:01	05°Sc58' R
Mercury Direct Station	Oct 28 2073 19:13	20°Li22' D
Mercury Retrograde Station	Jan 24 2074 16:04	20°Aq43' R
Mercury Direct Station	Feb 14 2074 18:02	05°Aq02' D
Mercury Retrograde Station	May 22 2074 15:25	17°Ge25' R
Mercury Direct Station	Jun 15 2074 12:51	08°Ge53' D

Mercury Retrograde Station	Sep 20 2074 22:03	19°Li38' R
Mercury Direct Station	Oct 12 2074 15:34	04°Li32' D
Mercury Retrograde Station	Jan 8 2075 12:54	04°Aq39' R
Mercury Direct Station	Jan 28 2075 23:55	18°Cp35' D
Mercury Retrograde Station	May 3 2075 05:41	27°Ta46' R
Mercury Direct Station	May 27 2075 01:57	18°Ta42' D
Mercury Retrograde Station	Sep 3 2075 17:54	02°Li53' R
Mercury Direct Station	Sep 26 2075 07:15	18°Vi30' D
Mercury Retrograde Station	Dec 23 2075 10:48	18°Cp44' R
Mercury Direct Station	Jan 12 2076 10:54	02°Cp28' D
Mercury Retrograde Station	Apr 13 2076 08:46	08°Ta52' R
Mercury Direct Station	May 7 2076 02:30	28°Ar33' D
Mercury Retrograde Station	Aug 16 2076 07:05	15°Vi33' R
Mercury Direct Station	Sep 8 2076 14:50	02°Vi10' D
Mercury Retrograde Station	Dec 6 2076 07:49	02°Cp53' R
Mercury Direct Station	Dec 26 2076 02:19	16°Sg36' D
Mercury Retrograde Station	Mar 26 2077 06:30	20°Ar48' R
Mercury Direct Station	Apr 18 2077 17:14	08°Ar56' D
Mercury Retrograde Station	Jul 29 2077 12:46	27°Le31' R
Mercury Direct Station	Aug 22 2077 10:09	15°Le21' D
Mercury Retrograde Station	Nov 20 2077 02:22	17°Sg04' R
Mercury Direct Station	Dec 9 2077 21:25	00°Sg52' D
Mercury Retrograde Station	Mar 8 2078 21:45	03°Ar25' R
Mercury Direct Station	Mar 31 2078 20:12	20°Pi07' D
Mercury Retrograde Station	Jul 11 2078 08:48	08°Le39' R
Mercury Direct Station	Aug 4 2078 13:01	27°Cn54' D
Mercury Retrograde Station	Nov 3 2078 17:09	01°Sg14' R
Mercury Direct Station	Nov 23 2078 19:01	15°Sc11' D
Mercury Retrograde Station	Feb 20 2079 02:32	16°Pi35' R
Mercury Direct Station	Mar 14 2079 08:31	02°Pi06' D
Mercury Retrograde Station	Jun 22 2079 16:30	19°Cn03' R
Mercury Direct Station	Jul 16 2079 20:53	09°Cn37' D
Mercury Retrograde Station	Oct 18 2079 03:22	15°Sc18' R
Mercury Direct Station	Nov 7 2079 17:40	29°Li30' D

2080-2089

Mercury Retrograde Station	Feb 3 2080 16:29	00°Pi09' R
Mercury Direct Station	Feb 25 2080 04:21	14°Aq49' D
Mercury Retrograde Station	Jun 2 2080 12:02	29°Ge03' R
Mercury Direct Station	Jun 26 2080 12:08	20°Ge24' D
Mercury Retrograde Station	Sep 30 2080 08:25	29°Li09' R
Mercury Direct Station	Oct 21 2080 15:24	13°Li45' D
Mercury Retrograde Station	Jan 17 2081 11:45	13°Aq59' R
Mercury Direct Station	Feb 7 2081 06:43	28°Cp05' D
Mercury Retrograde Station	May 14 2081 01:21	09°Ge06' R
Mercury Direct Station	Jun 6 2081 21:32	00°Ge26' D
Mercury Retrograde Station	Sep 13 2081 08:03	12°Li41' R
Mercury Direct Station	Oct 5 2081 10:01	27°Vi51' D
Mercury Retrograde Station	Jan 1 2082 09:22	27°Cp58' R
Mercury Direct Station	Jan 21 2082 14:55	11°Cp47' D
Mercury Retrograde Station	Apr 24 2082 19:43	19°Ta44' R
Mercury Direct Station	May 18 2082 14:55	10°Ta11' D
Mercury Retrograde Station	Aug 27 2082 01:28	25°Vi42' R
Mercury Direct Station	Sep 18 2082 22:37	11°Vi43' D
Mercury Retrograde Station	Dec 16 2082 07:04	12°Cp04' R
Mercury Direct Station	Jan 5 2083 04:05	25°Sg48' D
Mercury Retrograde Station	Apr 6 2083 06:09	01°Ta11' R
Mercury Direct Station	Apr 29 2083 22:05	20°Ar14' D
Mercury Retrograde Station	Aug 9 2083 11:34	08°Vi05' R
Mercury Direct Station	Sep 2 2083 01:40	25°Le12' D
Mercury Retrograde Station	Nov 30 2083 03:03	26°Sg15' R
Mercury Direct Station	Dec 19 2083 21:15	10°Sg00' D
Mercury Retrograde Station	Mar 18 2084 11:47	13°Ar27' R
Mercury Direct Station	Apr 10 2084 18:04	00°Ar57' D
Mercury Retrograde Station	Jul 21 2084 13:00	19°Le42' R

Mercury Direct Station	Aug 14 2084 14:42	08°Le08' D
Mercury Retrograde Station	Nov 12 2084 20:06	10°Sg27' R
Mercury Direct Station	Dec 2 2084 17:30	24°Sc18' D
Mercury Retrograde Station	Mar 1 2085 09:33	26°Pi19' R
Mercury Direct Station	Mar 24 2085 01:01	12°Pi28' D
Mercury Retrograde Station	Jul 3 2085 04:08	00°Le30' R
Mercury Direct Station	Jul 27 2085 09:22	20°Cn21' D
Mercury Retrograde Station	Oct 27 2085 09:10	24°Sc36' R
Mercury Direct Station	Nov 16 2085 15:38	08°Sc37' D
Mercury Retrograde Station	Feb 12 2086 18:46	09°Pi39' R
Mercury Direct Station	Mar 6 2086 16:51	24°Aq46' D
Mercury Retrograde Station	Jun 14 2086 06:58	10°Cn41' R
Mercury Direct Station	Jul 8 2086 09:02	01°Cn39' D
Mercury Retrograde Station	Oct 10 2086 17:25	08°Sc34' R
Mercury Direct Station	Oct 31 2086 14:07	22°Li55' D
Mercury Retrograde Station	Jan 27 2087 11:14	23°Aq21' R
Mercury Direct Station	Feb 17 2087 15:48	07°Aq44' D
Mercury Retrograde Station	May 25 2087 22:19	20°Ge37' R
Mercury Direct Station	Jun 18 2087 20:32	12°Ge05' D
Mercury Retrograde Station	Sep 23 2087 20:11	22°Li18' R
Mercury Direct Station	Oct 15 2087 10:56	07°Li06' D
Mercury Retrograde Station	Jan 11 2088 07:44	07°Aq14' R
Mercury Direct Station	Jan 31 2088 20:45	21°Cp13' D
Mercury Retrograde Station	May 5 2088 11:49	00°Ge52' R
Mercury Direct Station	May 29 2088 08:09	21°Ta55' D
Mercury Retrograde Station	Sep 5 2088 16:55	05°Li37' R
Mercury Direct Station	Sep 28 2088 03:28	21°Vi07' D
Mercury Retrograde Station	Dec 25 2088 05:41	21°Cp17' R
Mercury Direct Station	Jan 14 2089 06:58	05°Cp04' D
Mercury Retrograde Station	Apr 16 2089 12:31	11°Ta51' R
Mercury Direct Station	May 10 2089 06:33	01°Ta44' D
Mercury Retrograde Station	Aug 19 2089 07:21	18°Vi24' R
Mercury Direct Station	Sep 11 2089 12:28	04°Vi50' D
Mercury Retrograde Station	Dec 9 2089 02:59	05°Cp26' R
Mercury Direct Station	Dec 28 2089 21:53	19°Sg10' D

2090-2100

Mercury Retrograde Station	Mar 29 2090 07:18	23°Ar38' R
Mercury Direct Station	Apr 21 2090 19:32	12°Ar01' D
Mercury Retrograde Station	Aug 1 2090 14:21	00°Vi28' R
Mercury Direct Station	Aug 25 2090 09:55	18°Le06' D
Mercury Retrograde Station	Nov 22 2090 21:59	19°Sg38' R
Mercury Direct Station	Dec 12 2090 16:36	03°Sg24' D
Mercury Retrograde Station	Mar 11 2091 20:12	06°Ar11' R
Mercury Direct Station	Apr 3 2091 20:59	23°Pi05' D
Mercury Retrograde Station	Jul 14 2091 11:46	11°Le43' R
Mercury Direct Station	Aug 7 2091 15:35	00°Le46' D
Mercury Retrograde Station	Nov 6 2091 13:19	03°Sg48' R
Mercury Direct Station	Nov 26 2091 13:55	17°Sc42' D
Mercury Retrograde Station	Feb 22 2092 23:18	19°Pi16' R
Mercury Direct Station	Mar 16 2092 07:49	04°Pi57' D
Mercury Retrograde Station	Jun 24 2092 21:17	22°Cn13' R
Mercury Direct Station	Jul 19 2092 02:15	12°Cn36' D
Mercury Retrograde Station	Oct 20 2092 00:14	17°Sc53' R
Mercury Direct Station	Nov 9 2092 12:27	02°Sc02D
Mercury Retrograde Station	Feb 5 2093 12:08	02°Pi48' R
Mercury Direct Station	Feb 27 2093 02:32	17°Aq33' D
Mercury Retrograde Station	Jun 5 2093 18:40	02°Cn14' R
Mercury Direct Station	Jun 29 2093 19:14	23°Ge31' D
Mercury Retrograde Station	Oct 3 2093 06:09	01°Sc47' R
Mercury Direct Station	Oct 24 2093 10:21	16°Li18' D
Mercury Retrograde Station	Jan 20 2094 06:47	16°Aq33' R
Mercury Direct Station	Feb 10 2094 04:05	00°Aq45' D
Mercury Retrograde Station	May 17 2094 08:19	12°Ge15' R
Mercury Direct Station	Jun 10 2094 04:44	03°Ge39' D
Mercury Retrograde Station	Sep 16 2094 06:41	15°Li21' R

Mercury Direct Station	Oct 8 2094	05:36	00°Li26' D
Mercury Retrograde Station	Jan 4 2095	04:10	00°Aq31' R
Mercury Direct Station	Jan 24 2095	11:33	14°Cp23' D
Mercury Retrograde Station	Apr 28 2095	00:51	22°Ta45' R
Mercury Direct Station	May 21 2095	20:31	13°Ta24' D
Mercury Retrograde Station	Aug 30 2095	00:59	28°Vi27' R
Mercury Direct Station	Sep 21 2095	19:24	14°Vi20' D
Mercury Retrograde Station	Dec 19 2095	01:58	14°Cp37' R
Mercury Direct Station	Jan 7 2096	23:59	28°Sg22' D
Mercury Retrograde Station	Apr 8 2096	08:35	04°Ta06' R
Mercury Direct Station	May 2 2096	01:22	23°Ar22' D
Mercury Retrograde Station	Aug 11 2096	12:08	10°Vi57' R
Mercury Direct Station	Sep 4 2096	00:12	27°Le53' D
Mercury Retrograde Station	Dec 1 2096	22:21	28°Sg48' R
Mercury Direct Station	Dec 21 2096	16:34	12°Sg32' D
Mercury Retrograde Station	Mar 21 2097	11:36	16°Ar14' R
Mercury Direct Station	Apr 13 2097	19:28	03°Ar57' D
Mercury Retrograde Station	Jul 24 2097	15:08	22°Le41' R
Mercury Direct Station	Aug 17 2097	15:32	10°Le55' D
Mercury Retrograde Station	Nov 15 2097	15:58	13°Sg00' R
Mercury Direct Station	Dec 5 2097	12:25	26°Sc49' D
Mercury Retrograde Station	Mar 4 2098	07:12	29°Pi01' R
Mercury Direct Station	Mar 27 2098	01:04	15°Pi22' D
Mercury Retrograde Station	Jul 6 2098	08:04	03°Le36' R
Mercury Direct Station	Jul 30 2098	13:02	23°Cn15' D
Mercury Retrograde Station	Oct 30 2098	05:43	27°Sc09' R
Mercury Direct Station	Nov 19 2098	10:24	11°Sc09' D
Mercury Retrograde Station	Feb 15 2099	14:55	12°Pi19' R
Mercury Direct Station	Mar 9 2099	15:48	27°Aq33' D
Mercury Retrograde Station	Jun 17 2099	12:35	13°Cn51' R
Mercury Direct Station	Jul 11 2099	15:28	04°Cn42' D
Mercury Retrograde Station	Oct 13 2099	14:38	11°Sc10' R
Mercury Direct Station	Nov 3 2099	08:58	25°Li27' D
Mercury Retrograde Station	Jan 30 2100	06:23	25°Aq57' R

Mercury Direct Station	Feb 20 2100 13:39	10°Aq26' D
Mercury Retrograde Station	May 29 2100 05:07	23°Ge47' R
Mercury Direct Station	Jun 22 2100 03:55	15°Ge14' D
Mercury Retrograde Station	Sep 26 2100 17:59	24°Li57' R
Mercury Direct Station	Oct 18 2100 06:10	09°Li41' D

Zodiac Degree Index
Mercury Stations 1900-2100

While it's useful to review a chronological listing of Mercury stations to get an intuitive understanding of the long-term flow of the Mercury cycles that can modify market behavior and help set up profitable trades, there are also times when it's important to find out when specific positions in the zodiac come into focus through their associations with Mercury stations.

That's why this Degree Index has been created.

It can be helpful, for example, to know months or even years ahead of time when a stationary Mercury will conjoin the midheaven or a key planet in a First-Trade horoscope, and to plan trading strategies accordingly. The same advantage can be applied to the analysis of an astro-trader's individual horoscope, not just as an approach to seeing stressful times and important opportunities in advance, but also as a tool for reviewing key events in the past, with an eye toward anticipating reoccurring patterns which can be managed more resourcefully with an awareness of the Mercury cycles at work.

The application of this index is not limited to the markets and trading activities, of course. It can also be useful in understanding mundane affairs, geopolitical events, and even celestial phenomena. We can, for instance, gain a lot of valuable insights by comparing the zodiacal positions of solar eclipses with the Mercury stations nearest the eclipse, and with the Mercury stations that have taken place (or will take place in the future) at the same zodiac degree as the eclipse point or the eclipse antiscion. When we discover those correlations of zodiac position, we are then able to learn new things about key relationships in time.

Mercury Stations Listed by Zodiac Degree

Aries

0° Aries	03/06/1940, 04/12/1959, 03/05/2065, 04/10/2084
1° Aries	03/08/1907, 03/09/1953, 03/07/1986, 04/12/2005
2° Aries	04/13/1926, 03/07/2032, 04/13/2051
3° Aries	04/14/1972, 03/08/2078, 04/13/2097
4° Aries	03/10/1920, 03/10/1999, 04/15/2018
5° Aries	04/16/1939, 03/12/1966, 03/10/2045, 04/15/2064
6° Aries	04/17/1985, 03/12/2012, 03/11/2091
7° Aries	04/18/1906, 03/13/1933, 04/18/2031, 03/13/2058
8° Aries	04/19/1952, 03/15/1979, 04/18/2077
9° Aries	03/15/1900, 04/20/1998, 03/15/2025
10° Aries	04/21/1919, 03/16/1946, 04/20/2044, 03/16/2071
11° Aries	03/18/1913, 04/22/1965, 03/17/1992
12° Aries	03/19/1959, 04/23/2011, 03/18/2038, 04/21/2090
13° Aries	04/24/1932, 03/19/1959, 03/18/2084
14° Aries	03/21/1926, 04/25/1978, 03/20/2005, 04/23/2057
15° Aries	03/21/1972, 04/25/2024, 03/21/2051
16° Aries	04/27/1945, 03/23/2018, 03/21/2097
17° Aries	03/24/1939, 04/28/1991, 03/23/2064 , 04/26/2070
18° Aries	04/29/1912, 03/24/1985
19° Aries	03/26/2031, 04/28/2037
20° Aries	03/26/1906, 03/26/1952, 04/30/1958, 03/26/2077, 04/29/2083
21° Aries	03/27/1998, 04/30/2004
22° Aries	03/29/1919, 05/02/1925, 03/28/2044 , 05/01/2050
23° Aries	03/29/1965, 05/03/1971, 03/29/2090, 05/02/2096
24° Aries	03/30/2011, 05/03/2017
25° Aries	03/31/1932, 05/05/1938, 03/31/2057, 05/04/2063
26° Aries	04/01/1978, 05/05/1984
27° Aries	05/07/1905, 04/03/1945, 04/01/2024 , 05/06/2030
28° Aries	05/08/1951, 04/03/2070, 05/07/2076
29° Aries	04/05/1912, 04/04/1991, 05/08/1997

Taurus

0° Taurus	05/10/1918, 04/06/1958, 04/05/2037 , 05/10/2043
1° Taurus	05/10/1964, 04/06/2004, 04/06/2083, 05/10/2089

2º Taurus	04/08/1925, 05/11/2010
3º Taurus	05/13/1931, 04/09/1971, 04/08/2050 , 05/12/2056
4º Taurus	05/13/1977, 04/09/2017, 04/08/2096
5º Taurus	04/11/1938, 05/15/2023, 04/11/2063
6º Taurus	05/15/1944, 04/11/1984, 05/15/2069
7º Taurus	04/13/1905, 05/17/1990, 04/13/2030
8º Taurus	05/18/1911, 04/14/1951 04/13/2076
9º Taurus	05/19/1957, 04/15/1997, 05/17/2036
10º Taurus	04/16/1918, 04/16/2043, 05/18/2082
11º Taurus	04/16/1964, 05/20/2003, 04/16/2089
12º Taurus	05/21/1924, 04/18/2010, 05/20/2049
13º Taurus	04/19/1931, 05/22/1970, 04/18/2056, 05/21/2095
14º Taurus	04/20/1977, 05/22/2016
15º Taurus	05/24/1937, 04/21/2023, 05/23/2062
16º Taurus	04/22/1944, 05/25/1983, 04/21/2069
17º Taurus	05/26/1904, 04/23/1990, 05/25/2029
18º Taurus	04/24/1911, 05/27/1950, 05/27/2075
19º Taurus	04/25/1957, 05/27/1996, 04/24/2082
20º Taurus	05/29/1917, 04/26/2003, 05/29/2042
21º Taurus	04/27/1924, 05/30/1963, 05/29/2088
22º Taurus	04/28/1970, 05/31/2009, 04/26/2049, 04/28/2095
23º Taurus	06/01/1930, 04/28/2016
24º Taurus	04/30/1937, 06/02/1976, 06/01/2055, 04/29/2062
25º Taurus	05/01/1983
26º Taurus	05/02/1904, 06/03/2022, 05/01/2029
27º Taurus	06/05/1943, 06/03/2068, 05/03/2075
28º Taurus	06/05/1989, 05/03/1996, 04/09/2017
29º Taurus	06/07/1910, 05/05/1917, 06/06/2035, 05/05/2042

Gemini

0º Gemini	06/07/1956, 05/06/1963, 06/06/2081, 05/05/2088
1º Gemini	06/08/2002, 05/07/2009
2º Gemini	06/10/1923, 05/08/1930, 06/08/2048, 05/08/2055
3º Gemini	06/10/1969, 05/09/1976, 06/10/2094
4º Gemini	06/11/2015, 05/10/2022
5º Gemini	06/12/1936, 05/12/1943, 06/12/2061, 05/10/2068
6º Gemini	06/13/1982, 05/12/1989
7º Gemini	06/15/1903, 05/14/1910, 06/14/2028 , 05/13/2035
8º Gemini	06/16/1949, 05/14/1956, 06/15/2074
9º Gemini	06/17/1995, 05/15/2002, 05/14/2081
10º Gemini	06/18/1916, 05/17/1923, 06/17/2041
11º Gemini	06/19/1962, 05/16/2048
12º Gemini	05/17/1969, 06/19/2008, 06/18/2087, 05/17/2094

13º Gemini	06/21/1929, 05/19/2015
14º Gemini	05/19/1936, 06/20/2054, 05/19/2061
15º Gemini	06/22/1975, 05/21/1982, 06/22/2100
16º Gemini	05/22/1903, 06/22/2021, 05/21/2028
17º Gemini	06/24/1942, 05/23/1949, 06/24/2067, 05/22/2074
18º Gemini	06/24/1988, 05/24/1995
19º Gemini	06/26/1909, 05/25/1916, 06/26/2034, 05/24/2041
20º Gemini	06/27/1955, 05/26/1962, 06/26/2080, 05/25/2087
21º Gemini	06/28/2001, 05/26/2008
22º Gemini	06/29/1922, 05/28/1929, 06/29/2047 05/27/2054
23º Gemini	06/30/1968, 05/29/1975, 06/29/2093, 05/29/2100
24º Gemini	07/01/2014, 05/29/2021
25º Gemini	07/03/1935, 05/31/1942, 07/01/2060, 05/31/2067
26º Gemini	07/03/1981, 05/31/1988
27º Gemini	07/05/1902, 06/02/1909, 07/04/2027, 06/02/2034
28º Gemini	07/05/1948, 06/03/1955, 07/05/2073
29º Gemini	07/06/1994, 06/04/2001, 06/02/2080

Cancer

0º Cancer	07/08/1915, 06/05/1922, 07/07/2040
1º Cancer	07/08/1961, 06/05/2047, 07/08/2086
2º Cancer	07/10/2007, 06/05/2093
3º Cancer	07/10/1928, 06/07/2014, 07/10/2053
4º Cancer	06/09/1935, 07/12/1974, 06/07/2060 , 07/11/2099
5º Cancer	06/09/1981, 07/12/2020
6º Cancer	06/11/1902, 07/14/1941, 06/10/2027, 07/13/2066
7º Cancer	06/11/1948, 07/15/1987, 06/11/2073
8º Cancer	07/16/1908, 06/12/1994, 07/15/2033
9º Cancer	06/14/1915, 07/17/1954, 06/13/2040, 07/16/2079
10º Cancer	06/14/1961, 07/17/2000, 06/14/2086
11º Cancer	07/19/1921, 06/15/2007, 07/18/2046
12º Cancer	06/16/1928, 06/16/2053, 07/19/2092
13º Cancer	06/17/1974, 07/20/2013, 06/17/2099
14º Cancer	07/22/1934, 06/18/2020, 07/22/2059
15º Cancer	07/24/1901, 06/19/1941, 07/22/1980, 06/19/2066
16º Cancer	06/21/1987, 07/23/2026
17º Cancer	06/21/1908, 07/25/1947, 06/21/2033, 07/24/2072
18º Cancer	07/27/1914, 06/23/1954, 07/25/1993
19º Cancer	06/23/2000, 07/27/2039, 06/22/2079
20º Cancer	06/25/1921, 07/27/2085
21º Cancer	07/30/1927, 07/29/2006, 06/24/2046
22º Cancer	07/30/1973, 07/29/2052, 06/24/2092
23º Cancer	06/28/1934, 06/26/2013, 08/01/2019 , 07/30/2098

24º Cancer	08/01/1940, 06/27/2059
25º Cancer	06/30/1901, 06/28/1980, 08/03/1986, 08/01/2065
26º Cancer	08/04/1907, 06/29/2026, 08/03/2032
27º Cancer	08/04/1953, 06/29/2072
28º Cancer	07/01/1993, 08/06/1999
29º Cancer	07/03/1914, 08/06/1920, 07/02/2039, 08/06/2045

Leo

0º Leo	07/03/1960, 08/07/1966, 07/03/2085, 08/07/2091
1º Leo	07/04/2006, 08/08/2012
2º Leo	07/06/1927, 08/09/1933, 07/05/2052, 08/09/2058
3º Leo	08/11/1900, 07/06/1973, 08/11/1979, 07/06/2098
4º Leo	08/12/1946, 07/07/2019, 08/11/2025
5º Leo	07/08/1940, 08/13/1992, 07/08/2065, 08/12/2071
6º Leo	08/14/1913, 08/25/1919, 07/09/1986
7º Leo	07/11/1907, 08/15/1959, 07/10/2032, 08/14/2038
8º Leo	07/11/1953, 08/16/2005, 07/11/2078, 08/14/2084
9º Leo	08/17/1926, 07/12/1999, 08/17/2051
10º Leo	07/13/1920, 08/17/1972, 07/13/2045 , 08/17/2097
11º Leo	07/14/1966, 08/19/2018, 07/14/2091
12º Leo	08/20/1939, 07/15/2012, 08/19/2064
13º Leo	08/22/1906, 07/16/1933, 08/20/1985, 07/16/2058
14º Leo	08/22/1952, 07/17/1979, 08/22/2031
15º Leo	07/18/1900, 08/23/1998, 07/18/2025, 08/22/2077
16º Leo	07/19/1946, 07/19/2071
17º Leo	08/25/1965, 07/20/1992, 08/24/2044
18º Leo	07/21/1913, 08/26/2011, 07/21/2038 , 08/25/2090
19º Leo	08/27/1932, 7/22/1959, 08/27/2057, 07/21/2084
20º Leo	08/28/1978, 07/23/2005
21º Leo	07/24/1926, 08/30/1945, 08/28/2024 , 07/24/2051
22º Leo	07/24/1972, 08/30/2070, 07/24/2097
23º Leo	09/01/1912, 08/31/1991, 07/26/2018
24º Leo	07/27/1939, 09/02/1958, 08/31/2037 , 07/26/2064
25º Leo	07/28/1985, 09/02/2004, 09/02/2083
26º Leo	07/29/1906, 09/04/1925, 07/29/2031, 09/03/2050
27º Leo	07/29/1952, 09/05/1971, 07/29/2077, 09/04/2096
28º Leo	08/01/1919, 09/06/1938, 07/31/1998 , 09/05/2017, 09/30/2034
29º Leo	07/31/2044, 09/06/2063

Virgo

0º Virgo	09/08/1905, 08/01/1965, 09/07/1984, 08/01/2090
1º Virgo	08/03/1932, 09/09/1951, 08/03/2011, 09/08/2030

2º Virgo	08/04/1978, 09/10/1997, 08/03/2057, 09/08/2076
3º Virgo	09/11/1918, 09/11/2043
4º Virgo	08/06/1945, 09/11/1964, 08/05/2024, 09/11/2089
5º Virgo	09/14/1931, 08/07/1991, 09/12/2010, 08/06/2070
6º Virgo	08/08/1912, 09/14/1931, 09/14/1977, 08/08/2037, 09/13/2056
7º Virgo	08/09/1958
8º Virgo	09/16/1944, 08/10/2004, 09/15/2023, 08/09/2083
9º Virgo	08/11/1925, 09/17/1990, 08/11/2050, 09/16/2069
10º Virgo	09/18/1911, 08/12/1971, 09/17/2036, 08/11/2096
11º Virgo	09/19/1957, 08/13/2017, 09/18/2082
12º Virgo	09/20/1924, 08/14/1938, 09/20/2003, 08/14/2063
13º Virgo	09/22/1970, 08/14/1984, 09/20/2049
14º Virgo	08/16/1905, 09/22/2016, 08/16/2030, 09/21/2095
15º Virgo	09/23/1937, 08/17/1951, 09/23/2062, 08/16/2076
16º Virgo	09/25/1904. 08/19/1918, 09/24/1983 , 08/17/1997
17º Virgo	09/26/1950, 08/19/1964, 09/25/2029, 08/19/2043
18º Virgo	09/26/2075, 08/19/2089
19º Virgo	09/28/1917, 08/22/1931, 09/26/1996 , 08/20/2010
20º Virgo	09/29/1963, 08/22/1977, 09/27/2042, 08/21/2056
21º Virgo	09/29/2009, 08/23/2023 09/28/2088
22º Virgo	09/30/1930, 08/24/1944, 09/30/2055,08/24/2069
23º Virgo	10/01/1976, 08/25/1990
24º Virgo	08/27/1911, 10/03/1943, 10/02/2022 , 08/25/2036
25º Virgo	08/27/1957, 10/03/1989, 10/02/2068, 08/27/2082
26º Virgo	10/05/1910, 08/29/1924, 08/28/2003 , 10/05/2035
27º Virgo	10/05/1956, 08/28/2049, 10/05/2081
28º Virgo	10/08/1923, 08/30/1970, 10/06/2002, 08/30/2095
29º Virgo	09/01/1937, 10/08/1969, 08/30/2016, 10/07/2048

Libra

0º Libra	09/02/1983, 10/09/2015, 08/31/2062, 10/08/2094
1º Libra	09/02/1904, 10/10/1936, 09/02/2029 , 10/09/2061,
2º Libra	10/12/1903, 09/04/1950, 10/11/1982, 09/03/2075
3º Libra	10/12/1949, 09/04/1996
4º Libra	09/05/1917, 10/11/2028, 09/05/2042, 10/12/2074
5º Libra	10/14/1916, 09/06/1963, 10/14/1995, 09/05/2088
6º Libra	09/08/1930, 10/15/1962, 09/07/2009 , 10/14/2041
7º Libra	09/08/1976, 10/15/2008, 09/08/2055, 10/15/2087
8º Libra	10/17/1929, 09/10/2022, 10/17/2054
9º Libra	09/11/1943, 10/18/1975, 09/10/2068, 10/18/2100
10º Libra	10/20/1942, 09/11/1989, 10/18/2021
11º Libra	09/13/1910, 10/20/1988, 09/13/2035, 10/19/2067
12º Libra	10/21/1909, 09/13/1956, 10/21/2034, 09/13/2081

13º Libra	09/16/1923, 10/22/1955, 09/14/2002, 10/21/2080
14º Libra	10/24/1922, 09/16/1969, 10/23/2001, 09/15/2048
15º Libra	10/24/1968, 09/17/2015, 10/24/2047, 09/16/2094
16º Libra	09/18/1936, 10/25/2014, 09/17/2061, 10/24/2093
17º Libra	10/27/1935, 09/19/1982, 10/26/2060
18º Libra	10/28/1902, 09/20/1903, 10/27/1981, 09/19/2028
19º Libra	10/28/1948, 09/21/1949, 10/28/2027, 09/20/2074
20º Libra	09/22/1916, 10/30/1994, 09/22/1995, 10/28/2073
21º Libra	10/31/1915, 09/24/1962, 10/30/2040 , 09/22/2041
22º Libra	10/31/1961, 09/24/2008, 10/31/2086, 09/23/2087
23º Libra	11/02/1928, 09/25/1929, 09/28/1942 , 11/01/2007, 09/25/2054
24º Libra	11/03/1974, 09/26/1975, 11/02/2053, 09/26/2100
25º Libra	11/03/2020, 09/27/2021, 11/03/2099
26º Libra	11/05/1941, 11/04/2066, 09/28/2067
27º Libra	11/06/1908, 09/30/1909, 11/06/1987, 09/28/1988
28º Libra	11/07/1954, 10/01/1955, 11/06/2033
29º Libra	11/08/2000, 10/01/2001, 11/07/2079, 09/30/2080

Scorpio

0º Scorpio	11/09/1921, 10/03/1922, 10/03/2047
1º Scorpio	11/10/1967, 10/03/1968, 11/10/2013, 11/09/2046, 11/09/2092, 10/03/2093
2º Scorpio	11/12/1934, 10/06/1935, 10/04/2014
3º Scorpio	11/12/1980, 10/06/1981, 11/12/2059, 10/04/2060
4º Scorpio	11/13/1901, 10/07/1902, 10/07/2027
5º Scorpio	11/15/1947, 10/08/1948, 11/13/2026, 10/07/2073
6º Scorpio	11/16/1914, 10/10/1915, 11/15/1993, 10/09/1994, 11/13/2072
7º Scorpio	11/16/2039, 10/09/2040
8º Scorpio	11/16/1960, 10/10/1961, 11/16/2085, 10/10/2086
9º Scorpio	11/19/1927, 10/12/1928, 11/18/2006, 10/12/2007
10º Scorpio	11/19/1973, 10/13/1974, 11/18/2052, 10/12/2053
11º Scorpio	11/20/2019, 10/14/2020, 11/19/2098, 10/13/2099
12º Scorpio	11/21/1940, 10/15/1941, 11/21/2065, 10/15/2066
13º Scorpio	11/23/1907, 10/17/1908, 11/22/1986, 10/16/1987
14º Scorpio	11/23/1953, 10/18/1954, 11/22/2032, 10/16/2033
15º Scorpio	11/25/1999, 10/18/2000, 10/18/2079
16º Scorpio	10/20/1921, 10/19/2046
17º Scorpio	11/26/2091, 10/20/2092
18º Scorpio	10/22/1934, 11/26/2012, 10/21/2013
19º Scorpio	10/23/1980, 10/22/2059
20º Scorpio	11/29/1900, 10/24/1901, 11/29/2025, 10/24/2026,
21º Scorpio	10/25/1947
22º Scorpio	12/02/1913, 10/27/1914, 12/01/1992, 10/25/1993, 10/24/2072
23º Scorpio	12/03/1959, 12/02/2038, 10/27/2039
24º Scorpio	10/27/1960, 12/04/2005, 12/02/2084, 10/27/2085

25º Scorpio   12/05/1926, 10/30/1927, 10/28/2006
26º Scorpio   12/05/1972, 10/30/1973, 10/29/2052,12/05/2097
27º Scorpio   12/08/1939, 10/31/2019, 10/30/2098
28º Scorpio   11/01/1940, 12/07/2064, 10/31/2065
29º Scorpio   12/09/1906, 11/03/1907, 11/02/1986

Sagittarius

0º Sagittarius   12/10/1952, 11/03/1953, 11/02/2032, 12/09/2077
1º Sagittarius   12/12/1919, 12/11/1998, 11/05/1999 11/03/2078
2º Sagittarius   11/05/1920, 12/12/1965, 12/11/2044, 11/05/2045
3º Sagittarius   11/06/1966, 12/14/2011, 12/12/2090, 11/06/2091
4º Sagittarius   12/14/1932, 11/08/1933, 11/06/2012, 12/14/2057
5º Sagittarius   12/15/1978, 11/09/1979, 11/08/2058
6º Sagittarius   11/09/1900, 12/17/1945, 12/15/2024, 11/09/2025
7º Sagittarius   11/11/1946, 12/18/1991, 12/17/2070, 11/11/2071
8º Sagittarius   12/18/1912, 11/12/1913, 11/11/1992, 12/18/2037
9º Sagittarius   12/20/1958, 11/14/1959, 11/12/2038
10º Sagittarius 12/21/1925, 12/20/2004, 11/14/2005, 12/19/2083, 11/12/2084
11º Sagittarius 11/15/1926, 12/22/1971, 12/21/2050, 11/15/2051
12º Sagittarius 11/15/1972, 12/21/2096
13º Sagittarius 12/24/1938, 11/18/1939, 12/23/2017, 11/17/2018, 11/15/2097
14º Sagittarius 12/26/1905, 12/24/1984, 11/18/1985, 12/24/2063, 11/17/2064
15º Sagittarius 11/20/1906, 12/25/2030, 11/23/2078
16º Sagittarius 11/25/1920, 12/27/1951, 11/20/1952, 11/19/2031, 11/25/2045, 12/26/2076
17º Sagittarius 12/28/1918, 11/26/1966, 10/21/1967, 12/27/1997, 11/21/1998, 11/20/2077
18º Sagittarius 11/22/1919, 11/28/1933, 12/29/1964, 12/28/2043, 11/21/2044
19º Sagittarius 12/31/1931, 11/23/1965, 11/29/1979, 12/30/2010, 11/28/2058, 12/28/2089, 11/22/2090
20º Sagittarius 11/24/1932, 11/24/2011, 11/29/2025, 12/30/2056
21º Sagittarius 12/01/1946, 12/31/1977, 11/25/1978, 11/24/2057, 11/30/2071
22º Sagittarius 01/02/1945, 01/02/2024, 11/26/2024,
23º Sagittarius 11/27/1945, 01/03/1991, 01/02/2070,11/27/2070
24º Sagittarius 01/05/1912, 11/29/1912, 11/28/1991, 01/03/2037
25º Sagittarius 01/05/1958, 11/30/1958, 12/05/2051, 01/05/2083
26º Sagittarius 01/06/1925, 01/06/2004, 11/30/2004, 11/28/2037, 11/30/2083
27º Sagittarius 12/01/192501/08/1971, 12/06/2018, 01/06/2050, 12/01/2050
28º Sagittarius 01/09/1938, 12/03/1971, 12/08/1985, 01/08/2017, 01/07/2096, 12/01/2096
29º Sagittarius 12/04/1938, 12/03/2017, 12/09/2031, 01/09/2063

Capricorn

0º Capricorn   01/11/1905, 01/11/1984, 12/04/1984,12/04/2063
1º Capricorn   12/06/1905, 01/12/1951, 01/11/2030, 12/06/2030

2º Capricorn   12/07/1951, 06/06/1968, 01/12/1997, 01/12/2076, 12/06/2076
3º Capricorn   01/14/1918, 12/09/1918, 12/07/1997
4º Capricorn   01/15/1964, 12/09/1964, 01/14/2043, 12/08/2043
5º Capricorn   01/15/2010, 12/10/2010, 01/14/2089, 12/09/2089
6º Capricorn   01/17/1931, 12/11/1931, 01/16/2056, 12/10/2056
7º Capricorn   01/17/1977, 12/12/1977
8º Capricorn   01/19/1944, 12/13/1944, 01/18/2023, 12/13/2023
9º Capricorn   01/20/1990, 12/14/1990, 01/18/2069, 12/13/2069
10º Capricorn   01/21/1911, 12/16/1911, 01/21/2036
11º Capricorn   01/21/1957, 12/16/1957, 12/15/2036, 01/21/2082
12º Capricorn   01/24/1924, 07/20/1967, 01/23/2003, 12/17/2003, 12/16/2082
13º Capricorn   12/18/1924, 01/24/1970, 01/23/2049, 12/17/2049
14º Capricorn   12/19/1970, 01/25/2016, 01/24/2095, 12/19/2095
15º Capricorn   01/26/1937, 12/20/1937, 12/19/2016, 01/26/2062
16º Capricorn   12/22/1904, 01/27/1983, 12/22/1983, 12/20/2062
17º Capricorn   01/28/1904, 12/22/1904, 01/27/2029 , 12/22/2029
18º Capricorn   01/29/1950, 12/23/1950, 01/28/2075, 12/23/2075
19º Capricorn   01/30/1917, 12/25/1917, 07/27/1960 , 01/30/1996, 12/23/1996
20º Capricorn   02/01/1963, 12/26/1963, 01/30/2042, 12/25/2042
21º Capricorn   06/26/1967, 02/01/2009, 12/26/2009, 01/31/2088, 12/25/2088
22º Capricorn   02/02/1930, 12/27/1930, 02/02/2055, 12/27/2055
23º Capricorn   02/03/1976, 12/28/1976
24º Capricorn   02/05/1943, 12/30/1943, 02/04/2022, 12/29/2022
25º Capricorn   02/05/1989, 12/30/1989, 02/05/2068, 12/29/2068
26º Capricorn   02/07/1910, 01/01/1911, 01/01/2036
27º Capricorn   07/01/1947, 02/08/1956, 01/01/1957, 02/07/2035, 08/04/2078,
                01/01/2082
28º Capricorn   01/04/1924, 02/08/2002, 01/02/2003, 02/07/2081
29º Capricorn   02/10/1923, 01/04/1970, 02/09/2048, 01/02/2049

Aquarius

0º Aquarius   02/10/1969, 02/10/2094, 01/04/2095
1º Aquarius   02/13/1936, 01/05/1937, 02/11/2015 , 01/05/2016
2º Aquarius   02/13/1982, 01/07/1983, 02/11/2061, 01/05/2062
3º Aquarius   02/14/1903, 01/08/1904, 02/14/2028 , 01/07/2029
4º Aquarius   02/14/1949, 01/08/1950, 01/08/2075
5º Aquarius   01/10/1917, 02/16/1995, 01/09/1996, 02/14/2074
6º Aquarius   02/17/1916, 01/11/1963, 01/10/2042, 02/16/2041, 01/10/2042
7º Aquarius   02/17/1962, 01/11/2009, 02/17/2087 01/11/2088
8º Aquarius   02/19/1929, 01/13/1930, 02/19/2008, 01/12/2055
9º Aquarius   02/20/1975, 01/14/1976, 02/19/2054
10º Aquarius   01/15/1943, 01/14/2022, 02/20/2100
11º Aquarius   02/22/1942, 01/16/1989, 02/21/2021, 01/15/2068

12º Aquarius   01/17/1910, 02/23/1988, 01/17/2035, 02/22/2067
13º Aquarius   02/24/1909, 01/18/1956, 02/23/2034, 01/17/2081
14º Aquarius   01/20/1923, 02/25/1955, 01/18/2002 , 02/25/2080
15º Aquarius   02/25/2001, 01/20/2048
16º Aquarius   02/27/1922, 01/20/1969, 02/26/2047, 01/20/2094
17º Aquarius   01/23/1936, 02/28/1968, 01/21/2015, 02/27/2093
18º Aquarius   03/02/1935, 03/02/1981, 01/23/1982 , 02/28/2014, 01/21/2061
19º Aquarius   01/24/1903, 03/02/1981, 01/24/2028, 02/29/2060
20º Aquarius   03/03/1902, 01/24/1949, 03/03/2027
21º Aquarius   01/27/1916, 03/04/1948, 01/26/1995 , 03/03/2073, 01/24/2074
22º Aquarius   01/27/1962, 03/05/1994, 01/26/2041
23º Aquarius   03/06/1915, 01/28/2008, 03/05/2040, 01/27/2087
24º Aquarius   01/29/1929, 03/06/1961, 01/29/2054, 03/06/2086
25º Aquarius   01/30/1975, 03/08/2007, 01/30/2100
26º Aquarius   03/08/1928, 02/01/1942, 01/30/2021, 03/08/2053
27º Aquarius   03/09/1974, 01/31/2067, 03/09/2099
28º Aquarius   02/02/1909, 03/11/1941, 02/02/1988, 03/10/2020
29º Aquarius   02/03/1955, 03/12/1987, 02/02/2034, 03/11/2066

Pisces

0º Pisces   03/13/1908, 02/04/2001, 02/03/2080
1º Pisces   02/05/1922, 03/14/1954, 03/13/2033, 02/05/2047
2º Pisces   02/06/1968, 03/14/2000, 03/14/2079, 02/05/2093
3º Pisces   03/16/1921, 02/08/1935, 02/06/2014, 03/16/2046
4º Pisces   03/17/1967, 02/08/1981, 02/08/2060, 03/16/2092
5º Pisces   02/09/1902, 03/17/2013, 02/09/2027
6º Pisces   03/19/1934, 02/11/1948, 03/19/2059
7º Pisces   03/19/1980, 02/11/1994, 02/09/2073
8º Pisces   03/21/1901, 02/12/1915, 03/20/2026 , 02/12/2040
9º Pisces   03/22/1947, 02/12/1961, 03/21/2072, 02/12/2086
10º Pisces   02/15/1928, 03/22/1993, 02/14/2007 ,
11º Pisces   03/24/1914, 02/15/1974, 03/23/2039, 02/14/2053
12º Pisces   03/24/1960, 02/17/2020, 03/24/2085, 02/15/2099
13º Pisces   03/27/1927, 02/17/1941, 03/25/2006 , 02/17/2066
14º Pisces   02/18/1987, 03/25/2052
15º Pisces   02/20/1908, 03/27/1973, 02/18/2033 , 03/27/2098
16º Pisces   03/29/1940, 02/20/1954, 03/28/2019, 02/20/2079
17º Pisces   02/21/1921, 03/30/1986, 02/21/2000, 03/28/2065
18º Pisces   03/31/1907, 02/23/1967, 02/21/2046
19º Pisces   04/01/1953, 02/23/2013, 03/30/2032, 02/22/2092
20º Pisces   02/24/1934, 04/02/1999, 02/24/2059, 03/31/2078
21º Pisces   04/02/1920, 02/26/1980, 04/02/2045
22º Pisces   02/26/1901, 04/04/1966, 02/26/2026

23º Pisces	02/27/1947, 04/04/2012, 02/27/2072, 04/03/2091
24º Pisces	03/01/1914, 04/05/1933, 02/27/1993, 04/05/2058
25º Pisces	03/01/1960, 04/07/1979, 03/01/2039
26º Pisces	04/07/1900, 03/02/2006, 04/07/2025, 03/01/2085
27º Pisces	03/04/1927, 04/09/1946, 03/03/2052 , 04/08/2071
28º Pisces	03/04/1973, 04/09/1992
29º Pisces	04/10/1913, 03/05/2019, 04/10/2038, 03/04/2098

Online Resources

www.BasicMarketCourse.com

The Basic Stock Market Astrology Home Study Course, including 31 hours of audio instruction, a 250-page workbook, and a bonus DVD.

www.FinancialCyclesWeekly.com

Subscriptions to the ***FinancialCyclesWeekly*** newsletter, the FinancialCyclesWeekly Gold-Plus Elite Astro-Trading membership program and the free Astro-Traders' Tip of the Week.

www.TimBost.com

Schedule confidential appointments for personal astrological and astro-trading consultations with Tim Bost, in person, by telephone, or on Skype.

www.PracticalSpiritualAstrology.com

Free monthly guidance for establishing a personal spiritual focus for maximum effectiveness in maintaining emotional balance.

www.GannPlan.com

A free site featuring a variety of comments and resources on the life and astro-trading career of W. D. Gann.

www.HarmonicResearchAssociates.com

Direct ordering from the publisher; a wide selection of Tim Bost's publications, including books, e-books, monographs, audio recordings and DVDs.

Made in the USA
Charleston, SC
06 October 2012